Fil Bufalo is an engaging writer who loves travelling, reading, music and architecture. While everyone around her was taking poloraid pictures or slides by the rolls full, Fil could be found writing or sketching in her journal as a means of recording life. She loves meeting new people and is prone to exaggerating when relating stories—just to add that little bit of spice! The bigger the audience, the better. Her only reservations are restrictions on the number of words permissible.

Dedicated to Nino and Gabriella – my parents who, sadly no longer with us, both loved Italy almost as much as Verdi. Almost!

Fil Bufalo

A Suitcase Full of Olive Branches

Austin Macauley Publishers™

LONDON • CAMBRIDGE • NEW YORK • SHARJAH

Copyright © Fil Bufalo 2022

The right of Fil Bufalo to be identified as author of this work has been asserted by the author in accordance with sections 77 and 78 of the Copyright, Designs and Patents Act 1988.

All rights reserved. No part of this publication may be reproduced, stored in a retrieval system, or transmitted in any form or by any means, electronic, mechanical, photocopying, recording, or otherwise, without the prior permission of the publishers.

Any person who commits any unauthorised act in relation to this publication may be liable to criminal prosecution and civil claims for damages.

A CIP catalogue record for this title is available from the British Library.

ISBN 9781398428409 (Paperback)
ISBN 9781398428416 (ePub e-book)

www.austinmacauley.com

First Published 2022
Austin Macauley Publishers Ltd®
1 Canada Square
Canary Wharf
London
E14 5AA

My acknowledgements goes to the Holy Trinity-Amanda-Jane, Colleen and Marcello – all three had a part to play in my writing of the book.

Chapter 1
Life in the Fast Lane

What is pure coincidence? Was it coincidental that the first man we encountered in the lead-up to our flurrying flight to Milan from Heathrow Central was Milanese? Had he been our pilot, then perhaps it would have been less coincidence and more logical step. Perfect plausibility for a Milanese pilot to have been flying a British plane from London to Milan every day of the week. Yet, the first man we met was not our pilot, nor was he a flight attendant on the plane. He was the effusive yet quiet, engaging yet reticent, and chatty yet brushed with sadness gentleman assigned to push my friend Alice all the way to Runway no Five, Gate 28, Terminal 2. Heathrow International.

Contrary to what one might assume, it wasn't brute force the man was exercising to propel the unfortunate Alice along the ugly Heathrow linoleumed walkways. His sidekick was a slick chrome wheelchair accessorising and enhancing his sought-after craft. One would be hard pressed to find as skilled a 'pusher' in any international airport. In Alice's case, the wheelchair was precautionary. Alice-of-the-injured-left-knee could walk, granted with a limp, but she could not run, and we were late.

Without the tenacity of the assistant, and the propulsion of the wheelchair, we would never have made the plane. Without the plane, we would never have made the ten-day coach tour, and without the coach tour, we would not have seen the Northern Italian lakes, nor the snow-studded Swiss alps, would not have bonded so easily with the other twenty passengers on our tour, and most certainly would not have had the opportunity to hand out little fragments of Australiana to perfect strangers in the John O 'Groats of Italia'—La Dolce Vita!

So, I say 'Gràcia tante' (thanks very much) to the lovely Luigi for pushing Alice and for urging me to "fait presto" whilst I struggled along behind the air-bound chair, handicapped considerably with our copious collection of hand luggage, backpacks and coats.

Why hadn't we left home earlier? A fair question, but not one which elicits an easy response. Short answer was that we did leave early enough. Two and a half hours before the flight, both Alice and I were two sleepyheads shivering on the porch of her south London home, awaiting the taxi we had booked three days ago and had double-checked on the prearranged time with the taxi company the night before.

Yes, we had booked! Yes, the taxi would be in our driveway at six-thirty and yes, we could pay by credit card, once we'd reached our destination—Heathrow International. As far as we knew, all was well with the world.

It was early, Alice had a bung knee and grumpiness was my perpetual morning state. (I'd been awake most of the night tossing and turning in anticipation of the big trip to Italy.) Apart from that, we were good. The cat from next door, Crewcut, appeared and wound his fat, furry body around my legs, probably for warmth more than undying affection. It was chilly for May in London.

Six-forty, and the taxi was still a no-show.

"I think we should ring and find out where the taxi is." Alice was taking no chances on our missing the plane. Having lived in the 'Capital' for more than thirty years (Australian-born but married a Londoner), Alice was well aware of the distance to Heathrow, and the possible thwarting to our trip in terms of traffic, roadworks, diversions and general London clogging. She was suggesting ringing the taxi because she was an organised person, used to delegating and meeting deadlines in her work as teacher of the deaf. I was the complete opposite.

Prone to lateness myself, I knew I would have no place chastising the taxi driver. That task had Alice's name all over it. I was well aware that friends and family saw me as displaying a more than healthy slug of casual indifference towards people not honouring commitments or keeping to timetables. I really did make the worst kind of companion one could hope for in a twin-share bedroom for ten days in Northern Italy. But we were friends, and we were going—Alice would make certain of that, now we had come this far. All the suitcases, flight bookings and coach tour arrangements were in place.

I sashayed around for a bit on the porch, trying to pry Crewcut from under my feet. He wouldn't move, so I resorted to shaking my left leg forcefully. This time he sprang to attention as if I had been conducting a pre-dawn inspection of his barracks. I could tell he was none too pleased with my can-canning motions, as he let out a loud hissing noise, as if to say, "I'm glad you are going to Milan, and I hope you never come back." Which was a real shame, as Crewcut and I had bonded over the week I'd been in London.

Having arrived from Australia the week before, I was, as usual, overwhelmed with jet lag and my sleeping patterns had been all over the shop. I'd found myself sneaking out of the house for a pre-dawn walk whilst the rest of the household slept (Alice, Patrick and their two small dogs). The master and mistress of the manor (Alice and Patrick, not the dogs) were sound sleepers, so I hadn't disturbed them, even when I'd turned on taps, banged doors and rattled windows.

I would have liked a walking companion in the early mornings to show me the best parks to circumnavigate and the best lanes and alleyways through which to shortcut. But, over the five days I had been early morning walking, I had failed to rouse either Alice or Patrick and, as noted, I tried my very best. I was, however, successful in rousing all manner of animals at four am. Call me Doctor Doolittle, it was something uncanny how many of the creatures slept with a shotgun on their laps. Hence the expression, 'watchdog'.

The dogs in residence at number Four-Looby and Holly, were constantly ready for 'walkies' but I dared not take the risk with them. A definite pattern over the first few days of jet lag. The moment I left the house, Crewcut and a neighbouring crony would unfailingly trip me up at the front door, and once I was actually walking, I became the Pied Piper of the suburb. Dogs and cats from every second house I passed greeted me with much enthusiasm and early morning delight. They yelped, they barked, they howled and they followed me. Here was someone mad enough to be up walking at five am. Food may have been up for grabs, or even better still, the mysterious stranger in the hooded green tracksuit might be up for a game of 'Fetch'.

I didn't want to play. Not Fetch! Not nothing! All I wanted to do was restore my circadian rhythm by walking around in circles for an hour (minus the menagerie of cats and dogs who had attached themselves to me) and then crawl back into bed until lunchtime.

My long-winded explanation of how I came to be on a first-name basis with Crewcut has been to set the scene, and essentially this impresses upon the reader the sheer volume of cats and dogs in one tiny little pocket of South London. I was thick in dog country, and the cat population wasn't far behind. Alice was already upset about leaving her dogs for a couple of weeks, so I dared not mention them and reignite her separation-anxiety. Again! We'd been through the pangs of how Alice would cope without 'her babies' for hours last night, and for the moment at least, it seemed she had more pressing issues to think about; namely, were we going to make the plane in time, and had we definitely booked a wheelchair for our hike to the boarding lounge?

Would Looby and Holly be skulking around inside the house, already missing Alice? I doubted it, in fact I would lay bets on their exact location as being in the lap of luxury on Alice's side of the bed in the master suite, sleeping peacefully underneath the lavender satin sheets Alice loved so much. (Patrick wasn't that fond of them, so they would probably be replaced by tomorrow morning with the more functional, and more masculine, navy flannelette sheets he preferred to sleep in.)

Alice was speaking to me. "Fil, Leonard's cat seems to have taken a fancy to you, he's all over you." Alice had lived next door to Crewcut for more than ten years and still didn't know his name. She knew Leonard, and his wife and kids, but not their treasured family heirloom—Crewcut. It was all on a need-to-know basis with Alice, and she hadn't really needed to know much more than the fact that the bundle of fur beneath my feet was 'that cat from next door'.

I didn't answer her, or give her any leeway with her implication that I was overly attracted to cats. I wasn't. It was the cat who had sought me out, not the other way around. It was a good thing though, because for about forty years, I had an irrational fear of cats and dogs, not unfounded, but nevertheless annoying, because it meant I would find myself in a position of being invited to stroke cats, pat dogs and even worst-case scenario, forced to wash and blow dry the creatures.

We were still waiting for the taxi.

"That's it, Fil. We can't wait any longer. I'm going back inside to wake up Patrick and he'll just have to drive us." I wasn't really sure that would be a wise move, since Patrick was never at his best in the mornings. He consistently came good after his first gulp of caffeine followed by a brisk walk with the dogs—sacred time he cherished every morning, rain hail or shine. Getting him up would be a feat in itself, and Alice was so slow on her own feet these days, it would be another twenty minutes at least before we could leave. Assuming, of course, that there was enough petrol in the Jag to ferry us to Heathrow.

Patrick was one of those men who lived with everything ordered and economically accounted for. The Jag was seldom out of the driveway, since Patrick walked, bussed or trained it around London. As he insisted on more than one occasion, "I can't abide being cooped up in a vehicle in a traffic jam when I could be on a bus or train with my nose in a book." It was a wonder Patrick's nose was not as long as Pinocchio's, so joined at the hip was he to his beloved books.

"You wait here with Crewcut, Alice. (I was determined for her to learn Leonard's cat's name.) I'll go and prod the sleeping bear with a stick and tell him the taxi is late. I'll be quicker than you." Not that I wanted to be the one to raise the alarm.

Five days ago, I would have delighted in the opportunity to furiously shake Patrick until he awoke with a start. It just hadn't seemed appropriate then, but today, as it got lighter and later outside on the porch, I would not need convincing. Patrick was a good chap. He would take it for King and country. And for Alice. He knew she needed a holiday with her bosom buddy from Australia (me).

I peeled Crewcut from my ankles and turned to open the front door. The second coincidence occurred. At that exact turning of the handle moment, we heard a honking of a horn and witnessed a big black taxi mounting the kerb and landing in the driveway right alongside Patrick's precious Jag. A man of exaggerated roundness, shortness and baldness in a crumpled black suit and black jockey cap, jumped out and ran up to Alice, who was still leaning on the rail on the bottom step.

"You are waiting for a taxi?"

No, we were just hanging around the outside the house in the streaky greyish yellow light of morning, twiddling our thumbs, looking for some entertainment. Would this be the rhetorical question of the day at such an early hour?

Neither of us answered, so he shut up. He offered no excuse for his tardiness (not even a remorseful or slightly apologetic look) and began loading the large, straining-at-the-edges suitcases into the boot. We had one each, but apart from one almighty heave, accompanied by an echoing double-Sumo-wrestler grunt, his work was done. He was ensconced back in the driver's seat before Alice could implore for assistance with her hobbling. Just like that, the age of chivalry took a beating for Latvia, or whatever his home country turned out to be. It wouldn't be England.

I'd lay bets on that just judging by appearance alone, but, as Patrick always maintained, books should never be judged by their covers alone, and if there was anyone who knew about the covers of books and significance of title—it was Patrick. I knew the ethnicity of the driver didn't make the slightest difference to his turning out to be a decent person, or even a capable driver, but it's what we do—stereotypically box people. This trip I would be making a concerted effort to wipe out my 'country of origin thought patterns' when meeting someone for the first time. I needed to alter my brain patterns so that I would not immediately and involuntarily start to guess a stranger's nationality by their appearance, actions or accent. (I was actually complimenting Eastern European citizens on their success in weightlifting).

Perhaps though, Italy would not be the best country to begin my New Year's resolution, as historically, it was not a land to which migrants flocked, but of late there was much concern with Africans and Libyans attempting to cross the Ionian Sea to the Italian coast. I would be on my best restraint behaviour on our trip, should I meet anyone who did not look Italian. (I know, double conundrum—failed already with the tacit Italian stereotype.)

Our stateless driver appeared to have gone to sleep, clearly not here to make things easier for us this morning. After much faltering and deliberation, Alice reached the taxi doors and triumphantly claimed the favoured front seat. I shared a tiny portion of the backseat with our cabin luggage, backpacks and coats. Looking back towards the porch, I noticed that Crewcut's companion-cat from next door had joined him in the valedictions. I was warming to cats in England. They would never be my favourite bird or animal—that category being reserved for a swan—but thanks to Crewcut and his offsides, the status of the feline creature was definitely on the incline in my eyes.

Once Alice and I were settled and seat-belted, the driver took his cue, woke up and began to manoeuvre the car down the gutter at an angle so that the jolting was not too severe. That was a point in his favour, and although he did not speak for the next ten minutes, he was humming softly along with a folk song dribbling out from his compact disc player. It was a language I had heard before, but not one I would have been confident enough to have joined in with by either humming or singing. Dare I say it was from some far-flung European mountainous village, and that it became louder and louder with more than necessary whooping and clacking? I was imagining a full-on folk dance going on in the foothills of the Slovenian alps, cowbells and all!

Alice didn't like the music. "Excuse me, but would it be possible to turn off the music? It's making my headache worse."

The driver did not respond, but he did reach down and eject the compact disc. He then resumed humming the folk tune, rapping his gloved knuckles on the steering wheel as he did so. Alice turned her head to the window, and I busied myself with my phone, trying to work out how far we had to go and whether we would make the plane. The driver must have, at some stage in his driving career, attempted to pass the 'Knowledge', as he certainly knew a few shortcuts to Heathrow. (We were crossing precariously close to a brilliant green park on a service road, dotted with white uniformed cricketers scurrying out of the way as we hurtled past.) I was privy to the secret of the 'Knowledge' even though we have nothing remotely like it in Australia. The 'Knowledge' is a series of difficult tests concerning road rules and streets of London a cab driver must commit to memory. Unless the driver passes the 'Knowledge', he or she will not be the lucky recipient of a black cab licence and operating as a black cabbie would be breaking laws.

The vehicle we were riding in was a taxi, and not a black cab, even though it was black in colour. I really had no knowledge of whether or not our driver had passed the 'Knowledge' but he was possessive of real 'inside Knowledge' which was more than useful in our rush to the airport. (He may have picked up some tips from the soapie *EastEnders*, where the entire Slater family join in helping Kat pass the knowledge so that she can drive the family heirloom—a precious black cab.)

Regardless, he knew his stuff, and we were already halfway to the airport. (Alice and Patrick lived only thirty minutes from Heathrow—directly under the flight path.)

Just as we came out of a short rail ridge tunnel, Alice let out a shriek, "Stop! Stop the car please, driver! I think I've forgotten my tablets."

The driver slammed on his brakes as if trying to avoid running over a little child, and we all fell forward in a heap. Myself, the driver, Alice and the assorted backseat luggage.

"What do you mean, Alice? Why did you suddenly remember? What are we going to do?" Thinking about it later, I concluded it had been foolish of me to fire question after question at Alice without giving her time to explain. The driver said nothing. In fact, he was smiling, with his eyes fixed on the metre. The pound signs were flashing across! Alice wanted her cabin luggage, backpack and suitcase.

I handed over what I had, but I couldn't reach into the boot, so the driver had to jump out of the car and hurry around the car to the large boot. Of course, he didn't know who owned which suitcase, so he repeated his performance of half an hour before with added confidence, complete with overexaggerated grunting. Both suitcases ended up outside the boot. Cars, motorbikes and push bikes were weaving in and out around us like bees to a honeypot. The couldn't all have been late for planes, but not one person stopped to ask if we needed assistance. The driver could have had us captive in his taxi and might have been in the process of heaving suitcases with dead bodies into the nearby canal.

Back in the car, it was all happening. To be on the safe side, I had snapped down the lock on my door and had urged Alice to do the same. Things were just not adding up this morning. The late taxi, the erratic driving through playing fields and on service roads, the music, the metre stopped and finally the driver with the suitcases. I was just feeling a little uneasy.

Alice seemed oblivious to potential danger. She had tipped the entire contents of her cabin baggage onto the driver's seat and was furiously rummaging and flinging her possessions around. I was just sitting there, watching her and listening to the grunting of the driver, wondering what I could do. If Alice would just open her mouth and let me know what was missing, I might have been able to assist, but as it was, both the driver and I were in the dark about the missing tablets.

"Alice, how many of your tablets are missing, and can we get more in Italy on prescription?" There! Two questions rolled into one, and a real likelihood of obtaining an answer this time.

Alice did answer, and it was not looking good for the three of us.

"No and yes. I can't find them, and yes I need them." Was this the imperative of imperatives? Would she die without them?

"Alice, is it worth opening your big case and looking in there? Are the tablets all together?"

Valuable clue number one. Alice was perking up and nodding. "Yes, I remember now, they are all in the pink and blue striped makeup bag. I think I left it in my bedside drawer."

Well, at least that was something. Had she left them on the bed, it would have been the end for both Holly and Looby. The tablets would have been mistaken for lollies and wolfed down while Patrick snored on. Nothing surer.

"Well, that's a relief! Holly and Looby get to live another day." Alice was regarding me curiously, as if she were unable to make head or tail of my innuendo. The next thing she'd be asking me would be my stance on euthanasia, which I'd be fully prepared to give—and elaborate on.

Time was ticking on, and the bewildered driver was still waiting outside with the suitcases, probably cursing the taxi company for having given him the first shift of the day with the kooky customers from Kingston on Thames. I glanced over at the metre to see if it was also ticking away, but the driver must have turned it off with the engine. That was a relief!

"Try ringing Patrick, Alice, he might be able to jump in the Jag and meet us halfway."

Alice snapped to attention and began fossicking around in her bag for her phone. Once retrieved, she beckoned with her free hand for the ping-ponged driver to jump back into the car, should we need to make a fast getaway.

Alice finally got onto Patrick after two attempts. Upon hearing his bleary-toned voice, she made that fatal mistake of chastising him for not picking up earlier, and consequently, Patrick was not as helpful and sympathetic to her plight as he might have been had she been all sweetness. Alice, being Alice, had an ace up her sleeve which she pulled out swiftly and thumped down on her chastising. It was one word. It was 'Darling'. It worked a treat with Patrick every time.

As soon as he heard the magic word, his bleary tone changed to one of loving efficiency, and loud rummaging could be heard coming from Alice's mobile. (She had put Patrick on speaker so that all three of us could act hastily on whatever the plan of action turned out to be.) Patrick was continuing to pacify Alice, assuring her (and the driver and I, although he couldn't have known we were listening) that he was searching through her bedside drawers, but to no avail. "Oh Patrick, look harder." Alice was not giving up, now she was convinced she knew the location of the tablets.

Suddenly, she called out, "What? You found them? They are in there? In the striped bag? Are you sure? Can you meet us at Rafferty's corner in ten minutes? Why not?"

It turned out the 'why not' was because Patrick had not thought to fill up the Jag with petrol in case it needed to be on standby on the morning of our big trip to Italy. This morning. And the tank was all but empty.

Once Alice heard the dreaded news, she slipped into her third rotation from sweetness to "Listen carefully, Patrick, this is what's going to happen now" mode straight away.

The long and the short of it had Patrick springing up out of bed (tablet-bag in hand), locking the dogs in the laundry, thus preventing them from getting upset when our taxi pulled up outside the bedroom window (which was at the front of the house), throwing on slippers and a dressing-gown and waiting on the porch with Crewcut and his crony till our taxi appeared. The last leg for Patrick would be to run out to the road and baton-pass the striped bag to Alice, whose only part in the pantomime would be to wind down her window and outstretch her left arm. The driver's part would be to drive as fast as he could back to the house, and I was assigned to watching for green lights ahead and alerting the driver to any potential hazards, such as children crossing roads.

We were all set. Alice kept assuring the driver that we would pay him for the extra miles we clocked up, so he was sorted. She also kept apologising to me that she had left the tablets in the drawer. "I'm sure I put them into my hand luggage, but I couldn't have. I just can't remember now. I'm really sorry, Fil. If we miss the plane, we'll just have to sit at the airport and wait for the next one."

She needn't have kept on apologising. I wasn't fussed in the least. I was disappointed, because I had form with planes, and was well aware that the Milanese pilot who made the same flight every day of the week from Heathrow to Milan and back would be waiting for no one. It wasn't only Patrick who relished order and routine.

Speaking of whom, there he was, pacing up and down the 'Widow's Walk', clutching something small and striped. From the top of the cul-de-sac, with my limited vision, he appeared to be wearing a dressing gown. (I had taken off my long-distance glasses when reading the fine-print directions to Heathrow on my phone.)

As we got closer, I could also make out Crewcut and the other cat, but Looby and Holly must have been left inside. There was no sign of them on the porch.

Patrick must have seen us, as he suddenly leapt off the porch, stumbling and then steadying himself. (He may have tripped over one of the cats.)

On his last leg (literally), Patrick passed the baton (striped tablet bag) to Alice, who had stuck to the plan and outstretched her left arm. As soon as Alice had clasped the bag to her chest, she turned to the driver and uttered (loudly) only one word—"Drive!"

Which he did. Patrick was left standing on the side of the road waving us off and putting on his best smile. That was the last we saw of him until we returned some two weeks later. Many a time throughout the trip, Alice tried unsuccessfully to face-time him, but the connections just weren't happening. Not that Patrick was in the least concerned. He was well set to enjoy two weeks sabbatical without his wife or her best friend. The night before, he had let slip that he was looking forward to a glass or two of red wine with his evening meal, followed by a nip or two of port. (We have been discussing the Italian national pastime—'drinking the vino'—and Patrick had put his foot in it).

As children with an Italian father, we had dabbled with making wine in the backyard from the grapes we grew in our small backyard vineyard. Every year, dad and his sister Lucia (who had also come out from Italy to settle in Australia), her husband and a handful of dad's Italian buddies—Mario, Matteo, Giovanni, Umberto and Giuseppe—would congregate in our yard, and we would trample on the grapes trying our best to squeeze out some liquid.

The whole ordeal was totally unfruitful, year after year, but we had so much fun, jumping and screaming and squealing in delight at the goings on, that it didn't seem to matter that no wine was produced. There was plenty of wine to be drunk though, since every person who passed through the side gate appeared with a yellow-streaked raffia bottle of Chianti, loaves of crusty Italian bread, tomatoes swimming in oil, anchovies, olives and salami. We had the same vino-fest every year. The men would drink and play cards, the women would prepare the meal and clean up and we kids would crucify the grapes by trampling them to a pulp. An Italian childhood in Australia—one to be envied!

After Alice had barked out the order to the driver to "drive", she turned around to me and apologised for her shortness. "I was desperate to get the tablets and I thought we'd miss the plane. I'm really sorry for panicking." She then turned directly to the driver. His apology was next. "I'm very sorry for ordering you, especially when you are doing us a favour coming all the way back here. I was very rude, and I have no other excuse." The driver looked shocked, as though no one had ever apologised to him before. He said nothing, but rewarded Alice with a wide smile, which she seemed to accept.

I felt relieved that peace had been restored in the front seat, and a tiny bit thrilled that we were going to Italy after all. The driver had made good time in the mercy dash back to Alice's and the traffic was still light as it was only seven am. Two hours until we were airborne and on our way to the land of romance and song. Confident that Heathrow would be our next stop, I took the opportunity to close my eyes for forty winks. Alice looked to be doing the same, as her head was flush up against the window and she wasn't talking. The driver had resumed his humming, although I couldn't hear any music.

Twenty minutes to go, and we would be inside the terminal at last. It was a big thing—flying to another country, especially a country where one did not speak the language. I did know some Italian and could make myself understood with the help of mime and gesture, but Alice wasn't as confident, although it was Alice who was taking weekly Italian lessons and she who wanted to live in Italy forever and a day. Patrick was warming to the idea, but it was still a few years off. Alice had told me that our trip to the Italian lakes would seal it for her. If she loved Italy as much as she had on her last trip over with Patrick, it would be a fait accompli, and the moving box collection in the carparks of big department stores would begin.

The more I thought about it, the more I realised we had a good deal riding on this trip. Alice might move to Italy and spend her retirement years sipping chilled chianti and visiting churches, and I might take the opportunity to reconnect with my heritage in my father's country—his beloved Italy.

We ended up paying the driver double what we had planned, but he had done such a sterling job of delivering us and all our luggage to the terminal by seven-thirty that it seemed a small price to pay. He was thrilled with the bonus and assured us that he would be available to collect us on our return in a couple of weeks, handing us his card and urging us to ring him—'any time'.

Given that he had been the perfect driver, gone above and beyond his duty of safely delivering us to Heathrow, without once complaining or shirking his responsibilities, I would be racing off to an Italian version of *Office Works* as soon as we hit the shops in Milan, and printing him off one hundred new cards with a brief description on the back accolading his uncanny ability to teleport passengers. The whole trip had only taken forty minutes, and here we were shuffling towards the counter with an enormous trolley laden with our suitcases and the hand luggage. Yes. The humming man would be duly rewarded. It would just be a matter of time.

Chapter 2
Fast and Furious

From my vantage point at the end of the departures counter, it was possible to take in the chaos that was early morning departure in any international airport anywhere in the world. Earlier this morning, I had been wondering about the possibility of coincidence. Now, I had moved on to the possibility of chaos. Spreading out before me, amoeboid-like, the crowd was fast and furious. Alice, who had given me the slip once I'd deposited her at the Disability Enquiry Counter, was now in deep conversation with a tall dark-haired woman seated on a high-backed, black metal stool.

The woman was dressed in impeccable British Airways uniform (my clue to her airline affiliation was the sign above her head and the British Airways printouts in my hand imprinted with the identical logo). Alice seemed oblivious to time being of the essence, and the precious little time we had for sweet-talk. The fact remained that we were not yet comfortably seated on the plane. Far from it. Once the tickets had been secured, there would still be the dash to the Departure lounge to anticipate, not to mention the ablution stops, Duty Free and the settling of ourselves in our prepaid seats. Something would need to be sacrificed, and my guess was Duty Free, which would greatly disappoint Alice, who had been looking forward to purchasing a couple of bottles of Limoncello for our nightly nattering on the highlights and pitfalls of the day.

Speak of the devil!

Alice was hobbling over to me. "Fil, can you please line up in the ticket line, and I'll go and sit over on those seats and wait for the wheelchair?" She was indicating across to where three elderly gentlemen were already seated, one of whom must have fallen asleep against the wall and was now perpendicular to the bench. I toyed with the idea of helping Alice limp over to the bench, but one experienced look at the extensive line to the ticket desk had me reconsidering.

Our wheelchair requirement had negated checking in online as an option, as the conditions for disability check-in differed from normal booking procedure.

I compromised and hastily half-dragged Alice over to the bench, throwing her down beside the sleeping gentleman as nonchalantly as one would throw a pot in a pottery class. The sleeping man awoke with a start, seemingly mistaking me for a wheelchair attendant, as he stood up and asked if he should follow me to where the wheelchairs were stored or would I be coming back to him with the chair?

I took the cheat's way out, splaying my hands and nodding my head in denial of all airport wheelchairs, and leaving Alice to deal with the befuddled gentleman. Startling the old man was regrettable, but my first priority was to make the plane. My second priority was clasping our tickets and praying the other two bench residents were his mates and not genuine disability cases in their own right. (The trio being together would place Alice next in line for a wheelchair).

Taking up my place at the end of the queue, still dragging all our hand luggage and pushing our suitcases (for which I had not found a trolley), I cursed myself for my lack of foresight. Why had I not dumped it all with Alice? Apart from my handbag, which contained our passports, my glasses, licence and all my cards, thus rendering it indispensable—nothing else needed to be disturbed until we boarded the plane. There were about ten people in front of me, but at least five of them appeared to be one big happy family—parents, two children and a grandmother.

Forgetting my pledge to myself regarding impure stereotypical thoughts, I had them pinned as Italians. They weren't talking, so language was no clue. It was more their looks, gestures and the fact that they had a 'bent-over-in-black' grandmother with a black scarf tied under her chin in tow. The matriarch of every Italian family. The woman who refused to be snuffed out, at least not until her secret recipes for soups and sauces had been interrogated out of her.

I never knew my own grandmother on my father's side. (My father himself hardly knew her.) Dad had only been six years old when she'd passed away. What I did know was that she had died in childbirth and that Nonna had been grief-stricken. They had lived in a tiny walled village close to the coastal port of Brindisi in Southern Italy, and even closer to rows and rows of olive trees which studded the otherwise dusty barren fields behind their stone house.

Seeing the family with the grandmother and thinking about Nonna Filomena made me remember that my handbag did not only contain all the necessary paperwork and gratuities required for entry into Italy, but also fifty sealed plastic bags with fifty tiny olive branches from the wild Olive Grove in a copse behind my home in Melbourne. I had brought the tiny tokens with me from Australia to hand out to perfect strangers—Italians I intended to meet on my travels.

The reasoning behind bequeathing olive branches was simple. The grove had been planted sixty years ago by a group of Italian community gardeners, and for at least a decade I had participated in the annual olive-picking festivities, trying my hand many a time at cold-pressing the olives. Even though the olive pressing endeavours had been some thirty years after the grape and tomato stomping of my childhood, my skills in food processing had not improved, and no oil was forthcoming.

There were stalls where one could purchase bottles of oil which had been lovingly fashioned by experts, so I didn't miss out. Just never made it as an artisan in the Italian food department. When Alice and I had planned the trip to Italy, I had babbled out my dream of handing out olive branches to the Italians, and she'd agreed it was an ingenious idea. (Probably just to shut me up).

"You're simply giving back to them what they gave to you, and keeping diplomatic relations and the cultural ties going, aren't you, Fil?" I was. It was also my hope that some over-intelligent recipient might actually 'get' the significance of the olive branch and how, historically, it has been a symbol of peace and love. I would be thanking the Italians for their unwittingly shaping Australia, and also complimenting them on the economic success of olive groves in many parts of our country.

I really wanted to hand the Italian family up ahead the first olive branch, but technically, they were not in Italy (even though they may have lived there) and as an added dissuasion, I wasn't sure if the family would be unduly detained at the luggage carousels, had plant materials been discovered in their luggage. (The coast was clear for me, since I had already obtained permission from the Italian Consulate in Australia, allowing me to bring the olive branches into the country.) The more I thought about it, the more it became apparent to me that it wouldn't do to rock the boat at this point in time—with only twenty minutes till boarding and multiple tasks still pending. The family would be missing out!

Suddenly, I was at the head of the queue and the woman behind the counter was indicating for me to step forwards. I was having difficulty balancing, so I kicked the luggage up towards her, using alternate feet in the forward propulsion. The sour-faced woman had a good thirty seconds to observe my novel approach and she was now regarding me curiously. I wanted to defend myself and call out that it wasn't all my luggage, and that my friend couldn't walk properly as evidenced by her sitting on the Disability bench awaiting a wheelchair.

Or, I could have strung the woman along once I'd reached the desk and convinced her I really was a football coach and was not a timewaster in airport queues. The woman herself had put the notion of football coach into my head when she'd enquired about whether or not I supported FC Milan, and was I on my way to Milan for a match? She could not have been further from the truth had she enquired about my devotion to Star Wars. I am at complete opposite ends of the spectrum to both sport and science fiction. We have nothing in common, and I intend to keep it that way.

When I reached the counter, I pretended to have misunderstood her question. Consequently, I was of no real interest to her, and Alice and I were never going to be in the running for an upgrade on the flight. I was dealt with efficiently and despite her overzealous examination of my passport, no mention was made of the fact that I was an Australian tourist, and not an English citizen—as was Alice. (The disgruntled woman didn't even look twice at Alice's passport).

I felt sorry for the woman, as she was clearly unhappy with her job and I hoped something more up her alley would materialise. But she was discontent, oldish, greyish and disgruntled, and I knew by the law of averages that the most likely thing to be looming up on the horizon for her would be retirement—and in the not too distant future. She had my sympathy, and I wished she'd qualified for an olive branch, but again, she was not standing on Italian soil. (Her accent gave her away as Italian, but she was still not eligible, according to my plans.) Still, I had a feeling someone would be eligible, and very soon.

The time was ripe for the first coincidence.

Enter Luigi. Blessed with the gracious qualities already elaborated on—and the rest. The honourable Luigi would be the first recipient of an olive branch, even though he lived half his month in Milan and the other half in London. From the moment we laid eyes on him to the moment the plane door was slammed shut in his face, Luigi was nothing short of magnificent—a trooper to the end.

The basic problem was that we had wasted too much time. Wasted taxi time, wasted airport line-up time and wasted washroom time. No sooner had Luigi appeared on the scene than Alice had taken flight and jumped into the wheelchair he was pushing towards her, hanging on to her handbag for dear life. I thought I glimpsed a flickering, knowing exchange between the two of them, and Alice's face was quite red, but I put her extreme colouring down to blood pressure and the stress of almost not having her life-and-death tablets.

Whatever was happening, it all looked above-board, and the two of them were off like Taylor and Burton, even before I had time to sherpa my way behind. Alice called back to me that they were bound for the Ablution Block. Luckily, Luigi had a key to a close-by disability bathroom, and doubly luckily, it was on the direct route to our designated 'Departure Gate'.

Tackling the conveyor belts with our copious amounts of hand luggage had been all that easier because of Luigi. Working at the airport for over twenty years, and being super skilled at his job, had earned him gold status with most of the airlines, to the point that many of the disability passengers would register a special request to be turned and churned by Luigi of the swift 'passagiato'. Here was a true Italian with a reputation to uphold.

He even admitted to me his weakness of being swayed by the ladies. His eyesight could not have been the best, as neither Alice nor I were spring chickens. Undeniably, Luigi had chosen Alice, not the other way around. There had been four to choose from, propped up on the bench against the wall like injured footballers, and Luigi had shown no hesitation in making a beeline for Alice—whisking her away faster than anyone would have thought possible in a crowded, chaotic airport.

The crowds were no problem for Luigi. Regarding them with approval was his trick. (I was quick to work that one out!) Approval for their choice of taking to the air over train and bus transport, approval for their understanding of what it meant to be hurtling along in a disability-wheelchair obviously late for a plane and lastly, approval for the 'disability condition' in general. When Luigi had first picked us up, there had been no enquiry as to Alice's disability, or as to whether she was able to take even the smallest of steps. Luigi simply assumed she had a disability and accepted the fact that he was there to take care of her.

Luigi's 'Achilles heel' was always going to be his overenthusiasm for the female form—his subsequent unashamed shunning of the three elderly tenors perched on the bench alongside of Alice letting him down big time. In his defence, the man was Italian after all and no harm done. The other three 'disabilities' had all been good sports—respecting of women and graciously accepting of their fate of an even longer wait.

Our first stop after the luggage search was the 'Disabled Toilet'—not somewhere outside of which I would have chosen to have been caught loitering, but Alice and I had come as a package and I found myself an unwilling loiterer. Walking around in circles and trying to look as though the attendant and his wheelchair had nothing to do with me was possibly not my best move, as it had just made people stop and stare more.

What was that woman doing? Pacing out the circumference for the next 'Time Team's' chipping and scraping of the ground to reveal London's long-lost archaeological remains? Or was she one of those characters in costume emulating the part played so convincingly by Tom Hanks when he spent three days wandering around an airport? My plan to look casual and disinterested was backfiring. Next step would be to rush into the toilet myself and hide my face, far from the ogling crowds.

Luigi was indifferent to my uncomfortable squirming. Alice being out of the picture gave him the opportunity to scrutinise me—the slow, overladen, circle-pacing donkey. I felt like a horse with colic. Being a voracious reader in my childhood, and of discerning literary taste even then, Enid Blyton stories had been amongst my favourite. In that respect I was an ordinary working-class child. But there had been one major difference—my childhood addiction to reading.

My sisters would be out gallivanting on billycarts and scooters, having mountains of wild, reckless, tomboyish fun in the fresh mountain air, and I was nowhere to be located. The daily search party would be dispatched, and most days I would be unearthed, kicking and protesting, from under a bed, or from the highest shelf in a cupboard, or sometimes even from the treehouse on the plantation across from our house—my nose in a book, living out someone else's life.

That was how I came to think of Luigi and the surging airport crowds may have assumed me to have had colic. (That, and the fact that I was pacing around outside the "occupied" Disabled Toilet.) In the Blyton books, a colic-ridden horse was forever being led around in circles in English stables. The phrase, "If the horse stops circling and lays down, he dies", had stayed with me for years, and was now back to haunt me. I didn't have any pain to speak of, my only source of anxiety being that in fifteen minutes time, our plane would be boarding and we were still twenty minutes from the boarding gate.

I wondered, had I been the invalid on the bench, would Luigi have been so quick off the mark in scooping me up with the wheelchair? Alice, blonde-haired and blue-eyed, was the perfect English rose, even though she was technically Australian, and I was dark, feisty and olive-skinned, courtesy of my Italian heritage. Looks alone should have had me up there with a fighting chance in the selection stakes.

Luigi was still staring at me. It was time to break the ice and allow him the opportunity to speak. Because that was it. I realised he was being overly polite and waiting for permission to speak.

"So, Luigi, you have been a wheelchair attendant for…how long? Do you have to do a lot of training to keep up to date with all the shortcuts down the corridors to the planes?" Luigi was off like a cannonball once I had tacitly opened the gates to conversation. I heard all about his tiny garden flat with the gigantic willow tree in the front courtyard, an hour from Heathrow—where he lived for two weeks out of four. I also heard about his villa in Milan where he spent the alternate weeks. Alone. His wife had died two years ago, and he was left with one daughter, now living back in Milan, whom he emphasised was very good to him. No grandchildren, and a life tinged with grief for his beautiful, departed Graziella, cremated over Lake Como, her favourite swimming hole.

Lake Como was to be a highlight on our itinerary, but I was loath to point this out to Luigi in case he wanted us to pay Graziella a visit, and it would be difficult to know where to begin looking. I was jumping in blind with the Italian Lakes, but I hoped to come away from this trip to the North more informed about the beautiful north of the country where I could no doubt spend days delving into Ancestry.Com.

Ask me about Southern Italy, and it would be straight to Master Mind with 'Southern Italia' as my special subject, but Northern Italy…well, that was an entirely different kettle of fish. Of course, I'd heard it was mountainous, and that there was snow and churches, and more snow and more churches, but I was still pretty much in the dark about the whole place. I probably wasn't alone either. Northern Italy just wasn't somewhere I had ever really thought much about.

Luigi was simultaneously looking at his watch and gazing at the closed door to the Disabled Toilet. He then turned to me with more than a hint of anxiety in his voice. "Do you think we should knock and hurry the Signora? I have some of the influence to get us to the plane quickly, but I cannot stop the plane from taking off without you. Only God can do that."

Here was my clue from a Milanese man that we were about to embark on a holiday in a country soaked in religious heritage. And I had forgotten to pack my rosary beads and mantilla! I smiled at Luigi and was on the cusp of knocking on the door and calling out to Alice "Fait presto!" (Alice had learnt this phrase in week 1 of Italian AO1 at the weekly night classes she and Patrick had been attending.)

Presenting coincidence number three. My knuckles were poised to knock (thump actually) on the paint-peeled (oh so Heathrow) door, when Alice suddenly burst out, looking flustered and grasping and falling onto me. "Phew. Fil. Thank heavens it's you and not Luigi. I couldn't get the door to open, and I've been calling out for ages. Didn't you think to check where I was all this time? Now we're really going to miss the plane!"

It was a long-winded speech from Alice, and we were frozen in 'Madonna and Child' position. I had expected Luigi to come rushing over to help, but he was standing stoically beside the wheelchair, staring straight ahead, guarding the chair with his life. I suspected many a wheelchair had gone missing from Heathrow International when left unattended outside Disabled Toilets, if even for only a few seconds. This particular Disabled Toilet directly abutted the main thoroughfare to eons of tired linoleum encrusted Departure lounges, and the amount of traffic ebbing past the door was a fast-flowing river.

We were in peak morning period, and many of the passengers were businessmen and women, late like us, and caring for no one, where their midday meetings in Brussels were concerned. The traffic was so thick, Luigi was momentarily obscured from my vision and the very real fear of having to carry Alice to the plane, hand luggage, handbags and all, was beginning to roll in like a dense fog. In a panic I let go, and Alice tumbled forwards onto a luggage-laden family pushing past. (There was a real Alice in Wonderland surrealism about the whole incident.)

It was the best possible outcome for Alice, as the father was of ample flesh and did a brilliant job of cushioning her fall. Slowed down, the choreography would have been exquisite. Free falling Alice, being passed from my arms to his. If being filmed, the shot would need to have been in slo-mo, but the finished vignette would have been colossally Instagram-able. In real time, Alice was being passed from the ample-fleshed father to Luigi, who had emerged from the fog with his wheelchair. Alice was once again the dumpy, perpetually demanding Queen Victoria being lowered from her bathing-machine directly down into the sea.

The family had gotten ahead of the father, so he wasn't sticking around long enough to be thanked. He did look back at our little ménage-a-trois and shook his head, but I was not sure whether this meant approval that we had been reunited, or bigoted disapproval at our supposed lifestyle choice.

He would have been right with the first supposition. We were, all three of us, happy to be reunited. Even though Alice and I had only known Luigi less than half an hour, it was a deep bonding—one which we would not forget in a hurry. Sometimes this happens. We meet a perfect stranger, and it is as if we have known them forever, yet unaware, they had been part of the fabric of our lives. Part of the air we breathe, the food we taste, the earth we smell. But not consciously. Always that layer below.

Luigi was one such person, and when I began by explaining the coincidence which was our meeting, I had the sense of faintly grasping this secret manifesto of energy. Whist at university I had studied Jungian theories, and the plausibility of both synchronicity and coincidence was not lost to me. Luigi was my divine nudge at this early hour.

Alice was my earthly nudge. "Come on, Fil. We only have ten minutes to get to the Departure Lounge. It doesn't look like we'll be making it to Duty Free on the way over. Maybe it will be open when we get to Milan?" I doubted it. Alice would be tired out by the time we made Milan, and if we bought the Limoncello and perfume she had been on about for days, it would end up in my hand luggage, along with everything else.

"Don't worry about Duty Free, Alice, we can buy Limoncello in Milan. Let's just focus on getting to the plane." Luigi had been a silent presence, pushing with all his might up the incline to the travelator which mercifully extended for a healthy length of aluminium and plastic towards the end of the airport, where floor to ceiling glass revealed a troop of planes to be lined up like Thomas the Tank and his engine buddies, awaiting customers.

Once we were housed on the flat travelator, Luigi again found his voice, and began pontificating the marvels of his hometown—Milan. He really came alive when he mentioned 'Il Duomo', as it had been the place where he'd met Graziella almost forty years ago. "It was Christmas eve, and I was waiting for mia amigo Gino. We were going to buy presents for our mothers. Gino was late, and there was a pretty girl looking for her sister. But the sister had gone into a dressa shop, and she did not return. It seemed the sister was trying on every dress in the shop, and she was behind the curtain when Graziella had gone into the shop to look for her."

"Because she hada lost her sister, and it was freezing and snowing, I gave her my jumper. She was beautiful, and I fell in love with her as I putta the jumper arounda her shoulders. I will never forget how I felt that evening. My heart was melting and turning to a-thicka-lump at the same time. Mia coupa, mia coupa." Luigi's free hand was thumping at his left breast.

It seemed we had set Luigi off into a tirade of first love/ last love, and there was no stopping him. His having met his wife by default through her sister on a snowy evening reminded me of the storyline in the Disney film, 'Frozen'. We pretended to listen, whilst anxiously scanning the Departure Lounges for Number 27-British Airlines-London to Milan. Thankfully, it was up next.

"Luigi, stop! Please! We're here." Alice had meant stop with the frantic racing, but I hoped Luigi would take it to mean he need also stop with the serious lamenting and focus on getting us safely onto the plane. He had come to a screeching halt when Alice had called out. So screeching a halt, in fact, that Alice was propelled forwards, and cue coincidence number four for the day.

Who should be sitting up like skittles in a row of five in the Departure lounge to Milan, but the family with the grandmother, towards whom I had toyed with the idea of presenting the first olive branch! Alice was again air-bound. Down she tumbled, this time into the folds of the grandmother's bosom. She wasn't hurt, just stunned, and the grandmother saw the funny side of the incident and burst into peals of cackling laughter.

The kids also started laughing, and that set Luigi and I off. Everyone was laughing. Some even began hyperventilating. It was mass delirium. Relief that we had arrived at the Departure lounge. Relief that Alice wasn't hurt, and relief that from this point onwards, nothing would be interfering with our sailing off into the early morning mist on the big bird that was a Boeing 747.

It was a quick 'cut to the chase' with Luigi, as no sooner had the collective laughter petered out to a trickle, than the announcement for boarding came over loud and clear. Everyone scrambled to their feet at once (except Alice) and raced off to declare themselves to the hostesses lined up at the gangway. It was a big enough plane to warrant an internal walkway, so there would be no need for Alice to be winched onto the plane. Some years ago, I had been travelling with two friends to Venice from Heathrow (one of whom had a bad leg like Alice), and a lift and a winch had been involved. Thankfully, we were spared this morning.

Our return trip was in the distant future, and the plane might not be as big as this one was, but that was almost two weeks away. Alice's leg would surely have healed by then. We would be able to parade proudly onto the plane with the best of them. Luigi was still standing to the side with the wheelchair in case Alice wanted to hop back into the seat, in which case he would push her all the way to the plane door. She did. He did. We ended up saying goodbye at the plane door. As he turned away, clutching the ten-pound note Alice had handed him before she'd hobbled down the aisle to our assigned seat, I slipped the plastic bag with the olive branch into his spare hand.

There was no need for explanation, as I had inserted a carefully translated script into the bag alongside of the olive branch explaining the significance of the branch, and instructions for planting. (I hoped he would do so at his home in Milan.) I also hoped he would be able to get the olive branch through customs, but given his sway and standing with airport officials, that should not have proved too difficult.

Luigi barely had time to smile at me before the door was closed on his face, and the chief-hostess was urging me to hurry and find my seat as the plane was about to take off. As I shuffled down the aisle, overburdened with our cabin luggage, people were looking up from their belted positions and urging me with their hands to make haste towards my seat. I could see Alice a few seats ahead also waving me towards her, as the engine had started up. We were off at last. To infinity and beyond!

Chapter 3
Plane Sailing

Our seats were roughly halfway up the aisle, and by the time the food trolley reached us, 'famished' would have been a best-fit description. In all the rush of our early morning departure, and the lateness of it all, breakfast had been forgotten. Even though it was only nine thirty in the morning, we had been up for almost five hours, and that was a long time between drinks in any language. At last I heard five words that were music to my ears, "Anything from the food trolley?"

Alice was ready with her response. Had been for the last half hour, when she had first begun to crane her scarf-embodied neck up and down the aisle on a sedentary food safari. I hadn't had the heart to point out to her that we were sitting smack-bang in the middle of the plane, and that unless we had pre-ordered our meals (which we hadn't), we were in for a long wait. I had cruelly wanted to rub salt into the wounds, adding that it wouldn't have made a scrap of difference where the hostesses started, our row was always going to be the last row served. (Ours and the row opposite.) But I'd held my tongue and we'd waited patiently, building up our appetites.

"I'll have the breakfast roll with egg and bacon, and a cup of hot tea please." Alice's order was in, and I was next.

It was easier just to make it easy for the hostess. "I'll have the same please, but without the bacon. Thanks." The window seat in our row was empty, so it was speedy service from the hostesses. The food, lukewarm but edible, was certainly not Michelin star, but we were both so hungry it didn't seem to matter much. The Gods must have been smiling, because the three Asian travellers in the row opposite still hadn't received their meals by the time we had finished ours.

"What did they order, Alice?"

Sitting in the middle seat can be disadvantageous when eavesdropping, and Alice had been closer to the action, so I assumed she may have heard them putting in their requests and would remember the contents of their order. She certainly wasn't hearing me, and I was sitting right next to her.

"Alice, did you hear me. What did they order?"

"Who?"

"The people opposite you. What did they ask for?"

"Oh them!" Alice shrugged her already hunched-over shoulders. "They wanted to know if there was Milanese rice with frog's legs on the menu, as they'd read about how good it tasted, but the air hostess didn't really understand what they were talking about, so they didn't order anything. They've got water bottles though."

Alice turned back to her reading. She was cheesed off because she hadn't been permitted to bring her stitching with her on the plane.

"No sharp needles allowed!" That had been the response she'd received when she'd politely enquired of the man at the other end of her mobile as to whether she might be permitted to do some of her stitching on the plane. If she'd had more time to loiter around the airport, Alice might have noticed the signs up everywhere explicitly listing what sorts of personal items might be brought onto planes, and what was categorically prohibited and would need to be surrendered at the checkpoints.

Interestingly, Alice hadn't put up any protest to the ban on needles when she had rung the airport with her enquiry, and had handed the phone meekly over to me so that I might find out about the process of importing my olive branches into Italy. Even though I had already prepared and packaged the branches, and had handwritten the accompanying instructions, complete with Italian tree blessing notes, I'd had Plan B up my sleeve, and had wanted to run it by the Customs officials. The plan didn't go down too well.

After I had explained my request to the first operator, I was asked to "stay on the line please and wait for the next operator." At least I hadn't been told that the wait-time would be two hours, and if I liked, I could request a callback by leaving my name after the beep.

The second operator (half an hour and two rounds of Phil Collins later) was even less helpful than her predecessor, and after ten minutes of Alice urging me to hang up and use my own phone as her battery was running low (not the case!),

I was finally connected to someone able to give me a definitive answer, and put a firm (double-locked) lid on my fanciful ideas.

"Ere, what yaw ganna do? Corblimey, yer wanna cart an olive tree around Italy and break off little branches and give 'em away? What for? It's not a Christmas tree yer thinking of, are yer?"

I had explained my idea to the man with the indecipherable accent in detail. No. I wasn't thinking of a Christmas tree. Yes. I did want to buy an olive tree in Australia, and have it sent over to Milan, where I intended to pick it up from the airport and carry it around with me on the bus. I would then happily distribute the branches to all and sundry in Northern Italy. (A tree would have far more branches than I would be able to individually package.) Yes, I was aware that the tree could not be over ten kilograms in weight, and yes, I did have a backup plan if my project proved to be outside the realms of possibility with either Australian or Italian Departments of Agriculture.

After ten minutes of pleading, and ten minutes of Alice's battery severely depleting, I realised that the hardened, hard-to-decipher man at the end of the line was never going to agree it was a brilliant idea, nor was he ever going to sanction the project.

"I think yer'd be wise ter stick ter yer first idea, lass. Seeing as yerve already gone to the trouble of packing the plastic bags, and yer go ahead is there. Ferget the tree. The Ities'd never go fer it, and yell end up in an Italian jail buried under an avalanche from ve earthquakes in ve mountains. Take my advice and steer clear of trees."

I knew in my heart of hearts the man was right, and that picking up the tree from the airport would have done no more than signal the start of our potential saga with a tree on a bus. It would have made a good dinner party story—meeting people along the way up to the lakes and inviting them to pick a branch from an environmentally-friendly living tree. It would have meant choice and ownership for them, but possibly obscured vision and frequent volatile outbursts from the driver when he was attempting to back the bus up on narrow mountain paths. (Which was definitely on the cards.)

That was how Plan B came to be scratched, and Plan A lived to see another day.

After the meals had been served, it went all quiet on the plane. Church quiet. I seemed to be receiving some sort of sign from the universe to visit a particular church on this trip, as all I could think about was churches whenever anyone mentioned Italy. I put the notion out of my mind, reckoning that I would recognise the church when I was standing in it. The old people had slipped into mid-morning siesta mode, the babies followed suite, fed and content with the lulling purr of the plane and the inbetweeners—the children and adults (Alice and I included) could be found reclining in their seats, eyes focussed on the small screens in front of them, or glazed over with built-up inertia.

I was partial to this quiet time on planes. The time when baby crying ceased, and all flight attendants were 'outa-town'. Alice was also very quiet, but I suspected her cloak of silence was more related to her not being able to engage in her favourite down-time occupation—needlework.

"Why don't you see if there is a movie you could watch, Alice? There might be one on houses." Alice loved watching house programmes such as *Escape to the Country* or *Grand Design*. She was forever making plans for renovations and improvements to both her town and beach houses.

"I think I'll see if I can find a programme on Italian villas or castle renovations in France. It'll get me in the mood for the beautiful architecture we'll no doubt see in Italy." Alice's face lit up when she mentioned Italy, and I was glad we had been able to make the trip. For a while there, it hadn't looked good for Alice. Her leg was making no improvement, and she was up to her eyeballs in tablets. The doctor had advised an operation, but that couldn't be scheduled until July. Almost two months away.

Italy seemed as good a place as any in which to squander away the hours until the Op. Alice had confided in me that she didn't fancy the operation, and that maybe we could stop off at Medjugorje in Bosnia-Herzegovina for a miracle cure. That way the operation could be avoided. (Lourdes would have been closer.) Finding a miracle cure at one of the healing hotspots would have been worth a shot, but unfortunately Alice was needed back at work in two weeks' time. She would be taking up light duties until the operation was completed. Then it would be back to full time slog out on the front for the poor woman. It seemed London was teeming with babies and students requiring the services of teachers of the deaf. Twenty minutes of channel surfing, and not an architectural programme to be found. There was a dedicated Lifestyle channel, but it was mostly reality television programmes, and neither Alice nor I had any time for that particular genre. I found it totally insensitive and bordering on cruel to sit criticising somebody else's lifestyle when we could be living out our own.

Time was moving on and we decided to have a little shut-eye before we landed in Milan.

Which lasted all of ten minutes.

The interruption was a swift bullseye.

"Ladies and gentlemen, please be advised that we have begun our descent into Milan. The flight attendants and stewards will be passing through the cabin to collect any rubbish you may wish to pass on. Can you also please ensure that your seat is upright, your tray table back in place and your window blind raised. Twenty minutes till landing!"

A few bumps and we were down. The inevitable grizzling tirade courtesy of the babies of the plane, and a few Italian nuns up the front furiously reciting decade after decade of the rosary was the only disturbance to our landing. The Captain was again quick to swallow the microphone. "Please remain in your seats with your seatbelt fastened until the red light is turned off, and it is safe to exit the plane."

Not one solitary person (with the exception of Alice and myself) took the slightest skerrick of notice. We were all up the second the plane was down. Seatbelts flying, hand luggage flying, people flying. It was pandemonium for a few minutes whilst the crowd arranged themselves into standing or bending positions in the aisles. Alice wanted to move with the rest of them, but I pointed out (sensibly, and for the second time) that we would be going nowhere as our seats were in the middle of the plane.

"I know that, Fil, I just didn't want to be last off the plane. Actually, we will probably have to wait for the flight attendant to tell us if they were able to get us a wheelchair at this end." She had a point. Jumping up would not get us out of the plane any faster. We might as well just sit back and wait. And wait. And wait and wait. Ten minutes later we were still waiting. The last person-a man carrying a sleeping infant's head swaddled in a huge pink fluffy blanket had disappeared around the corner of the exit door, and it was just Alice and I left.

"Now can we move, Fil? I think they must have forgotten us. They've all disappeared." Alice was correct, they had all vamoosed-off into the early morning bustle of the gleaming Milan airport. It took some manoeuvring to help Alice out of the seat, and I ended up having to climb over her to reach the aisle, from where I could pull her up to her feet. The next trick was to pull the luggage from above our heads and strap myself up with all manner of luggage like a suicide bomber.

Not that I had seen a living person in that guise, and not a healthy thought on my part. It was just all so cumbersome, and I felt so uncomfortable and weighed down. Alice was coping perfectly well with her walking stick and handbag and was already halfway up the aisle before I was ready to make tracks.

"Wait up, Alice. I'm all lopsided. Can you help me get my balance and distribute these bags properly across my shoulder?"

It took us another five minutes to get kitted out, and still no help had appeared. We had reached the end of the walkway, and were entering the 'airport proper', when a wiry, curly-haired Italian boy in tight blue jeans and a shirt with the airport logo jumped out in front of us. "Signoras, I am era for a you two. I ava the two-wheeler chairs." The two wheelchairs? Surely there hadn't been a mistake and a second wheelchair had been ordered? The pumped-up boy was indicating to the one he was pushing, but as far as I could tell there was no second chair. Alice was settling herself into the chair he was pushing with no invitation, merely entitlement. The boy looked at her and sunk his shoulders. "This is then for you?"

Alice nodded, and it was then my turn to be examined. "And you? We should get then another wheelchair?"

Time to speak up and defend my able-bodied-ness. "No. I'm good. Thanks, but I can walk."

I was tempted to ask him why he thought I could do with a wheelchair, or why he had intonated that two wheelchairs would be provided, but he seemed to be struggling with finding the correct English words, and he possibly had meant the wheelchair had two wheels-not that there were two lumpy seats on wheels ripe for the picking. As soon as I'd declined his kind offer of a ride in a wheelchair along the gleaming, lemon-scented linoleum of Malpensa Airport-he was off, zigzagging and weaving past people like there was no tomorrow. There was no way I'd be able to catch up with him and offload some of the hand luggage into Alice's lap, or hang it from the bars at the front of the wheelchair, so I slowed right down and took the slowest of slow steps.

Ten minutes later, I made it to the luggage carousel with 'Flights from London' marked in English on a huge fluorescent sign above the conveyor belt. There were only two people waiting there-Alice and the wheelchair attendant. Except that he wasn't really there at all but could be found leaning against a wall some ten metres from Alice and the chair, shouting into his phone in Italian. I could hear him as I approached the Heathrow luggage sign, and I could also understand perfectly well what he was saying. He was telling the person on the end of the line that he had been waiting for ages for the lady in the wheelchair to get off the plane, and that when she'd finally arrived, there were two ladies, not one, as he had noted down on his morning schedule.

The closer I got to Alice, the louder he became, to the point that Alice was looking very exasperated with him for disturbing the peaceful atmosphere of the airport. All I could think of was how different it was to Heathrow. And where were all the people? Not even a single person from our flight was to be seen, and the luggage carousel was looking empty and despondent. Round and round the belt circled in sullen solitary silence. Nothing appeared. I had a tiny red scarf in my pocket, so I whipped it out and placed it on the empty carousel.

"Let's just see how long the scarf takes to pop its head out of the carousel, Alice. That should give us an indication of how long we'll need to wait for our luggage—or even if it's on the carousel at all." It took three minutes for the scarf to reappear, and by the third rotation, we were ready to call it quits. Alice began waving her hands in an effort to summon the wheelchair boy, who had finished his conversation five minutes before, but had stayed leaning on the wall playing with his phone.

"Scuzzy, attentione, but can you please push me over to Lost Property? Our luggage hasn't come out and it doesn't look like it will appear today at all. We'll have to ask at Lost Property. Maybe it is already there, seeing as we were so late showing up here."

The boy came over tentatively towards us, his face reading that he didn't have a clue in the world what Alice had been on about. (I think it might have been the interchanging of 'here' and 'there' which was the source of his confusion. He was clearly neither 'here' nor 'there' with what Alice wanted of him.) I intervened by beckoning to the boy to push the chair and follow me. He wasn't the only one without a clue.

I had no clue where Lost property might be located, but I could read the universal language of pictures, icons and arrows, and if I could just follow my nose, the Lost Property Offices looked to be located along a very narrow, very long, glistening and gleaming marbled thoroughfare. It reminded me of Caesar's Palace in Las Vegas—everything was so clean, new and sterile.

The boy and Alice were following me, and I was a confident leader. Following arrows and little picture clues was right up my alley, and much easier than stopping to ask for directions in my limited Italian. The time I had stuck in my mind as I played tour guide to Alice and the boy was when I'd been at Fiumicino Airport in Rome a few years back, and we had wanted breakfast. I had assured my friends I was able to speak enough Italian to enquire as to where we might find the best place to eat. It seems I failed miserably.

After three attempts to convince an exasperated woman at the Information booth that we were looking for somewhere to eat, I ended up spitting out any old Italian words that popped into my head, and asking for 'burnt bread' instead of toast, and a clomp on the head instead of a cup of tea. Another story for the books, especially if, during the retelling, I was able to take off the accent of the woman who could make neither head nor tail of my request.

Finally, ten minutes after we had set off from the luggage carousels, I spotted the sign for 'Lost Property' ahead. It was only with eighty percent of confidence that I turned around and waved to my disciples to move faster. The twenty percent of uncertainty was nervously bundled up in the notion that I had misread the sign, and it had not been Lost Property, but an advertisement for a holiday spot in Spain or Portugal—'Los Palmos'.

For once, I was correct. We were indeed at Lost Property, and I could turn my head in pride towards the wheelchair and nod enthusiastically to the other two that we had reached our destination.

Chapter 4
Lost Property and Lost on the Trains

Lost Property was like a holding station en-route to hell. If the section of the airport from which we had just endured our long fifteen-minute pilgrimage was stark, pristine, and people-less, then this holding-zone into which we had stumbled aimlessly was the complete opposite. Dichotomous differences all round. The harlequin-patterned linoleum was faded, dirty and chipped, the pale blue walls shabby and paint-peeled-reminiscent of an eerie abandoned railway station somewhere in the desert. To add fuel to the fire, the queue to the booth with the one angry-looking official was endless.

"This can't be it, Fil. It looks like we've landed in another county!"

Alice spoke the truth. It was like being in another county, and also in another time-zone. I checked my watch, mistrusting the fishiness of it all, but it was 2019 alright, and we had not yet dematerialised, as was many a plot in almost every other Science Fiction drama I had ever had the misfortune to endure with my family on 'family film night'. Immediate action was necessary.

"Alice, you and your attendant stay here, and I'll go and find out what's happening. This is all very strange."

Alice didn't reply, so I directly addressed the boy. "I think she's in a bit of shock about how things have been going wrong for us this morning, can you please just keep an eye on her for me?"

The boy nodded, and started bending over towards Alice, eyeballing her. He was getting a little close for comfort and Alice was looking worried. I couldn't work out what he was doing, but I then remembered having asked him to keep an eye on Alice, and he was taking my words very literally. His left eye was on Alice, and Alice alone. It wasn't much use hanging around. I didn't want to embarrass the boy. "Okay, I'll go and line up now. By the way, what's your name?"

"Vincent, I'm Vincent."

"Oh, thanks Vincent, I shouldn't be too long. You can go if you like, we'll be alright from now on."

Vincent looked doubtfully at me. "Bot ow are you going to keep all the luggage?" He had a point. I hadn't thought that one through. Alice and I had one large suitcase each, as well as all the hand luggage. Our plan had been to buy a ticket and jump onto one of the fast speed trains into Milan. The airport was a good thirty kilometres out of Milan and a taxi would have cost a fortune. Way back in the first flush of impossible-to-be-contained excitement, we had meticulously planned our course of action, carefully considering time and cost. What we hadn't counted on was Alice's leg being as bad as it was, and added to this, I had imagined the wheelchair attendant to have accompanied us to the station and helped us with the boarding process.

Vincent was back on his wall (substitute mall?) cradling his phone again, babbling on in Italian. I stayed where I was, and waited for him to take a breath, mainly because of the overabundance of luggage and subsequent dilemma. Too much hand luggage, no wheelchair, and no way of communicating, put us in the midst of a dilemma of massive proportions. But good news was on the horizon.

When Vincent finally shoved his phone into the back pocket of his jeans, he was smiling from ear to ear, and jumping up and down behind the wheelchair. His erratic behaviour was making the crowds in the line to Lost Property stare at the three of us. I was a trifle embarrassed because I wasn't sure why he was so happy.

"What is it, Vincent? Why all the joy?"

This time he understood me perfectly, and the English in his retort was also perfect! "I ava my friend who willa 'elp you."

That was comforting. I hoped the friend would be leading us to the train station, and that he was bigger and stronger than Vincent. According to the map, he would be pushing the wheelchair for a long time. Cheered by the good news under my belt, I dumped the assortment of bags we still had in our possession at the foot of the wheelchair and made my way over to the line-settling myself at the end. The line looked to be longer than an overnight queue to a Nike shoe sale.

The next time I looked up, Vincent had disappeared and his elongated replacement was positioned in sedentary pose behind the wheelchair, a grim look on his face, but at least he had turned up. Alice had given up waiting by the looks of things. This time she had a larger and more detailed map spread out over her lap and was talking into her iPhone. I wasn't sure what she was saying, but knowing Alice as well as I did, I guessed it would have something to do with the map—probably dictating intricate directions to herself on the route from the railway station to the hotel.

Three irate strangers in front of me and it was already one o'clock.

The group leaving the front of the line were all men. Five of them—all theatrically outfitted in shiny bicycle attire. Tight blue and yellow-lycra-onesies with orange cone-shaped helmets. Black-slippered feet. From what I could gather, one of the cyclists had lost his bike in transit and was distraught. The unsavoury-faced attendant behind the counter kept shaking his head and waving his arms about, as if gearing up for a solo flight around the airport.

The bicycle group finally gave up, realising that the bike was 'lost in translation', and that they would be one man down in their team pursuit around Italy in the Italian equivalent of the Tour de France. They left dejected, the most forlorn faces I'd seen in a long time, and it would have been the perfect opportunity to jump out of my possie in the line, pursue them and hand them each an olive branch. Trouble was, they were Dutch! (I had recognised a few Dutch words being bandied around, and their physique also gave them away.)

It would have been the Good Samaritan thing to have done, but selfishly, I only wanted Italians, and they probably would have wanted another bike. Vincent and the new kid on the block who had taken his place would be the first two recipients of the olive branches on Italian soil.

And then there was one. One person left in front of me. Sadly, a person who had lost not only her suitcase, but also her hand luggage, which had contained cards, money and her passport. She was American, loud, and demanding. She was also up there for the long haul, which meant, so were we!

I tried to look patient but was taunted by the large black frowning clock above the attendant's booth. Patience is only easy when time is not involved. The longer I waited, the more impatient I became, until after twenty minutes I'd had enough. It was unlikely that the woman's case would ever be resolved in this lifetime, and we would still be standing here, waiting for the issue of our own cases to be resolved.

I was getting stronger at standing up for myself. Being in a foreign county sometimes allows one to alter one's personality to the point where it becomes difficult to revert back to normalcy. It was happening to me. I was morphing. Normally, I will wait for conditions to be rife before I can no longer tolerate impossible situations, but this morning I was tired and irritable, and what was probably only a ripple in the waters of life had for me, taken on tsunami proportions.

Pushing myself forwards, I bravely tapped the American woman on the shoulder.

"Excuse me, but I've been waiting behind you for ages, and you really have taken enough of everyone's time. Don't you realise there are other people here, other than yourself, with lost luggage? The guys before you lost a bike, and I get it that you have lost your worldly goods, but we've lost our suitcases, and my friend over there is injured."

The woman assumed mute mode. I wasn't even sure whether she had heard me. The attendant behind the counter was looking at the two of us, as if we were both a tedious distraction to his daily routine, and I could tell he had us tagged as being from the same geographical location. Not that I minded being thought of as American.

We had grown up with American television, American food and shopping malls, so I was quite comfortable with America. My fear was that he may have thought us to be together. (Not as a couple, just travelling together.) If I kept talking to the woman, I stood the very real chance of losing my place in the line and it would be another hour before I could plead our case. I looked over to Alice and the second attendant, but he was facing the other way, so I couldn't see his face.

Alice was reading and looked to be quite happy doing so. Why was I fussing? Neither of them seemed fazed and the tour didn't begin until Saturday. So, I laid off the American woman, apologised for my outburst and stepped back into my place in the line. I would wait it out like the rest of 'em behind me. And there was quite a line!

Ten interminable minutes later it was my turn. The man behind the counter was looking like a tornado had just crossed his path, and it was not just his voice which was giving him away as stressed to the hilt and fed up to the back teeth with complaints. His appearance was mainly what gave him away. Hair wild and bushy, and a crushed, crumpled uniform slick with sweat. I actually felt a little sorry for him, and seasoned traveller that I was, I knew better than to anger the poor man even further with an accusatory tone to my voice. I was well aware of one being looked upon more favourably when offering a teaspoon of honey than when offering a teaspoon of salt.

I tried the 'ever so cheery' nonchalant approach, as if standing in the line for the last half an hour hadn't bothered me in the slightest. "Oh, hello again. Buongiorno! Noi abbiamo perdto nostri valigi." I chose my words carefully, praying I had used the correct tenses, and that I had been telling him we had lost our suitcases and not our teeth. (A friend of mine actually did lose her teeth whist standing in the customs line in transit in the airport in Rome. She had sneezed, and her bottom plate had fallen out and disappeared down a nearby open drain.) My efforts at stringing a whole bunch of Italian words together to form a semi-meaningful Italian phrase were instantly rewarded. A fellow Italian—come to offer the weary attendant moral support in this endless line of foreign complainers.

"Cosa voi? Tu hai bisogne di valigi?"

I could see that the conversation was about to spiral into a 'tit-for-tat' of rapid Italian banter and I knew that even before we began the duel, I was dead meat. I decided to come clean. "I'm Australian and we have lost our luggage. We were on the plane from London Heathrow, which landed almost two hours ago now. Are you able to have a look out the back for us please? Here's my passport, and my friend's as well. She's in that wheelchair over there." I finished my extended monologue and stood still, pointing over towards Alice in the wheelchair.

I supposed he understood me, given that a decent understanding of English would have been a necessary prerequisite for working in Lost Property in any International airport. A gigantic form was being eased towards me, as if my signature on an Italian Magna Carta was required. The man was not saying anything, just looking at me through thick black rimmed double-glazed glasses which would not have been out of place in an Inspector Clouseau movie.

"Ava you ever been before with Italy?"

(Perhaps it wasn't such a high level of fluency on English that was required after all.)

"Yes. I've been to your country four times before."

"And what is it that you want us to make to find a-youra-luggage?"

That was just it. We needed him and his team to make our missing suitcases reappear so that we could be on our way into the city of Milan, where we would hopefully be meeting our fellow travellers. At this rate, we would be meeting them on day ten of the trip, when the bus returned to Milan for the farewell dinner. The Italians had the same word for hello, and goodbye, and if we were to miss the beginning of our tour, the first time we locked eyes with our travelling companions might be when we uttered the word 'Ciao' (meaning goodbye and not hello). Hand movements towards and away from our bodies might also have been required. Hopefully, it wouldn't come to that, and if I played my cards close to my chest, we would be reunited with our suitcases in a matter of minutes.

Five minutes passed, and the man still hadn't returned from the offices behind the front counter. There were a couple of meticulously dressed, shiny buttoned, yawning security guards standing to the side of the corridor which led back to the body of the airport, and when a dissatisfied customer in the crowd began yelling out, "Fai presto, fai presto" to the open office door through which the attendant had disappeared, one of the security guards stepped forward and immediately dragged the unfortunate yeller into an adjacent room.

Much yelling and screaming ensued, and the last we saw of the man was the thick row of greasy, black curls on the back of his otherwise bald head as the security guard had bobbed him through the doorway. (The same way police were always bending forward criminals' heads when depositing them into the back of police cars.)

No one in the line moved, or opened their mouths after the incident, and even the American woman, who was still waiting at the side of the counter for her personal travel items to be unearthed, resorted to whispering. The gist of her whispering was that she was glad the security guards hadn't stepped in and led her off to the torture chamber behind the doors when she'd caused a fuss, as she had tickets to the opera for this evening, and she wouldn't want to have missed out. No one looked at her, even though we all heard what she'd said. (She was one of those loud whisperers.) Who knew what was behind the doors? The Lost Property area was slowly emptying. Now there were three men behind doors. That only left one remaining security guard, a line of roughly ten travellers, the American woman and Alice and her attendant still standing.

(Technically, Alice was not standing.)

There was nothing for it but to wait. Five minutes or so later, the Lost Property attendant reappeared, shaking his head in despair and exasperation, looking directly at me.

"I'm a sorry. Mi dispiache Signore. We av notta fined your luggage. We can do nothing!"

I wasn't ready to accept his haltering apology. This was not good enough. The luggage could not just have disappeared into thin air. It must be somewhere, unless there had been a mix-up at Heathrow and the suitcases hadn't even made it to Milan. I hoped not. I'd read about Milanese high class fashion, who hadn't? But if I were to be expected to buy five new outfits in Milanese boutiques, who would be there to help me choose what looked good on me, and what made me look like a sack of potatoes? And it wouldn't only be me shopping. Alice would also need new outfits. Not to mention toiletries and makeup, shoes, socks, swimsuits and rain jackets. Not finding the luggage was turning into a disastrous result!

The man seemed not to be grasping the full extent of my quandary. Whilst he'd been searching, I had filled out the form he'd left with me as best I could, but it was paperwork, and I knew Italy to be notoriously slow and nonchalant with paperwork. Either slow or careless, or both. The likelihood of our luggage being found in under two weeks was looking very slim.

There was really nothing else I could do. The attendant had matter-of-factly turned his attention to the next customer, and I was forced to sidestep the counter, ending up alongside the American woman.

"You too, huh?"

I nodded in dismal agreement and made my sorry way over to Alice and the wheelchair attendant. Alice was still engrossed in her reading, so it was a safe bet that she had no idea of the agony I had just endured. It was going to be difficult telling her our luggage was lost, and that apart from the scant change of clothes we had in our overnight bags, we were not in the best of positions. I was going to have to spell it out for her—very slowly. "Alice, did you see what was happening in the line over there?" No response from Alice. "Did you see the security guard intervene when this man who'd had enough of waiting started yelling?"

Alice finally deigned to look up. "Nah! But you've been gone for so long, Fil. Did they find our luggage? Can we go now?" Did I mention I was going to have to spell it out for her—very slowly?

"Alice, our luggage is lost! Vanished. Vamoosed! Nowhere to be found! Gone!"

Alice looked shocked and disbelieving. "No. You're kidding, right? Haven't they got it, Fil? Are you joking?" Unfortunately, I was not joking, and after I spent the next three minutes explaining to Alice that I had filled out the relevant forms, and that all we could do now was to wait for a phone call, she calmed down a little. "I just don't see how we can go on the trip without our clothes and toiletries. I haven't even got a spare pair of shoes in my hand luggage. What if it's raining outside and we get soaked? Then what?"

It was raining outside. I could see the rain pelting down as I followed Alice's swishing, clanking wheelchair to the railway station entrance. (The station was connected to the airport, so we didn't need to venture out into the rain.) I was still lagging behind, because I was still lugging the hand luggage and the coats. At least we'd had the foresight not to have packed the rain jackets in the big suitcases. They would definitely become a popular item of clothing (in our skeletal wardrobe) once we reached Milan city—where there would be no wheelchair and no protection from the weather.

The boy pushing the wheelchair was on his iPhone as he pushed, and when we arrived at the ticket office, I realised that he had been organising a rendezvous with Vincent—the first boy who'd met us with the wheelchair at the plane. Vincent looked pleased to see us, but he must have been told the bad news about the lost suitcases as he was throwing his hands up in the air in disgust. His friend was explaining to him in rapid-fire Italian that I had filled out the necessary papers, and that we had been told to make our way to our hotel and wait for a phone call from Lost Property.

The tickets were purchased, and Alice handed the two boys ten euro each. They looked happy. I then handed them an olive branch each, and they looked puzzled. I explained the significance of the gift, and Vincent assured me that he would translate what I had explained to him to his friend Carlo, who "didn't speak the gooda English." They both then disappeared, leaving Alice and I standing in silence—the smaller bags and coats shrouded at our feet.

There were two steep escalators in front of us, and an arrow pointing down towards the lower platform, as well as a huge sign in gleaming blue letters indicating the direction of Milan city. I knew we still had a fair way to go, but we had come this far and were surely now on the home stretch. A light lunch, followed by an afternoon siesta, would invigorate us for the evening, when we planned to saunter the streets of Milan, rubbing shoulders with the locals in a 'passigiata' to take in the sights and sounds of our neighbourhood.

All that stood between us now was the train journey, and the drudge from the station to the hotel. If the scale on Alice's map turned out to be correct, the hotel could not have been more than ten minutes' walk from the station.

We lived in hope!

Chapter 5
Enough with the Mishaps!

The train to Milan was full. Chock-a-block full of tourists, students, farmers, families, babies, and businessmen and women. Someone for everyone. Alice and I did not look any different from the rest of them, and except for Alice's big white bandage on her leg, non-one would have taken us for anything other than what we were. Tourists. Except that we had boarded the train at the underground airport station and had no suitcases. Plenty of hand luggage but no suitcases, and that was possibly the reason for the stares. Who were we, and what did we want?

I tried to shake off the curious glances, and Alice did her usual job of ignoring all and sundry, by burying her head in her new guidebook of Milan. If I stuck to Alice like glue, I should be fine, as no authentic Milanese resident would be seen riding a train to the city with a guidebook of Milan propped up between his or her legs.

A little child had taken a shine to me and was hopping around my feet, trying to pry her grubby little fingers into the bag which contained my olive branches. The bag also contained a packet of shortbread biscuits, and I assumed the little girl was after food, as are most children. The universal quest for stomach gratification—unbounded by class or ethnicity. "Please Sir, I want some more" was alive and well in the North of Italy-transported from the East end of London and translated as, "Encore per favore."

"Sylvia, Sylvia, vieni qui, vieni qui!" Sylvia was going nowhere. She had settled herself at my feet as if I were Buddha himself, and I didn't have the heart to push her away and send her skittling back to her parents, grandparents and plethora of brothers and sisters who appeared to be occupying the three back seats of our carriage. It was a wonder they had even missed Sylvia, there were so many mouths to feed. Then it struck me. Sylvia might be hungry, and that was why she was, by now, rummaging around in my food bag. I needed to intervene.

"Sylvia, your mama and papa are missing you. Off you go, back to your parents." I had delivered my request in English, with the added effect of some gentle prodding, but Sylvia refused to budge. I tried adding, 'che bella' a phrase dad used on us as kids, when we were dressed identically in little sailor suits.

You don't see many of the sailor suits for children around nowadays, which is a real pity, as wearing the little navy and white top and white pleated skirt was something that had stuck in my head for years. I think dad had a hankering for a son from the moment mum was pregnant, and after a while the disappointment of mum churning out girl after girl just got too much for him. By the time I was eight, and my sisters-six, four and two, the miniature, all-girl-Italian navy of our neighbourhood had been formed. We mainly appeared in our 'uniforms' for mass or important Christmas parties. Ah, the good old days. Nowadays, the media is saturated with photographs of baby royals from England to Denmark in pretty pink dresses and culottes-the world is their oyster in terms of baby attire.

Suddenly, a large pink, hairy hand with blackened fingernails materialised in front of me, and Sylvia was plucked from the floor like a plump, wriggling fish from the river Po. The child-snatcher easily dangled her in front of me— triumphant with his prize—and the crowd of onlookers including his family up the back of the carriage all cheered. It was cheap entertainment for a Friday afternoon, but people seemed to be enjoying the show. Assuming the man to be Sylvia's father, I fished an unopened packet of shortbreads from my food bag and handed them to him. "Don't let Silvia eat them all at once. She can share them with the family." The man thanked me and heaved the podgy little Sylvia onto his shoulders. She didn't look too malnourished to me!

"Grazia tante, Signora."

That bit, I understood. Alice was also looking pleased with me, and I was fairly confident that my simple act of kindness would almost certainly have earned me brownie points with her.

After the excitement of Sylvia, we nestled back in our seats for the rest of our journey, comfortable and content. I must have been dozing, because I suddenly felt my shoulders being vigorously shaken and Alice's piercing voice urging me to hurry and wake up, as our station was up next!

It wasn't easy opening my eyes. Even though only ten minutes or so had passed, I felt like I had been drugged into a deep slumber, and that I just didn't have the strength to rouse myself out of my inertia, collect all of my belongings as well as Alice, and make my way to the doors awaiting their 'swoosh' which accompanied their opening at every station. Then it would be the added ordeal of jumping off the train and helping Alice do the same, although presumably there would be other passengers alighting at our station, and they might lend a hand. Regardless, I needed to act fast if we were to make it to the doors before the next station.

Luckily for us, there were two others pushing their way forwards towards the doors. They looked as though they might also be about to alight at the next stop. A boy and a girl, possibly in their early twenties. Their dress-sense was difficult to categorise. They were dressed in hiking clothes, and the boy had a red bandanna tied around his head. The girl's most distinguishing feature was her tangled mass of jet-black curly hair which framed her exquisite heart-shaped face from side to side. One could not help but notice her brilliant blue eyes. Putting two and two together, I had them pinned as young backpackers, and when I asked them for assistance, they were only too happy to oblige. Alice was escorted off first, and they then came back for me.

Once all four of us were safely huddled on the platform, I asked them where they were from. "Spain, we're Spanish and we have arrived here in Italy to make a hike around Cinque Terra. Have you heard of Cinque Terra?"

Had we heard of Cinque Terra? Absolutely we had. The featured day trip to the Ligurian coast, halfway through our Tour was to be the highlight of our trip. So important was Cinque Terra to our itinerary, that the tour organisers had proudly included Cinque Terra in the title 'Northern Italy with Cinque Terra included'. Before planning the trip, I will admit to sheer ignorance in the geography and history of Northern Italy. Having visited the big guns of Venice and Florence three times, I had all but ignored Milan, Turin and Genoa. It wasn't possible to visit every place in Italy, and the towns and villages surrounding Milan-or even Milan itself had never been on my agenda.

'Cinque Terra' had popped up in the brochures on Northern Italy more than once, and given that we wanted to have a crack at the North, the most economical and suitable Italian trip in terms of dates to fit in with Alice's teaching was the one we had selected, which included Cinque Terra.

The Spaniards were still hanging around, waiting for an answer to their question. Perhaps they were conducting survey on how many tourists had heard of Cinque Terra? When I explained our situation, they were impressed that we knew of the region. I suppose they were wondering where we were off to, with so few bags and no hiking gear or backpacks. I pre-empted the question. "We are joining a tour of Northern Italy tomorrow night, but the first couple of days are here in Milan. We'll be right from now on. Thanks very much for the help. According to our map our hotel should be just around the corner and up a bit."

They were probably also wondering why we were staying in a hotel so far out from the eye of the city, but we really had no idea where we were in relation to the centre of Milan, so I had no reason to explain our choice of hotel. I guessed it was because the tour bus drivers would have found it difficult to manoeuvre their enormous buses in the centres of large cities. Such over-sized people-movers would never have been thought possible in Da Vinci's days all those centuries ago when the laneways grew haphazardly out of a need to accommodate horses and carts.

It was time to move on.

If our map was to be believed, we would be going up the hill, and the Spanish couple had informed us they were headed downhill, towards an area of Backpacker accommodation. There were farewells all round, and Alice wished them safe and happy hiking.

"Make sure you hang onto the handrails, and don't hike in thongs." The boy looked at Alice as if she were mad, suggesting they would be hiking in anything other than custom designed walking boots.

"We have these boots. We now is wearing these boots. They never are to leaving this foots."

Upon close examination of his boots, and those of his partner, I understood him to be telling the truth when he asserted the boots never left his feet. They were so well worn and dusty, they looked as if they had just completed two circuits of the 'Camino Way' in Spain—and the rest! We watched the pair of them in their dusty, well-worn boots striding down the hill, two of the fastest tortoises I've ever seen! If we spotted a camping or outdoor gear shop on our shopping spree in Milan central tomorrow, I might just invest in a pair of those boots.

In Australia, people striving to be seen as dedicated walkers, fit themselves out in 'R. M. Williams' boots. Internationally, the brand was as iconic as Gucci, but the market more restrictive, appealing mainly to walkers, farmers in Akubra hats and grungy youth. I'm not much of a hiker but having been a member of a Walking Club for five or so years in my early twenties, meant there was always a pair of R. M Williams boots taking pride of place in my laundry. On the first Sunday of every month, we would walk for ten kilometres (mandatory) around the hills and dales of Melbourne, or further out into the countryside in our R. M. boots.

We were identical in our all-cotton hand painted tee-shirts, the Walking-club logo carefully inscribed on the back of every shirt. We were the 'Ramblers' (not overly original), and our theme song—'These boots were made for walking'—plucked from the archives of Nancy and Frank, and pumped out on a Walkman with linked-up speakers for ten minutes in the clubroom in a pre-walk call to arms. Nowadays walkers wear earplugs and wander off in small groups or pairs to 'find themselves' to the music of M and M or R and B.

Yes. A brand new pair of Milan-designed hiking boots would suffice as a wonderful keepsake of our time in Italy, and might even come in handy back in Melbourne when I revived (as I planned to do now that my memory of the boots had been jolted) the still living members of the 'Ramblers' from their Rip-Van-Winkle sleep of thirty years. Meeting the Spaniards had not been without merit, and with my new plans bubbling away, I picked up my pace.

Alice, the non-dreamer, had nearly had enough! "My leg is so painful, and I think I'm going to die of hunger. Can we find a café or something?" I gazed around the quiet, sleepy environs, and realised no shops would be open, as it was siesta time. We had spent so long at the Lost Property Department that it was almost three o'clock—hard-core siesta time!

"The shops are all closed, Alice. Remember siestas? There'll be food at the hotel. Can you survive till then?" Alice's face was ghostly white, and she looked as though she were about to pass out, so I handed her the last of the shortbreads. "Here. Eat these. They'll tide you over until we can find something more substantial." At least she was quiet while she was eating. My hands were all taken up with the bags, so I didn't even try to pry myself a biscuit. There would be plenty of food coming our way this trip, with all breakfasts and many of the dinners included. I would not be left to starve!

As we emerged from the underpass and rounded the corner onto a main road, I had my first realisation that we had arrived in a big city. This was no country railway overpass. According to the signpost, this humble, canopied, cobbled-stoned alleyway would eventually lead to one of the power-broking cities of the world. Milan. House of fashion. House of industry and House of architecture. Although Italy had been on my mind forever, courtesy of an Italian father and a spider's web of relatives down south; Northern Italy had never much had a look-in.

We had grown up with the idea that Northern Italy was in a different league to the south, and that if they had remained two different countries as had been the case before Garibaldi's efforts at unification one hundred and fifty years ago-no one would have batted an eyelid. One thing I did know was that the physique of the Northerners was completely different to that of their Southern kinsmen. And right here in front of us was the living proof. Standing six abreast at the lights, waiting to cross the busy road, there would have been no doubt on any drone footage as to which of us were English, and which of us Northern Italian.

The group with whom we were sharing the pavement were all Italian. All tall, and all lanky. All blonde. All well dressed, and all politely standing back from me with my keepsake of bags. (Two of the boys offered to carry the bags across the road but it would have taken too much effort to disentangle myself from the crisscrossing of straps across my chest, so I politely declined their kind offer. I did not fancy a round or two of frisking by the boys on an empty stomach).

On cue, we all crossed the busy road. I was excited to see the bright green flashing lights of our hotel at a direct diagonal to us-home for the next three nights. It may even have ended up being home for the next three days, while we waited for our suitcases containing all our clothes and worldly goods. I could think of worse places than a four-star hotel in Milan in which to be stuck, awaiting errant luggage. The worst was over for us—the waiting at the baggage carousels, and the waiting at Lost Property. In the hotel, we would have the luxury of beds, fresh air, cool drinks and a television. There would be room service and hot showers, and we had brought plenty of reading material with us-so a day or two or even three at a stretch on witness protection would not really be a sacrifice at all.

One the flip side of the coin, solitary confinement would mean forfeiting joisting and jostling with the other thousand tourists sightseeing in Milan. My carefully selected list of places earmarked for a brief visit was already a mile long, and there would be no opportunity at the end of the trip to bring to fruition our sightseeing plans. It was now or never, even if it meant venturing out in the clothes on our backs. No doubt there would be time this evening to wash out our light travelling clothes, and they would surely dry overnight in the mild Milanese breeze.

We had season-selected perfectly with late May. We might even be lucky enough to secure a balcony and hang our clothes out to dry on a string line. A befitting toe-dipping into life in Milan. The houses and shops we trudged past reminded me strongly of Nice in France. I was pretty sure Nice was on the coastline down from Milan, and similar architecture and the vegetation would make good sense.

For me, with my artistic eye ever turned outward, the most impressionable memory of Nice had been the hundreds of grimy apartment balconies (sometimes to a height of ten storeys) dotting the winding, mountainous coastline, swamped with rope clothes lines and straining with colourful garments all flapping furiously in the wind. I had been on a bus tour at the time, and as the bus had sped past the apartments, all that had been discernible had been an avalanche of colourful stringlines, zigzagging and twirling in the Nice wind. A merry-go-round of kaleidoscopic colour. Had it been a clear day, I probably wouldn't even have noticed the floats of colours parading by, but thanks to the wind, the sightseeing tour of Nice had come alive.

We were, at last, standing on the white marble front steps of our hotel. For Alice the decade of wide, white, steps were both welcomingly relieving and alarmingly insurmountable. A quick check up and down the street revealed there to be only a few die-hard trekkers out and about at this null and void hour. Everyone else was either still asleep or resting with a book or iPad. An old trick of mine, when resisting the temptation to run up endless flights of steps a-la-mountain goat with all my baggage in tow-was to feign light-headedness and lean at the bottom of the steps against the nearest wall waiting for a knight in shining armour to come along and rescue the said damsel in distress.

"Hang on, Alice, I just want to read this poster advertising a concert at La Scala tonight. What a pity we have nothing to wear, or we could try and get some tickets." Of course, I had no interest in blowing all our dough on tickets to La Scala tonight, and besides, as I had just pointed out, we had nothing to wear. Had we been in America, a Cinderella complex would not have been a problem. I had been listening to a radio programme on the plane on the way over to England—an interview with the founder of a multi-million-dollar American company specialising in renting out expensive designer-ware to the general public. Evening-ware, wedding-ware and outfits befitting salubrious occasions.

The company had made such accelerated growth since inception last year, that the projected plan was for it to be operational in sixty countries by the end of the year. Even if Italy were to be included amongst the proposed countries, it would have been of little use to us, as we would require ball gowns for tonight.

The best thing about the rental company was that one did not need to bother with the washing or dry-cleaning of the gowns once they had been worn.

The company took care of everything, and even supplied jewellery, should that also be required. It was a win/win company, and according to the interviewee, one with the US monopoly on dry cleaning. I filed the information away for next year, as Australia had been mentioned as one of the sixty countries to enjoy the rental service.

Alice was not to know I had no interest in attending the Opera tonight and that I was stalling for time. "Fil, you know they would never let us into the Opera in these travelling clothes, and even if we washed them out and ironed them, they would still never be good enough. And we haven't got proper shoes, or any makeup, or even any suitable coats. That would be a crazy thing to do." My plan was working. Alice was being waylaid whilst we waited for help to arrive. Or, I could leave Alice with the bags at the bottom of the steps and race up into the foyer for help. The porter wouldn't be asleep, surely? Then, he or she could carry up our bags, and I could assist Alice. She shouldn't need much help but given the miles we had gobbled up on an empty stomach it was understandable she was not coping with walking the last few kilometres.

"Alice, wait here, and I'll see if there is anyone in the foyer who can help us with this last stretch."

Alice looked relieved and immediately leant against the wall. Still no one was stopping to enquire if we were lost or just exhausted. Not that I was blaming the few people who did hurry past. They were not to know we had set off from London at six this morning, and that Alice was in extreme pain with her leg. I took the steps two at a time to show Alice that I was a strong and fit team member and that I would not be letting the team down. I was her long-time loyal friend who would be sticking by her through thick and thin. We would have no arguments on our ten-day trip together, and we would look back on our time away with a yearning to relive those good times in Northern Italy. Maybe.

Or maybe we would be so fed up with each other in twenty-four hours' time, having been cooped up in a poky little airless room on the top floor of the hotel, starving because room service was not operational, and dirty and dishevelled because there had been a problem with the plumbing. (Italian villas and hotels invariably have trouble with plumbing; I knew this because I was always watching television shows on castles and villas in Italy).

Time would tell.

Chapter 6
Hotel Life

The foyer was quiet and cool. Deserted would be another word for it. No porters. No receptionists. No background music. There was a large bell on the corner of the counter-larger than your normal household bell-more like the large brass school bell we would take it in turns to ring whilst running past classrooms, to signify the end of the school day. I picked up the bell and gave it two shakes. Obviously, I had underestimated my own strength.

There was a loud piercing tolling of bells, to rival the announcement of a royal visit to St Mark's square. Immediately, a tall man appeared behind the counter. His face was not what I would describe as agreeable, and he looked as though I had disturbed him from a very important nap. "Yessa. Can I elpa you, Signora?" I explained our predicament, and he listened patiently, but once I had finished my plaintive discourse, he turned away without a word of affirmation or dissent and walked back to the door from which he had appeared, moments before.

"Well, that part went well." I was working myself up into a state of delirium with all the goings-on. First no one was in the foyer, then the man had appeared and now there was again no one here. What was the go? It had to be a language thing. The man must not have understood my vague ramblings. I probably hadn't helped things by inserting in a few Italian words here and there. I figured I might as well get some practise in whilst there was no one else around.

While I was waiting for his second coming, I noticed a lounge-bar to the side of the foyer. A woman was in there, propped up on a high barstool. She had backed herself into the far corner of the counter and her eyes were downcast in intense concentration. Probably not a good idea to disturb her. It was three-thirty in the afternoon, and the woman was not asleep. I had her pinned as a local, even though she did not look anything like your typical Italian. It was unlikely for her to have been a tourist, or she would have been in the thick of tourist territory in the centre of Milan, ticking off sights never again to be witnessed in one's lifetime. (Unless one was a rich tourist who liked to keep returning to the scene of the crime year after year.)

Every few seconds, the woman would toss back her mane of curly red hair and loudly gasp, "Ecco bravo!" I had no idea what 'Ecco bravo' could mean—maybe that she was being very brave writing down whatever it was she was working her way through? Niggling away at the back of my brain was the thought that I had seen the woman somewhere before, but I had never been to Milan, so it was unlikely. She could have been a film star, but I could only see her back and the mass of red curls which framed her silhouette like a royal coat of arms.

I turned away, leaving the woman in peace with her secret machinations. No sooner had I done so than the speechless man from behind the counter reappeared with a younger, smiling bellboy, and the boy came straight up to me, asking in faltering English how he might be of assistance. "It's not me. It's my friend. She has hurt her leg and is at the bottom of the steps outside. Could you please help her up the steps into the foyer?"

The boy cocked his head from side to side and raced down the steps towards Alice. He then beckoned me from the bottom of the steps to join him. (The doors had been left open and I could clearly see Alice.) I took to the stairs, more sedately this time, wondering what grandiose plans the bellboy had in store for me. I shouldn't have wondered. In two seconds flat, he had stooped down in front of Alice and crossed over his arms. He urged me to follow suit.

I copied with sinking heart, cottoning on instantly to his intentions. We were about to carry Alice up the stairs to the foyer. I had little choice but to comply, and it served me right for having shown off my (virtual) strength to Alice ten minutes before, when I'd taken to the steps two at a time. The bell boy was puffing and groaning, but he was also taking the full weight of Alice, so I relaxed my grip a little on his hands.

Alice hadn't spoken a word until now. She had been as docile as a lamb when she had hopped onto our outstretched arms, settling herself as ceremoniously and 'matter-of-factly' as one would settle themselves onto the back of a smelly parading elephant. I had a feeling she had done this before. There were only ten or so steps, and because the bell boy was doing the hard part, I couldn't really complain. Had there been more people hurrying past the hotel, I might have been embarrassed at the spectacle we were making of ourselves, but it was still all quiet on the Western front, and only an empty tram rattled by.

"There you is. We 'av arrived." The boy had let go of my hands in the foyer a little too quickly and Alice went for a small tumble. Not a full-blown fall like the one at the airport Departure lounge. More of a slight inconvenience to her sitting position. I immediately threw out my arms to support her, and she was grateful. "It's like I'm always ending up on the ground. Isn't it, Fil?"

Hopefully, this would be the last time Alice would need to put the full brunt of her weight on her legs and knees for the next twenty-four fours. If we wanted to go out later tonight, the walking stick would need to be called upon, but looking at her pale, tired face, it was unlikely she would be leaving the bedroom for any length of time. There were a couple of high-backed, plush red velvet armchairs to the side of the counter, a tiny polished wood coffee table and a box with assorted tourist brochures and pamphlets. Alice heaven!

Once the boy and I had Alice settled, I handed him five euro, and gave him a hearty handshake. He reciprocated with a broad smile and disappeared via a back door behind the lounge-bar. I then approached the counter where the senior partner had again taken up his position. There was a fresh-faced boy of around twenty leaning forwards towards the one of the computers behind the counter. He glanced up at me as I approached, but just as quickly lowered his head back to the computer, giving his boss a sideways glace as he did so. I didn't get the impression they would be behind women getting the next vote.

Brushing my cynicism aside, I hurtled headlong into my carefully rehearsed monologue in my best Italian, hoping for a room with a balcony. I should have realised that the rooms were already pre-booked by the Tour Company, and that because we were travelling as a pair, our room would be a twin, and more than likely not possessive of a Juliet balcony (or any old balcony).

Then there is the age old 'Never judge a book by its cover' again rearing its ugly head. The boy wasn't ugly, but he did rear his head, and flick his hand expertly across the screen to locate where we had been placed. Things were suddenly looking up. My prejudgement prowess had taken a turn for the better, and I was solemnly presented with a gleaming silver key the size of a pair of shears, and informed that we would be sleeping on the first floor of the hotel in a room with twin beds and a beautiful balcony overlooking the street. Success!

Once I had secured the key, I wasted no time gathering Alice and our bags and seeking out the lifts. It wouldn't do for the boy to change his mind and stick us in the back blocks of the hotel with no fresh air. Alice was still white, and a few good gulps of pizza-infused Milanese air, inhaled from the height of our balcony, would be just what the doctor ordered until the real pizza arrived.

Pizza for a late lunch was my plan, and Alice would just have to go with the flow today. Not that I was laying any blame on her for the myriad of things that had gone wrong today. She had no control over the degree of pain her leg was dishing out. But I did have concern for her wellbeing, and I knew that paleness of face could be easily rectified with food. We were in Italy, so we would be having pizza. Very soon.

The lift was small, and there was only one operating, so we couldn't even go one-a-piece. The whole tiny area in front of the lifts reminded me of the lifts leading to the viewing platform of the 'Empire-State Building' in New York. After travelling up to what was thought to be the top of the building, tourists (myself included) needed to bundle out of one lift and into another to complete the last three storeys.

It was memorable because of the height, and because there had been two lifts involved. These lifts might have been designed by the same engineers, as the hotel was part of an American chain, and it was common knowledge that many American/ Italians were influential in the town-planning in Milan. Alice offered to hold two of the bags, and that helped slightly, by freeing up floor space. No one else was around, although I did notice two new arrivals—a very tall man and a very pretty woman with thick, dark shoulder length hair as I glanced back towards the counter, checking if I had left anything behind, as was my usual practice whenever I travelled.

Usually, it was keys I left behind, but there was no fear of a keyless entry today, as my entire left hand was taken up with the gleaming silver key. Some poor skivvy would have taken hours to polish the silver to perfection. (It was more likely to have been silver-plated but would have taken some time and effort to get the key to such a dazzling state).

As the lift doors closed, I could see into the lounge-bar, which looked to be deserted from our angle, but upon closer scrutiny, I could just make out a mane of red hair in the corner, still bent over, still foraging with her books. The mysterious redhead with the penchant for dark deserted bars mid-afternoon. Sticky-beak that I was, I had it in mind to wander down to the bar later this afternoon for an ice-cold lemonade and some crisps. If the woman were still there, some light might be shed on her identity. It was still bugging me that I'd seen her before—and quite recently!

A pleasant surprise awaited us as the lift door opened. We had arrived at a dark, cool, lavish foyer, complete with cream and pale green, glowing tiles. (Handy for optimum sliding of suitcases?) Directly opposite the lift was a grand circular staircase with twisted iron patterning trailing the balustrades. It was a magnificent staircase, totally unexpected, and totally out of place opposite the tired, dingy lift. I made up my mind there and then that the trip up in the lift just now would be my first and last.

From now on, I would be pirouetting up and down the exquisite baroque staircase whenever I needed to return to the lobby. I needed the exercise and it would be too good an opportunity to miss. Once the shock of the staircase settled, I noticed there were armchairs, to the side of the lift, matching those in which Alice had made herself comfortable in downstairs, and not one, but three little matching wooden coffee tables. There were also little Italian figurines and vases of lavender and clumped green sprigs, placed on the tables. Very chic!

Alice immediately dumped the hand luggage on the widest of the tables and plonked herself down on the closest chair. I was tempted to do the same, but someone had to do the scout for the bedroom, and I guessed that would be me. I then did that thing we all do when we first get out of the lift in a hotel and start the room search. I found a room number close to the number I had been handed on a small card (a difference of five) and began following the trail. I didn't have to go far, as our bedroom ended up being around a corner, but still quite close to the lifts.

"I've found it, Alice! It's over here. Can you manage the bags as well?"

Alice could, and did, and five minutes later, we were ensconced in our bedroom, a bed-a-piece, munching the last of the shortbreads. I knew it was not right to be so hungry when there were people starving for days and weeks on end, but we were not conditioned to such hardships, and it was only a couple of biscuits. Alice was talking with her mouth full. "Fil, do you think you could just go and check if I dropped my scarf outside the lift? It's not here, and I was carrying it over my arm."

Alice had such pathos in her voice that I burst out laughing. "Alice, you haven't lost a limb. You don't need to be so worried about it. I'll go and have a look now."

It was quiet out in the hallway. Quiet and dark. I hadn't noticed it being so dark when we'd been winding our way towards the bedroom, but now that I had time to focus, it really was quite dim. There was a glass plated notice on the wall outside the bedroom, which I couldn't read it even though it was in English. Part of the reason was my not having my glasses with me, but to retrieve them would have meant inserting the enormous key back into the door and rummaging around in my handbag for them. Too much like hard work. The notice would keep, and had it had been a declaration of great importance, something like "Benito Mussolini once hid away in this bedroom days before he was hung upside down in the city of Milan", then we would soon find out about it.

I left the wall and rounded the corner to the lift. Sure enough, the missing scarf was there! Not exactly outside the lift—more 'hanging at the top of the stairs'. I was about to pick it up and scurry back to our room, when the lift door opened and two large suitcases were pushed forwards. A tall man and a pretty woman followed directly. It was the couple from the foyer. It must have taken them a while to be assigned their rooms, because it was at least twenty minutes since I had glimpsed them. The man was so tall he was bending his neck to exit the lift. The woman smiled at me, and I smiled back, all the while reaching for Alice's blue scarf. I felt like I should offer an explanation as to why I was pulling my scarf from the wrought iron in which it had somehow become entangled.

"It's not mine. The scarf I mean." The woman kept smiling and gave the man a nudge. "Look Don. Someone else who loses scarves."

The man chuckled and extended his hand to introduce himself—a gesture entirely unexpected. "I'm Don, and this is my wife, Angelique. We're Canadian, and in Milan for the start of a bus tour. How about you?" It was a lilting accent overly pleasing to my ear, and being a singer myself, I had a great admiration for Canadian singers and songwriters. Off on a tangent again, I could clearly hear my alter ego asking me to ask Don if he could sing, and if he was by any chance here for the 'Northern Italy with the lakes and Cinque Terra tour'?

I dropped the singing question and dove right into the tour enquiry. "Nice to meet you both. I'm Fil. I'm Australian, and here for a tour a well. Does your tour include Cinque Terrra?" Bingo. I was on the bus with Don and Angelique. And Alice. I'd forgotten about Alice. "I'm not here alone though. My friend is travelling with me and she's in our bedroom down there."

I indicated towards the dimly lit corridor which led to our bedroom and dangled the large silver key in front of the couple. "Bet yours isn't as big as this!"

Don burst out laughing, and Angelique's eyes widened. "You're joking, right? That can't be a key to a bedroom. It looks like the master key to the Palace in the centre of Milan. We want to go there before we leave the city. I could drop the key back for you if you like."

Ha-ha Don. Too bad you don't have a key to rival this one.

Angelique had started freewheeling one of the suitcases down the corridor. "I'll just start looking for our room. See you later, Fil. Enjoy your evening."

Don hurriedly propelled the second case forwards and turned back to wave to me. "Until we meet again!" They were lovely, and if the other passengers on our trip turned out to be anything like them, we would be in for a happy time. I was really getting geared up now. Don and Angelique had fuelled my excitement, and I couldn't wait to get back to Alice to let her know what had just happened.

I gave the scarf (which was still tangled in the wrought iron of the balustrade) one last pull and it was free! I was on the floor, but the scarf was free. Mission accomplished. Giant key in one hand, worse-for-wear-scarf in the other, I strode back to our bedroom. I had left the door open so there had been no need to try out the key. Alice was still sitting on the edge of her bed with her leg propped up on what looked to be a tower made up of all the pillows in our room—if not our entire floor. It was leaning slightly to the left in true Pisa style.

"Hi Fil. I borrowed your pillows for my leg. It was throbbing." I wasn't too bothered, as I seldom use pillows provided by hotels. I find them too soft and end up with a crick in my neck the next morning. Not that Alice knew that, so it was more points notched up for me in the empathy stakes.

Alice had a surprise in store for me. Whilst I'd been on the scarf hunt, she had found the hotel book with room service details and had ordered pizzas and cokes. "A family-sized Margaretta Pizza, is that okay with you? I thought it best to get a big one and we can eat the leftovers for tea. Oh, and an apple each. That'll be healthy!"

Alice was looking anxiously at me, obviously worried that she had made an incorrect autocratic choice with the topping on the pizza. I let her off the hook after a minute or so of non-response. "Of course, that's alright, Alice. More than alright. Margaretta is my favourite. Did they say how long they would be?"

Twenty minutes was all it took for the pizza to arrive, and in the meantime, Alice and I took it in turns to wait on hold whilst the attendants at Airport Lost Property conducted the fruitless afternoon search for our suitcases. We were told to ring back again at nine pm this evening when they might have some news on the cases. I doubted it and rang downstairs to ask for extra towels and soap. The 'Washathon' was scheduled to begin at nine-thirty this evening.

After we had literally scoffed down all the pizza, it was siesta time. Granted we were a good three hours late for the kip, but it was a necessary part of the Italian ritual, and one entirely worthy of support. The tour would not be a problem because we would always either be on the road in the early afternoon, travelling to our next destination, or already settled in our hotel rooms for the evening. A perfect arrangement.

Alice fell asleep straight away, but I just lay there on the bed with the gentle balcony-breeze on my face. Nothing to do, nowhere to be, full stomach, thirst quenched—not bad for day one, and it was not over yet. While Alice slept, I gathered up my handbag and backpack, scribbled her a quick note letting her know I had gone for a walk and that I would pick up some nibbles for tonight. Alice was dead to the world, and she didn't even stir when the greasy doorknob slipped in my hand and the door slammed shut.

I stood in the corridor with my ear to the door just in case Alice had woken up and had wanted me to bring her back something specific. One never knew with Alice! It was all quiet behind the door, save for some heavy breathing. Either someone had been waiting on the balcony until I took leave of the room or Alice was the heavy breather. Hopefully Alice!

This time there was hazy filtered afternoon light in the corridor, so it was easy to read the sign on the wall outside our door. No. Mussolini had not frequented the bedroom! It was a warning sign in case of fire in the building, with instructions on where to meet and what to do in the case of emergency. On American television in times of crisis, people tend to run around in circles calling out frantically, "Call nine-one-one!"; in Italy it was one word repeated three times with increasing volume so that it had become a scream by the last utterance: 'Iutto, Iutto, Iutto!'

I hoped it wouldn't come to that.

The 'quiet' continued downstairs, and I purposefully stamped my feet as I walked through the foyer—just to breathe some life into the place. It must have worked, because people came running from all directions to see who was causing all the commotion. I just smiled at them and pointed down at my shoes. "Must have pebbles or something in them, I'm trying to stomp them out." I kept a look out for the mysterious red-headed woman, but she was nowhere to be seen. Probably at home in her villa cooking pasta for her grandchildren by now.

Outside it was still balmy. Beautiful weather to be sitting in a deck chair at the beach, sipping cold juice or white wine and reading. I was looking forward to seeing the Italian coastline on the trip. It looked spectacular in the glossy magazine photos, and I wanted to be able to take a dip or two. Without our suitcases, that was not going to be possible, unless we found a cheap clothing shop tomorrow, and just splashed out and bought whole new outfits. If there was no news on the fate of the cases by tonight, we would just have to cut our losses and start again from scratch. We both had travel insurance, so the money would come back to us eventually. It was more the inconvenience of not having one's own clothes and necessary travel possessions.

When I'd left the hotel (which was on a corner), I'd turned right. Directly in front of me was the longest, straightest street I had ever seen. It stretched endlessly to the horizon, and there was no way I'd even make it to the first set of traffic lights. The blocks were huge and squashed in with shops on both sides of the road. The shops were intriguing, but very deserted, as I had chosen the tail end of Siesta time to venture out. Had I waited an hour or so, the landscape would have been unrecognisable: the shops would have reopened and the early diners would be spilling out onto the pavements, enjoying the late afternoon sunshine.

As I passed a few shops which had reopened early, it was difficult not to be persuaded into entering the shops and making purchases I didn't need. Young men approached me from all angles, imploring me to cross the threshold into their den, and then presumably part with my money. Which would have been fine, had they been proprietors of food shops, but the three shops I passed with the spruikers outside were a shoe shop, a bookshop and a gun shop. It tickled my fancy that the owner of the gun shop could possibly think I would cross the threshold of one such establishment. I hurried on past all three shops, and thankfully a coffee shop with a wonderful aroma of freshly ground coffee and a stupendous display of cream cakes was the next shop along.

I lasted half an hour inside the coffee shop, and feeling full and satisfied with the delicious coffee and even more delicious cakes I'd consumed, I realised it was time to make my way back to the hotel. The streets were packed with commuters on their way home from work, and those who were not on foot or bicycle, were sitting or standing on the trams which rattled past. It was comforting to see the trams so far from my hometown of Melbourne, where trams are the main form of transport in the city. The Milanese trams were authentic old rattlers and added to the eclectic charm of the city. The tangled criss-cross of wires overhead gave the streetscape the appearance of a long, long disused car yard.

Alice was dressed and ready for our evening walk when I returned to the bedroom, so I didn't bother to make myself too comfortable on the bed, not even for a bit of a breather. "We won't be long, Fil. I just want to get some fresh air." I could identify with her wanting some fresh air, and it could not have been any longer than fifteen minutes and we were all ready to go.

Chapter 7
An Evening Stroll in Balmy Milan Friday

In the fast enveloping darkness, I could have been on the West End in Oliver Twist's London, but these cobble-stone streets were too narrow and uneven, and the buildings on the whole, more artisan and more lop-sided than any likely to encountered on busy London pavements. In London, there is a certain blank faced stoicism to the tall stately and uniformly creamy grey buildings, whereas here, the pattern was defiant irregularity, coupled with a certain coquettish antiquated charm, firmly favouring the atypical, rather than typical, in terms of building conventions in large cities. It felt more like a quiet country village competing in a flower show with like-minded villages, and yet, we were only around the corner from one of the busiest roads leading for a couple of kilometres into the Central Business District of Milan.

I'd seen it all before. Many a time, and mostly on the continent, but the peaceful co-existence of cream and green shutter-graced shops, tiny tobacconist and supermarkets, dwarfed by the pastel paint peeled tall, narrow apartment blocks-this was pure Italy.

The bright red scooters and chunky gleaming black motor bikes far outnumbered the small Italian cars, and the genti, strolling along in the fast-fading light outnumbered themselves. It was crowded, given the hour, but the 'No jostling allowed' tacit rule was in full force. Slow river, peaceful meandering was the go.

No one was in any kind of hurry. Not remotely. Ambling along, at home in their surrounds, the Milanese were out for an evening stroll with a difference. Slow, purposeful and directed inward as if out to impress themselves and not another soul on the planet. Most were meticulously dressed, as was the custom, and keeping up with tradition and custom was paramount by the looks of things. This was our first taste of Northern Italians and the way they embraced their world.

In stark contrast, this was clearly not the case for the uninitiated. The panting, bustling tourists, with their overfed backpacks stuffed full of important documents and keepsakes (not to be trusted to hotel safes) were unmissable as they bobbed and staggered along like buoys on the open choppy sea. I was on 'Team-Tourist', so I knew exactly why they were so guarded. We all had that, "I'm out walking on dangerous Italian streets at nine thirty in the evening" look. Slurping on creamy chocolate gelati, and leaning as nonchalantly as they could manage (without toppling over) against shop walls whilst tackling fast-melting cones, was a dead give-away, but the majority of my team seemed blissfully unaware of their sheer visibility as a tourist, or that they presented as sitting ducks to would-be pickpockets zooming past on smartly polished scooters. Completing the block was challenge enough for Alice, and she insisted she'd be fine to hobble back to the hotel, which was really just a block away.

"If anyone tries to pinch my bottom, I'll bop them with my walking stick." Those had been Alice's feisty parting words to me, as she had laboriously crossed the road at the roundabout covered in geraniums. I was torn. I knew I should follow her, but my selfish streak was hassling me to plough on to the next roundabout. And the next, and the next.

These streets were elixirs. It was impossible to get enough of them. Compromising with myself, I set my timer for ten minutes and continued on my merry way. Of course I ignored the beeping of the alarm ten minutes later, and more than likely outdid my welcome on Via-Marzone, lingering well past my bed time in the hope of drinking in more and more of the sumptuous smells of the jasmine, lavender, and masses of pretty pink roses and rhododendrons there for the picking on every little roundabout corner. It was heavenly, and quite intoxicating.

The Italians had marvellous connections with nature, especially in places like this Milanese suburb, devoid of the hustle and frenzied bustle of the city centre, yet Milan central was only ten minutes away by car. Tomorrow, I would hire one of bicycles I had seen chained up on the pavements like a cluster of offending convicts, awaiting liberation from someone just like me! I felt the pull of anonymity in a country so foreign, yet so genetically close to my heart.

I had grown up with Italy. Every day of my childhood a fascinating morsel of Italy would be revealed to me as my father tenaciously revealed his homeland. We ate Italian and sang Italian, we dressed Italian and we probably even smelt

Italian, on account of all the garlic and broccoli or meatball and cheese sandwiches we devoured in our school lunches.

Funnily enough, whilst recently on a commuter train in England, I overheard an elderly English woman commenting on how Prince George of the Royal family was commencing Prep school, and that risotto was on the menu for his lunchtime indulgence. I had my own childhood school food story. The one fateful day I defied the 'sandwiches only' rule and pulled out a plastic bowl of my favourite rice, potatoes and rich Italian sauce as my lunchtime indulgence, I was deftly seized from the lunch bench and ordered by the nuns to "clean my sauce-stained face".

Things have changed in forty years. Nowadays, I would have people licking my face for a taste of that prized 'Italian Nonna' tomato sauce. (My father always religiously followed his grandmother's sauce recipe.) Who knows? George could have had some Italian in him, way back, and that may have been how the dinner ladies got away with serving him risotto.

I had done the block twice, and despite the darkness, many apartments were still lit up, and I could see different, eclectic Milanese milieus as I wandered past. Someone was making a hot drink, someone brushing their teeth, and another watching television. They all looked happy and caught up in domesticity. I was warming to Milan. In these streets, it felt like a safe, bespoke village. Tomorrow would be the real challenge when we met the huge city face to face. I decided it was time to tun back, and ignoring my aching back and tired legs, I quickened my pace. It had been a long, long day.

Bed was a welcome relief, and by the time I crawled under the enormous white doona, I was well and truly wrecked. Alice was already fast asleep, and even my frenzied fumbling at the bedroom door hadn't woken her. I remembered she didn't have her own key, so she must have asked at reception for a second key. I would find out what had happened in the morning.

As I lay there with my eyes closed, I could feel my cheeks expanding into a wide smile. It was thrilling to be in Italy, amongst Italians and their customs and culture. Soon, there would be precious little time for any shuteye. The next ten days would be eye-openers for both myself and Alice. It was one thing to read about Italy in a book, or watch a film or documentary about the country, but something else entirely to be immersed here. Buonna notte. Fino a domani.

Chapter 8
Dreaming!

We were in the glorious breakfast room. A huge expanse of octagonal roof dominated the restaurant, and it was difficult to draw one's eyes away from the bespoke criss-crossing of verdant green wrought iron and thick honey coloured wood.

I love architecture, but was hard pressed to find words to describe such a spectacular canopy. As an added bonus, there were two tiny black birds who must have flown in through the open widows, and were now scurrying and scampering along the eaves, trapeze artists in a bonsai-rendition of 'Carnival of the animals'.

All that was missing was light percussion background music. I was aware of soft music playing. Soothing, meditative background sounds, but apart from that, and the racket being made by the two tiny birds, it was all done! All silent! Sold!

Where were the staff? It was still very early, but the restaurant should have been showing some signs of life by now.

We had waited at the tall, slender, wooden pedestal positioned at the entrance to the breakfast room for at least five minutes-but it was a no-show from the key players. A large child's blackboard of gleaming oak with a crisp white sheet of butcher paper had been freshly positioned to the front of the pedestal, and a dazzling pink iPad had been placed on the pedestal itself. Nothing else. No flowers no huge antiquated dusty leather ledgers and no little knickknacks of mini towers of Pisa or La Scala. It all looked stark and minimalist Italian-and the entire place was similarly deserted.

"Where do you think everyone is, Fil? I can hear a church bell ringing, maybe they're all at mass?" With ninety percent of Italians being Catholic and a church in the next street, it was a fair summation from Alice. Still irritable from my insensitive awakening, I steered myself into the position of first speaker for the opposition.

"I don't think they'd be at mass, Alice. We're in Milan and it's a big city. Not a small village in the mountains. People around here are young and energetic, and probably only Catholic for the census. No. I think they are probably all sleeping in, it being Saturday. The tourists like us, I mean. I have no idea where the staff are though!" As I had been talking, Alice had been peering at the blackboard announcing the breakfast specials in careful, loopy Italian script.

"Err…yuk! Fil, they have tripe and tongues for breakfast! And they call them specials!"

Alice made me laugh. Even at this early hour, she was able to assume a comical guise. Two hours ago, she had not been so forthcoming with the jokes. I had woken at five am with a start, to Alice furiously rubbing her arms and legs with sun cream—fully dressed and obviously ready for food.

During my cross examination as to her motive in applying so much sunscreen to the extremities of her body, she had replied in an exasperated tone, "Oh Fil, it's going to be so hot today, I just thought I'd get in early with the sunscreen."

I told her I thought it was a good idea, but wondered why it had to have been so early, as she'd beaten the sun into submission even before it had time to rear its head.

"Alice, it's still dark. Why sunscreen when there's no sun?"

Again, Alice looked exasperated with me, but this time with an added dose of extreme incredulity.

"Fil, it's sunrise in five minutes. We need to be prepared." That had been it for my brief affair with sleep. Having tossed and turned with the newness and narrowness of the spartan, blanket-less bed for most of the night, I wasn't in the mood for theatrics such as elaborately rubbing my arms and legs in white makeup.

"I'm getting up for a shower Alice. Do you want the bathroom for a while?"

No. Alice did not want or need the bathroom. She would be perfectly happy sitting on the edge of the bed with her painful leg elongated, studying the Italian news. I spent the next hour in the tiny, mosaic blue-tiled bathroom, readying myself for the day, glad of the peace. It wasn't Alice from whom I was hiding. It was refuge from myself. Being fully awake by then, I did that recrimination thing whereby one examines one's conscience for misdemeanours and poorly conducted interactions from the previous day. That loathsome, self-inflicted, gruelling which spitefully descends upon most of us at the most inopportune of times. Like right now.

I knew I wasn't living in the moment, but I was rattled and niggled by my irrational insensitivity to people, and their plight in life. Good advice to myself would have been to have a go at walking in their shoes. But that was just it. I couldn't even walk in my own shoes, because they were buried in the bottom of my suitcase, which by now was probably buried in black sand at the bottom of the Dead Sea. I had a very real feeling that we would not be seeing our suitcases again, and that my favourite pair of black jiffies would be lost forever. That's why I was so introspective. That's why I was hiding.

If I could just lay eyes on my suitcase, and rummage and ruffle my way through the clothes, shoes and little personal possessions I'd thrown into the case, I'd be right as rain and ready for a day in magnificent Milan. One thing missing in action was a photograph of my dad, in a small frame which I'd brought with me to show my father around the upper echelons of his birth country. I had wanted dad with me as I traversed the mountains of the North, because his early life in the South had been so different. (Dad had passed away on Christmas Eve last year, and he'd always wanted to see the Swiss alps.) I vowed that if my suitcase was returned, I would take his photo out of the frame, and carry it around with me in my handbag. That was one keepsake I would not be letting out of my clutches.

After about an hour of soul searching, and alternately turning on and off the taps so that Alice would not think I had topped myself in the bathroom, I emerged, bare footed but fully dressed. Alice was still watching Italian news with no subtitles and extremely low definition to the point of fuzziness. Given that it was still only six am, I suggested we have a game of cards until seven when the breakfast room opened. (If the room service book was to be believed.)

Alice, with her arms and legs lathered in a thick elixir of pearly white sunscreen, beat me in every game, and I wondered why I had bothered to suggest cards when I knew I was a hopeless card player. I was at my best playing solo on my app, where I could cheat my way through game after game and no one was ever going to find out. Playing against Alice, I was shamefully exposed as the inept novice that I am, and it wasn't a good feeling to keep losing on an empty stomach.

At six forty five, I stood up abruptly, urged Alice to wipe off all the sunscreen and get ready to go down for breakfast. She was reluctant to do so, her excuse being that the tube was almost empty. I insisted she do so, promising that we would locate a chemist later on, where she would be able to purchase more sunscreen as well as the deodorant she'd been banging on about. (Both of us had packed our deodorants and toothpastes in the big suitcases, so we'd had to make do without both items, although I had found a small crumpled tube at the bottom of my handbag.)

At six fifty-five we were all set to go, and at seven am sharp, we had taken the lift down to the breakfast room. At seven-o-five, after no one had presented to highlight our names on the iPad and show us to a table, we had taken it upon ourselves to make our way cautiously into the restaurant, selecting a table for two closest to the hot food buffet. It was a fair bet that the bus-people would be down at seven-thirty, and all hell would break loose. I wondered if there were buses other than ours based at the hotel. Judging by the laden breakfast counter, it would be wise to eat early. It looked as though the crowds were expected!

Miraculously, as soon as we were seated, a pretty Indian girl in full sari and black spot sidled her way over and enquired as to whether we would like tea or coffee. She spoke in perfect high-brow Italian, and I answered for both of us in perfect, monosyllabic, pigeon Italian. Yes. We would both like coffee. Thank you. Si. Cafe. Grazie.

Instead of feeling proud of myself for having mastered the three words to perfection, I felt a bit of a fraud. I knew much more Italian than that. I could have challenged myself to the full gamut of 'Most definitely we would like to partake of coffee this fine morning, and thank you for your interest in our beverage preferences'.

But, I shouldn't have been so hard on myself. Longer phrases would be something I could warm up to, and it was still early days on our trip. There would be plenty of time for manifestos in Italian.

At least Alice was looking at me with admiration.

"Fil, your accent was perfect. Say it again so I can hear the way you rolled your 'r' with 'grazie'." I couldn't tell whether she was having a laugh at me or whether she was seriously impressed.

I stood up abruptly. "Andiamo, fai presto, Alice. Noi siamo troppo tardi."

I lost her then, but she followed me into the little alcove which was being used as a makeshift breakfast room. That was a sign I knew very well. It could only mean one thing. The bus people would be on their way down the stairs.

Within half an hour, the breakfast room was bursting at the seams with bus people. Obviously not tourists on our bus (which was not due until tomorrow morning) They all seemed to know each other and wore bus company tags with their names in large print. I liked the idea of the large print. Too many times I had been caught out calling someone by an incorrect name because the print on their name tag was too small, and I had made a guess using the initial letter as a clue.

A friend of mine went one step better. She was at an educational conference, and on the first morning of the three-day event, had misplaced her glasses. Upon arriving at the registration desk, she had flicked through the alphabetical listing of name tags, and selected what she thought to be her name, going by initial consonant which was 'M'. It turned out she had selected the name 'Mick' from the rack of names, and had worn the nametag for the duration of the three-day Conference without any one having tapped her on the shoulder and informed her that she had someone else's name-tag pinned to her ruffled, paisley blouse.

The woman in question was my friend Maree, and we never found out whose nametag the real Mick was wearing. Maree said she'd thought she'd heard people calling her 'Mick' throughout the Conference, but had just assumed, as it was a Catholic event, that they were referring to her as 'Mick'—a Catholic. As for the strange looks? Well, she hadn't been able to work that one out. Moral of the story? One should wear one's glasses at all times!

Back to the bus people. They were so loud my ears were ringing, and even the two tiny birds had fled in a bustle and flurry of wings. Thanks to my entirely accurate premonition, we had finished eating and drinking by the time the avalanche of tourists descended upon the breakfast room, and with a few nods and smiles at the crowds we made a speedy retreat back to the solace of the bedroom.

Eight am and we were ready to hit the shops. Except that we didn't end up leaving until eleven, as Alice had insisted that we ring Lost Property at the airport to track our luggage before venturing out for the morning. It was already warming up, and my preference would have been to don our sunhats and backpacks and head out straight away, thus ensuring time for a well-earned siesta on our return. But Alice did have a point in her doggedness to make the phone call. The suitcases were still missing in action and our bus tour was scheduled to leave early tomorrow morning for a sightseeing day in Milan. We would need clothes for the next ten days, and today would be our last chance to buy up big.

"I'll wait on hold, and you can go on ahead if you like, Fil. I know you don't like being out too long in the sun. You once told me it brings out your freckles." I wished I hadn't once told her about my freckles-breakout, but it wasn't going to be something Alice would easily let me forget. Alice had a memory like an elephant. (Forty years had passed since the freckles fiasco.)

"No. It's okay, Alice. I can wait."

We sat in companionable silence on our twin beds, Alice with her phone placed on her pillow, and me with mine on my lap while we waited for the luggage attendant to search Lost Property for our cases.

Alice's phone was elevated on the pillow because she had put it on speaker, and mine was resting in the contours of my lap because I was googling directions to the centre of Milan, and having it in that position meant that Alice could also see what I was doing. Not that either of us had the faintest idea where we were in relation to the Central Business District.

One thing was for sure—we were on the outskirts, and it looked like a fair hike to the city centre. Even though Alice had her stick, it would be a struggle. We could always get a taxi, but I was wary of being either overcharged or robbed at knife point in a city where we knew no one, and about which we knew nothing-except Milan's reputation along with other large Italian cities for tourist muggings and scams. Not that the scum who performed such tricks on gullible tourists made up even a fraction of the total city population. Of the three million people residing in Milan, probably only a couple of hundred would fall into the low life category. The rest of the population would no doubt be unconcerned with taking what was not rightfully theirs, and content with just getting on with the daily grind.

If only our luggage could be found, we could give the shops a miss and relax all day in the hotel beside the pool. Twenty-eight degrees had been forecast, with a chance of rain later in the evening. Perfect toe-dipping weather. I bowed my head in a silent prayer to St Anthony to help the attendant find the suitcases. A few minutes later, there was a banging and crackling from the phone, and an excited high-pitched falsetto voice came bursting through the line. "We av its. We 'av the caresses. I find hit ata last!"

One-legged Alice started jumping up and down on the bed and hugging me. I didn't move. I was in an advanced state of shock. I had truly believed I was never going to see my suitcase again. I needed the facts.

"Alice, ask him if there are two of them. If there are two caresses." It would have been just our luck for only one case to have turned up but no, we were in luck, and a pigeon pair had been found. It was probably best not to ask questions about the who, what, where and when of the disappearance of the cases. As long as they turned up intact with our belongings, our silence would be assured. Alice had picked up the phone and taken it off speaker, so I couldn't hear what the attendant was saying, but it didn't matter. It was all good news. Alice just kept repeating, "grazie, grazie, grazie." It was elation all around!

When she finally put the phone down, Alice carefully explained the details of the find to me. "The cases will be delivered after midnight tonight, and the porter will bring them up to our room and leave them outside our door."

I wasn't altogether happy hearing this laissez-faire arrangement, as I knew Italians to be notoriously casual and prone to indifference, and an 'after midnight delivery' had a slightly clandestine ring to it. Why would the courier need to wait till then?

The only way to avoid a prolonged wait would be to retrace our steps back to the airport and pick up the suitcases ourselves, however, two obstacles were impeding this plan. Number one, Alice's leg not being up to the arduous journey, and number two, the entire day would be wasted, as the airport was more than sixty kilometres from the city, and we'd have to carry the cases back to the hotel ourselves. A taxi would be out of the question, and the train too crowded as it was a Saturday, with many more people out and about.

I would just have to put the dilemma out of my mind, and pray that the suitcases arrived safely in the dead of night-before tomorrow morning.

Alice was her usual nonchalant self. Unperturbed. She was focussing on the positive, and believing the hot-headed Italians when they promised to deliver the goods.

Alice was also changing our plans for the day now that shopping for new clothes would be longer be a necessity.

"Fil, I was wondering. How would you feel if I got my hair cut and styled today? I really wanted to get to the hairdresser before we left London, but I just ran out of time. Do you mind waiting for me while I get it done? I'm not sure I could make it by myself, and today's the last opportunity I'll have before we leave Milan. Please?"

Alice didn't realise it, but sitting around people-watching, sipping coffee, window shopping and dipping my feet into cool gushing fountains I was sure to stumble across while she was being pruned, suited me down to the ground. My idea of a perfect Saturday afternoon. (Second only to lazing by the hotel pool sipping cocktails.)

"Well…I'm not sure, Alice…oh okay. Fine." Alice looked relieved, and I smiled to myself. She would never know how pleased I was not to be subjected to a whirlwind morning of Gucci, Prada, Tommy Hilfiger, Armani and the rest of the boys. I retreated to the bathroom whilst she began her phone calls. After three failed attempts, Alice found a hairdressing salon only a few blocks away with a cancellation for this afternoon. She carefully wrote down the name of the salon, and the directions from our hotel, delivered to her by 'Tony' whose high-pitched seagull screaming down the phone to Alice in a fair attempt at English was hard to miss, even though I was, by then, standing outside on the balcony.

"Yes, yes, yes." That was the only part of the conversation I could make out, and that was from Alice. Tony must have been rattling off the names of every crossroad, hill and dale between the hotel and the salon as the 'yes' count had exceeded twelve. I stopped counting after that. Alice would tell me in her own good time what had transpired between them.

The hair appointment had been booked for twelve o'clock, and it was already past ten. We were in a quandary. It was too late to go to any Shopping Centres and get back to the hotel in time to freshen up, and too early to set off for the hairdressing salon following Tony's carefully explained directions. After a few minutes of deliberating, Alice came up with a compromise which suited us both.

"Let's just relax for an hour or so, read our books or watch television and then it'll be time to set off for the hairdressers."

Here was my kind of non-challenging plan, and I happily made myself a cup of tea and a coffee for Alice, and settled comfortably on the cool, concrete pavement of the balcony with my tea, a plump paisley-patterned cushion, my magazine, phone and sun-hat. Ah, the good life!

Exactly one hour later, Alice appeared on the balcony, informing me that we had better get a move on if we were to find the salon in time. "Do you have the directions in your bag, Alice? Don't forget them, will you?"

Alice assured me that she had the directions firmly planted in her bag and that she was ready to go. Five minutes later, I was also ready to go, and for the second time that first morning in Milan, we rode the compact lift down to the compact foyer and made our way out into the brilliant sunshine.

Chapter 9
A Hair-Raising Experience!

It was out with the sunglasses the minute we hit the pavement. The streets looked different this morning. And yet here were the same cobblestones, same flower borders, same narrow footpaths. The colossal difference was the light, which was full sun and glaring. Everything glistened and sparkled, as if a huge wand had been extended onto the pavements, shaken to liquid sparkle and sprayed over the landscape, coating everyone and everything in fine, pure, whitish, yellowish light.

"Alice, do you notice something different out here this morning?"

Alice was so preoccupied with getting herself off the last step and onto solid ground that she probably hadn't even had time to look up, let alone orientate herself to her surroundings.

"No Fil. I haven't noticed anything." She looked up at that moment. "Oh, the light, you mean?"

"Yes. Do you think it's unusually bright and shiny out here? It wasn't like this when I was out on the balcony before."

Alice was busy arranging her handbag and small backpack, and once again did not react to my revelation. My mind was buzzing. Here we were in a religious country, about as close to heaven as one could get in terms of altitude and proximity to some of the world's highest mountains, and it was the light which was drawing me-claiming me. I thought of old masters' paintings depicting celestial light. Then I thought of light at the end of tunnels, and light in one's heart when the first flashes of love strike alternately soft then hard. Finally, I thought of light emanating from beautiful rainbows and crystal prisms.

And then, in the wink of an eye, it was gone, and the morning was again ordinary. There was light, of course, but not anything mystical or biblical, not anything different from the daily cycle of the sun. Had I just had an epiphany in

Italy? I stole a look at Alice, but she was shifting her legs from side to side with single minded determination and seemed to have forgotten all about me.

Perhaps I was dreaming this whole scenario? But, if that were the case, why could I feel the sun on my face and the full weight of my backpack? This was madness! Now I could feel someone digging into my shoulders and shaking me. "Fil, Fil, wake up, we have to go, or we'll be late for my hair appointment."

I closed my eyes and then opened them again at once in a reflex reaction, and there was Alice, bending over me, shaking me into wakefulness. I was not out on the street at the front of the hotel in blinding light after all but had somehow been transported to our bedroom balcony. To make matters worse, I was slumped against a wall, with the full glare of the sun on my face. Thank heavens. It had all been a dream. I had not been walking along beside Alice and struck down by a blinding light like Saint Paul on the road to Damascus after all. I was not mad. I was not losing it. I had just been dreaming.

"Fil, what have you been doing out here all this time?"

I couldn't answer Alice because I had not the faintest idea what I had been doing all this time outside. Presumably dreaming. In a way I was relieved that it had all been a dream, as I was not in the mood for a calling into the great religious unknown. St Paul had not been ready either, nor had Joseph of the Technicolor dream coat, nor most of the saints.

In my teenage years, my mother had made possibly a hundred novenas, in the hope that one of her eight girls would heed the call of the Lord and take up the veil and the vow of chastity. The closest thing to a nun or a priest we had managed in our immediate family was a Chaplin in a jail. This sister had achieved chaplaincy, but unfortunately not demonstrated adherence to the vows of chastity, as she had five children in her flock, and yearned consistently for a sixth—or a foster child.

We dubbed her Mrs Pitt (a-la Angelina Jolie) and her husband eventually became 'Mr P' as his job was in politics and there had been a Prime Minister of the same name. The standard joke whenever the family turned up for a function would be for someone to be placed on guard awaiting their arrival in the people mover and for it to be announced to all in sundry, "It's the Pitts! It's the Pitts!"

Suffice to say, we were a religious family—just not that religious!

"Fil, are you listening to me? I've asked you twice now. You didn't crush any sleeping tablets into that cup of tea you had, did you? You've been asleep for an hour at least." I tried to remember why I was on the boiling hot balcony and not tucked up in my narrow bed; why I was fully dressed, sun-hatted but shoeless and whether or not I had drunk my cup of tea with the hemlock. No. I hadn't drunk it. The cup was right beside me, and when I put my finger into the brown murky water, the liquid was lukewarm, not hot. So, Alice was right. I had been on the Juliet balcony (aptly named in my case) for quite a while.

"Sorry Alice. I must have fallen asleep out here in the sun. Hope I don't have an outbreak of freckles today."

That made Alice laugh, and then we were both laughing.

"I had the weirdest dream while I was asleep. It was like Groundhog Day. I was living out what we will be doing in the next hour, and there was a strange, eerie light over the city."

Alice was looking at me in alarm. Obviously, she thought I had sunstroke or had overdosed on magic mushrooms at breakfast. I wanted to continue on with my mutterings and expand on the thought that perhaps I had unwittingly ingested some hallucinogenic substance whilst enjoying breakfast, but it would have been to no avail, and to Alice's turned back. She was already back in the bedroom fossicking around in her handbag. A sure sign of age. Or having lost something somewhere in the bowels of the bag. If I hurried, Alice wouldn't have to wait too long, and I would be in her good books again.

Ten minute later we were standing side by side in the Milanese sunshine, with Alice attempting to decipher her handwritten directions to the salon, and me pinching myself to make sure I wasn't still dreaming. The pain was real, so I had to assume I was wide awake.

"What's the name of the salon, Alice?"

"Ravishing Hair, I think. I'm just double checking now."

Alice was correct. The salon was called Ravishing Hair, but despite Tony of the falsetto voice having given us fairly accurate (if not circuitous) directions from our hotel it, still took us ages to get there, what with the frequent rest stops for Alice to elevate her leg, and my stopping to take panoramic photos.

It was a real workout—crossing busy vehicle-choked roads winding through back alleys, clambering over small stone walls covered in red and pink geraniums, and finally arriving in a wide shop filled street, teaming with tourists and natives-all out for a Saturday jaunt. At one stage in the epic journey we were following a stone wall which was more than likely built by the Romans. The wall was about a metre high and reminded me of Hadrian's wall in England. Everything about Milan was so old, and yet so new at the same time.

Dichotomous divergence. I knew from history books that Milan had been pillaged, burnt down and bombed during many wars over the centuries, and that many parts of the city had been rebuilt from scratch. It was a strange twilight zone we walked. Had we taken the taxi, the driver would have taken the main roads into the city, and we would not have seen anything of the fascinating backstreets.

When I say we finally reached the salon, it was not the actual door to the Ravishing salon we reached, but a pair of towering, thick, black, double-wrought-iron gates which protected the entrance to what looked to be a pretty paved courtyard with flowers, shrubs and shady trees. The gates were wedged in between trattorias and pizzerias to the left and right. There were people everywhere, on the street and in the cafes, but the gates were set back about three metres from the street, so that once we had stepped inside the alcove area which housed the gates, it was very shaded, still and quiet.

We had the correct number '287' and the correct street—Via Varone, but there was no sign informing customers that a hairdressing salon lay beyond the gates. The only outward projection from the wall was a row of gleaming old fashioned (like keys on an old typewriter) buzzers displaying apartment numbers. We worked out that a cluster of apartments must also have existed beyond the wrought iron gates.

"This must be it, Fil. We've been up and down this street three times, and this is the only place even close to the number Tony gave me. I'm going to have to ring him." Which she did. Twice. On the third attempt somebody who only spoke Italian picked up, and Alice asked, in English, to speak to the man who spoke English—Tony.

"E andato pranzo" was the sing-song retort Alice received, and the call was promptly and rudely curtailed.

"I think the boy was saying that Tony wasn't there. He was on pranzo, whatever that is. Would it be a walk?" A wave of insightful practicality with languages overtook me.

"It means he's gone to lunch. We still don't know if the salon is behind these gates, and we can't get in anyway. I'll go into the cafe over there and ask someone if there is hairdressing salon is in the courtyard." Just as I was about to approach the cafe to my left, a woman in expensive colourful clothing and a plastic cape draped over her shoulders and slicked down greasy red-conditioner lathered hair seemingly attached to the cape appeared at my side and punched in a long code.

Throughout the process she was looking stoically ahead, and her brisk manner conveyed annoyance (or embarrassment?) at finding two bumbling vagrants obstructing her pathway. She spoke not a word. The gates slowly ground open. Unless the woman had popped away from the set of the "Handmaiden Tale" for a cafe latte and was still in full costume, there had to be a hairdressing salon somewhere within the gated community.

The gates were slowly folding back into their original position, and Alice and I still hadn't moved. At the last possible moment, Alice stuck out her good leg and stopped the gate from fully closing. "Quickly Fil, squeeze through."

I gazed at the tiny opening in the gate, doubting very much that I would be able to squeeze my hips through without tearing my clothes, and at this stage, these were the only clothes we had left to wear. Alice was already through in the time I had hesitated, and given that we were roughly the same size, I copied her movements. Turn. Bend. Breathe in. Ease out. Not too different to a square dance. It wasn't that bad after all. Not that I'd want to be squeezing through gates and cracks for a living.

Were we in for a pleasant surprise!

Beyond the gate was an Italian Brigadoon. A fairy-tale courtyard with spongy soft green grass, wide branched leafy green trees studded with fairy lights, extensive beds of every coloured flower imaginable, little wooden seats and tiny free-standing cottages dwarfed by blocks of pastel-coloured apartments similar to the ones I had peered up into the windows of last night. Many of the rustic shutters on the apartment windows were all closed-up, and for some lucky apartment dwellers, Siesta time must already have been in full swing.

Directly in front of us, as we exited the small tunnel leading from the iron gates was a shopfront with oodles of sparkling glass, high cloister windows to die for, and a flashing sign which read 'Ravishing Hairdressing Salon' in English. More pastel-coloured apartments leant over the shop at peculiar angles reminiscent of the nursery rhyme, 'There was a crooked house'. For the second time today, I questioned whether or not I was dreaming. It was all very surreal, but maybe that's what being in a foreign country was all about.

I had no precedent for this courtyard with the hairdressing salon. Most hairdressers in Australia are in the Main Streets, or on second floors of a shopping malls, but this salon was a law unto itself. I thought of private islands and private towns and even private yachts, but a private hairdresser was something new. There must have been a regular clientele, as Alice had only managed to secure a spot because someone had cancelled. We would definitely be the odd ones out.

"Well. This is it. I'm feeling a bit nervous now. It looks all posh and swanky, and what if they won't take credit card? We don't have any lire."

Alice was working herself up into a tizz. Referring to Italian money as 'lire' was a dead giveaway. Lire hadn't been around as legal tender since the last century.

"Alice, calm down. Of course, they take credit cards, and even if you have to pay it off for the rest of your life, we're here now and there's no turning back. If you won't take the appointment, I will." Threatening to step in and take Alice's place had been just the right thing to say to her. Concerned that I might actually follow through with my threat to trade places, Alice hurriedly pushed open the heavy honey-coloured wooden door to the salon.

The inevitable bell tinkled, and the inevitable gushing girl in overalls and short cropped pink hair, ruby red lipstick and large loopy silver earrings came rushing up the runway, welcoming us into the folds of the funky salon as if we were long-lost relatives. The interior of the salon had a grungy, shabby-chic warehouse feel to it. A narrow warehouse, definitely alternate in aesthetics. It was painted in Rainbow colours, and there were at least six swivel chairs lined up facing show biz mirrors. All spots were occupied except the very last one, and it was to this swivel chair that Alice was led, the moment we finished hugging the maître d', and the gamine-looking girl who had appeared to ask us if we would like a tea or coffee. Both of us opted for water.

Once Alice had been whisked away to be prepped for the operation that would involve cutting into her unruly curls and liberating her face from her bushy bangs, I found myself a nice quiet bench at the front of the salon near the door, and guzzled my water until the glass was empty. It was a hot day, and we'd walked miles. After about twenty minutes of flicking through glossy magazines with the names Prada and Versace on every other page, I decided I would go for a stroll around the courtyard. I didn't dare venture out into the street, in case no one came by to let me back into the little community, and I knew Alice would be panicking if she could not find me.

I slipped out easily. Alice had been talking ten to the dozen to Marco, her stylist, about our anticipated holiday, and the entire salon had been listening—

probably trying to pick up an English word or two. Had it been me, and knowing I had a captive audience, I would have been throwing in lots of fast gibberish to entirely confuse them. It wasn't only the words which were different between English and Italian. It was the intonation. The singsong exaggerated delivery of words when Italians attempted English the first few times. We were probably the same when we tried to speak Italian. I dreaded to think what I sounded like when I shouted down the phone to my relatives in Southern Italy.

Alice was holding court like there was no tomorrow. At this rate, I would be lucky if we were not still in this salon when the tour left Milan, so slow was the pace.

Some fresh air out in the courtyard would be a wise move. It was stuffy in the salon. Obviously, air conditioners were still a novelty in Italian shops. The compromise in this establishment was two big industrial fans, like ones I had seen in films, but they had not been placed anywhere near the seats at the front of the salon, and I couldn't feel even a sniff of a breeze.

Outside was literally a breath of fresh air. It was cool, shaded and peaceful. I was the only one out there, except for the birds and a sleeping black Labrador curled up at the entrance to the salon. Usually I am afraid of dogs when I'm alone, but this one looked harmless and lifeless, so I steered clear. I found a bench and closed my eyes to meditate.

I couldn't have been in meditative state for more than two minutes, than the tinkling bell above the front wooden door went off into a frenzy, and I looked up to see two women floating out of the salon, capes flying in the wind they had created with the slamming of the door. The sleeping Labrador had also been disturbed, and was jumping up and down around them, yelping in delight. He must have known them, or else he was on staff, paid in bones and dog biscuits to guard the premises, and to greet or farewell customers as they entered or exited the salon.

Typically, the women came right up to the bench on which I was sitting and plonked themselves down next to me. I was forced to shuffle up to the very end of the bench, as one of the women had been eating for two for quite a while by the looks of things. I decided straight away that despite their uncanny resemblance to Handmaid characters, with their stance and slicked hair and red bonnets, neither of them were of the desired age or physique, and neither of them would have been in a position to bump up the dwindling population of a fictional Massachusetts town from any position, let alone lying on their backs. Playing the parts of old crones in Harry Potter might have been more up their alley. I kept my ideas to myself, and my head down.

The pair were not in the least interested in me. I could have been an overfed stray cat curled upon the bench for all the notice they took of me. I didn't mind. I had been enjoying my solitary meditation and was not feeling gracious. For the third time I was reminded of the 'Handmaid's Tale' as I examined them out of the corner of my eye. It was the capes and the slicked down hair which was so convincingly Atwood.

Then, they lost all credibility.

One of the women (the less plump one) began fishing around in her pocket and shrieking to her companion that she had lost something. I silenced the slit in the corner of my eye, which had also begun to flutter involuntarily, and ushered in the yellow darkness. With no visual clues as to the shape or size of the lost possession, I could only surmise it must have been something she needed outside and had left in the hairdressers. A sunhat? No, both she and the friend already had white handmaiden bonnets encasing their heads (probably part of the 2019 fashion statements cooked up by Ravishing Hair).

If it wasn't a sunhat, then maybe a water bottle? But I would have seen a water bottle, or it would at least have been bulging out of her pockets. Why would two women be so desperate to leave the fan-cooled comfort of the salon, with magazines and cups of coffee, little bowls of olives, wedges of cheese and crunchy breadsticks to bask in the sun in their costumes?

I was sorely tempted to open my eyes and see for myself, but was saved from doing so by my senses of smell and taste. Cigarettes. The dreaded nicotine known to contain over seventy cancer causing chemicals. (I was privy to this alarming statistic from having studied causes of lung cancer when my father was diagnosed with the condition in 2018.) The women may have identified as 'social smokers', but the fact that they could not do without a cigarette for three hours whist their hair was being coloured, cut and styled was not a good sign. More than likely they were addicts. As were a fair whack of mainland Europeans according to the guidebooks. I wouldn't have minded if they had set up camp in the next copse and left me to my meditation. I could have prayed for them. But to sit on my bench and puff away like steam engines in the five free minutes they had been granted was a bit much. I opened my eyes and leapt up from the seat.

My main concern was the smoke getting into my hair, and me being dubbed a heavy smoker for the duration of the trip, because someone had smelt the smoke in my hair and on my skin when they'd been introduced to me at the 'Welcome drinks', which were scheduled for tonight. Damn the women and damn my having scuttled outside for some fresh air. Those hopes were well and truly dashed.

It was more like a smoking ceremony performance than it was a peaceful sweet-scented garden of Eden. The women were being friendly now. Calling out to me in Italian to sit back down on the seat, and to tell them about myself. They couldn't have known I was a tourist, as I'm dark-haired and olive-skinned, and I had left my backpack inside with the gamine girl to store in the coat room. I didn't want to talk. I had every right, as Alice's companion, to be sitting on the bench enjoying the sunshine, and it was the pair of them and not me, causing consternation.

I spoke in defiant English. "Would you mind moving to another bench and smoking over there please? I can't breathe with all the smoke in my face."

I don't think they understood a word of what I was saying, but my added arm movements and fits of coughing should had been their cue to move away from me, the deranged tourist in the courtyard. One of the women got up to move, the second woman looked as if she were about to follow her, when she swivelled around and pointed to a sign which had been carved into the wood. I hadn't noticed the scratching when I'd first sat down on the bench as the women's caped backs must have been obscuring it from my vision whilst they'd been sitting there. Now that she was pointing it out to me, I could clearly see and read the sign. 'Posti a sedere per fumatori'. In other words, 'Smoker's seat'.

I felt my face redden, and the only thing I could think of to do was to apologise to the woman, race back to the salon and hide. The women were laughing by then, chain-smoking and gabbling to each other in rapid-fire Italian. More than likely they were discussing me and would no doubt have had me in the category of 'a peculiar English eccentric' even before I reached the salon door. The dog was back in his position, and feeling sorry for the creature, I called out, "good boy!"

My reward was frantic tail-thumping on the warm pavement. The creature probably thought a juicy bone was on its way, but I had nothing except water to offer him, and that was boiling hot from having been in my lap during the micro meditation and billowing smoke incidents. I did the best I could for the dog. I left him alone to do what dogs do best. Sleep!

Inside was a current of hairdresser energy. Washing, drying, sweeping, cutting, blow drying, pouring tea and pouring over the ledger, hanging jackets in the cloak-room, flicking magazines, more cutting, more blow drying and finally, the holding up of mirrors so that customers might admire their newly styled hair from the back.

Why did hairdressers include that last step? What was one supposed to say if the fashioning of the back stalls was not to their liking? And who cared what the back of their head looked like anyway? It was the same with tasting wine at a table before the glasses were filled up. How many people had actually, ever said to the waiter, "Err, no, I don't think so. It's dreadful! Take it away!"

Alice was almost at the finishing post by the looks of things. Her stylist, a tall man with a ponytail, overalls and copious amounts of heavy makeup was talking to Alice in slow halting English. His voice was very loud, and I could hear him from where I was sitting. (I had resumed my place near the door.)

"Ava you ever tinker ova usie condition? Your airs izzy very dry."

Alice was nodding, and as the man coaxed her, he was extending his free hand to a shelf above his head which conveniently housed bottles and bottles of lotions and potions. He grabbed the biggest bottle and shoved it at Alice. "Is izza ita?" Alice was nodding gratefully, and I knew that meant I would be struggling all the way back to the hotel with the enormous bottle of bright green liquid. I prayed she wouldn't buy me a present and then there would be two bottles to carry. Even with both of us conditioning our hair twice a day, we would be hard pressed to get through even one bottle on the trip.

The next time I looked up it was to Alice pirouetting around in front of me twirling her curls through her fingers and appealing to me to demonstrate my approval of her new cut and style by clapping, or perhaps even calling out to other patrons to look at her, because they too could look like that—if they had a few hundred euro to spare.

Once I had exclaimed in delight, "Oh Alice, your hair looks wonderful," she was satisfied and paraded proudly towards the cash register to pay her bill. Truthfully, Alice's brand-new Milanese haircut did look swish and chic. The stylists were top notch and they knew their craft. I felt a tiny twinge of jealousy that Alice would now be the favoured one when it came to men offering us seats on buses or in restaurants, or drinks in cocktail lounges, but I wasn't about to part with one hundred and twenty-eight euros, which was what Alice had just paid.

It was time to say goodbye to our new-found friends in the salon, and with promises that we would return in a few years' time, and that the next time I would also be parting with one hundred and twenty-eight euros, we took leave of the premises. Secretly, I thought Alice had taken leave of her senses, paying all that money for a cut, colour and blow-wave, but one man's meat is another man's poison, and she was deliriously happy with the result.

Chapter 10
Gelato, Gelati!

The least I could do was to offer to buy her lunch, as we hadn't eaten since breakfast and I for one was starving. Exiting the wrought iron gates was child's play, as there was a big button with a large red knob at the side of the gate. I pushed down on it, and 'Open Sesame', we were out, back in the real world of restaurants and souvenir shops, clothes shops, gelaterias and more tourist shops. We didn't have to walk far before we turned a corner and came upon a large piazza, packed with outdoor eateries and crowds of people. Not just tourists by the looks of things. Many families with young children and babies in prams were walking up and down the perimeter of the square or sitting in small groups eating under the shade of the trees, chatting and laughing, really enjoying their Saturday afternoon passagiato.

Quite a number of the restaurants also had short black pedestals at their entrance displaying the 'House Specials' and because it was already four thirty, many were already welcoming patrons for an early dinner.

We were both hungry, but wary of eating too much, as later on tonight we would be meeting our future travelling companions with whom we would be touring Northern Italy for the next week at least. A 'welcome dinner' had been booked at a mystery restaurant, reportedly not too far from our hotel, and we would be driven there by bus and given a city sightseeing Tour along the way.

With these plans in mind, it was easier just to walk into the first restaurant we saw, sit down, and order two calzones and two cold Cokes. Once we were settled, it was time to sit back and people watch. The square was a never-ending catwalk of colour. I attest to the fact that the easily discernible Milanese we observed passing us by as we munched on our delectable calzones, displayed a passion of fashion-every single one of them. It was as if there were an unwritten law forbidding residents to venture into the heart of the city if they were not prepared to dress to the very high standards displayed. Even the babies and older children were dressed to the hilt.

Alice and I had the best excuse for looking like slobs. We were tourists who had lost our luggage and were forced to appear in public in shabby garb. But even if I had changed into an 'out-for-a-Saturday-afternoon-stroll-outfit', I would have been no competition for the fashionable, expensive wardrobes sported by the average Milanese.

Alice had been craving a gelato all day, so as soon as we'd finished our light lunch, we wandered up and down the square on a gelato hunt. The shop that took our fancy had the added bonus of being the most crowded, which could only mean one thing—they made the best gelato. After ten minutes at the end of the slow-moving queue, the gelato man with the red and white cap and matching apron was ready to take our orders. There were more flavours to choose from then there had been rainbow colour choices for hairstyles at the salon we had left less than an hour ago.

I finally chose a scoop of lemon and a scoop of pistachio. Alice was more conventional, and opted for Neapolitan —chocolate, strawberry and vanilla. They were to die for, and even though I had sampled gelato in many parts of southern Italy and in Rome and Venice, the pistachio was the best and creamiest I'd ever had the pleasure of swirling down my throat. The sun was searing, and we were tired, so the sugar and the cold creamy mixture did the trick. After two gulps, I had found my second wind.

The young man serving us was listening as we badgered each other, and he must have had an ear for accents, because he asked us (in Italian) if we were Australian. He then told us he had an uncle in Australia who came home every year, bringing Australian presents and souvenirs with him. My Italian wasn't good enough for me explain the significance of my olive branches, but I gave him one, nevertheless. (The first of the branches to be handed out in Milan, as I wasn't really counting airports.)

He was excited. "Thala your, I will plant this in my Giardino." He was also excited to discover I had Italian heritage, and we ended up singing a Gianni Morandi song together. He wanted to give both Alice and I free gelati, but we didn't want to do him out of his livelihood, so we left fifteen euro on the counter, and quickly left the premises. The man's name was Umberto, and I was off to a sterling start with my gifting.

Although still hot and steamy, spitting rain had begun to fall when we left the shop, and neither of us had thought to bring an umbrella. Alice hobbled into the nearest tourist bazaar and emerged with two identical fold-up umbrellas. She presented one to me. "Here you are, Fil. This will probably come in handy in Italy." We erected them immediately and set off with a spring in our step. (One of us did. The other moaned and hobbled along. Which of us was the 'other', you might well ask!)

For some peculiar reason, a return journey is invariably faster than any arduous venture into the great unknown. This was true for us after the calzones, the gelati and the sudden burst of warm, stinging rain.

The route we took was slightly different, as once we'd established our bearings, it was easy to follow the crumpled, colourful (slightly sodden) tourist map Alice had picked up in the shop where she'd bought the umbrellas with 'Milan' splashed over their canopies-decipherable only when the umbrella was fully expanded. Whilst Alice had been in the Souvenir and Knick-knacks bazaar, I had been sheltering from the rain under the eaves of a nearby flower shop, and the colourful plastic tubs and wooden buckets of flowers crowding the wet pavement smelt glorious.

It was the expert arrangement of pots, buckets and tiny painted Terracotta saucers which caught my eye, and made me think immediately of weddings, parties and religious occasions-events where flowers such as these would claim star billing and cost a fortune. Corsages, table arrangements, bouquets, sympathy bunches, Posies-the humble flower catered for all. The glistening rain-drops on the foliage only added to the charming display. Sniffing in the heady scent of the flowers was where Alice found me, when she returned.

"Are you alright, Fil? Do you feel sick? Why are you taking big gulps of air outside this flower shop?"

I had no real answer for her. I was there for the shelter, and because the vibrant colours of the flowers—reds, yellow, pinks and purples had attracted me towards them. Again, the reference to the rainbow. The spectrum colours were everywhere in Italy—in the signs above dress shops, in the rows of ice cream tubs in the gelati shop and now here in the colourful array of cut flowers. I looked up into the overcast sky, and what should be there? A brilliant rainbow! Definitely something to write home about! My mother would think we were in Ireland, and not Italy, after all.

Back on the route to the hotel, I noticed there were not as many people on the streets. In contrast, every café or restaurant we passed was brimming with patrons, and many of the families with prams and children were sheltering from the sudden outburst under shop canopies or in Park rotundas. Crossing the last road was the most difficult. Because of the route we had taken, the road just before our hotel was a main one, and the traffic was relentless. There were lights, but we'd ended up at the other end of the park to where we'd been this morning, and it was too far to traipse up to the lights to cross.

We ended up taking our chances with a dash between cars, and it was a gamble, but we made it safely to the other side. A foolish move in retrospect, and one that would have been better taken at the end of the trip when we'd seen what we'd come to see. It would still have mattered to have been mown down by the Fiats and Alfas, but not as much.

Our hotel was finally in sight, and we could not have been happier. My agenda for the rest of the evening had been set for the last thirty minutes—a cold glass of wine, some peanuts and my guidebook. What else was there to hope for in life? (Except clean clothes.)

Alice had informed me she would be having an hour's rest before we ventured down to the foyer at six-thirty for the 'meet and greet' session. My main concern was our attire, but with a bit of luck, no one would take any notice of us. We were on holidays after all.

Chapter 11
Meet and Greet and Meet Some More!

And what were holidays for if not taken up with eating, drinking, swimming and lazing about? The epicurean delights one enjoys when on holidays—the carefree, happy go lucky disposition which often causes one to act out of character, and to buddy up with perfect strangers. Since I had already ruled out swimming, only three wedges of the quadrant (eating, drinking and lazing about) had been ticked off, so I decided to go for another round, this time 'snazzing things up' a little by starting with the drinking.

The cool, dark lounge bar was deserted when I slipped in from a partially coveted side door close to the lift. It was just after five, and only an hour before the 'Meet and Greet' which had promised to include drinks and canapés. Following the initiation ceremony (and depending on how long it took to complete all the paperwork, cheek kissing and hand shaking with perfect strangers), there would be the option of proceeding to a local trattoria for dinner, again with the dependence clause attached, regarding the number of people who actually showed up in an hour's time.

Having been on many a coach tour, I was aware that the number of guests at the Welcome drinks could vary dramatically, especially if the function was held the evening before the trip was due to commence. Determining factors might have included guests' times of arrival and potential plane delays. For varied reasons, some groups arrived late in the evening, and consequently missed the Welcome Drinks. Or, guests chose to arrive in readiness for the bus, early on the morning of the trip departure. I doubted that would have been the case with our Northern Lakes and Cinque Terra trip, as the departure time for Day One had been clearly designated as eight am in the brochures. Arriving in the dead of night, or even early morning on the departure day would have been cutting it extremely fine.

Given that I was the only potential customer in the lounge bar, I had my choice of seats and lounges. I chose neither a seat nor a comfy position on the lounge, instead settling myself on a high stool at the bar, close to the drinks and nibbles. Someone had already done a good job of laying the table, as spread out along the bar were bowls of olives, tiny rectangles of cheese, peanuts and what looked to be baby artichokes. There was a pile of plates and a tower of serviettes, but no signs of human life.

Until…the woman who had been sitting in the corner of the bar on the last two occasions I had passed by enroute to the lift, appeared suddenly at the front entrance and proceeded to walk straight up to me. She might have been the waitress or bartender, but she was not dressed in waitressing or bar tending attire, and neither was she positioning herself behind the bar which would have made sense. The woman was carrying a large clipboard and a laptop. When I'd seen her yesterday, I had assumed her to be a businesswoman escaping the madness of Friday afternoons, relaxing in the bar before her commute home—wherever that may have been. But today was Saturday, and most businesses took well-earned weekend breaks.

The woman sat herself down at one of the little tables and spread out her laptop and clipboard. She then took a sheaf or pamphlets from the satchel she still had over her shoulder, and carefully placed the pile in front of her. She looked to be setting up a pop-up shop in the cocktail bar. Instantly, it hit me where I had seen her before.

Of course! She was the tour director for our Italian lakes sojourn, and she wasn't setting up shop, but preparing herself for the onslaught of guests who would be bombarding her with questions at the welcome drinks, scheduled to start in just under three quarters of an hour. The pamphlets must have been maps and brochures tempting guests to optional extras such as palace visits and sumptuous three-course meals which were not always included in the basic price of the tours. So that's where I had seen her face before! In the glossy travel-magazine advertising our trip.

The woman was looking over towards me, propped up at the bar like a clay pigeon awaiting my fate, and she was smiling. I smiled back, still not one hundred percent convinced that she was not an artist-in-residence or a pop-up stall-holder. I decided to approach her. "Excuse me, but do you know where the bartender has gotten to? I was going to order a drink, but no one has turned up."

The red-haired women smiled again, and then replied in perfect English. "I think he is on a break. We are very causal and trusting here in Italy. You can just make yourself a drink if you wish. Are you staying at the hotel?"

I let her know that I was staying here with a friend, and that this would be our second night in the hotel.

"Oh, and for how long will you stay here?" Even though the woman had spoken with a cross between an American and Italian accent, her phrasing and grammar gave her away as not being English. I knew that some Northern Italians had red hair, and green eyes, so her colouring, although not typically Italian, fitted the profile.

I told her we were leaving tomorrow on a tour of the Northern Italian lakes and Cinque Terra. Straight away, she guessed my identity. It must have been my accent and she must have done her homework. Well, she almost cottoned on.

"Yes. Exactly. You must be Alice and you are from Australia, si?"

I told her she was half right. That yes, I was Australian, but no, I was not Alice.

Alice was fast asleep upstairs, knocked out on painkillers she had swallowed for her injured leg and knee, and that I was Fil and my only ailment was alcohol deprivation. The woman laughed, and introduced herself as Francesca, the Tour Guide for the trip we would be taking.

"I am happy to meet you and Alice, Fil."

With that she jumped up and asked me if I wanted a drink, and positioned herself behind the bar, urging me to name my poison.

"I really wanted a martini with an olive. Would that be possible?" Francesca flashed me a smile, revealing her beautiful teeth and healthy, pink gums.

"Fil, this is Italy. It is the land of love. Anything is possible in Italy."

With that Francesca began pouring, mixing and shaking the spirits with practised ease in a fair imitation of Tom Cruise in the movie, *Cocktail*.

"Do you like martinis, Fil?"

Truth be told, I had only ever tasted a martini once before, and that had been on my eighteenth birthday when my father had taken myself and a friend out to lunch, and allowed me my first alcoholic beverage. Dad being Italian, the special drink was naturally a martini. Apart from the olive, I don't remember much about the drink, nor the rest of the afternoon and evening. Today, I had ordered the martini from Francesca in honour of my papa—Nino—but I didn't want her to think that she would be burdened with an alcoholic Australian on her bus. I hardly ever drink alcohol at home, even though we have some of the finest wines in the world (after Italy, of course).

Francesca didn't appear to be concerned that I had ordered a strong spirit. She mixed and swished without any instructions, so she must have had some experience. As I watched her rattle the cocktail-shaker high in the air, she reminded me of a maraca-playing Tarantella dancer about to beckon a Congo line of patrons and shuffle around the hotel. I imagined many of the yet unknown guests clasping hips in a long haphazard line behind Francesca, cavorting around the foyer, picking up more hotel guests and staff along the way.

An impromptu Italian fiesta, all because the woman with the mass of red shoulder length curls had come alive behind the bar shaking a cocktail for me. And one for herself! She had handed me a perfect little half-moon sugar-encrusted martini glass, complete with two green olives on either side, and then, just as quickly, picked up another filled glass, encouraging me to chink glasses.

"Saluti!" Francesca then threw back her mane of red hair and swallowed the thick crystal-clear syrup in one satisfied gulp. This was followed by an elongated, "rrr" sigh of pleasure, a noisy licking of lips and finally a beaming smile directed towards me. She was still standing behind the bar, and more to the point, she was still standing. The whole ritual was so swift, I hardly had time to do more than sniff my own drink, as one would tentatively sniff milk which had been left out in the sun.

Francesca was coaxing me to swallow the concoction, but upon breathing in the strong intoxicating mixture of liquors, I had something strong of my own to contend with. Reservations.

"The martini is a drink you should feel in your loins. It will warm your blood and put a fire in your belly. Drink it now for the fire." She appeared to know what she was talking about, and the olives did look tempting. I popped both of them into my mouth at once and began munching. I chewed slowly as, given my luck, one of the pips would lodge in my throat and that would be the end of our trip. Either that or Francesca would jump over the bar and grab my chest from behind and perform the Heimlich manoeuvre.

Being a tour director, she would need to have had up to date first aid training. The manoeuvre wouldn't be necessary as it seemed the olives were pip-less and I was still breathing normally. Whilst I had been deliberating, Francesca had slipped out from behind the bar, and resumed her place behind the pile of brochures—back in yesterday's writing pose. I wanted to think it was one of the happy coincidences I was experiencing in Italy that the tour guide had set up in the very bar where I had been languishing. But it wasn't really coincidental. More just fate. Or the roll of the dice.

I decided I didn't really want to drink the martini after all. It was so strong and there was the warning about the potential bushfire in the pit of my stomach. If it raged for days, I would miss out on vital aspects of the trip. I would be the passenger up the back of the bus with the almighty hangover. No one would talk to me, and Alice would be embarrassed by me yet again. The martini was a wild card which needed discarding. To the side of the bar was a cluster of large terracotta pots with bushy indoor foliage. Very green, and aesthetically pleasing. A heathy slug of vermouth and gin could only enhance growth, and who had time to bend over and smell the flowers in a bar? It would be a safe, sensible solution, and next time, I would order lemonade. Safer, and easier to swallow.

I was quick with my watering, and Francesca was none the wiser. I left ten euro on the bar near the bowl of peanuts and raced towards the circular stairs which led up to the bedrooms on the first floor. Francesca's head had still been bent in homage to her writing pad as I had passed, and a few people were starting to trickle down to the foyer. They looked excited, which could only mean they were there for the 'Welcome Drinks'. I raced off to retrieve Alice.

It took a bit of assisting and fussing over the bandages, but Alice was ready twenty minutes later, freshly bandaged and more than ready for food and drinks. On the way down in the lift, I related the story of the martini in dad's honour, and she laughed when I got to the bit about how Francesca had tossed back her head and swallowed the martini in one great gulp.

"You realise it was probably lemonade she was drinking, don't you, Fil? She wouldn't be able to drink on the job, and it sounds like she was setting up shop early in case anybody was lurking around in the foyer or the bar. And there you were. How fortunate!"

I didn't quite get what was fortunate about my having been the first customer for Francesca, but I let it slip. Did Alice mean I should have stayed down there with Francesca and built up the crowds? I would have stayed, but she had seemed preoccupied with her note taking. Perhaps she had been writing notes about me- the first passenger she'd met. I hoped the notes would not include the words and phrases 'soak, alkie or worse still, 'check each morning for signs of inebriation'. When I had the opportunity, I would be scrutinising those notes, and woe betide if they were in code.

By the time we arrived downstairs the foyer was almost full. A complete turnabout from an hour before. Francesca was nowhere to be located, but there were plenty of bright-eyed people to meet, and I had not been jesting when I had mentioned double cheek-kissing. The canapés were delicious, and most of the platters adorning the bar had disappeared within ten minutes of our arrival. Drinks were plentiful, and after about twenty minutes, the buzz and hum of conversation was interrupted by a loud banging of a drum, as if royalty were being announced. Francesca had appeared on the scene, and it was her way of getting our undivided attention.

"Grazie tutti, thank you everyone for presenting yourselves at the welcome drinks for 'The Lakes of Northern Italy' tour tonight. I hope we will all be one big happy family as we live together for the next nine days. There are only twenty-two of you eh? The bus will be only half full. Nice and intimate. Now you have the evening to be free, and please make sure you take a map and itinerary and mark your name off the list. If you are not here, then don't mark off your name!" Francesca looked blank-faced after her joke about the name crossing, and I wasn't sure it was exactly what she had wanted to say.

People were laughing and nudging each other with comments like, "She will be a fun tour director" and "Can't wait to meet the other half—the driver." Alice and I had been chatting with Don and Angelique, the couple on our floor who had also arrived last night. As the party started to break up, Don suggested we go and get something to eat in a nearby restaurant. "It won't be a late night, but we gotta eat, right?"

An older couple had been listening to Don, and the woman asked if she and her husband might join us. Don was delighted. "The more the merrier I always say." Luckily, no one else wanted to come along, as we hadn't booked, and it was a Saturday night. Six was a comfortable number, but stretched to eight, it may have been more difficult to find somewhere close by. We decided to go straight from the foyer, as it was already seven thirty, and we just wanted a quick meal—nothing fancy.

Nothing fancy did I say? It was magnificent! Wonderful! Mouth-watering! All six of us ordered different dishes, and not one of us was disappointed. The chicken, veal, fish, steak, pasta and 'prawns with rice' dishes all did Italy proud. The restaurant we found was three blocks from our hotel, and it had only been a ten-minute walk. The table we managed to secure was outside, with a thick white tablecloth, three bottles of straw-wrapped Chianti and little red candles dotted across the tabletop.

Halfway through our meal it started to rain lightly, but there was a canopy overhead, and we stoically stuck it out. There were children everywhere, and I remembered that the bambini were an important component of social occasions, and that where the parents went, their children followed. That was the fabric of Italian society. The family. At one stage there were two tiny children hiding under our table, and I only found out because something was rubbing my bare leg. I thought it must have been a stray cat, but when I peeped down, it was a little boy with the shiniest pitch-black eyes I'd ever seen on one so young.

I left him and the other child there without alerting anyone, and the next thing I knew they had disappeared. Back to the family at the big table wedged in behind us. The boy had reminded me of the little girl we had met on the train into Milan yesterday. The waiter kept appearing, repeating 'prego, prego, prego' but no one took much notice of him. We were too busy eating, drinking and telling stories of our homelands—Canada, England and Australia. (The other couples were both Canadian.)

After the meal, it was back to the hotel without any digressions along the way and straight to bed. Tomorrow morning, when we saw Don, Angelique, Roy and Yolanda again, we would no doubt be discussing the highlights of the evening. Thankfully, that would be tomorrow!

Chapter 12
Morning Jitters

All I could think of was how glad I was that Alice and I hadn't chosen to sit in the first seat on the bus. The seat behind the driver. The seat where one was obligated to pick up the tiny cue card which had been carefully placed there by Francesca as she had glided along the aisle, hours before we had arrived, plumping up cushions and generally making sure everything was ready for the much-anticipated tour of the city. Seats brushed down and dusted, tray tables polished, tissue dispensers refilled and the tiny bathroom sink, which was almost flush to the road, washed down, sprayed with flowers of the forests room freshener and disinfected.

There were blinds to be adjusted, seatbelts to be checked and more air-fresher to be sprayed. I know it is unusual to see oneself as a fountain of information on the ins and outs of bus-business, but with more than ten bus tours up my sleeve—two of them exceeding a month on the road—I had some inside knowledge of the effort involved in opening the doors for the first time to a brand-new tour group.

Those doors had been open for business from seven this morning, which meant Francesca and the yet-to-be-named driver had to have been up since the crack of dawn.

I could personally vouch for Francesca having been a visible presence on the bus before opening hours. Earlier this morning, when Alice had been in the shower, I'd been taking my time preparing to go down to breakfast. Alice was slower. Granted, she had some heaving to get through, hauling that irksome, tiresome leg over the bath lip and manoeuvring herself into an upright position. Having told her she could call me should she need assistance, I'd thought it better to wait in the bedroom, rather than float down the magnificent staircase with the iron twirling to the glorious breakfast room with the show feature of its own-the octagonal roof and find us a good table.

It was very noisy out on the balcony, which was surprising, as the night had been still and quiet after the suburb had finally slept. Saturday night is 'going out night' whatever the country, and last night in our particular neck of the woods had been a late one. Although Alice and I had retired to bed almost immediately after we'd arrived back at the hotel, getting to sleep had been no easy task for either of us. The street below had been still busy with revellers, cars, and motor bikes at two am. The reprieve this morning seemed indicative of many of the night owls now being out for the count, as despite it being noisy out on the balcony, the street was lifeless. No people, nor cars nor scooters. There was only a bus! Big, gleaming-white with a multi-coloured sash. A real bruiser of a bus with the motor running, warming up for something momentous. Beautiful! Sleek! Stately!

The bus was parked directly below our balcony at a sharp angle, taking up the corner and almost the length of three adjoining apartment blocks. I knew the bus had to be ours, I just didn't expect it to be positioned directly below our balcony at such an early hour. As I watched, a few cars rounded the corner, patiently navigating their way around the monstrosity, which was, by now taking up half the road. Still the street remained devoid of people. Usually there would be one or two families out for an early morning meander, but this morning appeared to be the exception. From my birds-eye vantage point, I could see a huge sunroof running almost the length of the bus, and it was half open, presumably to air out the bus. I imagined Alice being slowly lowered from the balcony down into the bus, and the image made me smile.

As I stood there watching, the engine rattling abruptly stopped, and two figures emerged from the front double doors. One was Francesca, and the other an extremely good looking Italian, not young, but not old either. He was dressed in an immaculate grey driver's uniform, and I noticed his shoes were shiny patent black. Francesca was also dressed to kill, in tight black pants and a frilly white shirt. Her crowning glory, the unruly red mane was a free-flowing tangle of curls. They were chatting, teasing, and bantering with each other, and that was always a good sign, wasn't it?

One trip I had been on in America years back, had been spectacular—scenery-wise, the Grand Canyon and Niagara Falls amongst some of the magical sites visited, but it had been marred by friction, the constant bickering and snarling between the driver and the tour guide. Thinking about it later, the situation was possibly the complete antithesis of how the driver and the guide were presenting. My suspicion, along with many of my fellow travellers was that the pair had liked each other that little bit too much and were behaving in the complete opposite way.

"Me thinks thou dost protest too much."

I tore my eyes away from the nattering Italian duo, took a final gulp of the fresh balcony air, and sauntered back into the bedroom, carefully locking the French doors behind me. When we returned from breakfast, there would be no time for taking in air on balconies.

Alice was ready to go, and breakfast was waiting.

That had been an hour ago now, and after breakfast we had been in a hurry to get down to the bus and meet our companions for the second time. Last night had all been a blur of faces at the Welcome drinks. Dinner, having been a much smaller gathering had allowed us to get to know Don, Angelique, Roy and Yolanda in a little more depth, but there were still sixteen more strangers to meet, seventeen counting the dreamy driver.

And now we were sitting on the bus, three rows from the front, Alice by the window and me with a lap full of bags. Once I'd settled in the seat, my intention was to stand up and stow half our bags in the overhead locker, but so far there had not been an opportunity. It had been like sitting in a plane with people streaming past in desperate quests for their seats, and every time you attempted standing, someone else (usually carrying a baby) was pilgriming past. And you were the jack-in-the-box who never got to put the bags up, and the you were the mug reprimanded by the flight attendant for not having kept a clear lap nor having stowed luggage away. A normal scenario on bigger planes, but in comparison we were seated on a smallish bus. My chance to stand and stow could not have been far off.

It seemed it was my own private job to handle the luggage, and for the most part, I did so with good grace. Today though, I was annoyed that no one was noticing my uncomfortable overladen state, as they squirrelled their way along the carpeted aisle.

That's what I was getting at, when I hinted at the pros and cons of meeting people for the first, second or third time. As soon as Don passed our seat, he greeted us like long lost friends, and sensing my frustration with the load on my lap, did not hesitate in offering to heave the bags and backpacks up into the overhead space. Being so tall and lanky put him at eye level with the bulkhead, so moving the cabin bags and backpack was an effortless manoeuvre. "That should do it for you, lovelies. Anything else I can help you with?"

I assured him that I could manage from now on, and as he was holding up the line for the rest of the passengers trailing him in their struggle to claim their seats, he moved on. During the pit-stop, Angelique had blazed on ahead, and had found a seat for herself and Don about halfway up the aisle, opposite the middle door, and toilet. (A few steps down and on the same level as the door.) I could just make out her purple scarf as I extended my head down the aisle following Don's tall retreating back.

The bus was filling up quickly, and even though there were only twenty-two of us according to Francesca, the number of passengers lumbering past me seemed endless. Francesca was tapping the microphone, breathing out in a husky, hushed tone, "testing, testing, one two three," as though she were about to announce the arrival of Freddy Mercury or Elton John at Crystal Palace. Nobody was listening. Not in the slightest! They were all too excited about the first morning of the trip, and anxious to impress each other-everyone nodding and smiling like it was going out of fashion. Most people had that 'first day of a trip' fresh look. Perfect hair, smart new walking shoes and casual clothing was the go.

Alice and I also looked the part. Seven hours ago, we would have been a sight for sore eyes on our anticipated glamorous Northern Italy trip. Had our suitcases not finally arrived after midnight, we would not have experienced the elation we'd shared at six am when the errant luggage was found to be lined up outside our room. Alice had been first to remember that it was D-day for us and the missing luggage.

"Fil, can you pop your head out and see if the cases have been delivered?" It was so early that I didn't worry about my scant attire—a thin cotton T-shirt and shorts—the spare clothes I had stowed in my hand luggage. No one would be skulking around at six am, surely? The prowler turned out to be the room service attendant, on his way to the room next door with an early morning breakfast delivery. I was sprung! My excitement at having been reunited with my suitcase was overshadowed by my embarrassment at being discovered bending over in perfect pike position—bare-footed and resplendent in boxer shorts and T-shirt—an ensemble I would not normally be found wearing out in public on judgement day.

The Adam and Eve story, with both parties painfully ashamed of their nakedness, was playing through in fast motion in my sleepy morning brain. It was all in my mind though. The boy hardly glanced at me, but I have a gift for reading people's minds, and in my own mind, I could distinctly hear his sniggering, "Bit much for a Nonna to be out here in her granddaughter's skimpy pyjamas, putting out the cases!" It was obvious he thought I was putting cases out, and not bringing them in, as was the actual case. (No pun intended.)

The custom with bus tours was for luggage to be placed outside bedroom doors early on the morning of a departure, at least an hour before the coach's scheduled departure. I scanned the darkened corridor and noticed, with alarm, that nearly every door had one or two suitcases, strategically placed towards the side-awaiting pickup. The cases could not have belonged to any passengers on our intended trip, as the 'trip-proper' did not begin until tomorrow morning, so there must have been another group staying overnight in the hotel, and they must all have been residing on our floor. (Apart from Don and Angelique, who had, like Alice and I, arrived a day early, and had also been allocated a bedroom on this floor.)

Seizing up the situation, I threw my head up to the heavens and involuntarily began exclaiming, "Thank you, God! Thank you, thank you, thank you!" Heavens knows where our cases might have ended up, had I not dutifully obeyed Alice and poked my head out of the bedroom door around six am. Actually, I knew exactly where they would have ended up! In Switzerland. Lucerne to be exact, as when I had been cosying myself up the cocktail bar yesterday, I'd spied an itinerary pinned up on the Tours News noticeboard and had assumed it to be a 'posting reminder' for our Northern Lakes Tour.

It turned out to be the itinerary for another bus group. That bus had been scheduled to leave for Lucerne early the next morning at seven am, as Lucerne was over two hundred and fifty kilometres from Milan according to the information provided. I loved Lucerne, with the lake and the lion, but I wasn't prepared to go yodelling at such an early hour.

Before my arm splaying display, (air-punching in praise of the God for having saved our cases from a multi-leg trip), the room service boy had not given me the time of day, intent on his task, and possibly sharing my embarrassment at my blatant outburst of fashion ignorance and inappropriateness. My actions had disturbed him, had possibly even frightened him into thinking I was a hotel terrorist, bunked up the evening before, receiving a couple of suitcases full of classified-information, or worse still, weapons in the dead of the night.

The young boy was fumbling with the tray he had dropped. A tray containing two plates of a 'full Italian' breakfast—pizza and some milky substance which had spilled over the carpet. He had managed to push the pizza back onto the body of the tray, but most of the coffee was still a murky puddle. The boy's eyes were darting towards the lift, as if expecting a supervisor to appear from the lift door, size up the situation and promptly fire him, even though he probably needed the job to support his entire struggling family of rice farmers living in a field beyond Milan.

The ramifications of my outburst could have been far reaching, had I not acted quickly and called out to him that I had just finished morning prayer in the bedroom, that our cases had been lost and were now found, and that I was in my seventh heaven, because at last my status as an ageing fashion plate would be restored. Since I was in a hurry to deliver my less than convincing speech, and since the boy looked, and probably was, Italian, my deliverance fell on deaf ears.

He hesitated for a fraction of a second and then immediately gathered up the tray and fled to the lift, disregarding the carpet-stain, but buying himself time to brew fresh coffee and microwave the by then cold, pizza slices. Uncomfortable at the confusion I had yet again caused, there was nothing for it but to bang on the door and wait for Alice to appear and lend me a hand. (The door had slammed shut when I'd attempted to lug the first suitcase-mine, into position.)

Alice was slow, but to her credit, she falteringly helped me heave the loot into the bedroom, and up onto the beds. Time was of the essence, since the cases needed to be back outside our door within half an hour, in readiness for the seven am pickup. As today was to be the first day of the tour outside of Milan, and the first time the cases were to be picked up from outside bedrooms, the instructions had been to 'have them ready by seven'. I assumed that once the bus driver was able to gauge the amount of luggage which would need to be stowed and positioned in the bowels of the bus, a later pickup might have been possible from then onwards. Today, being the first day would be the driver's first opportunity to assess the luggage situation.

Inside our bedroom had been a hive of activity for twenty minutes, as clothes were strewn from one end of the beds to the other. Drastic repacking was the order of the day, as we would need to rummage through every possible clothing item to find suitably impressive travelling clothes for the first big day of the trip.

Eventually, we managed to meet the deadline, and the cases were hastily repacked with the crumpled clothes and repositioned outside the door for pick up. Next up was showering, and for Alice, ten precious minutes restyling her curls. Whilst she was in the bathroom fiddling around with the curling wand she had gratefully unearthed from her suitcase, I sat on my bed flicking through my Milan guidebook.

La Scala, Il Duomo, Piazza San Vittorio-Emmanuel plaza-all manner of marvellous Milanese landmarks beckoned me. I abruptly stopped flicking, totally confused. Hang on a minute, what was happening here? What was I thinking? Today wasn't the day we were leaving Milan! Today was the day we were touring Milan. The day when we would have the opportunity to see all of these famous places and more! We had been so excited with the news that our suitcases had been found that we must have become confused with the days. Well, I had confused the days, Alice had just gone along with me.

So, today was Sunday and not Monday!

The cases did not need to be put outside the bedroom door after all and, if I didn't hurry, they would be mistaken for suitcases belonging to passengers on the Switzerland tour, and in with a second chance for seeing the lake and the lion in Lucerne. Alice was still in the bathroom, so it was easy to poke my head out the door, praying all the while that the suitcases had not yet been picked up. Murphy's law slipped into auto-play in my mind before I had a chance not to panic. 'Anything that can go wrong, will go wrong'. And we have lift off!

The cases had disappeared. In ten short minutes, they had been whooshed away by some over-keen bellboy and were probably by now already on the bus to Switzerland. Without bothering to bang on the door again, in the hope that Alice would appear and let me back in, I raced for the circular staircase, gobbling mouthfuls of stairs, and narrowly avoiding knocking over two Chinese tourists, who must have been on their way back from breakfast. Crewcut the cat from next door in London came to mind immediately as I toppled down the stairs and into the street from the bustling foyer.

Crewcut must have somehow bequeathed me one of his nine lives, as wonder of wonders, the bus to Switzerland had not yet left, and doubly wonderful was the fact that the bus driver was lining every available case up in front of the bus, counting them with intense concentration. I raced up to him. "Excuse me, mi scusi, but I have lost my cases, and I think they may have become mixed up with these cases."

I indicated to the cases he had lined up in front of him, my eyes desperately scanning the neat rows for our suitcases. Sure enough, they were there. Lined up like skittles, in anticipation of the big trip to Switzerland. "Oh, I can see our cases. Here they are!" I wrenched the troublesome suitcases from the line up and dragged them over to the shoulder-height stone wall which made up the front façade of the hotel wall.

The driver was scratching his head and gazing at me in astonishment as I shuffle-dragged. It would have been far too complicated to have explained to the puzzled driver why I was acting in such an irrational manner, so I cheekily waved at him and dragged both cases towards the steps, where I left one case at the bottom of the stairs and lugged the other up into the foyer. Depositing that case, I raced back down for the second.

In that instant, I gratefully used up a second of Crewcut's lives, as no one had touched the outside case and it was exactly where I'd left it. It was an omen of good things to come! There could be no further opportunity for the suitcases to cause us consternation. In ten minutes, the Switzerland-bound bus full of excited yodelling passengers would have departed and the only suitcases needing to be picked up from outside people's bedroom doors would be those belonging to passengers bound for the bellissima Italian lakes, and that would not be for twenty-four hours. With the issue of the suitcases resolved, there was not much left to do but to relax and look forward to embracing 'la bella paese'.

Back in the room, Alice was looking perplexed.

"Fil, why have you brought the suitcases back? Shouldn't they stay outside the door ready to be picked up?"

She was incredulous at first when I explained the saga of the suitcases, and in the end, was throwing her hands up in exasperation at my long-winded account of the incident. "Maybe we should just put all of this behind us and head down to our bus. You said it was downstairs waiting, so we may as well get a good seat. I'm sure there will be lots to see that we missed yesterday when we were walking." Having said her piece in a voice which clearly meant she didn't want any more grief from me, Alice hobbled over towards the door.

Chapter 13
Morning on the Bus to Milan

We were ready to begin. A finely tuned orchestra on the brink of the overture; a new-born's first piercing cry upon entering the world; a tribe of trekkers leaving base camp for the expedition of a lifetime. It was impossible to contain my excitement and exhilaration at being in Italy, poised to embark on the adventure of a lifetime. My legs were literally leaving the seat in anticipation of the unknown. The bus was beautiful! Having ridden buses all my life, I was well acquainted with their ins and outs.

Mainly, accolades such as functional, practical and reliable came to mind but this sleek, purring, beautiful creature was no ordinary mode of transport. This was the baby-grand of bus travel! Extensively roomy with luxuriously soft leather cushioned seats, wide sparkling clean windows licking the length of its stately back and the added bonus of matching, gleaming skylights complementing every window. The outside world was welcomed at every angle. The clear blue sky, with not a trace of yesterday's streaky grey flooded the bus with colour, and I felt alive and ready for anything. This stirring, this thirst for discovering all that was enigmatic Italy, seemed to emanate from deep within me, and I felt the pull of Columbus as he left Genoa for uncharted lands.

None of us on the bus knew what to expect of this trip. More than likely, we'd all read the itineraries, and chosen well by the looks and feel of the bus, but every day would be a wild card in terms of having no precedent for the unexpected. Ten days of the unrevealed, the unpredictable, the unbelievable!

It was all I could do not to jump up and shout out, "Viva Italia!"

When we were kids, our father would, at the most inopportune of times, sporadically call out, "Viva l'Italia!" and we would jump up and down on the spot and echo him with, "e base l'Australia!" We had no idea what we were chanting, or why we were chorusing out like frenzied children on Sport Carnival days chanting for their teams, but our father seemed happy he had taught his children well and, as Crosby, Stills, Nash and Young so aptly observed with their soul stirring lyrics, he would "know we loved him." (And his country of birth.)

The fabric of my childhood was beginning to unfold here in Italy. I was living and breathing the intoxicating air of my ancestors, and so far, it was marvellous. Crisp, clean and full of palpable energy.

Francesca was furiously tapping the microphone. And so it began! The pattern we would slip comfortably into after a day or so on the bus. Soft background engine-purring, and the distant honking of horns and sirens from the outside world, mostly smothered by the double glassed windows. Cool air streaming onto our sweaty faces from unobtrusive vents recessed into the canopy above our heads, and hushed conversations as the passengers (ourselves included) settled back in their comfy seats for the day. Not forgetting the more than delicate microphone tapping and nervous coughing as the Guide-Francesca performed her morning act of greeting, followed by a short outline of the expectations for the day-generally what we could expect to be seeing and doing.

I thought Francesca's first greeting to us that first morning on the bus was by far her best quipping of the entire trip. With neither fuss nor precedent, she delivered her magnum opus line with an elongated earnest emphasis on the words 'Northern' and 'Italy'.

"This is the Northern Italy you have come to see!"

She was right, and it was a wonderful concise evaluation of what we were all doing there on the bus-having traipsed from the far corners of the earth to experience a taste of gorgeous, haughty North. After her punchy one-liner, Francesca proudly introduced our driver, Matteo, but he did not speak as he was too busy negotiating the twists and turns in the road. Francesca explained that Matteo was concentrating on finding a spot to perform one of his specialty U-turns, as many of the suburban Milanese side-streets were too narrow for a bus the size of ours.

It was a comforting thought to have an oversized bus ferrying us around Milan, because even though there was so much to love about the place, there was nevertheless a proven dark side. The Yin and the Yang—as with every large city. An element of subterranean diffusion which had Milan recently voted as the least safe city in Europe after Rome. That fact was good to know, but hopefully not one about which we would be forced to witness examples. We were safe on the bus, and when we did hit the pavements, I would be making sure I stayed glued to Francesca and Matteo for added protection.

Once we'd left the rabbit-warren, it was full steam ahead for the bus. There was room to breathe and glide on the highway, and within minutes the cityscape of tall buildings coated in silver and shrouded in greenery beckoned. According to Francesca 'Milan was still sleeping' and I had to agree with her. There was a peaceful stillness about the place, green shutters still down, and streets relatively empty. Compared to the number of people who had been out and about yesterday in the sunshine, and then in the light rain, today's streets were deserted.

The streetscapes were not dissimilar to those laid out in my hometown of Melbourne. Wide, tree-lined and dotted with typical European apartment blocks-not too short, but not too tall-slender and embracing of each other. There was a casual haughtiness to the place, and because it was so deserted and bereft of vehicles and pedestrians, it had the look of an exquisitely-coiffured ghost town. Even Francesca was surprised by the sleeping habits of the Milanese this morning.

"It is very unusual for the whole of Milan to be sleeping in this morning. When we arrive to the city centre, you will see the true Milanese on a Sunday—the tourist!"

It was what we'd expected to hear—Milan equated with tourists by the guide. This was her industry and her area of expertise. If Francesca was predicting an almighty influx of tourists for Milan this morning, once we reached the hub of classic, iconic Milanese sights and buildings-then teeming with tourists it would be! They had just left their run a bit late, because as far as my eyes could stretch, there were no other buses to be sighted, and only a few cars on this main tree-lined thoroughfare into Milan.

We were pulling up in the centre at a roundabout which directly faced the famous Milan Opera house and Museum, 'La Scala'. Opera was one of the interesting tributaries of the wide river of music in which I held enormous interest, but sadly very little knowledge. I was a 'quasi-opera' fan, meaning I loved opera, but had never really bothered to listen to operatic tracks as intently as I listened to other genres. I was really a bit of a fraud, as friends and family kept giving me opera music as birthday and Christmas presents, but most of these gifts were still cosy in their plastic wrapping in the back of my cupboard.

Nowadays, it wasn't such a problem, as the gifts tended to be vouchers and music-shop cards where I could choose my own music genre. Invariably, I chose scores from films. My most favourite was the score from the *Mission*, right up there at the top, leading the way for the other five hundred or so in my collection.

Opera scared me. It was such a powerful medium, and more often than not in Italian or German, so I was never really sure what was going on. I am ashamed to admit that my knowledge of operatic scores would never be my special subject on *Mastermind* or *Jeopardy*, but I could probably get by with a few simple questions such as, "Who composed *Aida* or in which country is *Madame Butterfly* set?" The usual stereotypical opera questions one might find on a game of *Trivial Pursuit*. But the name of the principal soprano in the recent Milanese production of *La Boheme*? Forget it!

Alice was slightly savvier, when it came to music. Her instruments included the flute, piano, guitar, and violin. Mine included the triangle, clapsticks, and a rippled-iron washing board which I had once played with gusto in an Australian outback nativity scene for a Children's Hospital Appeal. I wondered how many of the other passengers were Opera fans or proficient musicians. It would make an interesting survey. Then again, they could have been dancers, as La Scale was also home to world famous ballet performances-the arduous rites of passage leading to world renowned status for many a woman in a chiffon tutti or man in tights. Yes, La Scala would have something for everyone this morning, even the Art lovers amongst us. I had studied photographs in guide-books of magnificent oil paintings we would no doubt encounter in ample bundles of glistening flesh this morning. It always fascinated me-that compulsory accompaniment of operatic voice with more than ample layers of flesh. The Old Masters were at their best embellishing and magnifying-especially in the heaving chest department with the women.

As there were only twenty-two of us, it didn't take long to exit the bus. Alice and I waited until everyone had streamed past, in their eager anticipation of a first taste of one of the many fruits of Milan-spectacular architecture. We waited because of Alice's leg. Yesterday's walkathon was taking its toll this morning, and Alice had already digested four painkillers, with fifteen hours of Sunday to go.

"You go on ahead Fil, I can wait till everyone is off the bus!" Alice wasn't aiming for martyrdom in Catholic coated Italy with her statement-she was just in so much pain it would have been difficult standing up and allowing herself to be surged along with the crowd, down the front steps of the bus. "I'll wait with you, no hurry!" I meant it, there was really no hurry around these parts. It was so still and so quiet out there. No wind, and not a tree in sight. Even the red, white and green flags (which were everywhere) lay flat and lifeless on the roofs and top floors of buildings. Very apocalyptic.

White statues and sandstone monuments were in abundance, and with my face fixed to the window (I had again ventured to the back of the half empty bus for premium photographs using my iPhone), I was acutely reminded of the architecture and buildings strategically placed like giant chess pieces around the Arc-de-Triomphe in Paris. Possibly, Napoleon had dabbled in Milan as well as in the French Capital with his architectural feats and road building. There was something distinctly Parisian about Milan this morning. It was a placid place full of light, freedom, and space. The perfect Italian piazza.

When I'd hinted at practices evolving into rituals on a bus tour, such as Francesca tapping away at her microphone every morning, and thrusting a second microphone into one's face so that a life history might be revealed to all in sundry, I was not restricting the adoption of fairly rigid rituals to Francesca. Alice was about to develop a peculiar idiosyncratic ritual of her own. That of throwing herself into the arms of the driver (Matteo), whose job it was to stand at the foot of the stairs and offer a helping hand to those passengers unable to make it from the last (slightly elevated) step to the pavement (often stony and uneven).

Mostly, passengers were young and agile enough to manage by themselves, but on any bus tour I had ever undertaken, there never failed to have been a smattering of passengers requiring a helping hand to cross that troublesome River Styx. 'Hand' being the operative word. To speed things up, I overtook Alice and jumped down the stairs, politely reaching for Matteo's extended tanned, hairy limb. (So authentically Italian.) Alice was still behind me. Turns out I turned too late to help Matteo help her down; before I could pivot a full 360 on the spongy heels of my brand-new walking shoes, Alice was in his arms in a full embrace to rival Audrey Hepburn and Gregory Peck's coy coupling in *Roman Holiday*.

Matteo looked shocked and startled, as he would have had no idea Alice sported a handicap. He probably thought two of his most ardent fans had waited on the bus until the last possible moment so that they might gain his undivided attention. His immediate reaction was to graciously and delicately prise Alice from his personage and hurriedly triple jump the steps back into the body of the bus, sliding down in his driver's seat with his beetroot face. No one else seemed to have noticed, and Alice was busy arranging her bag across her shoulder and chest to the point where she resembled a Swiss mountain climber. All she needed was the cowbell.

That left me—the only one who was cluey and close enough to Alice to know her inside out, realising the embracing movement—the leap from the stairs into Matteo's arms—had just set the precedent for the next ten days. At an average five stops per day, more than fifty opportunities for Alice and Matteo to publicly embrace were on the cards. Matteo must also have been adding things up, as he had slunk further into his seat and was scribbling something on a sheet of paper.

Great. Yesterday, Francesca had been scribbling notes about me, and today it was Alice's turn with Matteo.

It would not have taken an Einstein to work out what Matteo was scribbling. Something along the lines of 'avoid the women with the walking stick at all costs. Note to self. Dangerous to take up the position at the foot of the bus stairs when said woman approaches!'

Luckily, Alice was still preoccupied and appeared to have forgotten all about Matteo. It was time to leave the bus behind and whet our appetites with art and opera. Francesca was already at the doors, handing out brochures of La Scala as each passenger processed past.

"There you are, Fil. I thought you might have decided to stay on the bus with a Matteo and not be joining us this morning. (Now there was a thought.) You would have missed out on one of the great wonders of the world. This will be something truly magnificent!" She was smiling and waving the brochure about in front of me with one hand, and gently nudging me forwards with the other. Once I had passed through the tiny wooden side-door reserved for tourists with bulk pre-paid tickets, Francesca picked up her brown-wicker basket brimming with brochures and followed me.

Her description of La Scala as being 'something truly magnificent' reminded me of another tour guide—a Belgian gentleman with whom I had spent thirty days touring Europe some years back. His favourite daily exclamation in his thick Belgian accent had been, "and if you look directly out of your window, you will see something truly wonderful!" That phrase has stuck with me for more than a quarter of a century. A marvellous turn of phrase-something wonderful. What was wonderful in this world?

According to Louie Armstrong, trees of green are wonderful, as are red roses and skies of blue. The optimist, the glass half full person on this trip would probably agree to everything in this beautiful country being wonderful, but this was Italy, with a head start on nearly every other country in the world. The Italy of foods such as rice, spaghetti, biscotti and pizza which feeds the world. The Italy of the Romans, who forged empires and created civilisations. And the Italy of over fifty tangible cultural World Heritage listings a global record. with the Italian Mediterranean diet recognised by UNESCO as a legitimate intangible world Heritage listing, practices and philosophies in Italy such as traditional folk-dancing and great story telling through dance and puppetry which might be taking a number in the very near future.

We were now inside la Scala. Nothing much to report in terms of mind-blowing architecture. A dingy lift into which Alice and I squeezed, along with Francesca, Roy and Yolanda (Roy also had a gammy leg) and a moody guard who kept exclaiming aloud to our little group and waving his hands about in frustration. I knew the said phrase to be blasphemous from the one solitary time dad had used the expression. This guard was clearly not a one-time user. It took the rickety old lift a couple of minutes to ascend to the second floor, and in those two slow minutes, the guard had excelled himself hissing and mumbling out many more profanities.

Francesca, being Italian, kept her head bent, and did not let on to the guard that she well and truly got the message that he was inconvenienced by our requiring the lift and not taking to the stairs like the other eighteen compliant passengers. I felt compelled to reprimand the guard for making us all feel so uncomfortable with his swearing and mumbling in the tiny grated lift, but he was big and hairy and angry and Italian, and this was to be our first cultural heritage tour.

I wanted to be part of it, not flat on the floor from a decking by the unfriendly caretaker-cum-security guard. I understood that we had disturbed him, but had he smiled at us, welcomed us, shown sympathy towards the injured and their careers, he might have received an olive branch from me in exchange for his glowing disposition. As it was, he would receive nothing but my best glare.

I reserved the glare until we had reached the second floor and had thanked him for his trouble (his job).

Then, once he was safely behind the bars of the lift, I went right up to the grate and whispered, "I could understand when you were swearing like a trooper in the lift on the way up here. Just so you know." Instead of flaying his fist at me, in an encore to his Act One anger, he smiled expectantly at me and held out his hand for a tip. He hadn't understood a word I had been whispering and thought I was one of those gullible tourists who put up with ridicule and rudeness and still ask for more. Not me! Not today! Francesca had appeared by my side, calling me to hurry up and join the others.

"You are becoming like the lost sheep of the group, Fil. Watch out for the 'Lupe' if you stay behind too much." I must have known more Italian than I thought, because instantly I was having images of being chased and then eaten by wolves, and I hurriedly turned away from the distasteful man in the lift who had not yet pushed the 'down' button. I would start making a concerted effort from now on to stay bonded with my group.

Tagging along at the end of a group can sometimes have its advantages. Today, it meant the opportunity to shadow Francesca, who was talking into her midget microphone, singing out the praises of La Scala, and what it meant to Italy to have in her possession such a wonderful national treasure. (Francesca would have been forced to change professions should the word 'wonderful' disappear without a trace from the dictionary.) As it was, she was having a field day labelling everything she pointed out to us as 'wonderful', like a fairy godmother casting a magic wand full of stardust and breathing life into all that appeared before her.

We had entered a large high-ceilinged ballroom, which looked like it might double as a practise-space for the resident dancers and singers. Whatever the function of the room, the acoustics were marvellous. With little effort on her part, Francesca had achieved gold status on the decibel metre rating. We were urged to feast our eyes upon the 'wonderful polished floors, the wonderful glass windows and cabinets full of busts and artifices and of course the wonderful ceilings which, according to biased Francesca who lived locally (at least in Northern Italy) "were something more wonderful than the pretty little roof of the Sistine chapel in Rome."

I was relieved to be standing alongside of Francesca, and hoped she had not noticed the way I mimicked her every movement and hung on every word she uttered. I had my reasons. Too right I did. Back on the bus whilst we were making our merry way into central Milan, Francesca had skipped up and down the aisle with her little wicker basket—Little Red Riding Hood on her way to grandma's cottage in the woods, handing out headphones to every passenger and stressing that we needed to be extra careful when we turned them on, as they were temperamental and extremely expensive to replace.

Whenever anyone puts those two thoughts into my head—overly expensive and irreplaceable—you can bet your bottom dollar I find some way to muck things up. I am notorious for losing or breaking things, mostly my own possessions, but sometimes possessions belonging to others. I had moved up to the back of the bus to take some photographs while the headsets were being handed out and ticked off as having been given to each particular passenger, so I wasn't sitting next to Alice. By the time I'd made my way back to our seat, Alice already had her headphones plastered to her ears and she was listening intently to Francesca, who had wasted no time testing out the headphones.

Her hearing tests involved asking passengers to do things like, 'raise your left arm, wave towards the window and clap hands in glee'. I quickly stuck the headphones on my head and copied Alice, not wanting to appear slow on the uptake and earn any 'prone to slowness' nicknames such as turtle or snail from any of the other passengers. Nobody knew I hadn't turned on my headphones, as I was a proficient copycat and Alice was right beside me.

I was learning from the mistress, as signing was a matter of routine for Alice when she was at work and signing on a bus a simple natural progression. I had gotten away with it on the bus, and before I'd had time to fiddle around with the sound and frequencies of my set, we had arrived at the roundabout directly outside La Scala. Now I was in exactly the same predicament, not having had a spare moment to make the necessary adjustments to the headphones. I surreptitiously tried fiddling and turning but nothing was happening.

The only thing I could think of doing was to invade Francesca's social space and keep lifting the headphones from my ears whilst she was talking. I vowed to adjust them once we returned to the bus, but I knew we still had hours to go before that could happen. Alice had found herself a seat in the far corner of the enormous ballroom. She saw me looking towards her and beckoned me over. I was loathe to leave Francesca and her commentary, but Alice looked like she needed me, and I had promised to look after her, especially for the first few days of the tour while we settled into a routine.

"Fil, what's the go with your headphones? I could see you pulling them on and off your ears while Francesca was talking. Do you want me to tighten the sockets for you?"

Here was my chance. Alice may have been immobile, but she was super handy with fixing things. Jammed doors, broken shelves, air conditioners on the blink? Call Alice for fast no fuss assistance. Alice would have made an excellent "cleaner" in the gangster movies when they send in the cleaners to give the apartments the once-over cleaning up all the blood and gore and having all appliances again working to full capacity. Today however, she appeared sluggish and in definite holiday mode. She had taken my headphones from me and was carefully examining them, one side at a time, as if they had been freshly unearthed from Pompeii.

She finally looked up and shook her head. "The sound isn't coming through them. I can hear Francesca talking through mine but yours are dead. You'll have to go and let her know they are not working at all." I didn't want to tell Francesca, I would gladly have forked out the cost of a replacement set, but when I really thought about it, I had no need to take any responsibility for the headphones malfunctioning. It was the principle of the matter. I would just have to swallow my pride and report to the boss that the contraption had never worked, and surely, they carried spares on the bus?

That would be a task for later though, because right now Francesca was still talking and I had already missed five minutes of the very important discussion. Back by her side, flashing my doleful puppy dog eyes, was a comfortable position for me. I decided I quite enjoyed employing disciple mode. It was so easy just to sit at the feet of the master (mistress) and hang on every word. No wonder there were so many paintings with dogs nestled at the feet of their owners.

In one way it was a cop-out, as I was not bothering with adjusting my headphones and concentrating on Francesca's every word in scrutinising detail, but on the other hand, being emancipated from the binding, ear-hugging head gear allowed me to explore other parts of the fascinating room without feeling obligated to always look in the direction in which Francesca was pointing. My laissez-faire position and disposition came to a crashing halt with Francesca's next command!

Chapter 14
Mid-Morning Milan Sunday

"And now we come to the show we have come all the way to La Scala to witness. Ladies, please step forward in a line and let the show begin." I looked around at the eager women of my tribe in a panic, cursing myself for not having adjusted the headphones in time and therefore not knowing what was going on. In my self-righteous fog, I had failed to live up to my motto of "be prepared" and was about to suffer the consequences big time.

Francesca was delivering further instructions. The rest of the women were all standing straight and erect, just as Francesca has requested, reassembling a line of Samoan or Tongan dancers poised to perform for the king. Francesca had them eating out of her hand. "Now, I want all the ladies to step forward and pirouette on the spot you stand. Try to be like a ballerina. Try to hold your head high and your back straight like the ironing board." Certainly, I had missed out on the previous instructions. Francesca must have informed the ladies of the tour that they would be required to role-play what it felt like to be a prima ballerina on one of the largest and most famous stages in Italy.

This run-through would have to be a practice one, as we were still in the rehearsal room, but who knew where it would lead? I didn't want to miss out on being discovered, should a talent scout for La Scala ballet company slip through the door and take notes on our technique. My swimsuit, which was amongst the mess in my case, had the look of a tutu, and my hair could be scrunched up into a ballerina-bun with a pinch. I also had my black travelling jiffies in my overnight bag. I was all set, should the scout recognise aging talent when he or she saw it.

I would possibly have some stiff competition from a few of the other younger women, Brielle in particular (now that I had managed to put a face to her) but disposing of her would be easy enough. (I would just need to stick my foot out as far as it would extend.) I decided to give it my best shot. For an annual stipend of one point five million euros, I could do it!

I glanced over towards Alice, who appeared to have fallen asleep on the bench. Good! At least she would not start behaving like one of those relatives and spectators, who hurled out alternate abuse and encouragement to the exhausted participant who always ended up on the ground in any football, soccer or netball match. With no one really knowing me and with nothing to lose, I threw myself onto the end of the line, and began kicking my legs up as high as I could in a frenzied imitation of the Can-Can Moulin Rouge dancers I had seen in Paris. They would have looked like mere amateurs compared to me.

It was only when I stopped kicking and started panting and heaving that I noticed the other women had abandoned the line. In fact, there was no line, only me, bending over trying to regain my breath, and feeling my face turn scarlet with embarrassment. It was all quiet and people were looking at me in awe. No talent scout appeared, and the next thing to happen was the echoing sound of 'one-hand clapping' as Alice must have woken up with the silence, and loyal and faithful companion that she was, had begun hammering her fist into the wall, in a mock clapping movement.

Francesca was speaking to the whole group. "Well, that was something marvellous, wasn't it, eh? Especially Fil who loves it so much she is not badgering from the centre of the stage." Everyone laughed and I joined in, just to make sure they were all laughing with me and not at me!

Francesca had moved on to Part Two.

"And now, it is the turn of the gentlemen. Normally, it is ladies before gentlemen, so we are good with this, yes. And it is a good thing today, because now you know what is in the store for you." Again laughter (this time tinged with nervousness) as the gentlemen crept forward to form a line where I had been standing. They looked to be a motley crew, mainly because of their attire and clumpy shoes. More suited to a German clod-hop than a Milanese ballet.

At least I was off the hook, with the gentlemen performing brilliantly to the audience, following Francesca's commands of "bow down and bend up and extend and turn" in perfect choreography. I marvelled at the mix of races on that dance floor, and the fact that despite their culturally different upbringings and experiences, these men knew exactly what to do-and were doing it well. The applause from the onlookers (we ladies) challenged the acoustics to the point that one of the guards who had been standing outside the rehearsal room burst in shouting something in Italian which I took to mean, "Is everything alright in here? What is happening?"

Francesca dismissed the guard in the typically Italian fashion with her hands and facial expressions. She then gathered us all into her fold, even the two injured parties—Roy and Alice—and praised us again for our efforts. "I am busting with the pride for you all. Just busting!" Most people looked pleased with themselves, and began making their way towards the door, readjusting their headphones around their heads. (All headphones had been removed when the dancing had begun.) Now would be the best chance I'd have to get my own headphones working and who better to ask for assistance than Francesca herself.

"Excuse me Francesca, but I'm having difficulty with my headphones. Can you help me adjust them so that I can hear you when I'm in the bus or at the back of the group?" Francesca gave me a half smile, a knowing look indicating that she understood now why I was constantly at her side hanging on her every word.

"Here Fil, look, it is easy. Even the child can do it!" Not this child, Francie. Not this one who is severely technologically challenged, but above average in the mishaps department. I gave Francesca an added look of helplessness and she must have felt sorry for me, because she deftly fished into her large Mary Poppins-type carpetbag and produced a new pair of headphones for me.

"Now you can be like the rest of us, Fil. Take these and keep them on your head until I tell you to take them off. You will be my special glory shadow for the day."

It was Karma day. Karma for me for all those times I had kept a student close to my heels on excursion days, despite their protests, despite their sulky looking faces and despite my not wanting to be burdened with them. Francesca seemed not to notice my reluctance to follow her every movement, nor the fact that I was slowing up, deliberately, waiting for Alice.

"Come on, Fil. It is time to move into the next part of our tour."

Outside in the gold-plated fresco-lined lip of a corridor, I managed to give her the slip, as there were so many others cramped in the small space, many of whom were firing out questions concerning the length and breadth of the stage, qualifications of the singers and dancers and queries about La Scale in general. Mercifully, I was soon forgotten.

An official was deep in animated conversation with Francesca, and she was wildly gesturing towards our group. He was dressed in a superbly fitting uniform, his chest adorned with what appeared to be military badges. Perched at an angle on his head full of black curly hair was a small red feathered cap. His matching black shoes were noticeably shiny. The man had Francesca by the elbow (just that tiniest bit too forcefully) and was guiding her towards an open door. She allowed herself to be dragged along by him, and like sheep we all followed. Alice and I were to the back of the group so we didn't stand much chance of entering the room, whatever it may have been.

About five or six people remained in the room (we could see the tops of their heads and baseball caps) and Francesca and the guard had reappeared at the door. At last, Francesca had found the opportunity to explain what was happening to the rest of us, setting our minds at ease as to the fate of our fellow passengers who were by now behind the closed door of the room.

"We have arrived to the 'boxes' where the people can watch the opera or the ballet. These boxes have all their own rooms, and the view of the stage is something wonderful." Of course, it was!

Alice and I were amongst the last of our group to be led into one of the little Confessional boxes. It was quiet inside and quite cosy, but the opulence of the 'snug' was not to be sneezed at, and Francesca had been right about the view of the stage. It was amazing. It was like being on top of a mountain in a hot air balloon, looking down on the stage, which, despite lacking performers, appeared to be already staged for tonight's opera. Only eight performances per opera, so exclusive was the place. Now that I had seen La Scala, I was definitely going to add attending an opera performance in this establishment to my bucket list. However, after this morning's fiasco on the dance line, I would be giving the ballet a big miss.

"Did you know they used to hold parlour game tournaments in these boxes, and also frequent them to get up to a little hanky-panky?" Alice was holding her guidebook of Milan right up to her face, trying to decipher the tiny print. "And they paid a small fortune for the privilege!" That part I got. The whole place was dripping with opulence. I just wasn't entirely sure to which privilege Alice was referring.

The next exciting episode on the agenda for our La Scala interlude was the opportunity to wander around the museum rooms at our leisure, and to purchase La Scala memorabilia. Alice was tired, and she had made her way back downstairs to wait for the rest of us in the foyer. She had her Guidebook with her, so she wouldn't be bored. It was probably a good people-watching position, and no doubt Alice would have some tales to tell when we reconnected. I had half an hour to wander around. Since there were three floors of museums to explore, I thought it best to stick with the rest of our group.

Although they were moving slowly, it would be difficult get lost or lose track of time if I stuck to them like glue. I was mesmerised. Every single room we entered had grander and more spectacular artefacts and paintings than had the room before. It was a real eye-opener for me. I thought I knew about art and sculpture, but my knowledge was a grain of sand compared to the magnificent displays before me. Our hour in the museum rooms was up before I knew it. The paintings of famous opera singers with their heaving chests and ruby red lips had been a sight to behold, and I found myself wondering why someone hadn't bundled them all up and taken the entire display on a five-year tour to the far corners of the earth.

And yet I also knew that these treasures were one small portion of what Italy had to offer in terms of an Aladdin's cave of Renaissance wealth. To truly showcase Italian art and sculptures, every church or museum in Italy would need to become a travelling circus of intangible heritage.

Alice was sitting exactly where she'd said she would be. On the bench by the rickety old lift which had taken us up to the second floor some hours before.

"Did you have a good time? Did you get some great photos? Did you buy anything from the store?" Yes, yes, yes! These were my three delivered responses as well as my gift from the souvenir shop—a framed photograph of Maria Callas, as I knew the singer to be one of Alice's favourite operatic sopranos. I had wanted to buy a framed picture of my beloved Pavarotti for myself, but they were no longer stocked on account of Pavarotti going out of favour with La Scala administration when he had an off-day in 1992 and his beautiful tenor voice had cracked on a high B.

The crowd had booed him when he took his bow, and that was the end of Pavarotti and La Scala. (Maybe he should have put more practise into his scales?) I had heard Pavarotti sing with his two chums in Melbourne some years back, and our seats were up so high in the stadium that Luciano could have been flat for the entire performance and those of us up in the "Gods" would have been none the wiser. Yes, I had wanted to hear the three Tenors, and yes, we would have been disappointed if they had not met with our expectations. But booing? That would have been un-Australian. Different culture, different mores and nuances. One item from the Souvenir shop was probably enough anyway. We had limited space in our luggage, and limited euro in our wallets.

"Come on, Alice. Andiamo!" Alice moved off the bench slowly and we once again found ourselves at the end of the line exiting the small side door. When we finally made it out into the open air, the bus was nowhere to be seen and the roundabout, statues and treeless piazza were all still deserted. The place looked like a set from Dr Who.

Milan could not still be sleeping! Francesca was talking, and this time I could hear her loud and clear through my speakers.

"If you will all just follow me, we will be approaching the Galleria Vittoria Emanuele the second. This four storied double arcade-mall was built in eighteen seventy-seven, making it the oldest shopping mall in Italy and considered by the Milanese to be the 'living room of Milan'. Here you can buy whatever your heart desires, but please, not too many big boxes on the bus. Matteo need to be able to see to drive us to the Lakes."

The glass domed roof of the shopping centre was criss-crossed in a thousand slashes, and the pavement an endless stretch of polished marble, dotted strategically with perfectly designed large-scale mosaics. Neoclassical! Spectacular! The group was quiet. Oohs and aahs resounded and amplified.

About halfway down the Galleria walkway, Francesca stopped striding and blew a loud whistle. She stood serious and straight-backed as she did so, reminding me of Christopher Plummer in *The Sound of Music* when he hit the exact same notes with his whistle. I called out to those closest to me, not really knowing if they were familiar with the iconic film, but willing to take a chance, given that we were in an Austrian-invaded stronghold from way back. "Do you want to be Liesl or Kurt or Birgitta or Fredrick when Francesca asks us to perform the 'meeting Maria' sequence, accompanying us with her whistle blowing?"

Everyone laughed, and although it had been a lengthy joke, I couldn't help remembering our ballet performance in a similar line, not two hours beforehand. Perhaps we would be performing in every city, town or village on the tour, with a winner to be announced at the end. He or she would be that person who had performed most consistently throughout the trip. The 'all-rounder' who had consistently managed to sing, dance and act their way through the lakes and Northern Italy. I hoped it would be me, but I knew I'd have some stiff competition from the Californian couple-Lizzie and Fillip, who'd already let me know twice that they were ballroom dancing champions in their home State of

California. It was a huge State, so they must have knocked out more than a few contestants to have earned the title.

Happily, we were spared!

The purpose of the whistle blowing had not been to initiate an impromptu song, but to gather the tour passengers together for a group photograph on the exquisitely marbled floor, close to the bulls' balls landmark where all manner of tourists were encouraged to spin around on their heels and make a wish. (Locals avoided the ordeal.) The bull, mosaiced on the marble floor of the shopping mall was a sort of landlocked Trevi fountain, or a ground-floor Blarney castle-kissing podium. It sounded adventurous and appealing, spinning on the 'balls of the bull', and we all wanted a turn, but there was no time left for loitering. After the photograph, Francesca used her umbrella to prod and push us onwards and upwards to the great Il Duomo Cathedral-adjacent to where we'd been standing.

Stepping back out of the Arcade and into the sunshine, a spectacular sight loomed up before us. An enormous Gothic Cathedral. A marvellous architectural feat. A towering testimony to Italian engineering.

In front of the massive Cathedral was a piazza. Not any ordinary piazza with tables or generous café umbrellas, but again, an expansive, sparse, lace tablecloth of concrete and stone walls, little humps of stone in a desert of concrete. Reminiscent of the prelude to the Vatican in Rome, and equally jam-packed with tourists. The whole scene was literally brimming with backpacks and sunhats. From where had they all materialised?

I glanced at my phone. Eleven-thirty. They had to be out for an early lunch, or maybe even midday mass in the Cathedral. Being Sunday, it had to be the most popular day for visiting the church. It was tourist city in all directions. It was their casual clothes and bags of souvenirs which gave them away. Had the piazza been populated by native Milanese out for a midday stroll, they would have been instantly recognisable with their fashionable attire.

As it was, the crumpled sea of caps and sunhats, shorts and slip-ons were dead give-aways, completely exposing the tourist for what he or she stood for-fashion ignorance. It was a strange enigma to be witnessed in Milan-the fashion capital of the world, but even bus-status did not grant us immunity to the "bogan-fashion" labelling, even though most passengers on our coach had made more than a concerted effort to appear well dressed. Francesca was handing out coupons for an hour of free time, and that if we wanted to visit the Cathedral, we would need to buy tickets from that booth over…there!

The booth to which she was indicating, the only booth within fifty metres, had a line longer than a queue for an Ed Sheeran and Andrea Bocelli concert. Alice and I decided there and then that we would be giving the much-adored 'Il Duomo' a wide berth this trip. Had we been staying in Milan for a week, the Cathedral would have been right up there with all the other must-see sights of Milan, but we didn't have a week. We had one hour; sixty short tourist minutes, most of which would be swallowed up with toilets, eating and making our way to the bus.

Alice had called for extended time-out, and was resting on the closest stone wall, whilst I jostled my way down to the ticket queue to see if there might be a second line where we could be fast tracked into the Cathedral-for a price of course! There wasn't, and I was back by Alice's side, sitting down for my own well-earned rest within ten minutes.

"At this rate we might as well make our way slowly to the toilets." Things were not going too well for us this morning. There was a queue there as well. I had seen it whilst racing past. Alice agreed with me that the ablution block should be our next stop, and we both stood up. As we did so, there was a commotion in front of us involving a lanky, beanpole man and a flurry of birds. The man was coaxing the birds towards him. The birds must have had some previous with the man, as they were scurrying around him, vying for the tiny morsels of bread he was offering. Loud squawking followed, and the crowd was building up encircling the immediate area. The lanky performer was about to perform a trick, I could sense it, but I was hazy on the details. We all were!

We need not have been.

Withing a minute the nature of his con was revealed. Two young unsuspecting female tourists had been standing close to the excitement, urging the birds to flight like the rest of us, and snapping away at the flurry of feathers and the performing man with intense delight. He was lapping it all up, parading around with gigantic strides in tiny circles, draped in strands of colourful materials. At the same time, he was offering his wares to the crowd for purchase.

No one was buying, only gaping, and in a sudden skilful swoop, the man coveted one of the two naïve girls with his best move. He waved her towards him, coaxing her to stretch out her arm with one hand, and with his free hand skilfully and deftly coated her arm with some kind of glue or gel. It was difficult to see exactly what he was up to, but I knew he was up to no good. In the wink of an eye, he had the girl's arm thick with gleaming white superglue, and the birds began attacking her flesh, probably after the sticky liquid.

The girl started screaming. The friend jumped in to help her, and the man with the 'colourful materials' cloak threw some of the material strands over the friend's backpack and snatched the satchel away from her after slashing the shoulder straps. Now there were two girls screaming and in the chaotic diversion, the man had thrown the backpack to an accomplice who was whisking by at that very second on a bicycle—brazenly escaping with the loot. Even though the crowd had built up, no none was really getting involved.

I remembered my mother having impressed upon me to be on the alert at all times for pickpockets in Italy, but she hadn't said anything about a circus performance such as that which had just unfolded before our very eyes. Both Alice and I were appalled at the audacity and insensitivity of the act, but neither of us moved. Suddenly, the girl with the birds still stuck to her arm let out an almighty terrified roar, and I sprang into action. If no one else was going to do anything to help her, that left me!

As quickly as I could, I began peeling the birds from the poor girl's arm. Their claws were stuck in the glue, but with a huge effort I managed to pry one bird and then a second from her arm. The whole scene was beyond belief. As soon as I had jumped in to help, a flood of Good Samaritans joined in, and within seconds, the traumatised girl was freed from the equally anxious birds. She was extremely shaken, and someone had called for a doctor or a nurse. A doctor stepped forwards and the next minute, the girl was being lifted up and carted off towards the ticket booth (which we all assumed must have housed a first aid area.)

I looked around for the two thieves and scumbags who had caused all the drama, but they had disappeared into thin air. The friend was last seen fleeing the scene after the injured girl, and people were just standing around the piazza in shocked silence. Broad daylight robbery was not something one expected to be taking place on the steps to Il Duomo. Alice was tugging at my arm. "Come on, Fil. Let's get out of here! We've probably only got enough time left to find the toilets after all this drama. Here, take some of this hand-sanitiser, and keep your money belt around your waist low and tight. Is it still there?" I felt my hips, and the comforting money belt was in its rightful place.

"Yes. All accounted for!"

The toilets presented the next challenge for us, on account of Alice not having the correct change and her insisting to the woman attendant that toilets should be free and that we were tourists and that we had rights. Exhausted from my efforts at bravery with the girl and the birds, I left Alice to fight her own battles and slipped into the nearest toilet block whilst she was still arguing.

Luckily for Alice, Yolanda appeared on the scene and graciously handed her two euro which Alice promptly handed over to the attendant. She had given up the good fight and was desperate by then. I called over to her that I would wait outside, and Yolanda, who was still close enough to hear everything, insisted on waiting for Alice and helping Alice down the stairs and back onto solid ground. "I'll do you a trade. You take Roy back to the bus, and I'll handle Alice. Deal?" I looked down the stairs towards where Roy sat huddled in his knee-length shorts on a stone wall totally surrounded by bright red barricades, plastic witches' hats and tons of thick plastic scaffolding signalling the ongoing (try five years and counting) renovations to the make-shift public restrooms.

Perpetual chaos was possibly the best description for the scene in general. Hordes and hordes of tourists lined up behind the scaffolding, and an air of heightened excitement as the crowd 'oohed' and crooned over the magnificent spindly pronged structure dwarfing everything in sight. Absolutely everything paled into insignificance in the presence of this house of God. Best house, best street—spoiled only by the scaffolds.

Roy was the only person sitting on the wall. Everyone else was too busy scurrying by or buying gelati and entry tickets to the Duomo. I had heard that the view from the roof was something not to be sneezed at, and I wondered how a bird's-eye view from there would compare to the scene in front of me. Alas, I would have to wait until my next trip to find out, as the clock was ticking and I still had my work cut out for me before I made it back to the bus pick-up point, which was where Matteo had set us down—opposite La Scala.

Yolanda was still waiting for my response. I glanced down at Roy again and decided it would not do to be stuck with him, as I wasn't really sure about his mobility status. Last night he had enlightened me to the fact that he was recovering from an operation involving both knees and would not be right for at least six weeks. It had been raining when we'd left the restaurant last night, so there had been no opportunity to properly assess the extent of his handicap. Would we make the bus in time? What would the general opinion of me be, when

I showed up with someone else's husband on my arm? Someone with gammy legs, a cane and thick black sunglasses to rival Stevie Wonder?

Once I had begun deliberating, the answer came swiftly to me. I would stick with Alice. The devil you know and all that! Yolanda looked disappointed that I didn't want to take part in the "wife swapping", but she hid her disappointment well. "It wouldn't really matter, as Roy can be quite slow and he might even need an ablution stop himself before you made it back to the bus. Then where would we be?"

My relief was enormous, but I could play her game, and did so with my non-committal retort of, "maybe next time, Yolanda". It was the right thing to say. Keeping that tiny window of opportunity open—not letting the other person know you had no intention of ever doing what they wanted. "We'll see…maybe…could do…there's always tomorrow… How many people in the world got through their days by leaving these tiny windows open in their conversations? Letting people down lightly was the best policy, and I had just made a winner of myself."

When Alice finally emerged from the restrooms, I was leaning against the scaffolding, playing over in my mind how I would carefully phrase my words to speed her up. The bus would be leaving in ten minutes, and we still had to traverse the glass-roofed shopping mall with the wall-to-wall people obstacles. I need not have worried, as Alice had emerged from the blocks a new person. Freshened up, slicked up and geared up for the next phase on our morning sightseeing escapades in Milan. She had even managed to find some muesli bars in the bottom of her backpack when she'd been rummaging around for lipstick, and we munched on them as we negotiated the crowds, past the scaffolds, past the Cathedral, past the piazza, past the Bulls' balls mosaic and finally through the shopping arcade. Our bus, patiently waiting at the end of the arcade, was a welcome relief, as were Francesca's words of greeting.

"Ah Fil and Halice. You are the first to return. You know to keep the rules and I am happy to see you." That was nice! It was also strange, given that we had not really planned the birds in the piazza and the incorrect euros in the restrooms incidents.

Where were they all? As we clambered onto the bus, I remembered that quite a few of our fellow travellers had been keen to see inside the Cathedral, and the promised rooftop view of Milan and the surrounding landscape. That would account for most of them, and the rest were more than likely still eating lunch in nearby restaurants. In a way, it was a good thing that so many passengers were late, as it gave us time to get settled back on the bus, and to come to a consensus on our plans for the rest of the day.

According to our itinerary, Sforza Castle was to be the next highlight, and after dropping us off at the castle, the bus would again find a resting spot in a neighbouring park, and we would have the opportunity to wander around by ourselves for the remainder of the day. The next reconvening would be at six pm this evening for the 'Welcome Dinner'.

I was looking forward to meeting the entire group in a more intimate setting. Not that being together on a bus for hours on end wasn't intimate, but apart from immediate neighbours, and those in the aisle-seats opposite, it was mostly backs of heads on display.

This morning three passengers had been given the opportunity to introduce themselves on the microphone Francesca had thrust into their faces, and that had been enlightening, although I was yet to fit faces to two of the voices. Even the backs of their heads had been too far away from our seats for me to recognise them in a line-up. The three who had spoken had done a great job, and we had their names, so as the trip unfolded, everyone would be able to match their names with faces. The other clue was that two of them had been married, and the other was a single woman from Jersey in the United States. Her accent was quite distinctive, as was her name, Brielle, and I had already identified her.

The married couple were farmers from the south of New Zealand with plans to travel around Europe for the next couple of months. They were quite comical. The man, Jerry, came on the mic first and introduced himself. He then addressed the second question (of which there were five.) The question asked of his reasons for choosing this particular trip, to which the jovial Jerry replied, "because my wife told me to come."

Everyone laughed and that broke the ice. He then handed the microphone over to his wife, Babette, and she bantered with him about being his wife and living in the same house as him "because she was his wife and that's why they lived together." Brielle was also quite the card, although I suspected nerves played a part in her comic delivery.

She introduced herself as Brielle and added that she was from Jersey in California. She then corrected her mistake with, "What am I saying here? Jersey is in upstate New York. Nowhere near California. Sorry everyone!"

The three stooges had set a precedent for the rest of us. Luckily, there were eight mornings to go so we had time to prepare.

Within ten minutes, everyone had returned like Brown's cows from their sightseeing and eating, and as soon as we were all settled and belted up, Matteo put his foot down. We seemed to be taking the long route to the castle, which according to my map should have been less than ten minutes' drive. Francesca explained why. "You will notice out of your windows that we are having another little glance at Milan while everyone is a-eating their lunch, eh? It is a good time to see some more of the sights, and tomorrow morning when we leave Milan, we will see more and more. You will be full of Milan, just like you will be full of the pasta, but we can never be too full of such a wonderful city."

There had been more to see!

Much more!

For the next hour, Matteo wound his way through side streets, back alleys and sometimes back out onto the highway. The traffic wasn't too bad as everyone appeared to be walking, scootering or cycling. It felt very laidback, and typical of a lazy Sunday afternoon in any big city around the world.

Chapter 15
The Rest of Sunday

Eventually, we pulled up outside the castle. It was expansive and imposing and it looked as if the crowds had beaten us there. The flat, red gravelled path leading up to the clogged entrance to the castle was simply thronging with people. And dogs! Most of the crowd were walking three or four abreast, suggesting they may have been families or groups of friends, and there was a dog or two to be found under the feet of many a family. I supposed the glut of canine creatures to be the norm with families out for a sunny Sunday morning stroll. The path seemed familiar to me, and then I realised it was reminiscent of many of the wide Parisian boulevards.

Alice and I were again towards the end of the line in the trudging stakes. Once we were through the gates, Francesca gathered our group together and began reading out the riot act, geared towards those passengers not ready to board the bus at the end of the castle tour. "It is very, very important, eh? Do not get yourselves lost. We have not even left Milan, and some of you are getting good at going missing. Three steps and you are lost! Please stick like the horses' glue with your regional guide!"

Like a group of guilty school children, we all chorused our promise to stick together. Satisfied with our earnest assurance, Francesca introduced the first of the regional guides to us. In the course of the trip, we would meet eight guides, and not one of them would be the same. All marvellous, all eccentric, all passionate about their job, and their towns and cities. In retrospect, some were overly informative, whist others were overly reticent. Some were laidback and others single-minded in their deliveries.

The woman in front of us was well selected as our first sampling of the local guides. She was bubbly, feisty, funny and very Italian. Her English was perfect, but one needed to get around the accent. Francesca introduced her as 'Carmella', and her first words to our group were, "Hello and Goodbye. I am glad to meet all of you people of my tour, and I hope you like dogs."

What was it with the dog thing around here? First the over-presence of dogs (again, we could have been in Paris) and now, this appeal to our animal preferences. I did like dogs, but was afraid of them, so I wasn't the best person to be asking. Alice was over the moon with the question, and although we were to the back of the group and it was unlikely that she would be heard, she nevertheless cried out, "We love dogs in England! Everyone in England has a dog."

She was probably right, judging by the number of dogs I had seen in the United Kingdom, but we were so far back that no-one heard her, except me and the couple of people directly in front of us. Knowing Alice, she would find a way of getting the guide to herself and confessing that the loves of her life were two little furry yelping creatures who answered to the names of 'Holly and Looby and that they had been left behind in England because we were on a bus tour, and dogs (no matter how small and inconspicuous) were not permitted. It was just a matter of time before Alice found the opportunity to buddy up with Carmella—a fellow dog lover.

We had no idea what lay behind the walls of the castle. Carmella was determined to make us guess what we would see, and finally in desperation, someone yelled out, a dog show?

"Yes. Yes. You are very hastute!" (She was correct. He was extremely hirsute!) The man who had called out the correct answer looked pleased with himself and a few people clapped. (Definitely the dog lovers of the group.) Alice was doubly pleased. "Fil, I'll be able to see two of my most favourite things in my most favourite country, castles and dogs in Italy."

Thrilling. Absolutely riveting stuff. The castle, I could relish, but a courtyard full of bouncing, yelping, barking dogs? Not really my cup of tea. But that's what was up for grabs as we emerged from the tunnel entrance to the castle. A wide, rectangular green lawn, dotted with canine creatures of all colours, shapes, sizes and long dripping tongues. It was an incongruous sight against the backdrop of the grey stone castle. Even more incongruous were the fashions sported by the dogs and their owners.

Milan had not earned the title of fashion capital of Europe for nothing. The dogs looked as if they were competing in a mini-pageant, especially those with oodles of curls piled high on their heads as they paraded past the sardine packed tourist entrance. This over-population of both people and their dogs was a complete turnaround from the deserted streets of Milan some five hours before. It felt as if we were sharing the castle with just about every other tourist who had selected Northern Italy as their holiday destination, yet I was aware that could not have been the case, having lined up for two days in snaking lines at the Uffizi Gallery in Florence, and Sistine Chapel in Rome.

Regardless, this little-known castle was up there with the best of them. Perhaps many of the tourists had included the castle on their list of 'to do's' because of its close proximity to the 'Santa Maria alle Grazie Basillica' home to one of the most famous of Leonardo De Vinci's paintings-The Last Supper. I would have loved to have seen the famous painting, but a visit to the chapel was not included on our itinerary, and if Alice and I set out on our own to find it, we might never be seen again. Francesca was right. We needed to stick together in a city which welcomed nine million tourists every year, making it the sixteenth most popular city with tourists in world ranking.

If time permitted in the castle, we would be able to view other paintings by Da Vinci and Michelangelo, many of which hung in the museum rooms inside the castle. It was not the Louvre, but the treasures were typically Italian and not to be sneezed at.

Carmella was 'doing a Francesca'—herding us together with the greatest of animation, flaying her arms and legs and screeching out in Italian, "Vieni, vieni, tutti." We obliged, and so did the dogs! Dogs on leashes and free-range dogs—there was no discriminating as a multitude of legs and tails whizzed excitedly around Carmella's feet. The owners were not as quick to respond, but as soon as they realised their dogs were missing, they too raced over to where we stood encircling Carmella.

"Please take your dogs away! Va-Via con questi." Carmella had only an hour in which to give us her spiel on the castle, and the presence of the yapping dogs was perturbing her greatly. Most of the owners were very apologetic, and quickly led their dogs back to the common, but a select few were angry with Carmella for having called them over, away from their real work.

Finally, the last dog disappeared, and Carmella was able to deliver her talk about the history of the Sforza castle. She was very lively, and informative for the first five or so minutes, and then she informed us that we would be doing some of the story telling through our acting, and could we please form a line to the left of her so that she might select suitable actors from the group to tell the story of the castle. For the second time in one day, audience participation was expected.

I began to panic about the rest of the Lakes tour which promised to include cheese, ham and pasta making and a visit to an enclosed order of nuns sworn to silence. I thought I might as well volunteer for Carmella today, and get it over with when she asked for volunteers, as it was clear we had no props or scenery, and if we were to be staging a history play, it could only always be better than grinding up pigs' tails or ears to make prosciutto (especially when I was a pseudo-vegetarian).

Carmella was already calling for volunteers. The impromptu play was intended to illustrate the story of the kings and rulers of Italy from the Middle Ages onwards. The main character was a king who had wives galore and thirty-nine children-so there were parts for everyone, and the need for some doubling and tripling up. One married couple offered to play the part of the king and his beloved queen in the story, but Carmella let out a loud protest at the husband's suggestion, exclaiming that they were already married and that it would be bad luck to pretend to be married in a play.

"And no holding hands when you are near each other. Okay?" Everyone laughed, and this ice breaker was a brilliant segue into the story. I really didn't have a clue what the epic poem (Yes! The words were rhyming.) was all about, and luckily, I was assigned only a very minor role by Carmella. That of the youngest child. It was child's play, that part!

Alice fared even more badly. She was chosen by Carmella to be one of the King's wives, but as soon as Carmella realised Alice was hobbling over to stand by the king (a good-looking Singaporean man on our coach, whom I had not yet met, but had heard whisperings about), Alice was dismissed. Scratched. Gazumped by another more able-bodied lady on the bus.

Carmella was quick with the excuse that Alice had been too tall for the part. Alice gave in easily and slunk back to her position next to me in the line. She really was hurt at having been overlooked, but I whispered to her that she'd had a lucky escape and that the king was so good-looking people might think she had been over-anxious to act as his wife. I then played the joker up my sleeve. "Don't stress, Alice. Matteo is still around, and we have eight days to go." Alice was happy with that comment!

After the play, we were granted half an hour to walk around with the Guide and view the museum artefacts and the glorious paintings-or given the option of sauntering off by ourselves, with the proviso that we were back at the bus on time. Erring on the side of caution, I suggested to Alice that we should stick with Carmella, and the other ten or so people who were already following her, but Alice had other ideas. "You go with her, Fil, and tell me all about the paintings. I just want to get a closer look at some of the dogs in the dog show. There might be some like Holly and Looby." Alice was beside herself with excitement, and I couldn't think of a way to inform her I would rather go to a circus than a dog show! Carmella's travelling show it would have to be!

Surprisingly, I really enjoyed the tour and half an hour was not nearly enough time in which to do justice to the wonderful sights and paintings on display. We were fast tracked into an auditorium with a mini-arena-designated wooden benches and treated to an interactive show depicting the history of Milan, with highlights of the Middle Ages and Renaissance periods, and the works of the great masters. It was a clever light-show production, with the focus of the action on a huge black screen. Every time a new epoch of history was highlighted, the next section would light up, until the whole screen had evolved from darkness to light. Very ingenious, and encouragingly informative, especially for the many children in the room.

Carmella bid us farewell at the gates where we had entered the castle, and most of us were quick to hand her a few euros for the grand tour and the play. (I included an olive branch with my offering.) She had been a wonderful local Guide, and if her performance was to be any sort of precedent, we were in for a very enlightening trip.

Francesca was waiting for us by the side of the bus.

"So, the pilgrims return, eh? Did you all enjoy the castle? And Carmella? She was good for you?" There was a slightly anxious pitch to Francesca's voice when she mentioned Carmella, and I felt a little sorry for her.

"No Francesca. She was rubbish!" I called this out loudly, and everyone laughed. Carmella hadn't been rubbish. She had been a very nice, very informed Italian woman, who had been totally professional in her deliverance. But Francesca had needed her confidence to be restored, and there was no harm in a little jest.

It took a few minutes to get settled back into our seats, and just as we were about to take off, Francesca began tapping on the microphone to gather our attention. She'd had an exciting new idea. "Scusi everyone, but I have an idea and Matteo agrees with me. Instead of driving you all back to the hotel for your free time this afternoon, we will be happy to take you on a short tour of Milan, and you will not even have to leave the bus. Just climb back and enjoy the scenery and the marvels of this wonderful city. If there are some of you who want to go back to the hotel for some rest, you can offload here. It is only a short hour's walk back, or you could take a taxi."

Alice was up on her feet in an instant. We had already made our plans for this afternoon and by the looks of things, Alice was not one to be changing them. I wouldn't have minded staying on the bus and relishing more of Milan, but I was also happy to return to the hotel and relax. There was still washing and packing to do, and the scheduled meal this evening had emphasised a six pm start.

It was already three-thirty.

Three other people also stood up and the five of us took to the stairs, waving our goodbyes to those who had elected to stay and be pampered by Francesca and Matteo. Not that it would be a forever parting. We'd see them again in three hours. The other three people turned out to be our old pals Yolanda and Roy, as well as an elderly gentleman whose name I didn't yet know. He was travelling with a woman around his age, whom I took to be his wife, but that was all I knew. Alice was a little better informed.

"That man is American, but originally from Armenia. His son told me." Son? Who was his son, and how old was he? As far as I could make it out, there were no children travelling on the tour, unless they had been sleeping the day away on the back seat of the bus and had yet to be discovered by the rest of us. If there were children on the bus, it was probably a wise decision on the part of the parents to keep them hidden until we were on the open roads with no chance of escape for anyone.

Memories of children on planes and long boat and plane journeys came flooding back to me. Having them on a nine-day bus tour would be a new experience, but I suspected the novelty would wear off as soon as we hit the open road.

If the Armenian gentleman had a child on the bus, he was keeping his cards close to his chest. And then there was the question of his age. At least seventy-five, with the countdown in full throttle.

I should have ignored Alice and concentrated on finding a taxi for the five of us. It turned out he did have a son on the trip. All true. But the son was at least thirty, and a soon-to-be-qualified doctor. The older man-Joe, had talked about his brilliant son all the way back to the hotel. We were all so squashed in the back seats, it was difficult to even nod. The taxi was a mini-bus, as we needed room for the two invalids-Alice and Roy. As 'carers-extraordinaire' Yolanda and I had sat in the two back seats, and that left the front seat opposite the driver for Joe. As soon as he was settled, Joe began his long-winded soliloquy on his son-Devo, the miracle doctor. According to the bursting-with pride Joe, Devo had the hands of an angel, and the face of a cherub. (Weren't they the same creatures?)

Joe didn't seem to notice that replies and accolades were not forthcoming from the back seats. Yolanda and I were too busy helping our charges with seatbelts and rearranging the cabin baggage at our feet, to interject with more than an, "Oh yes!" What with the souvenirs from the glass-domed shopping centre, the Cathedral gift shop and the castle, we were struggling for room. Not to mention Alice's walking stick and Roy's crutch. (Not Roy's actual crutch, rather, his walking apparatus.) The driver seemed to be taking the long route back to the hotel, because even with my poor sense of direction, I could tell we were going the wrong way. I tapped him on the shoulder and asked in my best pigeon-Italian if he had the correct hotel. The man pulled over to the side of the road and consulted his GPS.

"Of course. You are the smart signora. It is on the other side of the road." His English was better than my Italian, and a hair-raising three-point turn ensued. I should have kept my mouth shut and we wouldn't have all ended up very close to the floor. All of us in the backseat—not the driver and Joe, who were tightly belted up in the front. It took another couple of minutes to complete the second arrangement of seatbelts and baggage, and this time Yolanda and I made certain all four of us were as tight as rats in a trap.

The three-point turn incident had put the fear of God into Joe, and he clammed up for the rest of the journey. The driver steered the conversation once he had taken the brave step with his praising of my sense of direction. He described every building, park, museum and church we passed with enthusiastic pride in his city, and by the time we reached the hotel we were probably more informed about the Central Business District of Milan than our fellow passengers who had stayed behind on the bus with Francesca and Matteo.

When we arrived at the hotel, some thirty minutes later, the driver insisted on a flat fee of twenty euro, which worked out to be four euro each. We gave him a five-euro tip, and I handed him an olive branch. He was astounded with the gesture, impressing upon me that in his ten years of taxi driving, no tourist had ever given him a gift that wasn't a tip. Let alone something living. (Well, semi-living) Yolanda, Joe and Roy all wanted to know about the olive branches, and we sat in the little lounge bar and had a well-deserved drink, chatting about the morning and how exciting it had been to see such marvellous Italian architecture.

We were still there when the bus pulled up outside the hotel. As soon as he realised his wife and son had returned, Joe jumped ship and raced out to the foyer, promising to introduce us to the rest of the family tonight. We waited until everyone had disappeared up the stairs and lifts to their respective bedrooms, and then made our weary way towards the lift and up to our own rooms. Roy and Alice were exhausted, and Yolanda and I weren't far behind. An hour's rest, and a hot soothing shower would be just what Doctor Devo ordered.

Five fifty-five came soon enough.

Francesca was the first to congratulate us on our scrubbed-up appearances as we boarded the bus to take up the promised 'Welcome meal' in a well-known restaurant area of Milan known as 'Bresa'. Alice and I had deliberately hung around near the steps whist Matteo and Francesca greeted the group and helped the more elderly up the steps. Not that there were too many elderly passengers. The average age would possibly have been fifty, which is a respectable age for travelling in any country.

At last it was our turn to mount the stairs. Matteo smiled and extended his hand to Alice, and Francesca just looked at our clothing and refrained from commenting. (We had both had showers and washed our hair, but still hadn't had time to wash our clothes, so they were noticeably not in the league of the other passengers.) I wanted to explain the saga of our suitcases to both of them, but all the other passengers were on the bus, hungry and ready for an immediate take-off. It would not have been the time or place to start telling our sorry story.

People must have been really famished, because no one else seemed to notice that we were dressed in the same clothes we had worn all day. Francesca had started up some singing on the microphone, and before long everyone was joining in with *That's Amore*. We sang the song three times before we reached the drop-off point to the restaurant and were just about to launch into our fourth rendition when Francesca interrupted by announcing that we had arrived at our destination.

"It will only be a short walk to the restaurant, and a short walk back. But, on the return journey some of you will not even notice the distance if you have drunk enough Italian vino." I liked the sound of a glass or two of the 'vino-veritas' and thinking about the promised food and wine helped me put a spring in my step and find added energy to propel Alice through the streets towards the restaurant. When we arrived, Francesca again motioned us into a circle like a group of footballers about to race out and win the Grand Final for Milan.) But all she did was briefly explain the evening's plans.

"We will eat, we will drink, we will talk and get to know each other, and then we will come back to the hotel and sleep. Tomorrow we will be leaving very early, and the bus cannot wait for you if you sleep in. Remember that, eh? Now, Andiamo! Let's go in and have a good night."

We did! We had a fabulous night. Our group had been assigned a room at the far end of the restaurant-past acres of patrons, past the toilets, past the bar and past the kitchen. (The smells wafting into the restaurant from the busy kitchen were to die for. Garlic, onions and more garlic!) It was a squashed in, tiny area for twenty-five people, and there was barely room for the waiters to squeeze past the two long tables with course after course of delectable Italian cuisine.

Fresh fish, risotto, fritters, meat, vegetables, delicious, crusty melt-in-your-mouth bread and sweet mouth-watering delectable desserts of custards, liquor-laced cakes, creams and gelati. We ate and ate and ate. There were roughly twelve of us at each table, and someone quipped that it looked like two gatherings of the Last Supper. (The painting of the same name by Leonardo Da Vinci turned out to be just around the corner in a little out-of-the-way church.) But it wasn't our Last Supper, it was our First Supper together. We bonded beautifully, all twenty of us. The waiters did a superb job of serving and whisking away plates (sometimes even before we had finished) filling up our wine-glasses way past the plimsol--line and replacing serviettes and cutlery with practised ease). We left a substantial tip (as one does at the beginning of one's tour) and I couldn't resist placing an olive branch on the tipping plate beside the wad of euro.

The waiters had been good, very good, and I wanted to be able to return to the restaurant in five years' time and enjoy an olive tapenade from the tree which the proprietor would be sure to plant in a healthily soiled wine barrel outside the restaurant. I was certain that would happen, because I made up my mind right there and then that if ever I were to find myself back in Milan, that action-packed, high-energy restaurant in Bresa will be top of my list of things to do. Everyone enjoyed themselves, and even though we were all exhausted after the long, long, day, it was sad to leave the restaurant after such a bonding time together.

Francesca was delighted with our performances. "I can see that we all be good together from now on. This will be the best trip ever!"

Back at the hotel, it was time to rest. A few of the younger passengers were mulling around in the foyer, deliberating whether or not to venture out into the streets in search of a nightclub. Alice, Yolanda, Roy and I left them to their indecision and headed straight for the lift. Our last night in Milan, and a comfortable bed was the only fix we needed.

Chapter 16
And We Were Off!

How to force my eyes open? This was ridiculous. Every other morning, I had jumped out of bed, bright-eyed and bushy-tailed. Now this morning, the very morning we were to begin our trip into the great unknown-the lakes and the rocky coastal inlets of Northern Italy, I could not wake up! My mind wanted to perform all sorts of feats, but my body was sluggish, my eyes sticky and gluey with sleep. Perhaps if I just felt blindly for the glass of water on the bedside table, and poured the contents over my head, I would awaken to the sweet sound of birds, pipes rattling and water gushing its way down the rusty iron cylinders from upstairs showers.

I fumbled for the glass, but it seemed to have disappeared, and the semi-darkness of the bedroom was not helping. Finally managing to open one eye, I strained my head towards the balcony and Alice's bed, trying to squint and make out if she were still there. She wasn't! Her doona had been flung back, and Alice was missing in action. I looked towards the closed bathroom door and realised that the gushing water was coming from behind the door and not from an upstairs bathroom as I had first presumed.

Excellent!

Being able to place Alice in the shower would allow me at least twenty minutes of twilight-zone relaxation time, and precious downtime allowing me to adjust to the day ahead. It was still very early—five-thirtyish—but the bus was scheduled to leave at eight, and we had packing to complete, showers and breakfast to be fitted in, if time permitted. Alice was a little further advanced than was I, the evidence being her closed and padlocked suitcase and the fact that she had lain her clothes for the day ahead out neatly on her bed.

Too much!

Pulling the covers back over my head for the next twenty minutes seemed my BPS. (Best possible solution.) As long as I didn't give in to the temptation to close my eyes and have a micro sleep. If that happened, I would be in the doghouse with everyone on the bus on the first morning of our trip.

Thirty minutes later, I resurfaced to Alice standing over my bed, informing me that it was already six and that she was going down to breakfast. "If you don't think you will have time to come down, Fil, I can bring you back some cakes and fruit. Would you like that?" I thanked her and agreed it might have been somewhat of a marathon effort for me to make breakfast this morning, given that I hadn't yet packed and the suitcases were due to be collected from outside our rooms at seven.

"I'll be fine here pottering around, Alice. You go down and get yourself a healthy breakfast. You'll need your strength for walking around the gardens at Villa Taranto."

Just uttering the title 'Villa Taranto' sent shivers down my spine. Even though I have admitted to a scant knowledge of Northern Italy, I had long harboured a fascination with Taranto Gardens, and had always wanted to see them for myself. I knew they were in Italy, opposite a fairly substantial lake, and that they were exquisite. Gardens to rival the likes of Boboli, Kew and Givenchy. This morning I would find out for myself just how exquisite the Gardens really were. It was tremendously exciting, and enough to spur me into action.

Hungry Alice disappeared quickly, once she had seen me jump out of bed and shake the entire contents of my suitcase onto her bed. I was grateful she had promised to bring me back some sustenance and I realised (too late) the number of water bottles which had spilled out onto the bed were, in hindsight, totally superfluous. Not having been sure of the quality of Italian drinking water, Alice and I had each hidden six one-litre plastic water bottles in our big suitcases. (No wonder the suitcases had been dead weights.)

Fortunately, no random drug tests had been undertaken, and no suitcase-opening had taken place, or we may have been bombarded with questions such as, "Why bring these substances into Italy?" and "What is in the bottles?" On the topic of water bottles, one travel story which had kept us entertained through many a dinner party was that involving two friends and non-consumable Lourdes water. The 'Holy water' had been sourced from the miraculous springs at the grotto in France, and although it had taken two days of hard slog, they had managed to siphon litre upon litre of holy water in tiny little plastic bottles. The plan was to cart the haul back to Australia for redistribution.

On their return, it seemed the party was not yet over. Their actions caused no end of disruption and disbelief at the Melbourne airport, upon informing officials they were eager to dish out bottles of 'Holy water' to the sick and the elderly. The customs officials in those days (in any days) did not look too kindly on travellers attempting to bring large amounts of any substance or produce into the country, especially if it was professed to be only water. No one carried water bottles around with them thirty years ago.

Needless to say, my friends spent the rest of the day in Customs, made the news that night and the 'Holy water', all twenty litres of it, ended up down the gurgler. All the custom officials could tell them was that, "one could never be too careful when dealing with foreign substances." Not that much has changed in three decades, except that nowadays 'Holy' has been dropped from the title, and it is possible to order 'Lourdes water' online, direct from the grotto, for under twenty Australian dollars, including postage.

The middleman, Mr Customs, appears to have been bypassed. The importation of illegal drugs has pushed Holy water to the back stalls. A recent story in a leading London newspaper featured Prince William of Cambridge touring the Lost Property headquarters in the dungeons of London's Heathrow International only to find himself coughing and spluttering throughout the tour. When he emerged from the bowels of the building, he was reputed to have remarked that he could smell something distinctly cannabis-like-that it was a good strong smell, and that they should leave the depot they were touring which was full of illegal drugs, weapons and wildlife, before they were drug-tested. No stiff British upper lip for William. He could crack a joke with the best of 'em.

The timer was going haywire. I'd only set it for twenty minutes, as the suitcases still demanded their daily dose of dragging to the door. I'd had some practise with that particular routine, so I wasn't too concerned about how I'd manage without Alice to perform her duties as door-opener. I had to smile at Alice though. Suddenly, her leg was all better.

She had been up packing and showering with the birds, and her suitcase stood by the side of her bed, strapped and ready for the big trip. Come to think of it, Alice had practically run to the door once she'd confirmed I was awake, and that was probably only to ensure I didn't forget to drag her suitcase outside when I was dragging my own. On the upside, she had promised food, which at this rate, I would be munching all the way to Villa Taranto.

I was going for the record! Packing, case closing, case dragging, showering, hair-washing, tidying my side of the room and rearranging my passport, cabin luggage and handbag! Check, check, check! By the time Alice reappeared, all chores were completed and with time to spare, I had begun flicking and scrolling on my phone, shifting photos into folders, relabelling folders and deleting unwanted notes.

"They didn't have much, Fil. This was all I could get. The Indian waitresses were staring at me like I was a looter after an earthquake, even though I told one of them you were up in the room packing, and that breakfast was included with the room. She didn't seem to believe me." I peered into the calico bag Alice had dropped on the bed in front of me, but I had to look hard and deep to see the three long breadcrusts and the tiny shrivelled apple she had managed to smuggle out.

She would never make a proficient house burglar.

Outside in the sunshine, my hunger pangs were all but forgotten, as the adrenalin kicked in, and excitement and anticipation grew. There was a buzz in the air, and a warm breeze rippled the leaves on the nearby oak trees. Francesca was at the helm, excelling herself with welcoming salutations and praise for our appearances. She stopped when Alice and I approached, her beaming smile making any words redundant. "Fil, Alice! I could nearly not recognise you both. How well you look. How wonderful are your costumes!"

Costumes? Did Francesca think we were dressed in costume, ready for an eight-day historical tour? I was familiar with themed bus trips, where passengers choose their characters and costume for the tour and ended up playing their part for the duration of the trip. *Game of Thrones* tours were extremely popular, and I had also read articles about *Star Wars* and *Sound of Music* themed tours. The thing was, we were not dressed in costume. Just dressed in fresh, yet crumpled clothes which had been cooped up in our suitcases in an undisclosed holding zone at the airport.

Matteo, being a man of meticulous dress sense himself, was more appreciative of our attire. He smiled graciously but made no comment. Francesca soon recovered from her surprise at our outfits and helped us both up the steps onto the bus.

The gang were all back. Two couples whom we hadn't really talked to yesterday or last night were occupying the first four seats of the bus on either side of the aisle. Francesca must have been up at the crack of dawn preparing for this early morning take-off. I could see she had placed name tags on the seats so that we all knew where to sit. Not that it should really have mattered that much, as the bus was only half full. We were such a small group. Alice was ahead of me and had found our seats almost as soon as we passed the first two couples.

"Here we are, Fil. This is us!" Our positions—two seats behind the front rows (row three)—were both fortuitous and alarming. Fortuitous because being in row three meant we would be spared from having to speak on the microphone today, and alarming in that we had only two days in which to prepare our addresses to the nation. Gerry, Babette and Brielle had drawn the best straws. They were the three lucky passengers who had been totally unexpecting of the task they had been asked to perform yesterday and had been caught totally unawares.

Today's four passengers would be in a similar position, although I was uncertain as to whether Francesca had slipped them a handwritten note of forewarning. (Or a late-night email after our welcome dinner last night?) They hadn't looked worried as we'd passed by. In fact, all four of them had looked expectant and anticipatory. Must have all been extroverts. Alice was an extrovert, so she should be fine with speaking. I tended to doubt myself more, and for me, speaking on a microphone with my back to an audience did not hold any great appeal.

Give me a stage, a crowd to the front of me and a fistful of sure-to-impact jokes, and I'm happy. One thing I've learnt in life is that a performer needs to know how to 'play the crowd'. The audience should be putty in one's hand, and all that should be needed to ensure success would be to look them in their collective eye and play the game with supreme confidence-never faltering. I didn't see how I was going to be able to do that on this bus, given that my back would be to the audience. Even priests turned around to face the congregation, not to mention conductors of orchestras or bands in processions. 'All eyes on the leader' was not mentioned for nothing!

Still, my fate was two days away, and a lot could happen in that time. I might find a way to give Francesca the slip, by making a daily escape to a backseat with the excuse of travel sickness. I did not want to wish this condition on myself, but I was prone to the queasy disposition. Or better still, Alice would talk for me, as yesterday, Francesca had encouraged only one person from a couple to do the talking. 'Couple class' was turning out to be the best option all around. I settled back into my seat, putting my worries to the side and relishing the fact that finally, finally, finally-we would be off to the Northern lakes.

Francesca was completely ignoring the unwritten bus law of addressing the group. She was looking at us all directly, speaking loudly and with confidence, even wandering up and down the aisle with her roving microphone. Blatant, blazing disregard for the rules and norms. Perhaps tour guides had reached the status of diplomatic immunity?

'So, you are all ready, eh? All of you ready for the marvellous North? Matteo, are you ready to go?

Matteo floored the accelerator as if he had been green-flagged at Monaco, and we were off! So, we were in the clutches of a lead foot for the foreseeable future? Definitely something to look forward to for the next eight days. Caught unawares, Francesca was sent flying down the aisle, into the sunken cockpit, and landing almost on Matteo's lap. He swerved with the impact and we ended up on the kerb in front of the hotel before any of us knew what had happened. Francesca, obviously an old hand at defying gravity, was quick to regain her composure and, within seconds, had the microphone back in her mouth and had begun relating the Ten to the power of infinity Commandments of bus travel.

"When we are on the bus, peoples, there are some of the rules we all have to know and go by. The most important one is for everyone to know how to break the glass if there is an emergency. If you need to, you will all have to use your ice-pick and break the windows. Do not be afraid to smash hard."

Alice and I looked at each other incredulously. Ice-pick? Would mountain climbing be offered as an optional extra on the trip, and if so, would we be issued with ice picks with which to become familiar? Alarm bells were rippling down the aisle. Ice picks? Broken glass? What had we signed up for? Francesca was still speaking. "Don't be alarmed. It hardly ever happens. If it does happen, you will all be the ginny-pigs with the ice-picks. The lucky ones eh?" I would need to be a pretty damn sozzled ginny pig if I was to be using an ice-pick on the Alps. And hold the tonic! It was hard to tell if Francesca was kidding or deadly serious. No ice-picks were held up on display, and there was no sound of demonstration-glass breaking, so we had to assume she was kidding.

I couldn't resist calling out to her, asking for a demonstration of the window shattering, as I was one of those people who learnt by demonstration.

"Fil!" Francesca's voice was dripping with sarcasm now. "Fil, this is not the cooking demonstration. You will just have to use your imagination!"

There was more to come from Francesca, with the next instruction delivered in a state of heightened uncalled for stress. It was to make sure we were all on time every morning for the bus. "Otherwise, you will be left behind, and we cannot pick you up until the next trip." That broke the ice, so to speak, and the nervous murmurings of alarm turned to chuckles and snorts at Francesca's joke. She really was quite the card.

Liberated, Francesca proceeded to rattle off many more "suggestions", but most of us had tuned out by then. Despite being clouded in the thick of the Monday morning traffic, there was still so much to see, and so many wide gleaming windows through which to gaze. Francesca wasn't giving up though. Sensing she was fast losing the crowd with her endless list of dos and mostly don'ts, she cunningly switched tact.

"And a nowa, I know you will all look to the left and you will see the building where Mussolini, the great 'Il Duce' breathed his last breath. He was there with his mistress, but they were not on a date! It was the scene of the famous upside-down execution. Somebody really put their foot in it, eh?" Even though the whole ordeal—the shooting followed by the hanging—being described by Francesca sounded like a gory prospect, it was understandably historically significant for Italy, and we had come to Italy for the history as well as the architecture, the food and the scenery.

With the exception of those passengers who had already fallen asleep (those sleep-deprived few who took bus tours to sleep the days away), we craned our necks towards the windows to see the spot where Mussolini, who had founded his fascist movement in Milan, also ended it there when he met his fate. We saw nothing. Matteo, of the crisp white shirt, dark, dark designer sunglasses and little feathery cap was driving at such a cracking pace that most of us missed it. I had to smile again at the pride in Francesca's voice when she mentioned Mussolini and Milan in the same sentence.

The understated rivalry between Milan and Rome was still alive and well, and the likes of Francesca and local Guides were in the driver's seat when it came to extolling the virtues and importance of the North. No one else noticed this little enigma so I let it go!

I wasn't even sure what I was supposed to be looking for. I knew the upside-down hanging of the Italian dictator was embedded in world folklore, as my mother had related the story to me many times with precisely the same biased facts as her father had related to her. (My grandfather had listened to the whole ordeal on the radio.) I thought of significant moments in history which had taken place in my own lifetime. Martin Luther King and JFK's assassinations as well as Princess Dianna's car crash and Elvis Presley's death. Michael Jackson. The Queen-Mother! Francesca had moved on.

"So, you see-a we have the famous people in Italy. The next to come is the beautiful buildings where the rich and the famous live in the week. In the weekends they go to Lake Como or Lake Maggiore to the beach house. No, no to the Lake-house. Can you see all the beautiful gardens behind the walls?"

I tried to look behind the walls when the bus whizzed past a series of black iron grates, but all I could make out were flashes of green. It didn't really matter. The whole place had natural urban beauty, and the wide clean street we were hurtling down was practically devoid of traffic at this early hour. We had almost reached the motorway-about to head north. It was time to say goodbye to Milan and 'Buongiorno' to the beautiful lakes.

After about five minutes of droning on about the influence of the Austrians in these wealthy northern outskirts of Milan, supplemented with more rules on bus etiquette such as 'no arguing on the bus', it went quiet. Francesca had stopped for a breath, and most people seemed to be taking extended breathers of their own (code word 'sleep'). All that now filled the void was the quiet purring of the bus, the feint honking of horns from the nearby motorway, and a distant swishing of traffic, no doubt from cars crammed with commuters battling severe cases of Monday morning-itis.

Even when we took the ramp onto the unchartered frontiers of the motorway, and joined in the madness of Monday mornings, our side of the road remained relatively traffic free, save for a convoy of lorries in front of us, and a couple of bright red tractors visible on an arterial road lapping the motorway. (I had heard whisperings that speed limits were meaningless anywhere in Italy, or at least, no one with any sense of moral purpose was policing the motorways. I now believed the rumours to be true.) To take my mind off how fast we were travelling, I turned my attentions to the surrounding vista. It had not taken long at all to have left Milan behind, and the countryside had suddenly opened up like a parasol. Or a giant sunflower in slow motion. It was striking!

The best way to describe this almost lunaresque landscape was 'flat'. I had expected immediate mountains. Big, black volcanic mountains! In my fanciful imaginings there had been numerous tunnels carved through these mountains which we would traverse as we made our way towards the lakes, but there was not even the tiniest of earthy mounds for miles ahead. Brownish-yellow, flat and waterlogged was my best assessment of the landscape. It was an interesting layout and consulting my guidebook, I was able to correctly classify the segmented land as hydroponic rice fields.

Reading my mind, Francesca was back on the microphone to confirm my findings. "These fields that you can see are brimming with rice. They are full of the Milanese risotto. In Italy, we do it backwards. Milan is always first. We say, 'risotto Milanese'."

I had seen rice fields before. We have an abundance of them in Australia, but we call them terraces, and they are normally much greener and easier to distinguish from neighbouring crop fields. These fields were beautiful and peaceful, wedged between rammed-earthen farmhouses, dilapidated barns and assorted crumbling, ancient, triple storied out-buildings. People must have lived on the farms, because there were battered old, distinctly Italian cars and tractors, abandoned at intervals up the dirt paths which led to the buildings. No washing on lines though, nor any signs of life-human or animal. It was a strange sight. Perhaps, like priests, the farmers and their families (including the animals) had Monday's off?

It all looked as if we were visiting in the off-season. Once again, Francesca read my thoughts. We were becoming close-Francesca and I. Alice would need to pick up her game, and make more effort to join in the conversations, or I could well have a new 'bestie' before the end of the trip. One could never be too old for best friends! I stole a quick look at Alice, wondering if she realised that she would need to fight to retain her status in the friendship pecking order, but her eyes were closed and she was dozing.

Francesca was tapping on the microphone, leaving nothing to speculation. "I am thinking those of you who are awake are wondering why it is so quiet out there in the farmhouses. Where is everyone, eh?" I looked around the bus, and as far as I could tell, most people were sleeping. Francesca must have come to the same conclusion, because within seconds, she was at my side (dozing Alice had the window seat).

"Fil. I know I can count on you to stay awake and listen to me and my chitter-chat. I can tell you have the straight back, and you are very interested in the rice fields. Do you like risotto as well?"

As well? As well as what? Did I like risotto, did I like martinis, did I have any Italian blood in me? Francesca wasn't the only one capable of reading minds.

"Yes. I love risotto. Especially risotto Milanese with mushrooms." Would we be stopping to explore the farmhouses and rice fields? (Or maybe going mushroom picking, taking it in turns to fill Francesca's little wicker basket?) Francesca looked at me intently-startled at my interest in the rice fields of Italy. I didn't think it was such a rare interest to have harboured. Plenty of people were interested in stranger things than rice fields.

Most probably, Francesca was surprised because no one had ever bothered to show any interest in the fields before today. My intrigue was genuine though. I had been informed by a friend before leaving Australia, that the countryside through which we were now travelling, was the largest area for rice production in Europe. Even the rice fields in the South of America paled in comparison. I wondered if the Chinese or Singaporean passengers I had seen up the front of the bus were in their glory as much as was I, with the rectangular green fields of rice.

There seemed to be farm after deserted farm of them. My trump card in the rice debate was rice being my most favourite food of all time, hence my fascination. The canals of Milan had also fascinated me, and it wouldn't have taken much working out to realise that these rice fields we were speeding past were an extension of the canals, and a centuries-ago effort on the part of farmers at hydroponic self-sufficiency.

Mostly it was the monks of Milan who dug out the canals and tended their kitchen gardens. It really did put us to shame in the twenty-first century with our modern industrial and technological overload. What had happened to the connection with the land and the dirt on our hands? Where was Rudolf Steiner when you needed him? Still, I couldn't talk. Neither could any one of us one the bus. Life was too easy, and we had become too expectant.

I reclined in my seat, shutting off the rice fields, concentrating instead on how I might help save the earth by buying rice in bulk from these self-sufficient farmers. The trouble was, by the time the Italian rice reached us in Australia, it had tripled in price and was classified a luxury import. We had our own rice, and irrespective of the farming practices, I should be buying and eating Australian. There was really nothing I could do to boost the Italian economy but add to the pool of tourists who filled the Italian wheelbarrows with euro each year. Too much to think about without my early morning coffee-and that was leaving BREXIT out of the equation.

My chance to boost Italy's economy turned out to be just around the corner when Matteo, with little forewarning, lunged the bus into the last parking bay of a roadside café attached to a fairly large petrol station. Despite Matteo's skilful manoeuvre having been a natural progression from the motorway, Francesca must also have been unprepared for the pit-stop, as she and her little wicker basket both ended up on the front stairs leading down to the double exit doors. Not missing a trick, she swiftly regained her balance and composure, unruffled her feathers, and reattaching the microphone to her lapel announcing to all passengers, "We will now make the stop at this authentic Italian café where you will have twenty minutes to freshen up, and maybe eat something. Then in one and a half hour, we will arrive to 'Taranto Villa and Gardens' to see something wonderful."

Hearing we only had twenty minutes got everyone moving quick smart! Even Alice and Roy seemed to sprout wings, and within two minutes we were all off the bus, headed straight for the ablutions blocks and the coffee machine (in that very natural order). Inside the café it was like stepping into a bygone era. Think English High teas and substitute 'High coffee' with percolated Italian trimmings. And lots of red, white and green flags. Upon entry, the delicious smell of freshly brewed coffee hit hard, a blast of equatorial air so far north.

Hot and pungent, an irresistible 'must-have'. The counters were piled high with mouth-watering creamy yellow custard, cream cakes and little bread sticks wrapped in red cellophane. Packets of cigarettes were also piled high on the counter, and judging by the smoke in the café, patrons had been trying out the merchandise since the early hours of the morning. The décor, although hard to make out in the thick haze of smoke, was also distinctly Italian. Polished, gleaming wooden benches, framed photographs of Italian football teams and whole rows of black and white depictions of snow-capped mountainous countryside-not to mention the entire wall of smiling café owners, named and shamed and stretching the length of the counter. There were no photos with rice fields in the background, which indicated to me that we had left them behind with Milan.

The behaviour at the long bench-counter was fascinating. David Attenborough could have spent weeks secreted away in this plain, nondescript roadside café, filming the peculiar migratory and movement habits of the strange enigmatic species—the Italian male. Because, apart from the women on our bus (most of whom had headed straight for the 'Ladies'), there were no local women to be seen. I hadn't been far off with my High Tea comparison, just too many streets away from the Ritz. I should have thought of Prince Charles' Club in Piccadilly instead.

We appeared to have stumbled into a tiny Italian island colony off the motorway which may well have been the exclusive preserve of the male species. I had a feeling this café was not an only child, and that should we venture further up or down the motorway, we would discover scores of similar establishments. Furniture wise, there were no stools, chairs or even tables, and most of the patrons (all dressed in black) were leaning on the counter sipping from tiny coffee cups.

Not much talking was going on, but I could feel beady black eyes boring. Leaving high teas and a gentleman's club of London aside, the next best comparison would be a stereotypical American diner minus the booths. Alas, in the short time we were in the café 'Fonzie' did not burst onto the scene from his office (male toilets).

One thing was for sure. We were entirely noticeable as tourists. Clueless to the Italian etiquette required in out of the way roadside cafes, not one of us was willing to make the first move towards the territorial counter. Finally, someone spoke out.

"I think we need to go up there and pay first, and they give you a little ticket on a little plate, a card. Then you can just move to the side and wait for your food and drink." The fountain of information had been Roy of the injured knees. He and Yolanda had been standing alongside of myself and Alice, and as he appeared to know what he was talking about, we all followed his instructions (we all, being myself, Alice and Yolanda) and thanks to Roy, ended up with a steaming cup of coffee and a cornetto each. (Both of which disappeared in minutes.)

The cream croissant was so intensely sweet and buttery that I longed to re-enter the queue and purchase half a dozen or so for later on, but our twenty minutes 'visiting hour' was almost up. Some of the other passengers who had followed our lead were still lined up patiently waiting as we made our way back to the bus, and I feared they had missed their opportunity for coffee and cakes. Francesca's doomsday words, "the bus waits for no one", were still ringing in my ears, and I felt obliged to inform these fellow travellers that we had exactly three minutes till lift-off. But I didn't interfere. It was probably something Francesca was expected to do as tour leader, and it would have been pointless of me to have called for "last drinks" when they clearly had not yet partaken of their first ones.

We waited, of course! Francesca had performed her head count twice before she realised four of her flock were missing. She remained nonplussed, as it had obviously been a small café and understandably, twenty minutes wasn't going to be long enough for all of us to do everything we needed to do. A veteran tour director, Francesca had a suit of time-fillers up her sleeves. She opted for the 'Solution focus' pathway, providing some lively Italian folk music through the state-of-the-art bus speakers whilst we waited for our tardy companions.

Ten minutes later, the truants turned up, clutching coffee cups and white paper bags which, by the looks of things as they passed us by, might have contained cakes or some sort of Italian delicacies of unusual shapes. The bags were full and bulging. Maybe these passengers weren't taking any chances on finding more food any time soon?

When you are in a strange country and you are deposited in a strange male-dominated roadside café and told to eat, you eat! And, if opportunity presents, you stock up like there is no tomorrow. I started chastising myself for not having had their foresight. With a bit of luck, the latecomers would offer to host an impromptu picnic at our first lakeside photo-stop, and all twenty-four of us would be offered seconds. Something to look forward to, as the next part of the journey was forecast to last for one and a half hours.

It would be a good time to catch up on emails and consult my guidebook for out-of-the-way bookshops and florists. My two passions—reading and browsing nurseries for unusual plants. Villa Taranto should help me quench my thirst for flowers and plants. If the guidebook was to be believed, we were in for a treat.

Chapter 17
A Botanist's Dream

The ninety minutes it took to grace the glorious lakeside entry-gates to Villa Taranto the largest and prettiest garden in Northern Italy, flew by. The folk music of the road-side café car park had been replaced with the soaring voices of Andrea Bocelli and Pavarotti, rousing even those passengers vying for top-dog position in the Rip Van Winkle stakes, from the depths of midmorning slumber. Without the elixir of Andrea's angelic and perfectly pitched voice, I too would have succumbed to the demon sleep. It was hard to resist closing one's eyes on this sleek people-mover.

Matteo had settled down comfortably to an acceptable one hundred and twenty kilometres an hour of hurting, and as we had not yet reached the lakes, let alone the mountains, the terrain remained flat and hazy. The weather was not the best, but neither was it the worst, and the rain had held off for our intended gallivant in the gracious gardens.

At one stage, about thirty minutes into the journey, and on the third round of 'Nessun-Dorma', I felt a presence by my side, a slight brushing of my right sleeve and the faintest whiff of Chanel perfume. I kept my eyes tightly closed, assuming the voyeur to be someone on their way to the bus toilet, which was opposite my seat, down four wide stairs. (It was also the middle exit to the bus, so I was at least close to the doors, should the axe-picks be called for.)

The presence and the smell lingered, and I debated whether or not to open my eyes and scrutinise my mid-morning visitor. A gentleman caller was out of the question, as the perfume was distinctly Chanel, and I was an expert sniffer when it came to perfumes. (Unless it was a Mr metrosexual male, rooted on the spot with my beauty, and unable to pass until he had declared his undying attraction to me, and arranged a first date).

Which I would not ever be attending. I could do chatting, eating out, dancing and even flirting, but a full-on date? No way, Jose! I was here for the beautiful vistas, the history and the architecture. I had moved way beyond holiday romances, even though they did add thousands of bonus points to the stories one was obliged to relate about one's 'said holiday' upon returning to one's native shores. Enough fanciful imaginings.

Time to open my eyes and see for myself who had come knocking at my door so early in the trip. Someone with impeccable timing, eager to accompany me around the Taranto gardens and buy me my second cup of coffee for the morning? No-one! There was no one there at all! I ostriched my head into the aisle and scanned the carpeted stretch of thoroughfare, but it was a hotel corridor at midnight—deserted and dimly lit. I strained my ears towards the tiny bathroom at the bottom of the stairs, but no sound was forthcoming. (Not that I was eavesdropping, more just hoping to hear movement of some sort.) It was unlikely I had imagined the perfume smell, and even more unlikely that it had been a male admirer.

If I were to wake Alice and relate the incident, she would more than likely wave her arms around in a mock ghostly motion and tell me it was either a perfume-savvy ghost or wishful thinking on my part. Or both. Naturally, it was neither, and within minutes, I was back dozing, the mellow voice of Eva Cassidy urging me to continue to chase elusive rainbows and embrace our wonderful world.

The next thing I heard was Francesca's shrill voice, breaking the sound barriers with her animated outcry. "And now we have arrived to the shores of Lake Maggiore and the beautiful Villa Taranto. We will have two hours to keep for ourselves."

We all woke up. Apparently, we had all missed the quaint old-world town of Baveno with its peculiar mix of pre- and post-industrialism five kilometres back down the road. Francesca admitted to not having wanted to awaken us up then with her microphone, opting instead to wait until we reached the pretty perimeters of Villa Taranto on the western shores of Lake Maggiore. Which was now!

A few people even stood up to get their bearings and to admire the expansive shimmering, rippling blue lake, fed by the glacial waters of the Alps, from an upright position. I followed suit with my iPhone, eager to capture my first impression of Lake Maggiore, even though before this trip, I had always assumed the only Italian lake to be Como.

The lakes of Northern Italy hadn't featured highly on Australian schools' curriculums, and even though a rapid recitation of the Great lakes of the United States of America both forwards and backwards was common practice, the Italian lakes were unheard of in my day. Nowadays, the endless blue Italian water-pools, nestled at the feet of many an alp, have risen in status to match the likes of monster Lakes such as Victoria, Superior and even Lake Windemere in England.

A bridesmaid in the wings, Lake Como (cousin to Lake Maggiore), has George Clooney to thank for being the name on everyone's lips. No sooner had the suave George purchased his lakeside villa, than Lake Como became as synonymous with Italy as was the Colosseum or the Trevi Fountain with Rome. By the looks of things, Lake Maggiore would give Como a run for her money if more of the jet-set decided to move in. I did remember one thing about the lakes, and that was that many an English or American writer or poet had lain temporary (or sometimes permanent) lakeside roots in Northern Italy, especially in the post-World war idyllic times of the fifties and sixties. It would be interesting to hear what the local Guides had to say about the history of the Italian Lakes, when they wrenched the microphone from the feisty Francesca.

Listening to our illustrious tour leader dishing out instructions on how to best behave on our first unguided excursion of the trip-the elaborate Italianate gardens in front of which we were now parked, I realised that the process of scoring a local Guide might turn out to be more of a sweaty tug-of war than a docile handing over of the burning torch. Francesca did not look like a woman ready to give up her audience without a fight-even if most of them were sleeping most of the time.

The perfumed spring air was beautiful. A moist and dry co-existence, as if neither state needed to triumph when they could thrive side by side in this vortex of deep peace. After days of continuous combative Italian drizzle, the blue sky and balmy scented breeze made for a nice change. It was like tumbling off the bus into the garden of Eden-Italian style, which was strange because the Villa and gardens had been the much-loved abode of a Scotsman with Australian parentage. No seeming association with Mesopotamia there!

Since Alice and I were the only Australian travellers on the bus, I thought that must count for something in the souvenir shop. I whispered to her that I would be bringing up the finer details of Mr Neil Boyd McEacharn's heritage, but she was not interested in this associative claim to fame. (Possibly because she had lived in England for so long.)

One person was interested in my news. Francesca! "Fil, that is a truly marvellous story. How do you know this? Is the founding father your relative?" I had to laugh. As soon as anyone heard of anyone living in the same country as oneself, they were automatically a cousin or close relative. Or they lived in the next street to you. Ridiculous.

Francesca must have realised from the look on my face that I considered her proposals ludicrous, as she quickly turned away from me, shot her umbrella high into the air and began delivering her next set of instructions to the whole group, the first one being to, "Follow my umbrella." My marvellous, country-of-origin connections were about as useful to me as 'String theory'.

I was lingering at the end of the snaking umbrella line. From my distance, in the wispy haze wafting up from the stunning lake, Francesca resembled one of the entitled tigers in a story from my childhood-one I had stored in the back-blocks of my mind, unearthed until this very second. It was not the text I recalled, but the vibrant illustrations of a band of tigers, one of whom had stolen a small boy's umbrella, and paraded the jungle with the upright appendage coiled around his tail. I think it was red!

In an uncontrollable flood of memory, I relived that overload of colour-yellow trousers, purple waistcoat, blue shoes, and red umbrella. And here they were. All back and rebranded. The come-back tour! Guised as flowers and foliage of primary colours, now boasting offspring of pinks and indigoes, tangerines, and cobalt-blues. A symphony of colour dwarfed by the very same palm trees which had delighted me in the classic story book. To the left, to the right, ahead, behind and above in the trellises and hanging baskets-a festival of flowers, ferns and palms. I felt a sudden tugging at my arm and looked up from my kaleidoscopic daydreaming into Matteo's dreamy eyes. From one dreamy scenario to another.

"Signora, you are well?" Eagle-eyed Matteo must have spied me, transfixed and motionless by the garden-entrance from his lookout position, the driver's seat, and when I had failed to follow the group, he must have become concerned. Perhaps I had unknowingly been swooning and taking deep gulping breaths whilst abandoning myself to a micro-meditative nature session, and that may have looked bad to Matteo as an observer.

I tend to get a trifle carried away when I commune with nature, and the momentary epiphany I had just experienced had left me limp and lightheaded. I was very tempted to let go completely and collapse into Matteo's white-shirted arms. Had I been twenty kilos lighter, I may have considered such a rash action, but those days were long gone. Matteo had an important job to carry out. That of safely delivering all passengers back to Milan in eight days' time. It would have been poor form on my part to have pounced on him on the first day of our county-jaunt.

"It's fine. I mean, I'm fine, I'm okay, I was just stopping to admire and smell the flowers, and I think I ingested too much of the strong perfume. Thanks Matteo, I'll just run and catch up to the others." Not true. There was no way I would be able to run, with my bags and camera and rain jacket. I couldn't run at the best of times, let alone with Matteo watching me.

I turned to face him, nearly passing out with the heady feeling of being so close to such a majestic Italian stallion. Then I blushed and managed to babble out. "Or maybe just walk quickly! That's what I'll do. Walk quickly. Bye Matteo." I fled, even though it must have looked a cumbersome, hopping fleeing. I didn't look back, so I had no idea whether or not Matteo remained there watching me, but it didn't matter. I had saved face, and more importantly, Matteo had been saved from having to support my weight against him.

I thought of Bridget Jones, and the awkwardness of relationships. I then got my second wind and slowing down to coronation pace, flounced ceremoniously through the iron gates into the thin neck of the gardens which led into the hilly terraces of Taranto.

By the time I sighted Alice, she had made her way up the first incline, and I had to call out to her to stop, so focussed was she on her pilgrimage. It was going to be tough, walking and trudging up the steep slopes of the Taranto Gardens, but I was so thrilled to be there, so unbelieving that I was actually at the top of the world-in Italy and in a garden I had admired in Guide books for years, that I hardly noticed the extreme perpendicular gradation.

Alice had decided to rest on one of the wooden benches along the path, and wait for Roy to shuffle past, and then she planned to invite him for tea and cake in the tearooms. For two reasons. Firstly, because Roy shared a similar ailment, and the Taranto gardens were not the best place to be practising exercise and rehabilitation, and secondly, because Roy had shown his appreciation and understanding of Italian practice and etiquette back at the road side café when none of us had known what to do or what to order. Chances were, Roy of-the-dark-glasses would be up for an encore, and Alice would curb the hungry haywire butterflies in her stomach.

"I'm still not sure if it is considered rude to order a cappuccino before or after lunch, so hopefully Roy will know what to do. Do you want me to get you a takeaway coffee and wait at the end of the path with it for you, Fil?" I declined her kind offer as I wasn't sure how long it would take me to complete the sixteen-hectare circuit. Cold cappuccinos I could live happily without. I had my water and trail mix. The small packets of nuts and berries I had buried somewhere in the back-blocks of my backpack were a concession to the lady in the hiking and camping shop in central Melbourne who had thrown in a few packets of grazing food for me as a bonus for having spent hundreds of dollars on a waterproof fold-up rain jacket.

"You never know when they might come in handy when you're stuck out on an icy precipice near the Matterhorn." She had smiled approvingly when she mentioned the Matterhorn. Not that I intended to be anywhere near the Matterhorn unless I was able to view it from the comfort of an air-conditioned train. And that would be unlikely because we would not be venturing all that near to the Alps. And now here I was, unwittingly less than one hundred kilometres (as the crow flies) from the very mountain she had singled out, and not a drop of rain to be felt.

For prosperity's sake, and because it was heavy on my arm, I pulled on the jacket. One could never be too prepared. Francesca was nowhere to be seen, and Matteo was back on the bus. Alice was waiting for Roy, and possibly Yolanda, but the others must have been somewhere close by. Unless of course they had set off at a cracking pace and were by now, up and over the hill, in the thick of botanica. I remembered that a few of the younger couples had been dressed in tracksuits, polo shirts and runners. Perfect lakeside attire, and even more perfect for blending in with the locals.

I knew we wouldn't be the only group here this morning. Even though it was still relatively early, the crowds were beginning to build up. The tourists were easy to spot, but then again, some of the locals from nearby towns could also have been flitting up and down the terraces, dodging behind hedges and conifers in their tracksuits. Sixteen-hectare was quite an open space. I sat down on a wooden bench at the top of the first incline and began to read about the ex-pat

Scotsman with the Australian parents who had fulfilled his dream in establishing these gardens.

What an imagination, and how much money he must have had! He certainly had picked a spectacular spot to accomplish his 'magnum opus'. A perfect temperate micro-climate in which to cultivate the rarest of rare plants. He'd had to cut down two thousand trees to achieve his dreams.) All around me, the vegetation and flowers craved affection. I tried to give the ones to my left and right my undivided attention, but it was impossible to favour one clump over another in this garden-the largest in Northern Italy, and one of the most famous in the world.

It was hard to imagine there were over twenty thousand species of flowers and plants in the gardens. Surely Captain Neil, the original owner, could not have envisaged such a prolific crop when he'd cleared the land of all those trees more than three quarters of a century ago? Now, it would be like counting grains of sand to be able to account for every flower petal in every flower bed. I was finding it difficult to describe the beauty of Taranto, even to myself, let alone into the 'voice memo' section of my phone.

I would need to create quite a few folders if I were to do justice to the enormity and magnificence of the Gardens. I considered myself a gardener of sorts. How would it be possible to bottle these sights and smells and take them back home with me? The vast stretches of green, the mini forests and the marvellous elder and chestnut trees. It truly was a garden of Eden. I had seen some gracious gardens in my travelling days, from the Eden Project in Southern England to the sprawling lawns of Powerscourt in Ireland.

The immaculate, flat green Gardens of the Palace at Versailles would have to be up there somewhere as well, but this beauty, this stark paradise of greens and golds was something else with which to be reckoned. Luminous and earthy at the same time. Punctuated plantings of green and gold. The gorgeous lake in the distance could never be ignored. With every corner I rounded, the lake seemed to grow more expansive and a deeper blue, until, in my mind's eye I was so close, I could have scooped up a handful of soothing water, had my arms been long enough. It was really all about perspective, and I was summing up the nearness of the lake with my artist eye.

I would paint it with artistic perspective. In reality, the lake was more like two hundred metres away, but the distance dissipated with my artistic illusion of space and time. The Irish, with their own peculiar mysticism and spirituality speak of distance as being in the eye of the beholder, and their thinking is appreciative of a real 'time-space continuum'.

I was both Irish and Italian, and therefore doubly entitled to fanciful conjecture concerning the proximity of the lake. Speaking of which, I would need to pick up my pace if I were to cover the entirety of the gardens. That was the thing about bus-trips. No lingering allowed. If one fell in love with a place, as I had done this morning with Taranto, one would need to return at one's leisure, because the fact of the matter was, 'the bus would simply not wait!' I still hadn't seen anyone I recognised, and when I tried to look back for Alice—she too had disappeared. The Gardens would have been a choice background location for an Agatha Christie's murder mystery, as people just kept disappearing into thin air.

Not to be dissuaded by a lack of company, I left the comfort and solace of the resting bench with the background of sweet birdsong behind and set off on a solo circumnavigation of the gardens. Which took all of thirty minutes! I could have spent longer near the extravagant bubbling fountains, on the pale green spinifex-infested ridge overlooking the villa, under swaying coccus-palms or even dancing in the warm breeze with the 'carnivale' of fifteen hundred border plants and flowers which were everywhere-hydrangeas, azaleas, rhododendrons, marigolds, lilies, lavender, cottage plants and many hundreds more. Or, for an added touch of solitude and solace, I could have lost myself in the Rhododendron wood and Victorian Green house with the Vertical gardens.

All flowers and plants were in late spring bloom, and all putting on the show of their lives. It was spectacular. The only thing spoiling my absolute delight was the fact that I wasn't one hundred percent sure of the hour Francesca had nominated for reconvening, and couldn't find anyone from our bus to confirm the hazy notion I had in my head, which was an hour and a half from when we had been dropped off outside the Garden gates. (Remembering I had wasted twenty minutes drooling over Matteo.)

To top it all off, my phone rang and it was my sister CJ, calling to see how my trip was going. (As they do when you are at the top of a hill, overlooking a lake, in Northern Italy.) "We're all here, Fil. We're all gathered around the phone. Who do you want to speak to first, or will I put you on speaker?"

The 'we all' part was the most concerning. It could mean two people, or it could mean thirty (excluding the babies who couldn't yet talk). I thought fast. "Can I call you when we get back to the hotel this afternoon? Would that be too late? I'm just not sure how many hours Italy is behind Australia. I think it's nine hours, so it will be around eight that I'll ring you. It's very hard to hear you."

CJ was one of those people who just cruised along the river of life in a slow-moving houseboat. She was happiest when she knew everyone in her world was safe and happy. Me included. And I was safe-she had my assurance. Not to mention deliriously happy in the magnificent gardens of Villa Taranto which had been on my visiting wish list for as long as I could remember. We hung up with promises of a longer chat tonight.

As I went to slip my phone back into my pocket, I noticed another message flashing, even though there had been no alert. It was from Alice, who'd met up with Roy and was now texting to let me know that even though there was still half an hour of sightseeing to relish, some of the passengers were already settled back on the bus, herself and Roy included. In the next twenty minutes, I whizzed around the gardens like super-girl herself. The tortoise had become the hare, and nothing escaped my greedy eyes.

The terrain was decidedly hilly, and the grass a little wet underfoot in places thanks to the recent rains, but by and large, it was one of the more pleasant romps I had undertaken through any windy, hilly terrain. Anywhere!

Even with my lightning speed, I was the second last person to jump back on the bus, the last being Francesca, who had been blocking the bus-steps with her clipboard, ticking off people's names as they high-fived her on their way past. The back doors were still locked, so Francesca was not making the same mistake she had made at the roadside café this morning when the repetition of the headcount was threefold. I would have been earlier, but it had been difficult not to heed the call of the souvenir shop.

I was in and out of there in two minutes with trophies of two tiny Taranto plates and a chunky guidebook of the Lakes district. (I left an olive branch on the counter for the woman as a surprise, whilst she was tissue-wrapping the plates.) The gang were all there, smiling at me and waving as I made my way to my seat. Alice had already propped herself up against window with her travelling neck cushion and a thin rug around her shoulders and lap. All she needed was the rocking chair and a pair of knitting needles.

Once we were on our way, I remembered I had just passed a woman head bent in a pair of large wooden needles, and I wanted to ask her what she was knitting, and boast to her that Alice was an accomplished needleworker and seamstress who had won prizes and that her framed needlework had been exhibited over the years in many amateur needlework shows. Tomorrow would be soon enough for exchanging niceties and favourite past times with fellow passengers. For the next hour I would be dozing. I wished I'd had a 'Please do not disturb sign' to hang around my neck, but the eye mask I had saved from the plane would just have to do.

Chapter 18
More for the Garden Lovers

The mask must have done the trick because I knew nothing until we'd pulled up along the foreshore. Not even Francesca's voice had penetrated my subconscious. All that mountain-goat gallivanting up and down the inclines of Taranto gardens had done me in.

It was Alice who brought me back to this world. She too had been grabbing forty winks and had only woken up after the bus pulled up in a look-out spot for a photo stop as we cruised along the shores of beautiful Lake Maggiore. Apparently, there had been no takers for the chance to capture the sensational earthen and celestial views, and Matteo had not even needed to swoosh open the doors-most of the passengers having been dozing or reading. And it had started to drizzle again.

"Fil? What has gotten into you today? Why are you so sleepy?" I had no idea what had gotten into me, but I hoped I would be able to shake off the blanket of sleep before this afternoon's promised excursion to the island of San Giulio. (Not that I had much of an idea what to expect once we got there.) I was getting things muddled up in my mind, thinking it was today that we would be visiting the island of Isola Bella and exploring the palace-summer residence where we would be exploring the grounds and the castle. But that was scheduled for tomorrow, not today.

Taranto Gardens may have been the largest in Northern Italy, but the gardens of Isola Bella were reputedly beyond the superlative. Hard to imagine when we'd just left Taranto-but time would tell. To ease my confusion, I kept repeating over and over in my head, "today the island of San Giulio, and tomorrow Isola Bella", all the while keeping my head pressed to the window in readiness of my first glimpse of the Borromean islands. There was an almost supernatural mystique to the name. Borromean islands sounded like they should crop up in the sea of Tranquillity on the moon, not in the middle of Lake Margorie in Italy.

It was not possible! I had opened my eyes to a slice of heaven which ebbed and flowed for kilometres, ribboning the bus as we meandered past the shoreline. Not even the term 'Exquisite' (overworked to the point of floggings in these parts) could do justice to this unbelievable vista. It was just so picture perfect, so pristine, so tranquil, so magical that everyone on the bus, Francesca included, was muted into stunned silence. Books were abandoned, iPods flung afar, arguments suspended and journal writing disgraced, in the face of the real thing.

This 'Bellissima' sight was something to be savoured by the senses—compelling, heady viewing. I suddenly understood how our tour had escalated to the status-title 'Italian Lakes' and not just ordinary old 'Northern Italy'. These lakes were undecidedly the jewel in the crown. Every day from now on, we would be embracing them, from the shores to the water itself.

Undeniably, the western shore of Lake Maggiore had been a superb backdrop to the Taranto Gardens, but we had moved on-now brave enough to reach out and almost touch the lake-to tease, to taunt, to tantalise the senses. There was nothing ominous or foreboding about the bold blue body of water in front and to the side of us. It was pure painters' light—a flat blue canvas stretching to the horizon. We were ready to surrender ourselves to the majesty of Maggiore. (At least I was. I couldn't speak for the rest of the passengers, but I could safely include Alice, who had almost used up the entirety of her iPhone storage supply and we'd only seen one lake.)

The naming ceremony for the Lake had not been in vain. Lake Maggiore was the larger of the five big Italian lakes, hence—'Major'. It was fitting that we were embracing the largest lake on the first day of our Lakes district venture, as it would be setting the highest of high bars for the sister Lakes. If Francesca had it right, visitors had been flocking to the shores of Lake Maggiore since the late nineteenth Century. Once this view of brilliant blue water, with the three craggy islands in almost touching distance was truly digested, the siblings would never be more than icing on the cake.

None of us could manage to shut our gaping mouths. To the casual observer, we would have resembled row upon row of open-mouthed side-show alley clowns. After minutes of initial silence, a train of awed whispering and oohing began to echo the bus, until finally, Francesca found her microphone, and began furiously tapping away to snap us out of our collective stupor (equivalent to slapping us all across the cheeks)

"Nowa. Here is something to wake you, eh? Something to make the hair coming from your neck stand up! This is the true Lake Maggiore. We could see it from Taranto Gardens, yes, but now we can feel it. We can see it so close. We can truly smell and taste the water."

I was too dumbstruck to comprehend Francesca. I had felt this way before in my travels and recognised this strangely disconcerting feeling which required more than a stiff drink. (Now would be a good time for Francesca to don her frilly white apron, strap the drinks tray to her shoulders, and tiptoe up and down the aisle offering plastic cups full of Chianti.)

I was in the throes of a mega outer-body experience, from which it would take an overload of energy to recover. Sitting down might also work. I needed to stop the blood rushing to my head. Alice was quiet for once, her face still pressed to the window, busily snapping angle after angle of the lake. I could imagine her back home in London, agonising over which shot of the majestic lake stood out enough to warrant printing off and framing. If not a photograph, it would make a beautiful tapestry if Alice could pull it off.

I thought of other places of such incredible silent grandeur and grace-The Grand Canyon in the United States, The Taj Mahal in India and Uluru in Australia. I'd had the same feelings I was now experiencing in all of those places, and possibly many more. Stonehenge England, the Cliffs of Mohar Ireland, Niagara Falls Canada-come to think of it, there were a few about. I thought about the insightfulness of Giuseppe Verdi, reputed to have to have said he would grant his public the universe if he could only have his beloved Italy. Here was the essence of Verdi's' challenge.

Francesca must have noticed my sinking back into my seat, as she was by my side in a flash. "Fil, are you unwell? Can you walk to the front and Matteo will stop the bus?"

I wasn't unwell, I was just in the first flush of love again. Not with any tall dark mysterious Italian, but with a suave, smooth, flat, gloriously shimmering blue chiffon curtain which stretched out as far as the eye could see. Luigi had got it all wrong organising for Graziella's ashes to be scattered over Lake Como. Lake Maggiore should have been his sole consideration. Not having seen Lake Como before, I could not imagine any lake rivalling this beauty before us. But time would tell, and in six days, when we reached Lake Como, I might just have to eat my words, and the ashes could stay intact. Time would tell.

Interestingly enough, our tour was designed to have headed straight to Lake Como today, but because of the cycling tour around Northern Italy, the Tour Company in their foresight and wisdom had kindly rearranged the itinerary, rescheduling our visit to Lake Como to the last day of the trip. Again, a coincidence of circumstance that Alice and I had encountered the tall, lean quartet of elite cyclists at the airport, where one of the team had unfortunately lost his bicycle. Had we not encountered the group at Lost Property, we would not have realised there was a race on, and been none the wiser that our Lake Como visit and boat ride had been pushed to the back blocks on the itinerary.

Meanwhile, the bus had stopped and Francesca was guiding me out of my seat as if I had lost both my sight and my senses, down the aisle to the front doors and out onto the pavement. No one else moved from their seats, possibly fearful that I had been struck down with some dreadful, contagious disease, and was about to be escorted off the bus and ferried across the lake by speedboat to Switzerland. (We were only twenty-five miles from the Swiss border.)

Of course, there was not a thing wrong with me, but they were not to know that. I was surprised no one else jumped off the bus in hot pursuit, but they all remained in their seats-complacent and slightly suspicious. (Accustomed to frequent spectacle status, I could feel suspicious looks when they were fired at my back.)

Still, I didn't mind.

With the entire waterfront marina to myself, I was free to take as many close-up shots of the lake as my heart desired. It had not been my intention for Matteo to have stopped the bus on this boardwalk, or for Francesca to have jumped back on to inform the rest of the passengers that, "one of us—the Australian woman—is not feeling good. So, we stop the bus, eh! And we wait. It's the best thing to do."

I could hear her short, out-of-breath microphone soliloquy from where I was standing at the foot of the bus, and immediately put away my phone. Being lynched by irate passengers to whom I had not yet been formally introduced, was not included in my plans for Day One. Luckily, I was bending over at the front of the bus and not halfway along, or many more passengers might have seen me snapping away. Not a good look when one is supposed to be ailing. Quick as a flash, I mounted the bus steps and almost knocked Francesca over at the top. Matteo laughed, and Francesca looked startled. "You are all better now, Fil?"

I gave her my best smile and best assurance that I was perfectly refreshed from the blast of fresh lakeside air and scurried back to my seat. Normally, I can't scurry on cue, but I felt a trifle embarrassed that the bus had stopped and no one except me had alighted. Alice had returned to an upright position in my absence. Her iPhone was nowhere to be seen, which meant she had finished taking photos. Sinking back into my seat, I closed my eyes and prayed for the hotel.

I would not be opening my eyes until then, and it would be debatable whether or not I would have the courage to face the other passengers, especially those who had been at the front of the bus, and surely must have witnessed me selfishly talking photos of the Gulf of Borromeo and the magnificent lake. Francesca had put the microphone away, after informing us that the little hamlet of Stresa—our stopover for the next two nights—was only five minutes up the road and that as our hotel wasn't quite yet ready, we would be stopping for lunch at the little lakeside village.

Stresa, according to the guidebook, was over one thousand years old and had played second fiddle to Milan for as long as anyone could remember, when it came to providing lakeside accommodation for the aristocracy. Had 'Hotels.Com' been around in those days, many a count, earl, duchess or even a Queen in need of a holiday would have been blessed to have found themselves summer digs in and around these parts. As we approached Stresa, Francesca again interrupted conversations. She was certainly in fine form this morning.

"In two minutes, we will arrive to Stresa. It is a nice little place. We can have time to room around. Please don't be late back for the bus, and do not eat too much of the local fish for lunch, or you will be too heavy for the bus to take you, and you will have to walk back to the hotel. In the rain." Francesca had added the 'in the rain' postscript when a loud clap of thunder had reverberated over the roof of the bus, and an almighty downpour had followed suite. She was however, nonplussed, probably well accustomed to these lunchtime/maritime squalls. After all, we were on a lake, and lakeside weather was notoriously temperamental.

Francesca's parting words to the lot of us were, "And nowa run like goats througha the town. You must act like it is the mafia themselfes chasing you, and you will suddenly find the dry restaurants." This time, I was determined not to be last off the bus, even if it meant pushing and jostling my way to the front. Our seat was about seven back from the front doors, and it looked as though Matteo would not be opening the back ones. It would have to be fight or flight.

I realise it was no excuse, but I felt compelled to act in the way I did. It just wouldn't have looked good to have lingered whilst the others raced over the zebra crossing to the cobblestone paths on the other side, housing shops and restaurants. Matteo would have definite cause to think I was hanging back like a teenager with a teacher-crush. I didn't have a crush. I wasn't interested. Not in the market! It just didn't hurt to steal a glance towards the back of his tanned, muscled neck whilst on the way down the aisle, did it? Matteo did not move his head, and I was forced off the bus in the throng of passengers all eager for a daily soaking.

Stepping on to the pavement of the 'Lungomare' (promenade) at Stresa was exactly like being in Cannes, about to take up seats at the film festival. It was uncannily similar. To the point that there were similar baskets of cottage-impatience and bright red azaleas, and the smooth honeysuckle coloured concrete of the pavement. The balmy air was the same temperature too, even though it had not been raining on the long weekend when I had visited Cannes in a France some years back. The peaceful, trance-like feeling of the whole place was hard to resist savouring, but there was no way I was going to stand there rooted to the spot waiting for Matteo to appear.

"Come on, Alice. Chop, chop! We've only got an hour and there seems to be so much to see and savour on the other side of this zebra crossing. Are you ready?" The snooze on the bus followed by the frenzied photography must have done Alice a world of good, because five minutes later, we were taking shelter from the rain in Frederico's smart bag and jewellery shop in the cobble-stoned street directly behind the main one which had been crammed with restaurants cafes and souvenirs shops when we had hurried past.

We might have missed the handbag and jewellery shop altogether, as the front display window was high and narrow, and I had set a cracking pace for us in our circumnavigation of this tiny narrow-waisted hilltop town.

After the zebra crossing caper, where all passengers took to the stripes, it had been like the starting pistol of the 'Great Italian Lakes' race had been fired into the misty air. Alice and I had started off with the best of them, securing a pretty safe position by the middle of the crossing, but once safely across to the other side, the participants in the 'great lakeside town tour race' were not to be seen for dust. Had we been in a hot-climate environment such as a desert or similar terrain, the dust kicked up by the pack would have been as substantial as that from prize-winning horses competing for the Melbourne Cup race.

As it was, the water sent flying from the muddy puddles was worse, as both Alice and I were not fast enough to jump aside and we ended up soaked. That was also how we ended up outside Federico's, as the shop was adjacent to a little horseshoe-shaped covered arcade where we were glad to take shelter and a breather. A fatal decision for a recovering shopaholic such as myself.

Before this big trip (of which the Northern lakes tour was the first of four of my booked bus tours), I had scoured the shopping centres and online sites in Melbourne with a mile-long list of clothing and items, makeup and toiletries I may have needed in the two months I would be away. I had also watched countless YouTube clips in an effort to minimalize my packing and stop myself from procuring unnecessary items online. The clips had been useful, and my normal expenditure had been ever-so-slightly curbed, but I was still a woman with an addiction to buying.

The trouble with me was I just loved giving presents and gifts to people. The live olive branches would go part of the way to feeding my addiction in Italy, but the need to buy presents for friends and family back home could not be snuffed out in one foul swoop. Like a recovering alcoholic-it would take time and a great deal of patience. My umbrella was soaking—a big wet shaggy dog with the name 'Milan' splayed across the wired folds.

Whilst I had been shaking it, Alice had been busy peering through the glass doors into the bag shop. Alice loved bags almost as much as I loved perfume bottles. She collected and stored them, hardly using a handbag for more than a month before replacing it with an even bigger and better one from her enormous collection. Her cupboards were full of handbags, to the point where clothes were displaced onto the dining-room chairs she had dragged into her bedroom whilst the bags took pride of place on the shelves.

"Look at those beautiful bags in this shop, Fil. Shall we go inside and have a browse? Not that I intend to buy a new bag or anything, I just want to have a look. They'll probably all be out of our price range."

I had to admit the shop looked warm, dry and inviting, and it would be a break from the rain and the mad rush around the little town. "Sounds good to me, Alice."

I was doing it again. Surrendering to that voice in my head urging me to feed my shopping hunger. It would have been better to have left Alice there and to have made my way down the hill to the trattorias and restaurants, in search of lunch. It was just that the display in the widow of beautiful colourful leather and suede bags as well as exquisitely coloured glass jewellery was hard to resist.

Alice and I synchronised our phones and entered the shop. We had a good ten minutes to spare, but anything beyond that would be pushing it.

Anyone selling jewellery and handbags had to be a gentle soul, and Frederico did not disappoint. He left us alone to browse for a few minutes, and then quietly appeared beside me, commenting on the richness of the green glass in the tiny bracelet I was admiring. I was certain it was Murano glass, as I'd had a similar one from Murano beyond Venice which I had worn for years until one day it suddenly disappeared. Today might just be my chance to replace it,

"We call that Murano glass. From somewhere, not too far away from here. Do you like the glass? It has a wonderful shine to it."

Frederico was earnest and sweet. The kind of shop proprietor who isn't out to sell you what you don't need-but something which took your eye or tugged at your heart strings with a strong grip. I ended up with a small delicate green glass bracelet, and Alice with an enormous cobalt blue handbag which I had no idea where she would be storing. At least my purchase was tiny enough to wear on my wrist without causing too much fuss.

Whilst he wrapped Alice's bag in copious amounts of brightly coloured tissue paper, Fredrick chatted away in a soft, soothing, storytelling voice, relating the history of the little town of Stresa, and letting us into his world of retail in a blue-blood and tourist town. He told us that the rain, and the fact that it was a weekday, was the main reason the cobblestone streets were not flooded with tourists.

"If you come to my shop on the weekends, it will be much difference. Too many people and nobody buying much, just looking." I told him that the Australian term for this type of a person was a 'sticky-beak', and although he looked perplexed, he still smiled at the way I demonstrated what a typical sticky beak would be up to in his shop.

Just before we left, I handed him an olive branch, and he reciprocated with his business card, assuring us that we could order online from back home, and that we would both receive twenty percent discount for our troubles. It sounded like a perfect deal to me, and there were smiles all around.

Frederico promised to put the olive branch in water straight away, even though I had carefully cocooned all fifty of them in a moistened cotton wool ball. We left on a high, pleased with our purchases and ready to eat a horse.

Chapter 19
Soaking It Up in Stresa

It wasn't a horse as such, but I was close! The roll was stuffed with thin layers of something almost certainly equine. The vending stall from which we had made our purchases was a colourful addition to the little piazza upon which we'd stumbled, with the body of the restaurant positioned across the 'pedestrian-only street'. The connection between the two food outlets was unmissable-the identical name having been scratched flamboyantly in red and black across their respective coverings—the canvas canopy and red-tiled roof—Carlo's.

To continue the horse affiliation, it had been Alice's idea to purchase an extra-long roll filled with vegetables and salad from the street vendor, her reasoning being that we only had half an hour left in which to complete our exploration of Stresa, which could be accomplished on foot, eating on the run. Francesca had mentioned grandmothers ruling the roost in Italy, and I remembered my own grandmother on my mother's side to have held her own strong opinions on eating in public places.

She had always instilled in my mother—as my mother had in turn with her own children—the vulgarity of being observed eating in the street, and that if one could not afford a restaurant—or found oneself too far away from home to sit at a kitchen table—then one was to go hungry! Under no circumstances should one surrender oneself to vulgarity. No one had ever died from not eating for a day or two.

Ordinarily, I was able to live out my grandmother's dying wishes, but today I was exceptionally hungry, and I rationalised to myself that it hadn't been my idea, but Alice's, to eat as we'd continued to sightsee. I did, however, insist on a compromise, and that was how Alice and I came to be sitting directly opposite our locked, empty bus, munching on the last of our salad and mortadella rolls. A long-winded explanation, granted, but a necessary setting of the scene for what happened next.

We had crossed over the zebra crossing in total gay abandon. Not a soul in sight. Feasting on fresh lakeside fish and delectable lakeside crustations must have been the order of the day in any one of the many Stresa seafood restaurants. The trattorias (I had been practising using the Italian terms as they sounded more authentic) had been bulging with customers as we'd passed by, and Alice had spotted Roy with his leg propped up on a chair, in the midst of a flock of waiters.

I hadn't recognised Roy but had noticed quite a few of the meticulously dressed waiters fussing over a gentleman, their tight black pants, crisp white shirts with red and black suspenders being hard to miss. Very chic and snazzy, yet, at the same time-very provincial-Italian. At that stage we had been women with a mission, keen to find a quiet picnic spot where we could flop down and unwrap the edible treasures of Stresa for which we had just traded fifteen euro.

Beyond the striped crossing had been the bus, and directly beyond the bus-the deep glorious lake. We found a bench, plonked down, and each took a huge, greedy, bite from our portion of the bread roll. (The roll had been made up as a foot long roll and brutally hacked in half by the overworked vendor) She, of the ample bosom and bursting red cheeks, had halved the roll in one foul swoop with an overlarge, over-gleaming butcher's knife.

Bang!

The enormous thick wooden chopping board had reverberated, but not as violently as did the hungry crowd who had decided to imitate us in our novel idea of hosting a picnic. (A new busload of tourists must have docked in the marina carpark, and as it was right on lunchtime; they too would have been famished.) I made a note not to end up within cooee of the volatile vendor-woman at the day's end when inevitably she would be cold, wet, tired and fed up with tourists such as ourselves. Such arduous primitive outdoor conditions and large gleaming butcher's knives should, under no circumstances, ever be wed. (In retrospect, there was something very Hannibal Lector-esque about that woman.)

Apparently (I found out later from a local shopkeeper), the roll was a 'Stresa speciality'. The vending woman, who was "stressa…d" out herself, had been coveting the long roll as she'd piled on the vegetables, and for this reason, I had not noticed her deftly layering the mortadella pieces onto the top layer of salads and vegetables as one would lay out a suit of cards. It would have been one very ingenious way to get meat into a person if they happened to be low in iron. That wasn't me though.

Woe betide anyone who tried to tell me I was iron-deficient. I had iron literally oozing out of my pores. I didn't, would not, could not, eat red meat under any circumstances, and today would be no exception. As delicately as I could manage, I eased my mouthful of mortadella into my serviette and threw the offending remains into the nearest bin. Contrary-Alice was slow to react.

In fact, she was delighted the salad and vegetable roll was supplemented with meat. She knew my dietary habits like the back of her hand, but was enjoying her chomping and masticating so much that my unfounded aversion to red meat of any description must have somehow slipped her mind. When she did react, it was to question my whereabouts, the teacher in her coming out again.

"Fil, what were you doing over at that bin? Did you drop something in there?"

I wanted to tell her that I had deposited ransom money in there, but then she would have wanted to know what the money was for, and it would not have been worth the rigmarole involved in letting her know I was only joking.

I sighed inwardly and let it go. (My mantra for the trip.) It was best that Alice did not realise I had thrown away good food, and it was also best that Alice did not realise that she was eating semi-refined horse product. In Australia, we call the product mortadella, but it was more often referred to as 'sfilacci' in Northern Italy. In reality, it was no different to eating kangaroo, which was becoming more acceptable of late—or any manner of game in England, even French snails. I knew that. I just couldn't come at horse.

Horses were so big and loud, glistening and sweaty, and I was afraid of them. Horses were for patting and jumping backwards from in shock when they threw back their heads neighing and shuddering in fits of madness. That was my idea of horses. I appreciated the thrill the horse lovers of the world, experienced from being perched pertly up on the saddle, and I wasn't ignorant of the revered place held by the horse in society. Horsepower was indirectly responsible for industrialisation, followed by Google and for that I would be forever grateful. Life without Google had been intolerable, especially for the traveller. So, thanks livestock of the world for getting us kick-started.

By the time I had picked all the mortadella out of my roll and disposed of the small shredded pieces in the nearby bushes, Alice had returned from the lake, towards which she had ambled down to 'wet her toes'. I'd thought briefly about following in her lumbered footsteps, but had spotted a gelato vendor, and the thought of a creamy Italian gelato appealed to me greatly.

"Alice, do you want a pistachio gelato from that stall over there?" Alice agreed enthusiastically that she would love something cool and liquifying after the coarseness of the roll. She had it in a nutshell with her description of the Italian delicacy. The roll had been fresh and the infused oily flavour delicious, but the texture was coarse, which made swallowing difficult. I had felt like a Viking tearing at a chunk of hardened bread stuffed with vegetables. Or, going back even further, imagining myself dressed in a loincloth and sandals, a club in my spare hand, should invaders land on the lakeshore in primitive hollowed out tree-trunk canoes. A gelato would be the perfect refinement we needed to reinstate ourselves as well-to-do tourists, possible bluebloods, in a well-to do lakeside town.

There were two women lined up at the gelati hut, whom I recognised as fellow travellers, even though we hadn't yet been introduced. They recognised me too, and one of them had even remembered my name, having heard Francesca calling me to follow her when I'd performed my 'walk of shame' earlier.

"You're Fil, aren't you? And your friend is the one with the sore leg? The one who couldn't dance at La Scala yesterday?" Was it only yesterday that we'd been immersed in Milan? It felt like far more than twenty-four hours ago.

So much had happened since then. The three of us chatted easily for a while, but the gelatos were starting to dribble down my arm, and I told them I had to run back over to Alice with her ice cream. They promised to continue our chat this afternoon, in our free time, and then ambled off companionly towards the bus. 'Gloria' and 'Natarsha'—both American.

Even melted, the gelatos were sweet, creamy and heavenly, and after sucking the last remaining drops from the bitten down wafer-triangle, I turned to Alice and, with deadpan inflection, uttered one solitary word: "More?"

She laughed, and we both ended up giggling as we trudged our way back to the bus. I told her about having met Natarsha and Gloria at the gelato-hut, and she was excited to think that there might now be the opportunity for a foursome. I tended to agree with her, as two can be intense, three a crowd, but four? Well there would be just so many more chances for a greater division of labour when it came to helping Alice and Roy conquer the insurmountable steps and stairs we would-sure as eggs encounter in two days' time when we came face to face with the mountainous paths of Cinque Terra!

By the time we reached the bus, most people were already seated. The whole ticking off process was much smoother than it had been the first time round this morning, when the latecomers had been missing in action for ten minutes.

"So, we are all here, yes? Did you enjoy Stresa?"

The response was an enthusiastic "Yes!" Francesca looked pleased with herself, as if she alone had been responsible for spearheading the lunch/sightseeing opportunity in such a picturesque lakeside hamlet.

"Nawa we will go to the hotel directly, and you will have the afternoon to unpack and look around some more. The hotel is the mirror to the lake. In Italy when someone says to you, 'go and jump in the lake', you come here. It is a big lake and we have room for everyone."

I wondered if Francesca had spent the entirety of the last hour researching quips about Italian lakes on TripAdvisor. She was an expert at knowing just which titbit or twist to throw into any conversation at exactly the right time. With more than fifty tours under her belt, it was no wonder she knew how to play the crowd.

Matteo, who had been hunched in intense concentration behind the wheel for the past five minutes, suddenly reverberated into action, and swung the bus hard into a narrow circular driveway, punctuated with large terracotta pots, brimming with red and white flowers. He had to zigzag his way past the giant earthen vessels-but he made it. Francesca called out loudly on the microphone, "bravo Matteo" and we all joined in with a chorus of "bravo, bravo!" A woman in the seat behind was calling out, "brava, brava" but I did not want to show off by turning around to inform her that an 'a' tagged to the end of an Italian word denoted femininity. Again, I let it go, and it felt good to be non-judgemental for once.

The wide, white, pebbled, driveway, bordered with an overenthusiastic supply of silver twisted iron had been the thick ceremonious ribbon to a rather fancy looking hotel. Very grand, very county, very lakeside. The old Europe of Viscounts and Barons, Duchesses and Dukes. And now us! A bus-load of bedraggled tourists, come to admire the beauty of the lakes and savour the relative peace and quiet of the softly breathing old dame with her vast flock of bedrooms tucked neatly into her folds of ample flesh.

"We ava arrived!"

Francesca may have been astute at slipping gems of information and witticisms into her monologues, but she was also a wiz at stating the bleedin' obvious. (To be fair, it may have been company policy to describe as many intricate details as possible in case some of the passengers had slight vision impairment.) I should mention that I too was visually challenged, but my impediment was nothing genetic; more likely, I was stumbling around wearing the wrong prescription glasses.

I'm pretty sure I've failed just about every eye test I've surrendered to in the last ten years, mainly because I didn't understand the questions. "Fuzzy or non-fuzzy?" Why would an optometrist even bother to ask you that? On almost every occasion I was perched up in that universal chair, my face glued to the glass frame in expectation of a well-deserved beheading for my ignorance of ophthalmic vocabulary, I'd had not a clue in the world as to the "fuzziness factor" of the letters. The bold, black letters themselves were even more of a challenge for me, and for the sake of peace, I would guess. And guess some more. No wonder I couldn't see when I finally procured my glasses. But as I said, that was nothing genetic, more likely, the wrong prescription strength of the glass.

Francesca was looking pleased with herself for the second time in as many minutes, and it would have been poor form for us not to have shown our appreciation for her and Matteo having delivered us safely to the swanky, if slightly middle-aged hotel, which was to be our illustrious accommodation for the next two nights.

It took a while, but all possessions and suitcases were finally unloaded-courtesy of Matteo. He had been managing single-handedly until a gorgeous Italian Adonis, dressed in porter's garb appeared on the scene, obviously sent out by the management to assist with arrivals. The baton must have been handed over to him, because when I opened our bedroom door to polite hesitant knocking fifteen minutes later-it was to the handsome young Italian porter, informing me that two cases were here, and enquiring if he might carry them into the room?

I was about to tell him he could carry me back across the carpeted threshold, after which I would gladly drag the cases back into the bedroom myself, but he had not waited for my delayed response, and was already through the door. I was about to wheel them in, when he picked up both cases and made his way ceremoniously into the bedroom, as if he were transporting luggage containing the heads of beheaded Roman emperors.

He was so particular in his positioning of the cases in the corner of the room, that I thought there must have been some sort of alert attached to them, warning hotel staff that we were the 'couple' (the Thelma and Louise of the North) who had caused so much trouble with suitcases at the previous hotel. I had a couple of euro in my tracksuit-pocket so I hastily handed them over. It did the trick. He smiled and bustled off.

Alice had been busy obliterating herself in the bathroom when the cases had arrived, so she'd missed witnessing the boy lugging them into the room. After he'd left, I took five long strides over towards the balcony, and flung open the pale-green double French doors a-la 'Room with a View'. Some things never change. The view of the still-blue glassy lake, bordered with gorgeous pink, purple and red foliage was timeless. Immortality finally grasped.

Even though there was a narrow stretch of road defining the hotel and the lake, it was very low and very flat, and could have been easily missed. The traffic was light, and bicycles were the go. Bikes and Tour buses like ours! Alice had joined me on the terrace, and we languished back in the white wrought-iron chairs to admire the view. Only our tracksuits bellied us as the eager tourists that we were.

Almost thirty minutes drifted by before we were able to rouse ourselves from that spectacular, mind-numbing scenic view. It was entrapment of the most glorious calibre. I found it hard to put my finger on just what trapped the room and the balcony to the nineteenth century, but there was no mistaking the fact that the entirety of the hotel was fixed in a pre-war time warp. (Just which war, was still up for debate.)

Terms such as ambience, quaintness, old-worldly, and just plain unequivocal ugliness came to mind. The room itself was baronial. Garish and more garish at the same time. Layers of garishness. Pale pinks and washed-out greens with thick white baroque furniture. Not a room in which I would want to spend an enormous amount of time. It was probably a matter of taste, and if you were a person who had once enjoyed aristocracy status but had unwittingly and unceremoniously fallen from grace in the aristocracy stakes, then this bedroom would have been the perfect witness protection hideaway. The whirls and twirls of wrought iron everywhere did nothing for me. Nor Alice.

"Let's stay out here for a while longer, Fil. The air is cleaner and fresher than it is in the room." She was cluey, that Alice! It was decidedly stuffy in the room, and warm to boot. We were much better off sitting out here on the balcony sipping from our water bottles and trying not to choke on dried apricots and cashews.

We ended up lingering outside for another ten minutes, watching the action in the car park below, and tracking the yachts on the lake, far out towards the horizon. It was a quiet, peaceful time of day, around two in the afternoon, and still too early for any real action. Children would still have been in school, and Nonnas would have finished preparing the customary veal and sauce for the evening meal.

The world was ebbing and flowing along without much disturbance to a 'hundreds of years' routine. Had I been in possession of a guidebook on the Borromean islands and a real drink, such as the martini Francesca had concocted a few days back, I would have been in my seventh heaven, and not needed to have budged from my seat for the next twenty-four hours.

As it was, I needed to muster up some money from somewhere, and stumbling upon an ATM machine in the foyer of this old-worldly hotel was probably as unlikely as finding a golden egg under my pillow.

"I think I'm going to have to go back up to Stresa and look for an outside teller machine, Alice. Do you want to come with me?"

Even as I uttered the words, I realised the impracticality of my suggestion, as it was a good twenty-minute jaunt back along the promenade, and in the last five minutes or so of our patio-sojourn, it had begun to spit, to the point of making our seats wet, slippery and uncomfortable. As predicted, Alice chose to stay behind. Her excuse was wanting to take some painkillers, dry herself down, and have a nap. We were scheduled to meet down in the foyer at four. The afternoon excursion promised to be an eye-opener in terms of extended lakeside beauty, and Alice wanted to be prepared in both mind and body. Not that there would be too much walking involved, as most of the afternoon would involve bus and boat travel-both low-key sedentary occupations.

Checking my phone, I realised with dismay that I only had an hour in which to sprint up to the little resort village, collect my cash, and claim a chaise-lounge in the foyer in readiness for the bus. It could be done. I would just need to put all my efforts into time management. Fifteen minutes to walk up to the town, half an hour negotiating the foreign bank, and fifteen minutes to scoot back. it was a plan. Which would have worked, had it not been pouring rain by the time I got down to the hotel foyer, had the bank not been so difficult to locate, and had I been permitted to enter the establishment when I finally found it. Another micro-adventure was in store for me, the moment I left the hotel foyer.

The street was almost deserted, save for a few straggling tourists who looked to be in the exact same boat. The leaky one! My raincoat became an instant Midori-coloured tributary of the lake opposite, and by the time I reached the first Stresa café, I was ready to shake off all the water like a flee-ridden shaggy Labrador, and head back to the hotel. Being penniless and unable to buy any more souvenirs was looming up as an appealing option. This had been no dry-run!

But I needed to stick to my plan, which did not include being a 'woos' and taking shelter until my fists were full of euro. Every minute was earmarked, and my mission was to find a bank and return as soon as possible. Apparently, banks were not the order of the day up near lakes or mountains. I trudged up and down three muddy lanes crammed with shops, most of which bore the sign 'Cuidi', before I finally found a local to ask for directions to a bank, and even then, the bent-over old man sitting in a doorway smoking, was a little rusty in his response.

"Banca? Hai bisogno della banca?" I nodded and he pointed, and that was the extent of our intense interaction. I tried to recall more from my years of studying Italian at night school, but banco was the best I could come manage. (Even then I wasn't convinced the word ended in an 'a' or an 'o'.) More than likely, asking for directions for a bank had not featured highly in the Italian textbook I had been using as my bible at the time. Shops, food, theatres and alcohol had been the extent of my need for Italian translations.

The old man came good. Once I had steered myself in the direction toward which he had pointed. Squinting helped, and with half-closed eyes to block out the drizzle, I could just make out a large, decrepit, crumbling building sitting sadly, smack bang in the middle of a piazza, with a tired, faded sign 'Banca'. Had soldiers in army tanks rattled up the hill, and unloaded provisions to store in their headquarters—this ancient, fortified bank—I would not have been in the least surprised.

The whole building, which occupied more than half of the piazza, looked as though it had been bombed every year for the past fifty years, rebuilt, and bombed again for good measure. I seriously doubted there would be an ATM in the decaying concrete wall encasing the building, but it was worth a shot having a squiz.

I didn't have to look far at all. The clues were there, right in front of my nose. Long lines of bodies shuffling forward slowly toward the building. The ATM itself (if it was indeed a teller machine and not the entrance gates to Dante's

Inferno which was obscured by the line of shufflers) was obscured by mostly old women with walking sticks and headscarves, and hard-to-mistake nuns (complete with wimples and heavy rosary beads which looked to be made of tint boulders of marble).

The light at the end of the tunnel (literally at the end of the line) was a flighty young thing, hopping from foot to foot in eager anticipation of retrieving cash. In stark contrast to the religious procession of black upon black, the girl was barely dressed in a yellow crop top and skimpy tan shorts-an extension of her very, very long, tanned legs. The whole effect was one of a short, stubby row of dark, silent hedge, swaying in the wind and drizzle, and a bewildered duckling at the tail end, flapping and dodging with the universal impatience of youth.

I decided to try my luck at interrogating her in Italian as to whether I might fare better by making my way inside the bank, instead of waiting in line. I realised blending in with the queue of locals was not an option for me. I had neither youth nor Nonna-status on my side, and my attire was entirely unsuitable. A glistening green raincoat such as mine would have drawn immediate unwanted attention, and I was not in the mood for a mugging.

"Scusi signora, mai e possible…veni dentro il banco?" Okay. It wasn't the interrogation I had planned, and I may have had a better chance of success by consulting Siri or the Babble dictionary for decent a slug of purist Italian, but I wasn't even certain the girl was Italian. She could have been a tourist as was I, and similarly in the dark when it came to Italian banking practice. I had it in the back of my mind that getting money out of Italy was akin to getting blood out of a stone. This unhelpful notion seemed to be emanating from somewhere in the back-blocks of my mind—from way back in my childhood when my father had taken me into an Italian bank in Southern Italy, and we had emerged two hours later with probably just enough cash to buy the evening meal.

My father had later explained to me the peculiarities of Italian-finance negotiations, which inevitably involved undignified waiting in long queues for a paltry pile of money and fighting one's way through layer upon layer of security guards in an effort to escape. Next to contend with would be the triple bolted revolving doors, not to mention the last lowly security guard, positioned in street-isolation, whose job it was to perform the final fleecing of the defeated customer. Granted, that was some time ago, but it didn't look like things would have changed much in this little town of Stresa—coming up for its bicentenary times five in the very near future.

The girl must not have spoken, full stop! Not Italian, not English, not a word. I tried repeating my request in English, but to no avail. She did smile at me, and kangaroo around a bit more, but apart from that, she was useless to my cause. And time was ticking at a much faster rate than the queue of crows and corpses was moving.

Immediate action was called for! I would need to face my fears and childhood traumas and venture into the great unknown. There were no Security guards lurking, and the big heavy wooden door leading into the bank was to the side of the ATM, so at least there would be some witnesses when the Italian news reported the disappearance of an Australian woman in a small town on the foreshores of a famous Italian lake.

Most people would assume I had drowned in Lake Como (the only lake anyone has probably ever heard of—and only then, I repeat—courtesy of George Clooney). They would never believe I had disappeared into the bowels of a bank. There was nothing really sensational about banks, unless one was involved in a heist gone haywire, compared to a mysterious drowning, but stranger things have happened. I pushed with all my might against the heavy door and, hey presto! I was in. More marble and concrete everywhere, but there was no going back now!

Chapter 20
Islands in the Rain

Forty-five minutes later, I was perched on the edge of a puffy armchair in the hotel foyer, resplendent in dry clothing with just a touch of evening glitz, on the off-chance that we didn't get time to revisit the hotel before the evening excursion. My concession to 'glitz' was a top with sprinklings of silver, matched with black stove-pipe pants. I had stashed a necklace of comfy colourful beads in my handbag, in case more 'glam', was the go, but time would tell. Alice had not even bothered with glitz. She was convinced we would be returning to the hotel before the evening meal, and her track record for prophesies was not to be sneezed at. Time would tell.

After I had set foot in the bank, things had moved along pretty smoothly. None of my phobias had come to fruition, but then again, I left the expansive mausoleum of a room, penniless and with my head down. When I say 'smoothly', think of the 'smooth' running of the tube in London. About as smooth a rattlesnake's rippled spine.

Firstly, the door closed firmly behind me, and would not budge when I attempted to flee back outside. The ballroom come bank was extremely echoey, and of course, I faltered, tripped, and dropped my backpack. I was pounced upon immediately by two burly Security guards in soldier's uniforms and escorted to a side door where I was propelled, ever so politely, back into the street. In the thirty seconds I had been inside the bank, I had observed three tellers and two customers.

One was an old woman with a basket collecting coins from a teller, and the other was a priest, engaged in earnest conversation with a second teller. The third teller was staring blankly ahead. At me. I suspected it was that third teller who had rung the bell I could hear resounding around the building, but I had no proof- it all happened so fast. The ringing bell was a double-edged sword for me-I was never going to get any money out of this bank, but I was going to get out of this bank alive—and for that I was thankful.

I ended up outside alongside of the line, which had miraculously disappeared, save for the 'duckling girl' who was, by now at the head of the one-person queue. She looked startled to see me stooped at her feet and helped me to steady myself. I was so over the banking debacle, that I decided, on the spot, to wait until we reached a larger town-or even a city, before attempting to withdraw cash. Alice had plenty, swollen in all manner of orifices, and she had offered to share her fortunes with me until that time when I could claim self-sufficiency.

The girl had turned away from me and was busy punching in numbers on the huge keypad. (Probably only ever used regularly by nuns, priests and farmers.) I admired this girl. She may not have had much to say, but her actions spoke louder than words, and she had a friendly face. Impulsively, I reached into my backpack and produced an olive branch. She looked uneasy at first, but when I pointed to the accompanying explanatory note, and she scanned the words, her face lit up in a smile. It had been a good move, and if she did manage to plant the branch, her grandchildren would know her as the Nonna with the massive olive tree. A worthwhile legacy!

Ten minutes after the handing-over of the olive branch, I was back at the hotel, having run as fast as I could in the heavy rain—for the most part along the lakeside promenade. Crossing the road back over to the hotel was the hardest part, as I had to wait in the rain until a slow-moving tractor and a pack of speeding cyclists passed me at their respective paces.

And now here I was, balancing on the arm of the three centuries old armchair, listening to Francesca run through the itinerary for the rest of the afternoon. It would be a late meal we would be partaking of together this evening, as we were not expected to return to the hotel until at least seven, and the setting for our bus was scheduled for eight pm.

"You see, ladies and gentlemen, we have many of the buses so eager to join us tonight, and there are too many of us to feed all at once." No one seemed bothered that we wouldn't be back for the first setting of dinner, because all that could mean would be a longer time exploring the island—where we'd been promised a late afternoon tea. We had also been promised an additional guide, a local woman from Baveno, whom we would pick up on our way through the town, enroute to the Island of St Jules.

It was exciting to be getting back on the bus with a tangible destination in mind. Most people took up their former seats, and a couple of older men, who had buddied up already, made their way towards the back of the bus for a natter. I turned to Alice and mentioned that a couple of the men were down the back in the 'Men's shed'.

In Australia, we have 'men's sheds' in practically every backyard. These are the private domains of the Australian males, often stuffed full of lawn mowers, tools and 'eskies' brimming over with ice and bottled beer. It would not be unusual to have found a television or a radio buried in there somewhere. No self-respecting woman would want to go anywhere near that 'Men's shed in the backyard'. Not much washing was hung out on clothes lines when the flag was flying outside the shed.

We were close enough for me to hear the beginnings of the conversation between the two men-at least I was until the bus picked up speed and their voices were drowned out. The bit I did catch was priceless. One of the men was asking of the other, "What brought you on this trip to Italy?" to which the other replied, "my wife!"

The second man laughed and continued with his questioning. "Do you always do what your wife asks you to do?" The second man must have paused, as there was an extended silence before the first man piped up with, "If my wife wants to go…I just follow." I would have loved to have followed the conversation all the way to the island, but by then the bus was in full throttle, and all could hear was subverted laughing. The two men were getting on like a house on fire!

Alice was commenting on the beauty of our surrounds. "I'd love to live here Fil. I would be so happy!" I wasn't so sure I could concede to living so close to such cold mountains positioned so high up in the world, but I nodded in agreement. It was less taxing to nod than it was to find more compliments for this marvellous country. Matteo was slowing down, and once he had come to a complete stop, a young woman jumped onto the bus and grabbed the microphone from the unsuspecting Francesca, who must have been having forty winks, as we hadn't heard from her in the last few minutes.

"Gooda afternoon everyone. I am Rena. Baveno is my wonderful home, and I will be your travel guide for this afternoon. Baveno is two thousand years old, compared to Stresa which has half as many years. If you have any questions-anything at all, please ask me and I willa do my best to give you the answer. I cannot say it is the right answer, but it will be an answer, eh?"

The woman had stepped out into the aisle for her delivery, and it gave us all the chance to see her pretty face and flashing smile. She wore a mustard puffer jacket and tight black ski pants. Obviously, the uniform around these parts. Although we were only an hour or so from Milan, this landscape (including the sky and seascape) was a whole different ball game. The landforms, the colours, the smells and the slow ambience all contributed to the feeling of being cocooned away from the rest of civilisation in this pretty, pretty, pretty corner of the globe. I was loving Italy today!

Rena was giving Francesca a run for her money. She may have been diminutive in stature, but she had a healthy pair of lungs on her, and a wealth of knowledge about Stresa and Baveno, the extent of which would have put the town mayor to shame. She hadn't drawn a breath since jumping on the bus, and I was beginning to feel a little overwhelmed, trying to digest and make sense of all the history she was unravelling, and simultaneously marvel appreciatively at the spectacular scenery.

Something she mentioned about Queen Victoria having flown the flag for England in the rambling pink villa we were crawling past piqued my interest, and I made a note to read up on the stamina-Queen's holidaying preferences on the continent. I knew she had enjoyed visiting spa towns in England and Scotland, but I'd never really thought about the entitled amongst the English leaving their native shores and ending up on the continent. It would have been a feat in those days, even in a royal yacht or carriage.

Rina was able to whet my appetite into further investigation of the habits of Queen Victoria with the local insider's knowledge that in the Spring of eighteen seventy-nine, when Queen Victoria had come to Baveno, the whole town had come out to welcome her. "Now we are passing so slowly, to smell at the lovely gardens of magnolias." By the time I twisted my neck to take in the 'marvellous magnolias', Matteo was up over the next hill.

The only other real gems Rina had for me was the information that Ernest Hemingway had written his famous novel, "Farewell to Arms" in Stresa, and that Winston Churchill had spent his honeymoon in the surrounds in nineteen hundred and eight. After that, I must have tuned out, because the next thing I knew we had arrived at the little harbour which serviced Lake Orta which looked on my map to be at the far end of a peninsula. It was here that the private boat reserved for our tour group was waiting patiently for our late afternoon outing.

The gleaming blue and white boat looked to be large enough for all twenty-two of us, but we would have been hard-pressed squeezing in any other passengers. Not only Alice and Roy had needed a hand to mount the slippery wooden plank to the hull. We were bending our necks and half of our bodies as we negotiated the doorway. Suffice to say, it was no Onassis yacht!

The path which had led down to the sandy shore had been overgrown and lacking the pristine boardwalk sheen more often associated with Italian seafront marinas. (I had in my mind the Lido in Venice.) Rena must have realised the collective doubt amongst the group, as she was quick to assure us that the path was not used all that often, and that she had taken the liberty of showing us the backroads and paths of the little town of Orta.

She had referred to Orta as a little town 'frozen in time', and looking around at the desolation and inactivity, she may have been right. Since I'd been dozing, I had missed the town entirely, and the second 'note to self' I dictated into my phone in as many minutes read "stay alert on return journey!"

Sea sickness! The dreaded condition which strikes when one least expects. I should have remembered that boat transportation to the island was mandatory, and that I was no sailor! I think I did know what was in store for me, but I hadn't really thought of a harmless lake as being as choppy or in any way as calamitous, as the open sea. Travellers indulged in lake and river cruises all the time, and they lived to tell the tale. That was my big mistake.

I had some seasick tablets back in my suitcase at the hotel, but of course I hadn't brought any spares with me this afternoon. I thanked my lucky stars I hadn't been born centuries ago before the construction of roads and railroads, when the only method of travel around the lakes had been by boat. I also acknowledged that wonderful emperor Napoleon, who had almost single-handedly brought roads to these parts, and all the way to Switzerland.

A woman whom I had been with in the foyer of the hotel last night whilst waiting for Alice to return from 'fixing up Francesca for the additional tours', had told me all about the revered Napoleon Bonaparte (self-proclaimed emperor of France). The woman was very interested in the history of the lakes in Northern Italy, and she had come across a little morsel of information about Napoleon and his road building prowess when she had been perusing the history books in one of the Milan universities.

According to the woman, Marjory, Napoleon had been more than ruthless in his tunnel vision of connecting Milan with Switzerland. He was so driven and passionate in his vision that many of the villas around the lake district found themselves the proud owners of a major road running through their front gardens. Also, according to Marjory, was the warning that one did not ever, under any circumstances, argue with all five and a half feet of Napoleon!

Rina was back on the microphone, telling us all about Ocean-man and Dragon-Man competitions involving long distance swimming—eight and half miles of Lake Orta to be exact. That was one tourist attraction I could do without enrolling for. I had planned a swim for tomorrow morning in the hotel pool, but apart from that, I would be happy just to remain an armchair tourist when it came to lakes and mountains.

By the time we reached the tiny island of San Giulio in the middle of Lake Orta, smaller and more compact than Lake Maggiore at only two hundred and fifty-seven metres long and one hundred and forty metres wide, I was ready for a long bout of semi-consciousness, a wet face-washer on my forehead and bucket between my legs. I couldn't see how it would be possible for me to ever return to the mainland, not unless someone knocked me out first. It was such a shame, because I'd been dying to explore the tiny island, having acquainted myself with it back in Australia, when I'd discovered the island's inclusion on our itinerary.

The island's two claims to fame were a tight little community of Benedictine nuns who lived in silence in their hilltop convent, and the preserved body of the island's Founding Father (literally), Father Jules, who had come to the San Giulio as a missionary after having founded churches all over Italy and only stopping when he had finished his hundredth church, which just happened to be the one on the island.

He had lived out the rest of his life as an islander and was now preserved and on permanent display in the crypt below the Basilica on the hill. Which we were going to see with Rina, and which olfactory sensation I would probably recognise as the musty smell of death often associated with rotting bodies, hundreds of years later. Not that I would mind seeing Jules. I had been over viewing dead bodies in glass coffins for fifteen years now, ever since I had been forced to view, with no prior warning, the body of a three-hundred-year-old nun in full bride-of-Christ regalia.

Her glass coffin had been positioned carelessly and insensitively in the side chapel of a dime-a-dozen church in Rome (if I might be permitted this small slither of sarcasm, there being so many churches everywhere in Rome), which we had entered to take refuge from the eternal heat of the eternal city and say some prayers for the world in general. Prayers accomplished, I wandered over towards the little chapel to light a candle. My intentions had been noble, but unfortunately, I screamed too loudly when I came face to face with the dead body of that old, old woman in that glass coffin, her hands folded over her chest, her lifeless eyes staring straight ahead.

I screamed and screamed, and only stopped when my companion came rushing over towards me and joined in the screaming. Had there been security guards protecting the church from pillaging and looting, we both would have ended up thrown to the lions in the Colosseum for having disturbed the peace and showing little respect towards the dearly departed. (I couldn't add "recently" to the dearly departed phrase, as there was a tiny sign which we read when we calmed down—claiming 1597 as the year of her death.) Not recent enough.

We had no idea who she was, but we were both out of the church and back in the intense, blazing Italian sun quick smart. From that day onwards, I had never been able to go to a funeral with an open casket on display.

If I didn't start feeling better soon, it might end up being me in a glass casket beside Father Jules.

The boat had landed bumpily on the lapping shores of San Giulio, and all twenty-two of us made our way up the wobbly gang-plank and onto the shore. We were like refugees being transported to a desolate island in the middle of a lake. I had visited Alcatraz before, and felt heartened that there had been no overnight accommodation. The lateness of our arrival on this island, and the fact that I was not feeling well enough to travel back over the choppy waters to the mainland was making me think that an overnight stay here may have been a real possibility.

I had no idea whether there would be accommodation on the island, but I'd stayed in convents before, on more than one occasion, so kipping down with the nuns of the silent order shouldn't have been a problem. Communication would possibly have been the only hurdle, but I felt certain my rusty miming skills could be revived.

With a plan in mind, I began to feel better. As soon as my feet had touched terra-firm and I had been able to breathe the fresh mountain-island air, I could feel the colour seeping back into my cheeks, and my stomach felt less queasy. I wasn't cured, but I could probably make it back to the hotel in a couple of hours.

Eating bread would help. It always did. Either bread or a drink of soda water. Alice would probably welcome a sit-down in a café (if there were any on the island).

"Alice, I think I'll get something to eat. I'm not feeling all that well. Quite queasy actually. The lake was too choppy for me." Alice looked concerned and immediately agreed to sit with me whilst I rid myself of my 'sea legs'.

"If we could find Roy, that'd make three of us with bad legs."

Bad joke, Alice.

You can guess who joined us for the impromptu late afternoon tea. But you couldn't possibly guess who else turned up on the café's stone doorstep. Once some of the other passengers had noticed the direction in which the three of us were shuffling, they tagged onto the end of the group-a hearty little quintet- Brielle, Natarsha, Gloria, Don and Angelique. The rest of the tour group had faithfully followed Rena, who had given us all the option of taking the tour of the island with her, or wandering off on our own and meeting back at the bus in an hour and a half.

I felt a little guilty at having started up a faction group, but I rationalised the situation by telling myself that no one had forced my followers into discipleship. They had followed of their own volition, and although it was nice to have company, and it would be a good opportunity to get to know the women from the gelati-hut in Stresa this morning a bit more, I would have been fine with Alice and Roy.

Chapter 21
There were Jewels, and There was Jules!

Rena had looked a little chaffed that not everyone had chosen to follow her on the tour of the island, but she had nevertheless played by the rules, hoisted her umbrellas high into the air and called out impatiently, "Andiamo!" and they were off, even Francesca, whose job it was to shadow the local guides. That had left nine of us in the café unaware that we had hurt Rena's feelings, preoccupied with munching on huge yellow scones and sipping hot coffees. (There had not been any bread or soda water.)

The waitress was very down-to-earth and friendly, and eager to point out that the scones were freshly baked twice daily by the nuns of the silent order, and delivered stealthily to the back door of the café at eight am and midday every day of the week with the exception of Sundays. "We tell the peoples we ava the scones from the silent nuns, and they come back with their families to eat the delicious foods. They think it is the same recipe as the holy bread, and it will cause them to be more holy."

For a native Northerner, confined to country living, the woman's English was more than adequate. I made sure I ate two of the delicious miracle scones, and although I might not have emerged from the café a holier person, I did feel sustained, and ready to tackle the hill to the church where St Jules lay resting.

The sit-down had been a good chance to get to know some of the other passengers, and we could easily have lingered in that café for the next hour and a half, unravelling each other secrets and life-stories, and of how we came to be on the trip. Brielle had been the star attraction in the café, as her tall stature, thick blonde bouncy hair, and super white teeth caused a stir with three young Italians at the next table. They were all dressed in outdoor wear and thick working boots, and the waitress informed us they were gardeners of the island, whose main job it was to tend to the luscious gardens lapping the foreshore of the lake, and the little courtyards of the grand covered piazza where tourists sat and regained their composure.

"Every afternoon at Siesta time, they arrive to here." The woman had been proud to utter this phrase, just as we had been proud of Brielle, who had held her own with the little trio, despite not knowing a word of Italian. Fluttering eyelashes and extending one's tanned leg in the direction of the intended does it every time. The boys only stayed for ten minutes or so, but it had given us all a good laugh to have seen Brielle in action.

"My holiday persona," she had confessed this to me on the boat back to the mainland when I had quizzed her on her technique. "Just a bit of fun really."

It had certainly lightened all of our moods and coupled with the food and drink had set us in good stead to tackle the hill to the church. As good fortune would have it, just as we emerged from the café, Rena and her wet bedraggled flock were weaving their way past us, and I was able to tag onto the end of the group. The others remained in a clump, desperately seeking authentic creamy island gelati from one of the tiny shops in the arcade, and Roy and Alice found themselves a seat in the piazza, protected from the rain and drizzle.

I would need to keep an eye on those two in the next few days, as they seemed to be getting awfully chummy. Yolanda was in Rena's group-up towards the front as she had told me she was hard of hearing, especially in the wind and rain. She looked to be having such a good time, despite the pesky elements, that I decided not to mention the fact that her husband and my best friend were, at that very moment, huddled up together on a wet bench in the middle of the covered piazza exchanging stories about gammy legs. It wasn't my business who fancied who. It was my business to get on top of my irrational fear of dead bodies, and where better a place to do so, than on a small island in the middle of a large lake in the most Catholic country in the world?

Francesca was skulking around at the end of Rena's line, trying to look interested, but letting her eyes wander towards a couple of little boutiques with racks of (wet) designer clothes outside. When she saw me, she grabbed my arm and led me over to one of the racks. At this rate I would never get to eradicate my fears. "Fil. I'm so happy to see you. What do you think of this jacket? Nice, eh?"

It was a nice jacket as far as jackets go but we had left the fashionable malls of Milan behind, and I was in no mood for a clothes fix.

"Yes. It's lovely, Francesca. I just want to catch up with the rest of the group, but you stay here and browse." I would have liked a little poke around by myself in the cave-like shop at the top of the hill. The clothes looked to be designer labels, and it would have been something to boast about when I returned home. An outfit from a tiny cave-shop on a tiny island on a beautiful lake in Northern Italy. But the group were already halfway up the hill, and if I didn't hurry, they would have disappeared entirely. The island may have been small, but the number of pint-sized streets and roads, with stone walls and uneven pavements seemed to be everywhere. One wrong turn and I would be lost.

Francesca stayed, lovingly fingering the rack of clothes as if they were from the costume department of a film set staging *Romeo and Juliet*, and she had been chosen to play the nurse. I left her there, summonsed up all my energy and took to the steep incline which led to the church. I didn't stop until I reached Rena and the gang, who were, by then, congregating in the red-tiled porch of the Basilica. Rena was telling them all about the body of St Jules being there, and a few of them were gasping in shock.

It probably wasn't something they had ever encountered before, and they may have been apprehensive, or it could have been the dust form the foyer settling in their nostrils causing them to gasp and snort. Rena was a sensitive soul, and she did her best to enfold us in her outstretched arms and herd us into the church. There were long narrow honey-coloured pews inside, and we all flopped down, exhausted. The church smelt musty and strongly of incense, and it was dark and gloomy. We could hear the rain on the roof, and had I not known it was late afternoon and still daylight outside, it could have been midnight on a dark, saturnine night somewhere in Transylvania.

Quite ethereal, eerie and a trifle disconcerting. I made the decision there and then not to go down to the crypt to take a gawk at Jules. I'd seen his photo in the Guidebook and that would have to suffice. Rena was babbling on enthusiastically about the paint and the gold etchings, the beautiful mosaics and frescos and most importantly of all-the treasure trove of jewels and precious stones which lined the walls and roof of the crypt where St Jules lay in perpetual silence.

"And nowa we go down. If you cannot fix the stairs or if you will not breathe your best down there, please stay in your poo and awaita us. We will not be too long. If we never come back, then you must call the nuns, who are only next door, and they will 'elp."

I knew it would be to no avail to go door-knocking for the 'elping nuns, as they had taken a vow of silence, and unless they were au-fait with the finer details of Morse Code, 'elp would not be coming.

About five of us stayed dutiful in our pews, heads bent in prayer, with the other ten or so teaming up eagerly with Rena. Here were true tourists, setting a precedent for themselves to tackle new experiences headlong. The small following, who delighted in pushing the boundaries-in diving headlong into the unknown. On the other hand, those who were by now bending their heads and disappearing into the inner sanctum of the church might be seen as the brave intrepid risk-takers that we, who had remained behind, would never be. The gamblers, the adventurous, the curious. I remembered Francesca mentioning in her opening manifesto to the group this morning, that if one really wanted to explore Italy, then one had to be curious. I hoped, in this case, that curiosity was not about to 'kill the cat'.

Perversely, I could not tear my eyes away from the group, even though wild horses wouldn't have been able to drag me down there to join them. My gravest concern for my fellow travellers was that Rena being so pert and petite, it would have been easy to have lost sight of her. I was certain that some antiquated strict Italian rules of sightseeing in heritage-listed churches prevented her from holding up the umbrella as a guiding beacon. (Although, it was bad luck to hold up an open umbrella inside a building.)

A glowstick would have done the trick, it was so dark. The crypt did not appear to be an easy place to access, and as I watched the group bending their heads almost to their knees and crawling forwards, I was relieved I had opted to stay and wait it out. To pass the time, I picked up a pamphlet at the end of my pew and began to squint at the history of the church, and the circumnavigation-route around the grounds and nearby rocky enclaves. The route had been suitably named the 'meditative way' by the group of Benedictine nuns who practised their walking meditation around the island daily (in between baking scones).

Sure enough, ten minutes later, there was a commotion on the other side of the church, and head after head began popping up from a set of rickety iron stairs I hadn't noticed before. It's funny how you never look for something unless you have reason. Until now, I had not had reason to focus on the far-left corner of the church. In the filtered light, the small army of heads appeared to be floating towards the top of the stairs. Very eerie; it would have made for a perfectly ethereal Da Vinci painting, had I been the local artist in residence on the island. One could sit and wait, paintbrush in hand for days, even weeks, for such a scene.

The regrouping took some time, as Rena had not taken notice of how many of her flock had accompanied her to the viewing of the body, and of how many had remained in the pews. I could have told her, because I could pinpoint the exact number who'd followed her in the quest for an 'out-of-the-ordinary' experience. Nine. There had been nine hapless souls brave enough to follow their leader into the unknown, and six chickens (myself included) who had remained on 'watch and wait'.

The complication for Rena was that two other guides had brought their groups into the church in the time that she had been underground with our lot, and the entire population of one new group had already disappeared down into the chambers, with the second group on standby. At the exact moment that our group reappeared on the other side of the church, the group in the wings had discovered the stairs leading down from which our group was emerging. What their guide did not know (for some unknown reason) was that they were waiting at the 'Exit' and not the 'Entrance', which had no stairs, only a gaping stone hole. Signage was non-existent, and it sounded like German and not English or Italian they were speaking, so it was an excusable mistake.

The whole church interior had been transformed, in a matter of minutes from one of reverent, peaceful, meditative silence to one of intense pandemonium. Once our group were all back on board, there would have been over fifty people in the church, not to mention the forty or so downstairs ogling at St Jules. Rena finally managed to gather up our group, with a little help from the German guide, who could also speak English.

"If you came ina ear with me, please go to the front porch so that we can come back together." I got the 'inner ear' bit. My own inner ear was ringing with the echoey noise and confusion of the goings-on. Rena had a slight desperation ring to her voice and pleading in her eyes, as if imploring those of us still rooted to the pews not to inform Francesca or Matteo of these goings-on, or of how she had managed to lose control and incite pandemonium through bad timing. Had our group been faster at the viewing, we would have been out of the church even before the next two groups had arrived and this train-wreck may have been avoided.

Rena need not have feared. None of us were about to blab, and once she had regained her composure in the porch, it was not mentioned again. In fact, it was underplayed so cleverly by Rena that to the unsuspecting, it would appear to have been 'business as usual' in the famous church on the hilltop on a gorgeous rocky Italian island.

Composures regained all around, it was time to faction! Rena announced, sheepishly that the church fiasco had signalled the end of her tour, and that we were to be on our own for the next forty or so minutes-free to explore the width and breadth of the island. I couldn't help noticing she was breathing cavernous, almost hypertensive sighs of relief, probably because we had been such an unruly, untameable group and she never wanted to see our backs again.

We weren't really all that bad, just victims of circumstance-rain, seasickness, undying hunger and thirsts, desires for the unexpected, injuries-the usual tourist traits. Once we were back on the rocky, dirt path down to the little village harbour with the piazza where I had left Alice and Roy, most people had already split into little groups of two or three. I ended up with Lizzie and Fillip-the couple from California, and as Lizzie had announced to no one in particular that she and Fillip were going to have a crack at tackling the 'Way of Silence' I had agreed somewhat too enthusiastically, to make a threesome. We had ten minutes to complete the circuit.

For the first few minutes we struggled up the rocky hills in relative silence. I say relative silence, because Fillip, who had been a wild card to me (but clearly not to Lizzie) turned out to be a heavy breather, and the grunting and the panting emanating from such a small, round body was not a sound with which to be reckoned.

In fact, it was so loud that at the third wooden post with the helpful sign secured to the stone wall of a nearby house, urging the climber to a state of meditative silence, Lizzie could stand it no longer. "Fil…stop! You are driving me mad!" The puffing and panting from Fillip had been so loud that I only managed to hear the first part of the name I thought she was calling to me to stop. I stopped, and Fillip continued to climb and grunt. Lizzie burst into laughter. "No. I didn't mean you, Fil. I meant my unfit husband. You're alright. You've been very quiet."

Well, that was a first.

It wasn't often that perfect strangers described me as quiet. The circuitous meditative trek suited me. I wished we'd had another hour on the island, and I would have gone for seconds. But once again, time was racing. I had been on the lookout all the way around for the coveted convent door so that I might leave a couple of olive branches for the nuns. Just as I was about to give up, we chanced upon two big heavy wooden doors with a sign (in English) which read, 'Benedictine Convent. Closed order. Please observe the rules of silence'.

As silently as I could manage, I deposited two tiny olive branches with the little explanatory note outside the door. I was as gentle with the twigs as one would be with laying twin babies outside a convent door. I felt exhilarated to have left the branches, knowing that if I were to return to the island in twenty years' time, there would be an olive tree to show for my trouble. No one would be able to explain to me how the gnarled tree came to be there, because of their vows of silence, but the proof would be in the pudding (or olive scones) if things went according to plan.

Lizzie and Fillip had given up on me when they'd seen me bending over reverently at the convent door, and as it had again begun to rain quite heavily, I left the slippery scene of the crime as reticently as I could, and raced off down the hill to the piazza, where I spotted Roy and Alice, chatting away as if they were on a speed-date rotation, oblivious to the world and the rain, and the fact that we were five minutes late for the boat.

I gave Alice the sternest look I could muster and pleaded with her to hurry and hobble down the wet path towards our waiting boat. Roy was about as useful as a feather duster in a convent, as all he did was sit back and watch Alice attempt to struggle to her feet. The age of chivalry had not yet reached the island of St Giulio, or else Roy was just bone-tried and didn't have the strength to help a damsel in distress. I was tried too, but not so tired that I wanted to face an agitated Rena, Francesca and the skipper of the boat.

"Come on, Alice! We're late! Late!" Roy sprung to life when he heard the panic in my voice, and three minutes later, we were back at the little harbour, once again about to walk the plank which led into the cabin of our boat.

On the way over to the island, when I'd felt so felt seasick, we had enjoyed the peace and solitude of our group on our own private chartered boat. No one had said anything about the return journey, and it was 'shock, horror, and more shock' as I poked my head into the cabin. It revealed a veritable cesspool of children! Not even really small children, who could be sedated with dummies and warm milk, but young teenagers. Much worse because they were so loud and so excited and so hungry!

Bags of crisps, little Italian lemon and orange sweets and bars of Toblerone were being passed up and down the seats, and they were having a ball, talking ten-to the dozen in Italian. There was lots of laughter and plenty of squealing. There were probably only twenty or so of them, obviously a school twilight excursion, but they were noisy and they took up so much room, and there was not a teacher in sight. A dismal scene for the solitude-seeking tourist with which to be faced head-on, at any hour of the day, but on a wet, cloudy, late afternoon boat ride—perfectly intolerable.

I had an advantage over my fellow travellers (excepting Alice) in that I was a teacher and well-used to school children, but some of the other tour-passengers were complaining loudly to Francesca, pleading for a private boat to ferry us to the mainland and letting her know, in no uncertain terms, that 'boat children' had not been mentioned in the itinerary (not even in the fine print).

I thought they made a fair point, but we really needed to get back to the mainland and Matteo, who had been waiting patiently all this time on the bus, ready to take us back to the hotel for dinner. For some peculiar reason, I wasn't seasick on the very public, very wet boat, with the squawking students. It had been quite an excursion to the island, and one which would stick in my memory for quite some time.

The preserved body, the eighty (non-sighted) cloaked and cloistered nuns, the miracle scones and the blossoming friendship between Roy and Alice—not to mention Fillip's breathing issues. I worked out that out of the twenty passengers, including myself, I had already met and interacted with more than half of them.

Tuning out the students (as only a true teacher can pull off without getting too flustered), I began an internal audit of the passengers with whom I was, by now, well-acquainted. Quite an accomplishment on my part I thought, given that it was only our first real full day out of Milan. First up there had been Don and Angelique whom we had met on arrival day, and then Roy and Yolanda, when the six of us had gone out to dinner in the open-aired restaurant.

Also, the three brave souls who had been the guinea pigs with the microphone this morning—introducing themselves and giving us little interesting anecdotes about their lives outside of Italy—Barbara and Gary, the married couple, and Brielle-a single woman from the United States. Next up had been Gloria and Natarsha, with whom I'd buddied up this morning in the bathrooms of the roadside café just out of Milan, as well as the three latecomers—the Silicon Valley family from California—Devo, Joe and the twinkly-eyed old mother, Armenia.

Last on my list were the Singaporean quartet, the old and the young I called them. All four were delightful. Polite. Welcoming and beautifully presented in immaculate attire at all times. Both Singaporean couples had been with me on and off whilst I'd been trooping the Taranto Gardens, and it had been a pleasure to have discussed plants with them. They certainly knew their stuff, as both couples lived in 'eco-green apartments' in Singapore, and only had good things to say about the marvellous display of plants and six levels of gardens (Jewel) which had not long ago opened its doors to the public at Changi Airport, and was now a 'must see' for anyone on a Singaporean stopover.

Last but not least, Lizzy and Fillip needed to be added to my list. When I thought about it, there were really only two people with whom I still needed to acquaint myself. I racked my brains trying to work out who they might be, but they must have been very quiet people, as I couldn't put my finger on their identities. Looking around the cabin didn't help, as the young people were everywhere, and I could only see about half our group sitting on a long bench opposite me.

Alice was over there with them, this time chatting to Devo, but I had no idea where the others might be. I had read about the lake offering all manner of water sports in Spring and Summer, so perhaps a few of them had decided to row back to shore? Or jet ski? More than likely they were congregated on the upper deck in the wind and the rain with Rena and Francesca. Some people would go to any measures to escape children.

My audit completed, I turned my attention towards the open lake, and let my mind wander for a further ten minutes-exploring the connections between this beautiful Lake in Northern Italy with the Great Lakes of Australia. Forty kilometres north of Canberra, the city where I had spent my childhood and adolescence, lies a massive body of water—Lake George (named for the British king at the time of discovery).

Coincidentally, the lake runs for forty kilometres. The first peculiarity of Lake George was that it was not a lake fed by rivers or glaciers-as was Lake Orta or any of the other Northern Italian lakes. At one stage, in the late nineteenth century, Lake George was put forward as a suitable site for Canberra-the capital city of Australia, but this proposal was rejected on account of the erratic water levels, the inexplicable rising and falling of the water. Sketches of a waterfront city, compared to Venice were also bandied around, and similarly rejected. The town planners must have had some very strong psychic premonitions about the lake. Some years you see it, and in other years, the entire Lake completely disappears. Our very own Bermuda Triangle.

Over the centuries, many strange and mysterious goings-on have been associated with Lake George, and it is not a place which inspires confidence amongst swimmers and fishermen. In fact, Lake George is pretty much known as a 'ghost lake'-best left to its own devices. Whereas here, in beautiful North Italy, what you saw was what you got, and we had just enjoyed a wonderful skimming across the lake with the peaked mountains in the background, and the shore beckoning us back into her arms.

Leaving the boat was a much faster process than boarding had been, mainly courtesy of the much-maligned youth, who redeemed themselves by staying silent in their seats whilst we disembarked. Still no teachers had been sighted. Matteo had moved our bus, positioning it closer to the shore for a faster getaway, and for that we were all grateful. Tiredness, that state of profound lethargy, was beginning to sink in, and most people were very grateful to Matteo for having gone that extra mile (literally) and moved the bus.

Rena bade us farewell at the doors to the bus, and as was the expectation, many of the passengers slipped her some euro by way of appreciation. My contribution was an olive branch and twenty euro from myself and Alice. The little gift (and the money) cheered her up no end, and the last we saw of Rena was her tiny frame clutching her red umbrella in the rain, fully opened now that her job was completed, as she trudged her way across the soggy, marshy inlet—no doubt on another of her famous shortcuts on her way back to town.

Chapter 22
Dining In

We were a quiet lot on the bus back to the hotel. Francesca tried hard to involve us in her raconteur and running commentaries on places we passed, but everyone was done in. There was serious doubt amongst some of us that we would actually make it to dinner in the hotel tonight. The only saving grace was that the banquet was not scheduled to begin until eight, and it had just gone six. At the very least, we would have an hour to revive and embrace our second wind.

By the time we reached the hotel, half the group had fallen asleep and the other half could be found with their seats reclined, flicking through magazines, guidebooks and tourist pamphlets—the staple diet of the traveller. I was probably one of the few passengers with a foot in both camps-three camps if you counted half-listening to Francesca, who had found a romantic poem on the Borromean islands and was reading it aloud in her best imitation of Lord Byron to anyone who cared to listen. The first five verses had been bearable, but I'd had no idea how many verses were to come, or even it was English she was attempting, so I'd tuned out.

Then it happened! Francesca stopped mid-sentence and let out a bloodcurdling scream as Matteo swerved the bus to avoid the large bubbling fountain, strategically placed in the centre of the white-pebble stoned circular driveway. The bus lurched dangerously, and those in the front rows were propelled forwards with little warning. Francesca herself landed back in her favourite position-the front stairs, and Fillip and Lizzie, who had been sitting side by side in the second seat, somehow managed to land on top of Francesca in a 'stax' position.

With the microphone still in her hand, Francesca called out to the embarrassed Matteo. "Matteo! Are you trying to land us all in the fountain?" Lizzie looked horrified, but Fillip (who was turning out to be quite the card) managed to see the funny side of the incident and began shaking with laughter, calling out, "Again, Matteo! Again." Like a child urging a parent to perform the same trick for the twentieth time in a row.

Francesca was not letting go of that microphone for anyone. She continued her chastising of the unfortunate Matteo from her position on the steps, firstly, in rapid, heated Italian, and then in even louder and more raucous English. "Matteo. We are not here to collect the fountain and wash ourselves before dinner tonight. Please, please, take the care!"

Matteo was steadying the enormous bus as best he could, but because we had gone too far around the driveway, we needed to complete the circle, re negotiate the main road, and swoop in again for a follow-up landing.

The second attempt was marginally better. Matteo managed to avoid the fountain, but not the fanned-out branches of the luscious green palm trees which studded the neck of the driveway. Those of us in window seats of the bus, Alice included, were treated to a huge wave of green palm-foliage washing across the windows like over-sized bristles at a self-serve car wash. More screaming. This time from the window passengers.

As soon as the bus stopped moving, everyone jumped up at the same time- eager to leave Matteo in peace to get some rest. It had been a long hard day for him, and the responsibility of ferrying twenty paying-guests around the countryside seemed to be taking its toll. Francesca had mentioned that tomorrow we would be meeting a substitute driver so that Matteo might have some down- time in the lakeside hotel. The plans for tomorrow included driving to and collecting us from a mystery Train Station at the foot of the Alps, so it could have been a short or long ride-it was to be a surprise.

Alice was taking so long to get ready that I suggested I go on ahead of her and save her a place at the table. I was pleased we were dining in tonight as it had been a very long day, and weariness was setting in. it would be nice just to sit down and be waited on, not have to prepare the food or wash the dishes, and fall into bed at whatever time I chose to do so.

Leaving Alice with a face full of trickling foundation, I took to the stairs for some token exercise. Not that walking the hills of the island this afternoon hadn't been enough. My calves were aching, and I realised I should have rubbed them with some 'Deep-Heat' this morning. I also should have remembered sunscreen, as my arms were a bright red from having been in the sun all day. Milan's rainy weather had tricked me into believing that the drizzle would continue into the countryside, but it hadn't. and I was now a flashing red from the waist up.

I stopped on the landing of the stairs to pull my shawl from my handbag, a token attempt at covering the flashy red. As I was bending, an older couple appeared by my side, and asked if I would mind taking their picture in front of the lake. At first, I thought they wanted me to accompany them outside, and take their picture from the hotel carpark, but when I indicated towards the downstairs doors, they both stood shaking their heads vehemently. It was obvious that conversing in English would not be a viable option, as they were dressed in traditional Austrian or German costume and pointing excitedly to the wall behind me.

I swung around to see a vibrant, freestanding picture of a fair-sized lake with snow-capped mountains in the background, covering the entire wall. I realised that they wanted me to take their picture where they were standing, on the King's Landing, in front of the fake lake. I wasn't sure whether or not the clothes they were wearing were costumes for the photo-shoot, or their regular attire, but I kept my silence on that one. After about ten shots of the two of them in different poses in front of the lake scene, I handed their camera back to them.

More than likely there would be one photo which depicted them favourably, but if not—c'est la vie! I had given them no cause to assume I was a professional photographer (unless my bending and reaching for my shawl in my bag had somehow looked to them like I was retrieving a photographer's cloth to drape over my non-existent tripod). They seemed happy with my efforts, and extra happy when I handed them an olive branch each. So happy with the gift that they managed to coerce the next person to come bounding down the stairs (a young housemaid with a pile of linen more than twice her body weight) to take a snap of the three of us posing with the olive branches on the landing in front of the lake. The Austrian/German couple promised to send me a photo of the three of us with the olive branches, although no addresses or names were exchanged.

The excitement and bustle continued downstairs. Two giant wooden doors which led to the baronial Dining room had been opened in anticipation of three busloads of people partaking of their evening meal. There was already a queue, so I hopped on the end, and began the slow shuffle towards the doors. I could see Roy and Yolanda's heads about three people in front of me, but they couldn't know that I was behind them, so I didn't bother to call them. The line was moving fairly quickly, and in less than three minutes, the waiters beckoned me into their fold.

There was an army of them, all decked out in black and white, each little group of three assigned to a table. Training for this evening would have been stringent, as the waiters (all young boys) seemed to know exactly what to do without uttering a word, and their hovering was perfectly choreographed. Alice had finally appeared and had made straight for the smorgasbord of food. I wished I hadn't eaten two muesli bars earlier on, as that had taken the edge off my appetite, and there was just so much food. Pizza, pasta, ravioli, veal, chicken, mussels, fish, squid...Alice's eyes were popping out of her head.

"Looks like we'll be here till tomorrow morning getting through all this food." Alice was in her seventh heaven, as was the rest of the room. All tables were full, and there appeared to be at least a dozen of them with at least a dozen people at each table. That meant close to one hundred and fifty people in the room. Not that it was overly crowded. The room was enormous, possibly having been used as an army headquarters in one of the wars. I could imagine it set up with rows and rows of wooden desks, with radios and speakers and tangled wires positioned strategically throughout the room.

After we had all eaten enough to see ourselves through the next two wars, steaming hot coffee and sweet almond bites were deposited on each table, and the waiters continued to hover, pouring coffees, supplying sugar and honey sweeteners, and generally making themselves as useful as worker bees.

Half an hour, we were all well and truly stuffed like the proverbial turkey.

"I think I need to go upstairs and lie down." Alice was clutching her stomach and moaning to the entire table, but no one was taking much notice of her. We were getting used to each other and were practically family by now. I wasn't quite ready to go to bed, and the lure of the swimming pool was playing on my mind. I decided to follow the long corridor up in the direction of the promised pool. I had no intention of swimming, as a blind parrot would have been able to predict that I'd sink, given all I had eaten in the last couple of hours.

Brielle, Natarsha and Gloria offered to accompany me up the long, carpeted corridor towards the pool. It seemed we were all 'full as googs' and in desperate need of exercise. It also seemed that the pool closed early, as when we finally reached our destination, it was shut down for the evening-deserted and forlorn looking. On the way back down the long corridor, we stopped every now and then to admire the little artefacts displaying the history of the hotel and the Lakes District which had been placed in tiny glass cabinets at strategic intervals along the corridor.

There were plentiful conglomerations of treasures in the glass cabinets, and if we'd had more time, and it hadn't been so late, we could have spent the next couple of hours peering into the thick sparkling glass which housed everything from handwritten letters to maps, boots and brass bells. It probably took us twenty minutes to reach the foyer on the way back, whereas it had only taken half that time on our maiden voyage. As the other three had bedrooms on the ground floor, we bade each other goodnight at the doors to the lifts. I wasn't going to chance being roped into taking more photographs on the landing in front to the Lake painting, so I took the lift.

Our room was in darkness when I pried the door open. The large brass key which Francesca had been handing out when we'd arrived at the hotel looked as if it may have been the spare for the giant's castle at the top of Jack's beanstalk. Alice was in her bed, immobile. Since no loud breathing was coming from her direction, I assumed deep sleep.

I slipped into my nightwear and snuggled down into my own oversized bed with the bedhead straight out of *Charlie and the Chocolate Factory*. It was probably too warm for any intensive burrowing, but there is something primeval about snuggling up in a foetal position and shutting out the rest of the world.

The day was done! Time for sleep!

Chapter 23
The Alps Calling!

Last night had been the icing on the cake of a very long, very productive and action-packed day. Neither Alice nor I had anticipated such a heightened state of lethargy when we'd called it a night within an hour of each other. Just as Alice had been asleep when I'd crept into the bedroom, she was still dead to the world this morning. It was six thirty and I was wide awake. The curtains were slightly open, and I debated turning over and facing the balcony, taking in the splendid morning light of pink and gold which I knew (from experience) would be streaking across the skyline by the second.

I could just make out snippets of sky from the ornate mirror, positioned on the even more ornate pale green dressing table. The ideal would be to allow my mind thirty minutes of mindless musings, but there simply wasn't time. The musing would have to wait! The swimming pool was calling out to me—invading my consciousness with the primitive moan of a mournful, pregnant dolphin. Besides which, I had promised myself the morning exercise.

Downstairs, it was deathly still and quiet. As the main desk was around the corner, I hadn't bothered to make my way around there to check on the opening times for the pool. There hadn't been any signs up last night when we had completed our scout, nor had there been any information concerning the swimming pool in our bedroom (The kind of information in a frame of fine print behind one's bedroom door-directly below the fire escape directions) so there was no need for me to turn left, even though I wasn't one hundred percent sure they would be towels on hand at the pool. I was willing to take the chance.

The long tunnel corridor we had traversed last night stretched out in front of me and although I was demurely decked out in the customary white terry towelling robe, I decided to make a dash for it and not stop until I reached the safety of the pool. This decision was entirely unnecessary as I saw not a soul on my dash.

The corridor was so dark no one would have seen me either, had they been resting in the darkness on one of the benches along the corridor on the way up to the pool. It was entirely plausible that the swimming pool was in neighbouring Switzerland. It wasn't a corridor at all, but a tunnel connecting two buildings, and almost certainly a former escape route for nobles, politicians and kings staying in the hotel and used as a thoroughfare for executing escapes to the neutrality of neighbouring Switzerland.

When I finally reached the pool, five long straight minutes later, the thick aquamarine glass doors which had been firmly closed last night where now still firmly closed. A lone bird tweeted imploringly at me from its vantage point in the wooden rafters. Who knew how long it had been trapped in the corridor, or if it even desired to be released? I couldn't think of a way to set it free that didn't involve a towel and smuggling back past the front desk. The bird seemed happy to sit there staring down at me, and as I observed it, I remembered the tiny birds that had been overactive in the rafters of the breakfast room in our Milan hotel. Best leave well enough alone.

It was early but not that early and people needed to exercise. I had two choices. Either to sit down and wait patiently for the attendant to arrive, or turn and head back to the bedroom, take a quick shower and be down for breakfast before anyone else. Apart from the solitary bird, it was church-quiet in the corridor. A compromise might work. I was getting good at compromising. At home, I would never have sat patiently and waited, had the swimming pool not yet been open.

I would have moved on to the next matter of the day —or come up with an alternative way to exercise. As today was the day we were scheduled to embark on the adventure of a lifetime on a little engine train and end up in a mountaintop village, I figured that walking in the Alps would be exercise enough, and that the added bonus of all that fresh mountain air in my lungs would be just the tonic I needed.

Accustomed as I was to fresh air and mountaintop-trekking, having grown up in an Australian city surrounded by mountains, I could always do with more of what I was good at—hiking. Francesca had mentioned that there might be some hiking in the Alps involved on the day we were to take to the mountains, and that day was now well and truly upon us.

"Some of you will know what I mean when I say to you, 'hiking in the Alps'. Do you know these words, eh? Do you like these words? Do you like these two words together? Hiking and Alps?"

To be honest, I liked Alps. The kind of Alps one could comfortably admire from a train window or a chairlift seat, but hiking? I wasn't keen on some of the connotations of that word. When Francesca had mentioned hiking, there had been a collective shuddering in the bus. Francesca had picked up on it, trained tour leader that she was.

"Some of you are not happy to hear the words 'hiking in the Alps' eh? Which part do you not like, hiking or Alps?"

I had been bus-jester even then, and had called out brazenly, "We don't like either of the words, especially when they are put together." And just like that I had my first 'group laughing' response. I loved it and had tried from that day onwards (three days ago now) to crack jokes whenever the opportunity arose.

Today, the local guide would be forcing me to face my fears of mountains and hiking in a strange unpredictable land. A land of mud slides and earthquakes, volcanoes and quicksand, wolves, snakes, and wild bears. I quickly adjusted my thinking. My plan was now to compromise on the compromise, and just sit back and wait and see what the day brought in terms of perambulation. For now, I would make my way (more slowly this time, but not stopping for a second look at the memorabilia) down the corridor back to the foyer and enquire at the front desk as to the opening hours of the pool. If the answer came back as ten am, or that the pool was closed for renovations—as had been the case in our Milan hotel, then I had my compromise-walking in the mountains.

The foyer in front of the desk was over-crowded. It looked as though a tour bus was about to leave, and that many of the tourists who had either partaken of room service, or had drained the mini bottles of vodka or schnapps which were to be found in the bedrooms and could be purchased for five euros a bottle. I could see it would be useless lining up at the end of the queue. I would stand out like as sore thumb in my white knee-length terry towelling robe and fluffy slippers. Humiliation at this early hour was not something I wanted for myself.

Already, people had been looking at me curiously, nodding and pointing at me as if I had escaped from a nearby sanatorium, or that I belonged to a Scientology group who had booked one of the meeting rooms for the day, and that I was early for the conference. There were a million reasons why I might be skulking around a hotel foyer in a white fluffy dressing-gown but I didn't want to think about any of them.

I was hungry and just wanted breakfast. The swim would just have to wait for this afternoon-if time permitted. When I got back to the room, Alice had opened the curtains and let in the full morning sun, and she was back on the balcony drinking in the morning dew. Alice planned her exercise indulgences perfectly. A little bit of this, a little bit of that, and then rest. Rather like a session of yoga, with the rest periods more frequent than the yoga itself.

"Alice, I'm back."

Alice turned around sharply when she heard my voice, and I could see that she was stitching. "Oh Fil. I'm all ready for breakfast. How was your swim? Have you had your shower? Where did you go?" Alice had long ago perfected the art of asking questions and not waiting for an answer.

By the time she'd fired out six in rapid succession, she had forgotten all about the first one, and I had learnt not to answer any until she stopped to take a breath. Which was now. "And have you showered?" No. I had not showered, because the pool had not been open, and my presumption had been that the showers (or probably Roman Baths if the swimming pool had remained untouched for centuries) to have been behind the locked doors.

"No, I haven't, but I will now. I'll meet you down at the breakfast room in ten minutes. Does that sound like a plan?"

As I gathered toiletries for my shower-soap, shampoo, toothpaste, body mists, lotions, potions and perfumes-it struck me that I had managed to avoid answering any of Alice's questions, save for the last one, which had let me off the hook and offered safe entry into the bathroom. Definite progress! The next hour passed in regular monotony. Shower, stairs to the breakfast-room, more hovering waiters, back upstairs to overcompensate our backpacks and check passports for the 'Great Alpine Train Ride', and then down to the foyer to claim a comfy armchair whilst waiting for the newbie-driver to show up.

Francesca was getting herself into a right pickle. Clapping her hands loudly, stamping her feet even more loudly and town-crying out to the crowded foyer, "Northern Lakes and Cinque Terra my group-please come over to here!" With reluctance I surrendered my post on the comfy plumped-up armchair and sidled over towards Francesca. Alice did not move a muscle.

"Fil, when you get over there, can you point towards me to let Francesca know I'm here? It's too comfortable to move right now." What was this, defiance from Alice? This was not a pain in the knee or leg rooting her to the spot! More like a pain in the neck!

I stopped and waited for the rest of the questioning tirade, but Alice had buckled up and buried her head back in her needlework. Exactly what she was stitching, that project taking up such a huge amount of her free time, I would need to investigate this evening when she was asleep. I had caught glimpses over the last few days of a mass of red crosses, and Alice's usual preoccupation was with flowers and fruit bowls and sometimes dogs. It was a good thing Alice had not been let loose in the Palace a couple of days ago, or she might have taken hundreds of orders for 'dog tapestries' and set herself up for life.

Alice still hadn't looked up, so I approached Francesca who had ensconced herself behind the 'Loan Shark' desk she'd set up last night, seizing her one last opportunity to elicit money from those passengers who had not yet prepaid the added extras, or were taking too long to decide if they wanted to take the trips. Since not all passengers opted for every optional extra, Francesca's job had added complications—getting it right just who was going where, and when. For her part, Alice had made it easier for Francesca, deciding last night that she would rest her legs this afternoon and not join the majority of us on Isola Bella, the grand Palace on the pretty little island which could be seen from the hotel foyer, and the bedroom with balconies facing the lake. (Such as ours.)

"I just want to relax on the veranda with my tapestry and rest my knee. I'll wave to you all!" That tapestry and that knee had a lot to answer for!

Francesca must have forgotten that the new driver was expected, as while I was hovering near the desk with a few of the others who had also obeyed her first instructions to leave the foyer, and await her next instructions, I was signalling madly to Alice that I'd made it to the desk. Of course she didn't look up, and I looked a right dingbat standing there flapping my arms about like a penguin and bobbing my head up and down to somehow let Alice know that I'd heard Francesca telling Gerry and Babette in no uncertain terms that, "Matteo was late!"

Babs was a smart woman with pink nails and a sharp tongue. I'd liked her right from the minute I'd heard she was a dairy farmer from a remote farm in the South-island of New Zealand. She was a no-fuss, down-to-earth, gutsy Kiwi, and a woman who knew how to get what she wanted. Not unlike Jacinta Arden who, for the last couple of years had made so many marvellous decisions and shown excellent leadership in the small double-island country. Knowing Francesca was misguided in her maligning of Matteo, Babette was quick to come to his defence. "Francesca, what on earth are you on about? Matteo has every right to be asleep. He's not on the shift this morning, remember?"

If Francesca had remembered, she was not about to let on, and she kept her head bent, scribbling away furiously as if she was onto Part Two of the 'National Testing for Tour Guides'. (Part One more than likely having been undertaken on the day I first met her in the Milan hotel—the day of the martini and the mix-up with the suitcases.) Babsie was like a dog with a bone, and Francesca, sensing her hostility, finally looked up.

"I'm sorry, I just had to finalise one last payment or some of us may have missed out on going to Cinque Terra, and that would be the biggest of the big shames, wouldn't it?"

Babs had to agree that the welfare and wellbeing of the passengers always came first, and she let it go graciously. An admirable quality which far outweighed her dogged persistence with doing the right thing. With that said, Francesca closed her ledger and shut down her laptop. Nothing more was said on the matter. The makeshift desk was left standing upright, but on her command we all moved away from there and headed back into the foyer, where the other half of our party had congregated around Alice and Roy, who were taking up both armchairs.

I waved to Alice as I approached her chair, hoping she would jump up and join me, saving me from having to stop by the little cluster of puffed-up armchairs with their picture-perfect view of the glistening lake, on my way to the bus. Someone had seen our bus flash by the huge glass foyer windows, and it was now parked territorially, directly behind the fountain. The positioning was excellent, and extremely considerate of passengers, in that there was plenty of room to manoeuvre oneself and one's worldly goods between the walls of the hotel and the wide opening onto the bus stairs.

The substitute driver had courteously opened both the front and side doors, and, relying on the fact that yesterday's seat had been located more than halfway up the aisle, I took a punt and boarded from the middle door. Alice was still way behind, just out of the foyer, and talking ten to the dozen to Roy. He appeared to have lapsed into a catatonic state-save for the occasional grunt and loose-head movement, but Alice was, as usual, oblivious to his non-communicative pose.

The occasional nod from Roy was high praise indeed for Alice, and it meant she would, by the looks of things, be betrothed to Roy for the duration of the journey. (The fact that he already had a perfectly adequate wife, Yolanda, must have slipped her mind in all the excitement of the bonding over the bad legs.)

Once I'd boarded the bus, I strained my neck forwards to catch a glimpse of our driver for the half-day. With my short-sightedness, all I could hazily make out was a shock of black curly hair and a very smartly pressed uniform which looked to have stiletto-shoulder pads. I could see and hear those passengers getting on via the front stairs greeting the new driver in a friendly manner and tone of voice, and someone must have asked his name, as when everyone (Alice and Roy included) had safely boarded the bus, the new boy on the block leapt up on his seat and took to the microphone, introducing himself as Antonio from Turin.

I wondered if it would be acceptable to address him as 'bello' as Francesca had let us know on our first day out of Milan that we should greet Matteo each morning with the so-very-Italian salutation of "Ciao bello!" I decided to wait until I'd gotten to know him better. It was best to work one's way up to such matters, and I wouldn't want to end up attached to Antonio in the same way that dear Alice was to the sexy Matteo. He turned out to be a man of few words, as that was the last we saw or heard from him.

Regardless, Antonio was a driver par-excellence, and he managed to back the bus out of the tight spot with the stupendous obstacle of the fountain, with the utmost of ease. I felt like I was back on the jumbo jet taking off from London, when it had been impossible to pinpoint that precise moment when we had become airborne. Thanks to Antonio, all we heard was a light beeping of reversing lights, and a soft purring of the engine signalling that we were away— off to conquer the Italian Alps!

Francesca was determined to hog the microphone when the new guide jumped onto the bus at a bus-stop five minutes down from the hotel. The two women were well matched, both possessive of a fierce determination and an unabridged passion for the perilous mountains of Northern Italy.

"You will see mountains on your left." (That was Francesca)

"And you will see more mountains on your right!" (That was Raffaella)

"The best view is from the left-hand side." (Francesca again)

"The best view is from the right-hand side." (Raffaella)

This banter, describing not only the mountains, but the fields, flowers, buildings and even extending to the state of the sky continued for five minutes or so, until one of the passengers at the front shouted out that he wanted a bit of peace and quiet, and could they please stop yelling so loudly into the microphone? That shut them both up and a sulky silence ensued for the next ten minutes.

The bus was quiet and as if on automatic pilot, as we purred through two or three little towns. By the fourth town, Francesca could bear it no longer. My immediate thought was that she feared losing control and respect from the group by handing over her authority as tour leader to Raffaella. I felt a little sorry for her and wanted to race up and yank the microphone from her clutches, assuring her that it could be a confident and happy handover to Raffaella, as our loyalties would still be with her—Francesca—at the end of the day, when Raffaella had returned home to her family for the evening meal and familiar nightly rituals.

Raffaella would be group-guru for the next five hours or so, true, but Francesca would be our true leader for the duration, and even though none of us had voiced our undying allegiance to her, it was a solid, tacit commitment. I couldn't really speak for the others, but in my heart of hearts I knew that to be true for them as well. But, with Francesca having been snuffed out for at least five hours, Raffaella took up residence at the helm.

We had arrived at the train station in the centre of the town, and it was truly a magnificent sight to behold. A beautifully preserved Italian hamlet, nestled at the foot of the imposing Alps, brimming over with culture and history. Again, I had to pinch myself to prove I was really there.

Alice and Roy were last off the bus, and Yolanda and I were getting a little antsy, as the rest of the group had marched off after squadron-leader-Raffaella towards the station. Francesca and the new driver had remained 'in Trieste' on the bus, and from where I stood waiting, I could see them huddled together conspiratorially, focussed intently on a wad of papers. With Raffaella out of the way, Francesca had reclaimed her voice and her turf and despite the fact that her audience had been reduced to one, she was, nevertheless again in her element. As any psychologist will tell you, it only takes an audience of one to precipitate adrenalin overflow.

"Come on Roy, hurry up, there's a lift to the downstairs platform, and if we get our skates on, we'll beat the others. They're going down the escalator." Yolanda hadn't been married to Roy-of-the-bad legs for fifty odd years for nothing, and if there were tricks of the trade to be learnt, I had before me the perfect mentor. Alice and I followed in respectful silence. Down on the underground platform, an eerie serenity was in full yoga position. Not a breath of wind nor a person in sight.

Yolanda looked a little taken back at the lack of life down there, but rallied quickly, as just as we were about to splinter into search-party configuration, there was a sudden flurry and fuss from the escalators, and our extended bus-family, led by Raffaella, storm-trooped the platform, emerged noisily from around a corner to the side of the lifts. (The escalators must have been hidden there.)

When Raffaella saw the four of us standing there, probably looking like we were bound for the lost dogs' home, she shouted over towards us to come and join them near the next platform. Rafaella must have recognised us from the bus, but as there weren't really any other people around, it would also have made sense that we were with her group.

"Come quickly now the disability peoples. All the fours of you. We are ready to leave off five minutes. The train will be coming!"

I was a little confused really. How could a scenic train be leaving from such a sleek, glossy underground station when every logical bone in my body was telling me that a slow-moving, steam-puffing wooden, open-carriage steam train would never in a million years grace these gleaming steel tracks? It didn't make sense. Alice was equally confused.

"I thought we were going on the Edelweiss train up into the mountains. (She meant the 'Centovalli Panoramic Train' we had read about.) What are we doing here? Do you think this is just a transfer train to the little red and green open-carriage train we saw in the brochures, Fil?"

I hoped the train on which we were travelling turned out to be just a substitute train just as Raffaella was our substitute tour guide, but I very much doubted we would be transferring to a third mode of transport this morning.

"I'm not sure, Alice. Let's just get on and hog the window seats just in case."

It was a wise move as it turned out, as there was no little train, and there was no steam, and no leaves brushed against our faces. Nor did any water from plentiful industrial-looking sprinklers saturating the nearby fields supply us with any refreshing spray. We had emerged from the underground station almost immediately after the train slunk into motion, and the official-looking conductor had been on the microphone before you could say 'Jack Robinson', announcing to all and sundry that in twenty-five minutes, we would reach the summit village and that we should all sit back and relax and try to take in the scenery.

On the plus side, the train would almost certainly have been amongst one of the top ten trains in the Guinness Book of Records when it came to the slowness stakes. Inebriated Italian tortoises would have been stiff competition. I now understood why five hours had been allocated to the pleasures of mountain pursuits. It would be pushing it for us to arrive in under a day.

The conductor threw some light onto the state of affairs on the train. "Goda morning to youa alla. This is the alpine train to the foot of the alps, and we wosh ou to see and breatha the best of the mountain air. Please sitta back and enjoy the climbing ride."

I feared he had proposed we would all be undertaking a breath-test, which to me meant a breathalyser test, and I spent the next five minutes trying to work out just how much alcohol I had consumed at the table last night when the waiter/patron ratio had been at a premium two to one (two patrons per waiter, not the other way round), but it was still heavily weighted towards the patron's glass being filled at every possible lull in between conversations or courses.

I decided I was under the limit this morning, and in my favour, a full twelve hours had passed. Surely the conductor wouldn't be conducting spot breath-checks? It was best not to wallow and hope for the best. I would just sit back and concentrate on the ride.

And what a ride it turned out to be. Flat at first-as flat as an ironing board, and then so steep a climb that I felt trepidatious at having to face descension on the other side when the time came for our return journey. Hopefully, that would be so far into the future that the worry beads could remain resting in my pocket. I had overheard Briella and Natarsha debating whether or not our bus would be waiting for us in a particular mountain-top village to drive us back to Stresa via the autostrada, and I'd liked the sound of that plan. My eavesdropping was paying off!

Alice was busy taking photos, as were most of the other passengers. The Singaporean couple had taken umbrage and were relishing the opportunity to rest, and the petite, silken-haired wife had fallen asleep on her husband's tanned shoulder. It was such a lovely pose! I wished I'd brought my pastels with me on the outing this morning. I could have sketched the way her delicate head dropped gently onto the expanse of shoulder. Her flat black hair was spread like a tiny baby blanket against the whiteness of his shirt, and her painted pink lips resembled two delicate rose petals in full bloom. I thought of the painting above my bed back home in Australia-Vermeer's "The Girl with the Pearl earring," and immediately dismissed the possibility of sketching in this carriage, packed with pseudo-paparazzi. The subject was ripe, but conditions remained poor. We were squashed in the rattling receptacle, and the light was not reliable, fluctuating between bright sunshine and tree-shaded semi-darkness.

The landscape was also changing, the higher we climbed. A kaleidoscope of springtime colour and texture, twirling and swirling slowly past, like coloured fairy floss. There was no way the train was going any faster, nor did there seem to be any hurrying on the part of the conductor to supply any explanations regarding all that our senses were digesting. Even Raffaella had clammed up. 'Best seen with eyes closed and an appreciative penchant for slow movement' pretty much summed it up for the train trip.

We saw intermittent waterfalls, crumbling stone-huts with rocky roofs, shepherd-shelters and rambling farmhouses. We passed valleys and gorges and ravines. And finally, we pulled up in a pretty little station with one solitary concrete pre-war platform, and a mass of pink, red and buttercup yellow flowers spilling out from wicker hanging baskets. The 'Hanging Gardens of Babylon' on herbaceous Holodeck. Who would ever have imagined such a glorious apparition at the top of a mountain in Northern Italy?

Most of the group were exclaiming loudly and congratulating themselves on having selected a bus trip, with such a plethora of surprises. I kept quiet, seasoned traveller that I was, as I knew full well that villages such as this pretty one could be discovered everywhere around the world if one just knew where to look. As soon as we had all safely alighted from the train, Raffaella tossed her umbrella high up into the air, threw back her head, and disclosed to the group her surprise news of the day.

"And now we will go to a small restaurant in the village where we will have our 'tea of the morning'. An Italian festa in an alpine village in the mountains. Andiamo tutti!"

Chapter 24
Some Grub and Some Grandeur for the Afternoon

The path leading down to the village was rocky and barren, reminding me of black-and-white feature films of Greece and Italy. Or Corfu. Not that I'd been to Corfu, but that was my expectation-of Corfu terrain. Had I been blindfolded, and then led to the windy rocky path, I would have been hard-pressed to have drawn a line in the sand between the countryside of Greece or Italy when my blindfold had been released. The sun was warm, but not blinding like it should have been in Greece in late May, early June, and it was almost balmy, with a fragrance of frangipani in the air, and I knew I had to be in Italy.

Naturally, there were no blindfolds-just my over fervent imagination, conjuring up the unnerving experience of being kidnapped on the lowlands and all being revealed in the mountains and highlands some hours later. If I kept up this self-harming (pinching myself) every time we encountered a new and wonderous sight, I would end up black and blue. It was just so hard not to. Everything was so spectacular and so very Italian. It really was Villa Taranto all over again. Ground hog day revisited. The flowers trees and shrubs were less plentiful, and there were many more villas than the one solitary towering abode, the visionary Neil had built for himself at Taranto, but it was concordant as far as sights, smells and tastes were concerned.

Raffaella had promised us a morning feast-a culinary delight at a local restaurant, but that was not scheduled for at least half an hour. An air hug would have to suffice. Already I could taste and swallow the fresh mountain air. It was like honey and the taste of fresh snow rolled into one.

"Totter down this little pile of steps here, my group, and you will see the side entrance to the church." None of us knew anything about the church Raffaella was about to lead us through (there had been no mention of a tour of a mountain-top church on the printed itinerary) but it looked very, very old and cracked from the outside, and extremely tiny, which could have been on the plus side for us, as we wouldn't be restricted to spending the entirety of the next hour in the church as we had done on the Island of St Giulio yesterday.

Inside the church, the walls were crumbling, the paint was peeling, the frescoes fading and the candles glowing. Some bright spark of a 'useful-of the village' must have crept in at daylight and lit all the candles adorning a tiny side-alter, as they were blazing like a proverbial Guy Falkus bonfire. Field mice scampered along the pews, a family of whom had already settled on a pile of aging yellow church pamphlets, undeterred by the hundreds of tourists who must have traipsed around the church on a daily basis. Winter would have been their holiday-sojourn from the tourists, as I couldn't imagine visiting the mountain-top village in the depths of a snowy winter. The roads would have been treacherous and the mountains perilous. Winter in this tiny village would have been the true meaning of Christmas. Snow and more snow.

Australian Christmases, on the other hand, were at opposite ends of the spectrum. Blisteringly hot, relentlessly stuffy and hopelessly long, often encompassing more than fifteen hours of daylight. Time enough to be burnt to a crisp whilst picnicking or cricketing on the beach on Christmas day. No wonder it had been a cool relief to have taken up the European custom of an afternoon siesta on Christmas afternoons. I had settled back to sharing my pew with the (possession is nine tenths of the law) mouse-family, when Lizzie let out an ear-piercing shriek.

She had found a dead body in an open coffin. An old man and, according to Lizzie, "Just like the one yesterday on the island of San Giulio." This macabre discovery was made as we were nearing the end of the church tour. Until then, apart from the usual suspects of frescoes, sculptures, broken mosaics and crumbling statues, nothing had really been out of the ordinary for Italy. With the discovery of the body, it was all oohs and aahs and "oh my God, look at this!" We were so noisy and jilted, Raffaella couldn't get us out of the church quickly enough.

The church was smack bang in the middle of the village, right next to the school and the bakery with the delicious smells wafting from the doorway. Immune to the novelty of crumbling churches, witness protection schools and artisan bakeries, Raffaella steered us past at a cracking pace, but I really wanted to leave an olive branch or two on the doorstep of the school-a sort of token gift from Australian school children to the little Italian bambini who were running around the school yard with their satchels, pinafores and little brimmed hats, screeching and pointing at the steady stream of tourists who passed their gates on their way to the real businesses of the village-the restaurants and cafes. It only took me a couple of minutes to leave two olive branches, with instructions and salutations for the nuns and the school children. If I were to return to the village in ten years' time and be greeted at the entrance by a row of olive trees gracing the ground, I would be a happy woman.

We had arrived at the restaurant. It was a typical alpine affair, and because it wasn't raining, we were encouraged to load up our plates from the over-abundant smorgasbord, settle ourselves outside in the front courtyard, and watch the world go by. The world was really a whole bunch of bedraggled tourists stopping at the little souvenir shops—buying trinkets and flags and mini dioramas of the alps. It was pleasant sitting outside, listening to the church bells peeling, sipping spumante and nibbling on all manner of Italian antipasto. Very civilised. Very cosmopolitan. Very chic.

It would have been easy to have stayed lounging in those wicker chairs with the plentiful bundles of flower-filled hanging baskets overhead. Too easy to have fallen asleep or to have picked up a favourite book and in a reclining position and a second flute of prosecco in one's spare hand-continue to allow the world its natural ebb and flow.

And then, God made Rafaella!

Raffaella, who had almost certainly completed her work experience days in Colonial India, where she had no doubt learnt how to blow a whistle in the challenging key of D Major, hoist a red velvet umbrella upright into the hot, steamy air and shepherd and regiment a wayward, bewildered crowd with the utmost of ease. She was more than good at her job, this one. With the simple clapping of hands and trilling of voice on the last syllable of 'andiamo', she managed to steer our whole entire group (and many of the local customers who had probably sipped their morning coffee in the cafe on the mountain-top for the last half century) away from the café, down the cobble-stoned main street and out behind the church where, lo and behold, our bus sat waiting to take us back down the mountain to Stresa.

It was all done and dusted in a matter of minutes, and as we had been bonding in the café, there had been no waiting for anyone, not even Roy, who had exceeded his personal best for making it back to the bus. (The locals who had joined our procession waved us off and then ambled back to their café.)

Less than a quarter of an hour after we had been eating and drinking, we were all tucked and belted up on the bus. Stresa-bound once more. Antonio drove so carefully and so cautiously that gobbling up the hairpin bends leading down to the little lakeside town where we'd slept last night was barely noticeable. Francesca had been a no-show until Raffaella had jumped off the bus at her stop, but once the doors had swished shut on her retreating back, it was as if a truckload of history-laden adrenaline had been injected into the good Francesca (who had appeared from the back of the bus with a stack of pamphlets tucked under her arm).

Once back in her rightful position with microphone in hand, she began talking ten-to-the-dozen about anything and everything. There was a desperation to her voice and again, I would have liked to have run down the aisle and shaken her into elective mute state, urging her to comprehend that we were all on her side, and that Raffaella was by now, relaxing with a glass of chianti and fingering the olive branch I had slipped into her palm when we'd been leaving the café. She had been surprised to have received the gift (probably hoping for money), but gracious to the point of placing the cutting carefully in the side of her tote bag.

I closed my eyes briefly, and when I opened them in what seemed like only a few minutes later (in actual fact, more than thirty minutes had passed) it was to the familiar, circular, gravelled driveway of our hotel, complete with the fountain still intact. Ours was the only bus taking up the space in front of the fountain-the other tour buses probably having gone off on day trips and not returning until late afternoon. I appreciated the way our day had been segmented. Very thoughtful and considerate planning! First, the Alpine train, then the meal, and now, our return to the hotel for a little R and R. It was taxing, this touring caper.

I was last off the bus, because I wanted to jot down some notes on a story Raffaella had related to us whilst we'd been sitting in the pews of the mountain-top village church. It was a fascinating story, and one which would, almost certainly in my book, have trumped every other story about Italy I had heard to date. But, as the tour was not yet over, I would stockpile it until day eight. Then I would decide.

The story concerned a young chimney sweep who worked for a master chimney sweep responsible for the mountain-top church's maintenance. (The ancient, crumbling church we'd visited.) The boy was around eight years of age, and small for his years. One day, the master needed a chimney to be cleaned out. The particular chimney was directly above the Confessionals. The older man helped the slip of an apprentice-boy squeeze up into a shaft beside the original chimney with his brooms and brushes so that the boy would be able to complete the job in such a tiny space high up in the roof.

When the boy finally returned to his master, covered from head to foot in thick black soot, he was bubbling over with excitement. He was a clever boy, despite having had little education, and he had something important to tell his master. Some news which would impact and ripple through the village like a mountain-fire as it concerned the government.

The boy had been scraping and sweeping in the chimney above the confessional when he had heard raised voices, followed by intense sobbing. He had stopped sweeping straight away and crouched down in the corner of the chimney, not wanting to be seen nor heard by either the *historical gem* priest or the confessor. He could see quite clearly down the confessional. The man confessing wore a soldier's uniform overladen with military badges, and he was telling the priest, in between gasps and sobs, that he was a General in Mussolini's army and that Il Duce himself had, just that morning, given him the orders to have his soldiers change sides from allegiance with the Nazis to the side of the Allies.

The General was deeply disturbed by this order and was now imploring the priest, under the seal of confession, to advise him. Should he go along with his leader's orders, or should he turn a blind eye in defiance and treason? Just as the priest had been about to give a response, some of the soot came tumbling down like a fluttering of black snowflakes, tickling the boy's nostrils and causing him to sneeze loudly.

Both men had looked up and the priest had gotten a good look at the eavesdropping urchin. The boy had fled the scene, reclaimed his master and related his tale. The cluey master, realising he had collateral richer than gold, had gone straight to the priest and threatened to disclose the secret if he and all his workers were not paid an exorbitant amount of lire. The silence was bought and it was rumoured that the whole chimney sweeping clan moved to England where their descendants now live as the filthy rich landed-gentry. Being from chimney sweeping stock, 'filthy rich' had a certain authentic ring to it.

Raffaella had loved relating the tale. She had then stood up and led us over to the wood-panelled confessional where the said conversation was said to have occurred, urging us to look up into the rafters and try to imagine what went on that day in the this little church in the mountains.

It would have taken me too long to write the whole tale, even though my fingers were itching to make contact with the gleaning letters on my iPad and disclose the juicy historical gem there and then. I would also have liked to have pencilled out a couple of rudimentary sketches whilst I had the little chimney sweep and the layout of the church vibrant in my mind's eye. But with no pastels or grey leads, I would have to make do with my memory when I came to write the explosive tale. It couldn't be there and then. Antonio was just about to lock the bus, and everyone else, including Francesca had disappeared. Time to seek out Alice.

Up in our bedroom, Alice and I spent the next fifteen or so minutes repacking and rearranging bags and backpacks. "I've made a definite decision not to come to the palace this afternoon, Fil. I've got a slight headache, and I think I need a bit of a lie-down." Which literally translated as, "I want to finish off my needlework in peace."

Alice knew that I knew that she had no intention of lying down all afternoon, but it didn't matter as it was her holiday, and she was free to spend the afternoons in any way she saw fit. I would have stayed with her and we could have had a lazy afternoon on the balcony sipping limoncello, but I had my heart set on viewing the palace where European Princes and Princesses married, and white peacocks and golden pheasants roamed the tufty green grounds, grazing and gazing in their idyllic surrounds.

The New Zealand couple on the bus, Jerry and Babette, had mentioned in their little talk about themselves that they had been to the palace on Isola Bella a few years ago, and that it had been one of the highlights of their tour. I thought about different things appealing to different people. It would be a pretty boring old world if we all liked the same things, dressed in the same fashion, and ate the same food.

"I'm still going, Alice, you'll be OK here, won't you?"

Alice did not look in the least chaffed that I would be in absentia all afternoon, and she promised to find a way to meet us on the island where we would be dining tonight. "I'm not sure yet how I'll get there, I may have to swim, but I wouldn't miss a three-course Italian meal for the world." Food was often foremost on Alice's mind, especially when it was Italian food—and who could blame her?

The menu for tonight's dinner had been set on the first morning when we had left Milan. Francesca had ended up extremely frustrated because every time she conducted a preference-headcount (who wanted chicken and who wanted veal for the main course), she came up with that different number. She had accused some passengers of putting up their hands for both chicken and veal, and had, in the end, thrown up her hands in exasperation, stating that it would be a lucky dip, and people would just have to eat the dish that was placed in front of them. Or swap! Too bad for the vegetarians, and the vegans. It wouldn't have been worth your life to have informed Francesca that you had turned from meat overnight.

Down in the foyer, it was typically peaceful and still, and someone had magnanimously opened the double doors leading out to the carpark and the lake beyond, so that the full force of the breeze rippled through the foyer. Only Brielle was there. I assumed the others to already be on the bus, and I was correct. Brielle had waited patiently for Alice and I to appear, and she looked relieved to see that I was alone. I quickly explained that Alice was doing a 'Matteo' and snatching some down-time this afternoon. "Sore leg. You know."

Brielle nodded knowingly and dragged me out through the doors to the bus. "Looks like it's just you and me from now on, kid." Which was a funny turn-of-phrase, because she was much younger than I, but being American appeared to be the coupon to chivalry and perfect persuasion.

We were all sitting and waiting patiently on the bus, but after ten minutes or so, when neither Francesca, Antonio nor Matteo had appeared, Fillip stood up with an address to the nation. "It looks like the Holy Trinity have abandoned us for the rest of the day. Is there any one amongst you who can drive a bus?" That could have been my moment to show the rest of them the stuff I was made from. I could drive a bus! And a tractor. And a backhoe!

I had learnt to drive a school bus when I'd worked at a private school with a student bus, and I'd learnt to drive a tractor and backhoe when my father had taken me out on the job with him on the weekends when he was coating Canberra suburbs in concrete. Canberra ended up with whole suburbs covered in concrete. It would be easy to stand up and make my way down towards the driver's seat, but just as I was about to push past Brielle and bound down to the aisle, someone pipped me at the post. That someone was Devo's father, Joe who had suddenly been resurrected from a three-day sabbatical when he heard the phrase, 'Drive the bus!'

I didn't have the heart to steal his thunder, so I slunk back into my seat next to Brielle. She didn't say a word, but it was clear she sensed my disappointment. I could tell by the way she was looking at me.

I got in first. "Brielle, I know you probably think that everyone in Australia can drive a bus because we have such vast expanses of land that's not settled on, but that's not really true of all Aussies. The only reason I learnt to drive a bus was so that I could drive school children to excursions. We all got a bus license back then. Now, kids don't go on excursions anymore. Just watch YouTube clips and never move from their classrooms." It was a sad reflection on the world if one stopped to consider it. Children with their eyes transfixed to a screen when they could have been out in the real world exhausting all five senses on a day-excursion.

It had been a detailed retort, and I could tell by the look on Brielle's face that she feared she'd awoken a sleeping tiger when it came to the state of education in the world today, and how technology was doing its best to eradicate the human touch. I should have reassured her that I wasn't really as passionate as I might appear, and that if it wasn't technology to blame, there would be another cause breathing down its neck. Progress and rapid change were just difficult concepts for me to grasp.

I decided to close my eyes and keep waiting. It was extremely unlikely that Devo's father would be permitted to drive the bus, and without any sign of the drivers and Francesca, there wouldn't even have been keys. The problem actually solved itself, because no sooner had I closed my eyes than Brielle was shaking me, urging me to listen to the instructions Francesca was dishing out. Yes. Francesca had reappeared on the scene, and was busy lecturing us that we had not listened to her instructions for the day and that had we done so, we would have realised the bus would not be taking us anywhere that afternoon, or even in that evening for the promised meal of chicken or veal, as we would simply not be travelling anywhere by bus.

We would be alighting and walking across the road to the little ferry-jetty, where a boat would take us to Isola Bella, the Borromean Island with the palace and the flag flapping in the breeze. "This, of course, means that the royal family are in residence, and who knows, one of you might be lucky enough to see one of the family roaming around." I hoped it would be me. The lucky member of the public to encounter royalty.

If my track record was anything to go by, the last time I had toured Europe on a bus and we had been in Monaco for the afternoon, I had glimpsed Princess Stephanie of Monaco (daughter of Prince Rainer and Princess Grace) backing out of her hilly, rocky driveway in an enormous grey four-wheel drive. She had been wearing equally enormous black sunglasses, and I hadn't even really been convinced that it was the princess herself, but according to the tour guide, the princess was a creature of habit and she did the same thing every day after lunch. A paltry claim to fame, I agree, but at the very least, I had a good chance of glimpsing a member of that very same family this afternoon (inter-marriage and all that).

Some of the passengers were embarrassed that we had been sitting like stunned mullets on the bus, entirely oblivious to the fact that we were off the Borromean islands, and that no bridge the length of the Golden Gate in San Francisco (my favourite bridge) had yet been built across the lake to the palace. Brielle, Natarsha, Gig and I saw the funny side of a busload of tourists sitting and waiting for twenty minutes on a bus that was going nowhere. We jostled and hustled our way down the back stairs, a tangle of laughing bodies.

There was a pleasant breeze coming off the lake, and I was glad I'd listened to Alice and had thrown my jacket into my backpack.

Francesca continued to wear her heart on her sleeve and express her disappointment at the fact that not one of us had listened intently enough to her to know that the bus would not be moving until tomorrow morning. Brielle tried to cheer Francesca up by walking alongside of her and whistling a tune from Snow White and the seven dwarfs, *it's off to work we go*, but Francesca wasn't having a bar of it. After she'd pointed out the boat which was to spirit us over to the island, she buried her head in her phone, and only reappeared when the last passenger (Roy) had been helped onto the boat by a tall tanned boatman with a red scarf knotted around his neck. (Or was it a large red scar? I couldn't tell, but he looked the part.)

Once we arrived on the island, we were given further, elaborate and painstakingly slow instructions from Francesca as to how much free time we had to explore the island, the exact time the tour of the palace would conclude, and where we would be required to assemble to catch the boat over to the neighbouring island, where we would be dining this evening. (The next island did not look to be too far from where we had landed, so that was a relief, as I tend to get very seasick in choppy waters.)

The tour of the palace was first up. Never, in all my years of touring have I stood face to face with such a beautiful palace, surrounded by such stunning gardens. Possibly it was the verdant setting (Topiary World headquarters by the looks of things)) but the palace itself had a magical feel, and I instantly and hopelessly fell in love with the island itself-the palace and the gardens were an added bonus to the stark beauty of the exquisite parcel of land. It felt like a little slice of heaven.

It was, to borrow a well-used cliché describing nowhere in particular, 'jaw-droppingly beautiful'. Nothing could even come close to the sheer ecstasy of this exquisite island. It was called Isola Bella after the wife of Carlo Borromeo the third. The Borromeo's were, and continue to remain, a prestigious Italian family of great nobility and wealth. Some time ago, I had worked in a school in Melbourne with the same name. St Carlo Borromeo. How blasé I had been about that namesake. How could I have been unaware of the importance of the title, or the fact that the Borromeo family still retained this island as their summer residence? Sometimes ignorance is bliss, and sometimes knowledge is even more blissful. Which brought me to where I stood, at the foot of the flight of thick stone stairs leading up to the palace, about to enter Nirvana.

The rooms in the palace stretched on endlessly-marble floor after marble floor of elaborate baroque furniture, iron spiral staircases stretching up to heaven, beautiful marble busts, and extensive dining tables set for fifty, with perfect blue merino-glass plates, cups and saucers. The whole scene was almost a movie set—half-moon rooms with soaring ceiling painted in the palest of blues, etched with real gold, and none of us would have been surprised to see James Bond catapulting through the French doors-cum-windows for a spot of afternoon tea. It was peaceful and awe inspiring. On the lower levels, the guide introduced us to room after room of cool stone and shell-covered grottos. I have never been in a catacomb, but I felt I was close in this palace.

The guide left us in the underground section, and she accepted a well-deserved round of applause, a handful of euro and of course, a tiny packaged olive branch which I was more than happy to part with for a guide so smart and so young. This woman, Kiki, had demonstrated a passion for the history and architecture of Italy, and that was to be commended. She had taken us into rooms inhabited at various times in their lives by both Napoleon and Mussolini and had given us time to take photos of a famous signed document bearing the signature of Mussolini himself.

I was still wandering around the underground stone rooms when I noticed a man huddled in a far corner, loading his camera and taking shots of the paintings on the stone walls—some of which appeared to be nudes, but in the half-light it was difficult to see properly. As soon as I approached the man, he quickly put away his camera and began hurrying towards the exit, his face scarlet. I wished Alice had been with me, as I knew we would both have burst into fits of laughter on the spot.

Of course, it would have been our turn to have blushed like mad the next time we saw the man. I was pretty certain he was not on our bus, as by now most of the passengers were quite familiar to me, but I did recognise him from somewhere. It might have been as far back as the day we visited La Scala, as there had been many other buses at the Opera House that day, besides ours.

I waited until the 'voyeur' had well and truly left the building, and then made my way out into the bright sunshine. I still had an hour in which to explore the gardens, and as Brielle and the others had not cared to venture down to the stone dungeons—I was on my own.

Without a map and no Wi-Fi with which to summons Siri, I took to aimless wandering. Carefree automatic pilot in the garden of Eden. The tour of the palace and underground bunkers had been a sombre affair, with Kiki doing most of the talking, and Fillip asking the occasional question. To his credit, Fillip's questions had been insightful and thought provoking. He had queried the number of place settings at the long table in the blue room, and got us all thinking about how Mussolini had managed to perfect such an idiosyncratic signature, which had been the flamboyant focal point of the framed declaration, hanging in prominent position in the Music room.

The young guide had also been impressed with Fillip's quizzing of her knowledge, causing her to hijack him as a sidekick for the next tour she was to conduct. Lizzie had told me the girl had begged Fillip to tag onto the next group to tour the palace and to ask the very same questions. That way she (the guide) would be assured of heightened interest by the crowd when she delivered her well-rehearsed monologue. They would split the tips.

As far as Lizzie and I knew, Fillip was still living it up in the Palace with Kiki and their next audience. That left Lizzie to also fly solo in the gardens, so inevitably, we joined forces. The arrangement with Fillip had been to meet at the departure point on the little island jetty at the designated hour—five-thirty.

Chapter 25
In the Midst of the Borromean Gardens

I had found Lizzie squatting on a little stone wall, staring down into the pit of the ten terraces, where there appeared to be an awful lot of movement, and an awful lot of commotion. There was also a bushel of a bride down there, resplendent in white taffeta and a laced veil which trailed halfway back up the path. Tourists were snapping away at the bride in the beautiful garden of juxtaposed English hedges and European cypress. It was a sight for sore eyes alright. Fussing around the feet of the blushing bride, like fattened altar-boys at a Coronation, were the white peacocks and golden pheasants of which the New Zealanders had spoken.

Faint music was drifting up the terraced cliff face, barely audible from where I stood beside Lizzie, but my ear for music is good, and I would have bet ten euro on it being Pachelbel's Canon. All that was missing were the white doves, which Lizzie eagerly informed me were behind the hedge, in a cage-awaiting release. "I saw some gardeners carrying a wicker-cage full of white doves and hiding it behind the hedge. Sit down here next to me, Fil. (Lizzie was patting the stone wall to her left.) We can watch the doves being released together. I don't think I'll see Fillip again till this evening. He seems to have run off with the guide."

At that stage I hadn't really understood what Lizzie had meant by Fillip having deserted her for the guide. Which guide? Francesca? Rena or Raffaella? Or, to add spice to the tale, Antonio who had guided us back down the mountains from the little village of this morning?

I didn't for one second think it would be the impeccably dressed, thin young guide who had just finished ushering us around the palace for the last hour. But, in the course of our conversation around the bride and the assorted birds on show, Lizzie disclosed the identity of the guide, and it all made sense to me. I had come to know Fillip a little better over the last few days and could well imagine him hitching up with the pretty, slender girl for the rest of the afternoon. He would have been flattered with her appreciation of his astute questions, and overeager to please her by repeating them verbatim with the next group. Harmless ego-striking. "Nothing to worry about", according to Lizzie. "In fact, I can finally get some peace. Fillip's questions are usually directed towards me."

We had sat in relative silence after that, watching the goings on at ground zero, a decade of terraces below. The releasing of the doves was spectacular, and I was left wondering where they disappeared to, and would they, like Fillip, be making a reappearance any time in the near future? It seemed fitting that the birds had been released in the gardens of a palace, as breeding was the key to their selection. In truth, there was little difference between a bunch of pigeons squawking at the seaside, or speaking glass windows and windscreens, and these silent types, especially bred for repeated release from wicker baskets. It made me think of the difference between the blue bloods of this Borromean Island, and the tourists, like myself, who came to from humble beginnings to admire the exquisite setting and triumph of nature in the world-famous gardens. No difference. There was no difference between them and us, except perhaps for an exorbitant stash of jewels, an endless pile of gold and a plum in the voice. The blood bit was rubbish!

I remembered another thing about Isola Bella. It was the island in Northern Italy on which Prince Charles and Princess Diana had stayed, and the garden was, reputedly, the most magnificent garden park in the whole of Europe. In the 'Dianna days' the Royal visit had been the talk of the town.

Leaving Lizzie to sit and people-watch on the stone wall surrounding acres of flowers and foliage, I set off for the steps which led down to the gardens where the bride and groom were still being photographed. It was getting chilly, so I stopped to put on my jacket, and as I was straightening up, I heard Australian voices to my left. As Alice and I were the only Australians on our tour, I knew it must have been a group from another tour. Probably a group who had just finished a session with the guide and her lovely assistant 'Fillip'.

The Australians were marvelling at the spectacular gardens, and the fact that the air was so fragrant and crisp at the same time. I wanted to tell them I was also Australian, and that I too could smell the frangipani-filled air, but I felt like there were five of them and one of me, and I would have needed to have addressed all five of them when I spoke. Too taxing. I would just leave it and go down to the garden. I turned to mount the stone pavers and tripped over a long plastic and metal object. An umbrella!

Someone was helping me to my feet and apologising for having lost his grip on the umbrella. I looked up into the wrinkled visage of an elderly purple-vested gentleman with a hat covering most of his face. He continued with his apologising in a toffy voice. "My goodness, my dearest. I'm frightfully sorry about that. The umbrella just seemed to slip out of my hand. It's fortunate I was not holding my dog leash with my other hand. We would have been in real trouble then. I always find it such a challenge when I'm out waking with Patsy and it starts to bucket down! I just never know what to do with my hands."

Speaking of which, he suddenly extended his dripping wet hand out towards me. "Allow me to introduce myself, Charles Shepherdson the Third." What were the odds? I had spent the last five minutes mulling over the differences between the landed gentry and the serfs, the red and the bluebloods, and now lo and behold, a man who tagged 'the third' on to the end of his name. And what did that mean? The third what? Third born? Third in line to a hefty inheritance? Last in a race of three contestants?

I was smiling as I recovered my equilibrium, but I didn't reply to Charles the Third, who had not yet drawn a breath. (Maybe I could introduce him to Francesca?)

I finally found my voice, and muttered to the gentleman that I was okay and there was no harm done. He asked if he might accompany me down the slippery stone steps to the garden, and he hoisted his umbrella into full bloom. Together we negotiated the steps—all sixty of them—and at the bottom, in the hedge-garden, he informed me that he was leading a small tour of rich eccentric Italophiles, who were waiting for him on the jetty. He was a pleasant man, and I wanted to bequeath him an olive branch, but it was more than likely he lived in England and I couldn't take that chance.

So, I didn't mention the olive branches, and he left me in the bottom garden, none the wiser. I was grateful he had sheltered me with his expansive black umbrella, as it was still drizzling and I didn't want to catch a cold. The bride and groom were still chasing each other around the miniature hedge maze, and the paparazzi were still snapping away. If I looked up, I would probably see Lizzie still sitting there on the stone wall, but I didn't bother, as then she would recognise me and almost certainly quiz me about Charles the third and why I had been under his umbrella for so long.

I spotted a pile of handbags and jackets close to where the 'two who had become one' had been having their photographs taken, and it seemed like a good idea to leave two olive branches next to their belongings. Hopefully, they would find them and get excited about a gift from a perfect stranger. Or, they might assume that one of the Borromeo family members had been watching the wedding ceremony from a bedroom window and had sent a servant down to gardens with a simple wedding gift.

It was nearing the witching hour-five o'clock being the designated time for meeting up with the rest of my group. I wasn't too far away from the jetty, and I could see the path leading down to the water up ahead. Along the way I zipped into the island's tourist souvenir shop. Clever positioning on the part of the island's town-planners. Where else would the chocolate bars be placed but at the end of the counter leading up to the check-out counter?

The placement of this shop was no different. The interior was different though. Once I'd crossed the threshold, I found that I had entered a souvenir shop in the league of Harrods and Bloomingdales. (Complete with a delicious coffee aroma permeating the entire premises.) The shop-fittings were gold edged and there was gleaming honey-coloured wood everywhere. The merchandise was exquisite-perfect pieces of memorabilia in a pristine arrangement of opulence. I had never, to my knowledge, been in such a gracious tourist outlet. The sales assistants, two dark haired young Italian women, were impeccably and identically dressed in colours I assumed to be reflective of the Borromean crest.

There were only two other customers in the shop, and once I had chosen a handful of gifts for some of my extended family, I hurriedly moved on towards the pretty little jetty. The shop would have been a lovely spot in which to have lingered and sipped strong, overly-sweet, Italian coffee. But, as usual, I was late.

With Alice by my side, time management was never an issue, but on occasions such as this afternoon, when I was a solo traveller, it was easy to forget that the clock striking midnight was imminent. Fortunately for me, I was not the last person to board the boat. That honour was taken up entirely by Fillip, who, according to Lizzie "must still have been up at the palace with the Guide."

Lizzie looked relaxed and unperturbed that her husband was a 'no show'. Francesca did not look anywhere near as relaxed, and with the looming reality that she might be losing one of her passengers for good-she raced back up the gangplank and began shouting out the tourists who were minding their own business-waiting for their own boat to arrive to take them to their next destination, that our tour was missing a passenger, and had anyone seen him? Ten minutes later, she had established that no witnesses were ever going to come forward, and that Fillip would need to be left behind. Once the rest of us had been safely deposited on the next island, Isola Madre, our evening dining destination, the boat would return to Isola Bella for the defector—Fillip. Still Lizzie showed no concern for the fate of her husband. "He's a big boy. He can look after himself. If he misses the meal, well, he'll have to go hungry."

Cruel, but fair, I thought. Fillip had brought it all on himself when he'd fallen for the guide's fluttering eyelashes and slim coquettish charm. Now he would be left waiting for the boat—alone—at close of palace.

"Grumm-umm, Rmm-umm" the boat spluttered and coughed along the short stretch of choppy water towards Isola Madre. As we'd pulled out, another three boats had arrived, and the collective displacement of water in the little jetty-harbour forced our boat into a continuous see-saw bob all the way to the next island. I was glad to get off. A queasiness was claiming me, and the erratic motion of the boat had affected me to the point that I felt giddy and disoriented. Brielle was walking beside me, and when I faltered slightly, she had my arm in a jiffy. "Fil, what's wrong? Are you boat-sick?"

I assured her I would be right as rain in a few minutes, and that I just needed to sit quietly on the wall and take in the air. I wasn't having a 'fit of the vapours', I was just a fraction unnerved by the hectic, erratic motion of the boat. Brielle fussed over me for a few more seconds, and then quickly raced up the path to join the others who had disappeared around the rocky bend. She promised me she would inform Francesca I would be along very soon, and that I was not ill-just seasick.

I imagined Francesca's response to the news that yet another passenger, had gone missing. Four out of twenty was almost a pandemic! We were dropping off like flies. One fifth of all the passengers-gone by the by. Francesca would fear she was losing her touch, which wasn't the case at all. Alice and Gloria had stayed back at the hotel for health reasons, I had been nauseous, and Fillip had flown the coup of his own volition. Francesca really had nothing to do with the decisions any of us had made.

I was sitting on the rocky wall with my head between my legs, wishing for a paper bag, and trying to remember how to breathe from the brace position when the plane was about to crash, when I was disturbed by the almighty roar of a speedboat surging along the lake, hurtling at a speed I deemed a little too fast for comfort. The boat looked to be heading straight towards me. Apart from the crazy driver, there looked to be three others on the boat. Judging by the speed, they were, like the rabbit in the Alice-in-Wonderland tale, late, late, late for a very important date. When the boat pulled up on the pebbly shore, I was astounded to see that that it was Alice herself sitting there clutching her handbag. Not Alice in Wonderland, but Alice from London, of the windswept hair, and petrified gaze. One of the other two passengers was no further surprise. Once I'd seen Alice it made sense that Gloria would be with her as they had both remained at the hotel whilst the rest of us were exploring the palace, but the wild card on the boat was Fillip. What on earth was Fillip doing on the boat and how had he managed to get onto the boat so quickly given the last tour of the palace would still have been in progress?

The answers were simple once we were reunited.

"I suddenly realised the time, and I left Kiki to finish off the last group by herself. Such a sweet girl, and so knowledgeable." Would Lizzie agree that the beautiful Kiki was a fountain of knowledge, or would she fly off the handle in a fit of rage once she realised her husband and the guide were on a first-name basis? Time would tell, when they were placed beside one another at the dinner in less than half an hour.

I turned my attentions to Alice and nonchalantly questioned her on what she had been up to in our absence.

"Nothing, really!" I tried asking her about her prized needlework, but she seemed distracted by the beautiful island, and I gave up. Who could blame her from being smitten with the flowers, the lush vegetation, the palm trees and the acres of terraces? We had already enjoyed Isola Bella for the last two hours or so, but Alice and Gloria were novices at this late hour. One hundred plus minutes of immersion into the luscious, ornate palace gardens had given us that slight edge over Alice, Gloria and Fillip.

I spent the next five minutes with my head in my hands on the stone wall, and the other three took over Brielle's spot of fussing and dousing me with cold water from their water bottles. I began to feel better. Wet, but better.

Just as we'd been about to set off up the hill in search of our group, another boat chugged into the tiny sheltered cove, and a boatload of Germans tumbled ashore. I recognised their voices as a German, and some of their faces from yesterday when we'd been on the island of San Giulio.

"Let's hurry and catch up to the others. They're probably already sitting up eating their entrees by now." Feeling slightly revived, I had assumed command because it was my fault Alice, Gloria and Fillip were late. They didn't seem in all that much of a hurry to climb the steep incline to the restaurant and some of the Germans were already overtaking us. I repeated my concerns.

"Let's go now, shall we? The meals will be getting cold." Both women jumped up and began climbing the steep incline, but Fillip didn't move at all. He just stood there with his hands in his pocket staring down at the fast-approaching Germans and waving to those amongst the group who were looking up to him.

"Are you coming, Fillip?" I didn't care either way whether or not Fillip was coming with us, but I knew that Francesca would be bounding back down at the jetty any minute now. She, like many of the other guides, must have had genetic engineering inclusive of an inbuilt honing device, alerting her as to when the next bigger boat was about to grace the island's fair shores.

Sure enough. Right on cue, Francesca made her appearance from behind a tall cypress tree.

"Oh, there you are, Fil. We thought you might have been snorkelling in the lake you have been missing for so long. Alice, Gloria, what are you two doing here? And Fillip? Ah this is the true Italian hospitality at work. We have you all now, eh? For the feast of a lifetime on a beautiful island. Come on, andiamo e fa presto tutti."

I followed Francesca and the others followed me. At the top of the hill there was a health, bulky vine-covered canopy with a spider's web of trellises branching out in all directions, groaning with roses and sweet orange flowers. To the side of the trellis was small grove of orange and lemon trees brimming with fruits, ripe for the picking, and beyond the trees were rows and rows of enormous, flaky terracotta pots filled with flowers of every conceivable colour. Francesca had stopped in the doorway behind the trellis, over which hung a 'seen better days' sign in English. 'Pirate-restaurant'. As soon as I saw the sign, I remembered having read about the famous Pirate's Restaurant on Isola Madre. We were in for a real treat tonight!

"Keep you bending your ear when you a walk reroute the doorway, and welcome to the pirate restaurant." This jovial conundrum was delivered by a fully-fledged pirate, right down to the parrot on his shoulders. Yes, a real parrot, but one that wasn't helping out with any of the greetings. (Possibly saving his voice for a later performance?) As the pirate-man addressed us, the parrot flew away squawking loudly. How could we bend our ears, and didn't the pirate mean "bend your head"?

To keep the peace, and to appear eager and obliging customers, all four of us bent our ears back and lowered our heads as we passed though the low, narrow arched doorway. This really was Alice in Wonderland territory! Francesca was last to enter and I noticed she was refraining from pulling and bending her ears back into a "Mr Spock" configuration. The pirate-man had simply gotten his words muddled, mistaking head for ears.

Undoubtedly, we looked peculiar to the group of German tourists hot on our heels, but they must have been booked in for a pre-dinner island exploration walk, as none of them followed us through the archway. The inside of the Pirate Restaurant resembled a large man cave, that enigmatic phenomenon that has of late begun to spring up in your typical Australian backyard, possessive of a garden shed.

The man's cave is stereotypically crammed with kegs and flags, beer glasses by the dozens, trophies and knickknacks, framed photographs and more framed photographs. The room we had just entered was more of a bar room, with one long bar-bench stained in dark wood, and every bottle of alcohol under the sun one could care to name, lining the dusty wooden shelves above the bar. The bottles looked as if they hadn't been touched in a thousand years, and although I was aware of the saying, 'the older the better' I was a little doubtful in this extreme case. The black-eyed pirate was introducing himself to us as Eduardo and assuring us that he was to be our host for the evening. "If there is something you want, and it is not right there in front of you on the table, please call out, or sing, or clap your hands and we will attend to you. We are true pirate servants for the evening. My brother is the chef in the kitchen, and he is the pirate who will meet you all later."

Eduardo then flounced forewords with his elongated feather and his cap and sword, swishing his way into a much larger room, where I was grateful to see so many familiar faces sitting up sipping wine and munching on breadsticks. They were all happy to see our little quartet-the lost sheep of the fold, and Eduardo was quick to place a full glass of red wine in each of our hands. (Only one glass per person, not two.)

Normally, I'm not all that partial to red wine, but I was cold from the boat and having sat on the cold stone wall for so long that it was with welcome relief I accepted the drink. I quicklopy threw back half of the thick red liquid in my wine glass down my throat, relishing the warm buzz as it slid down into my stomach. It'd been a fair while since I'd eaten, and I felt the burning sensation of the liquid grapes. Much better. A bit like Communion wine, but with more punch!

With fortification in place, I was able to put my best self-forwards and entertain the table with stories and songs. Francesca kept stopping by to ask if everything was going well, and none of us had the heart to tell her that although the food had been perfect, none of us had received the meal we had selected some days before. We had laughed about the fuss Francesca had made, writing people's names down and attaching a big 'C' for chicken and an even bigger 'V' for veal next to the name.

The main course had really paled into insignificance once we had tasted the entrée, which was the same for everyone—Polenta.

I was completely ignorant to the properties of polenta, and although I knew risotto to be a specialty of the North, I wasn't really as aufait with polenta. It was sticky, and as yellow as about the extent of my knowledge, and before the dish had arrived, most people at my table shared my sentiments. Alice was the only one with a morsel of extra information. "It's usually quite filling. That's why they give it you as an entrée in case the main course doesn't come up to scratch." The polenta was perfect. Delectable and delicious. The pirate chef (Eduardo's brother) appeared as soon as we had all polished off the polenta. (His timing was so precise he could only have been waiting in the wings for his cue from big brother.)

Garbed in full pirate costume, with the incongruous addition of a crisp white chef's apron, his carefully rehearsed lines, illustrating the cooking process were delivered in mock Shakespearean guise, with lots of throwing of hands and variation of voice. Clearly, English was not his first language, but there must have been a sufficient run of tourists and enough nightly sittings providing him the opportunity to practise his English. I assumed the guide from the next group would assist with the translation into German.

Here is how his English sounded, but one had to be there on the idyllic island in the middle of the soul-stirring lake, in the smoky room with the big chef jumping around from table to table, and the gophers rearranging the set between sets (courses) to truly soak up the atmosphere of the place. (A mask or two, or even a pirate's scarf to wrap around one's face wouldn't have gone astray, as the wind must have changed, and the sample from polenta headquarters was wafting in big time though the open French doors all down one side of the restaurant.)

"We cook the polenta on our fire in the fresh garden air. You can taste the earth and the smoke. This is a very old dish from the mountains where they sleep like bears. In the war-times, there was nothing to eat except polenta. So, we have made the recipe to 'perfecto'—the creamy, yellow colour you saw in a front of you."

As the brother had been spouting his soliloquy (the same lines every night to a different group of tourists?), Eduardo and a petite, dainty female waitress, the size, shape and colouring of a black and white butterfly, had been swiftly and silently collecting our empty bowls. When the chef saw the stacks, which had been scraped clean, his smile widened.

"I am so very happy you all enjoyed our traditional polenta" were his parting words as he mock-slashed his way back into the kitchen, presumably to stick a wire into the heart of the dessert to test its moistness and readiness. Promised on the menu we had been handed on arrival, had been authentic Italian cassata with fig and almond log-cake.

I thought about the firing process of the polenta and could well imagine the rounded conglomeration roasting in a fire pit in the glorious garden. A sharp parallel memory from my childhood was that of dad kneading pizza dough, and then wrapping it in a thick, checked baby-cot blanket, and placing the rounded mass on the kitchen table overnight, so that it might rise. The information pamphlet which doubled as a placemat on our tables described a similar process. That of polenta being swaddled in a rough-hewn cloth and left to settle overnight by the shepherds on the hills and mountains of Northern Italy. Old customs die hard-if at all!

During the eating sessions, the room was abuzz with conversation, and the evening was turning out to be one of the highlights of the trip. (Every night was a highlight in Italy!) Hunger, anticipation, and wine on empty stomachs will do that every time. Following the pirate chef's speech, whilst we awaited the promised chicken or veal lucky dip, Mario Lanza and a mystery Italian woman with a shrill, trilling voice kept us entertained. (The parrot did not appear, and hopefully was 'resting') During the singing, everyone joined in the chorus of "Santa Lucia" and it could have been that we'd all indulged in too much Chianti, as the gusto of the chorus, "Sa…an…ta…lu…chi…a" would have rivalled many a Gilbert and Sullivan light opera troupe.

The final course was cheese and crusty bread sticks, which we also polished off. It could be a feast or a famine when embracing restaurants in unfamiliar countries, but tonight we had struck it lucky with a feast fit for Italian Royalty. All that was missing was dancing, but Francesca promised dancing at a monastery when we reached Parma, and I knew that was something I could wait for patiently. I'd heard of the 'singing priests of Ireland' with their beautiful tenor voices, but dancing monks of the Italian mountains? Reserving judgement might be best.

It all ended far too abruptly!

"Everyone please, gather up your belongings. The boat is waiting to take us back to the hotel, and the next group is ready for their food." Francesca had appeared at the side door (a different opening to the one we had entered through some hours before. I looked at my phone. It was already eight pm, and time for the Germans to eat. I wondered what they'd been up to all this time on the tiny island. Perhaps there was a movie room and they'd been living it up with Italian movies and polenta-popcorn? No opportunity presented itself for me to question them, which was just as well, as I had failed German in my first year of high school and switched to French. The only German I knew came from binging on countless episodes of *Hogan's Heroes* as a child, and lately, in my prime. My minimal vocabulary would not have gotten me past hello and hurry up!

"Fil. You are behind again. Hurrying please!"

As I was on the end of the line, I took the opportunity to duck back into the restaurant and leave three olive branches for the pirates and the dainty waitress. They would find them on the tables, when positioning the place, for the Germans. I didn't have time to go through the restaurant to the little bar at the front and explain my gift. I'd just have to take potluck they would be discovered. With careful tending and watering, olive trees might spring up, and the entree in five years' time might end up a choice between polenta and olive-tapenade. That would throw Francesca into a tailspin when she tried for the orders for 'P' or 'T'.

A 'G and T' or two or three might have been more appropriate.

The boat was waiting, and the night was closing in. It wasn't yet dark, but the light was fading, and all the lakeside painters would have turned for home at least an hour ago. The singing and revellers had also ceased, and all that we wanted was bed. What a long, long day. I feared for the Germans making it back to their hotels by midnight. By ten pm there was not a sound in our corridor on the first floor of our grand hotel. Save for the twittering birds. Who never seemed to sleep!

Chapter 26
Genoa Bound

The starter's pistol had been released very early this morning. No swimming, a scant breakfast, and a whole bunch of bleary-eyed travellers making their sad and sorry pilgrimage to the bus. The large cases had been collected at the crack of dawn, but it seemed we were a busload of shoppers, because almost everyone had acquired a second bag, and as these were not included in the complimentary case pick up, they needed to be hauled onto the bus-courtesy of our own lily-white hands. Most people were managing, but I was aware of Roy and Yolanda struggling up the steps, and it seemed the right thing to do to offer assistance.

"Can I help you, Yolanda?" Picking up the two hessian bags with which she was wrestling, I was impressed that Yolanda had singlehandedly suffered the long hike from their bedroom, which I knew to have been two doors down from ours. I should have been proactive an hour ago and offered to 'sherpa' the extra bags downstairs for them, but as already alluded to, we were on a short time fuse.

Yolanda was effusing gratitude towards me in cup loads full enough to rival Jamie Oliver adding salt to his signature dishes. It was a trifle embarrassing, because a few of the other passengers were looking at me curiously, as if to say, 'Why are you always helping Roy and Yolanda? You're not after their money, are you?' I guess stranger things have happened on bus trips. If Roy had been a rich eccentric American, travelling alone and next in line to the fortunes of Randolph Hirst, then the onlookers would have had cause for alarm. Playing my cards right might well have seen me flying out of Heathrow International with a suitcase full of dosh to replace the suitcase full of olive branches I had carted into the country.

Sadly, Roy wasn't rich, and any spare money they had was converted into doctors' fees and operations on his legs before there was time for gaining any interest on their savings. Besides which, I enjoyed helping people. It was something I could do, and it made me feel good about myself. Testing my strength and stamina with these few bags was not going to hurt me. The hardest part about carrying Roy and Yolanda's extra bags onto the bus turned out to be heaving them up onto the wire racks above the seats. They weighed a tonne, and if I didn't know better, I would have thought either Roy or Yolande had knocked off a couple of statues from the Pirate Island last night, and I had, by my act of kindness, lain myself open to aiding and abetting.

The last thing I wanted was to end up in an Italian jail. I had watched enough episodes of Inspector Montalbano, the Italian police detective—meaner, much meaner than either Inspectors Tom Barnaby or George Gently from the fair shores of England—to have known that life in an Italian cell would never be without mafia connections. My second theory was that the bags each contained a slab of Corona marble, which the guide on our way to the island of San Giulio (Rena) had pointed out would be excellent for kitchen benches, and who had joked that if anyone was strong enough to heave some of the pink-coloured marble into their suitcases to take home would be bargain shopping.

It was worth a peek in the bags.

I just hoped I wouldn't discover a prosthetic leg—or two!

Alice had gone on ahead to claim our seats, and Roy and Yolanda had stopped for a rest halfway along the aisle and were now chatting away happily to the young Singaporean couple. They were so happy all the time-the young couple from the equatorial island. I made a mental note to commit their names to memory so that I could put a name to their faces and not need to continue referring to them as the 'Singaporean couple'. I had mastered the names of the older Singaporean couple who had been sitting opposite me at the Pirate Restaurant last night.

The woman had been so interesting, telling me all about Singapore island, and the wonderful new attraction "Jewel"—five floors of terraced gardens with light shows and waterfalls which had recently opened up at Changi airport. Karina had insisted I pay them a visit on my way back to Australia, as I had mentioned my eight-hour stopover in Singapore. I hadn't promised her anything, but it would have been nice to have seen the streets and green parks of Singapore with a local.

With the coast clear, I gently folded back the red towel which was concealing the contents of one of the bags and peered in. Sure enough, there was a white statue head inside the bag. The head of an angel. The mournful eyes of the statue stared up at me, and I hurriedly replaced the towel. As the second bag was exactly the same size and weight, I assumed it to contain a matching angel, but I was not about to look inside. Already trust had been broken, and my guilt was causing my face to redden.

It was a case of curiosity as having killed the cat, and I was cursing myself. It had been none of my business-the contents of their bags. I wished I could take back my actions and unsee what I had just seen, but the damage was done, and there was no turning back. I would however need to come clean to Yolanda. Roy would not have minded in the least, but women were different, and I had transgressed big time. They were approaching me.

"Yolanda, I was trying to get the bags up into the overhead racks, when the towel slipped back, and I couldn't help seeing what you had in one of the bags. I'm sorry. I didn't mean to pry."

There!

Done it!

I had confessed with a half-truth, and the ball was now in Yolanda's court as to whether she would react favourably or angrily. Yolanda was unfazed. "Oh. The angels. We bought them yesterday on Isola Bella, and I was just thanking Jimmy and Yvonne for carrying our bags onto the boat last night. We left them on there while we were in the restaurant, and then Jimmy and Yvonne helped us carry them back to our room for us."

I was relieved there had been no secrets surrounding the angels, and that other passengers had been involved in the cartage of the heavy moulds. I was thinking about how they would get them back to the United States without having to pay extra baggage, but sometimes, when you really want something-it's worth it. When I got a chance, I'd have a D and M with Yolanda about angels, as it was a subject in which I had been invested a great deal of energy some ten years back. I'd now moved on in my life journey.

At the moment, indoor plants and vegetable cultivation was consuming me, to the point that I couldn't walk past a wheelbarrow of plants outside a nursery without wanting to buy at least three of them, and usually the whole barrow full. It was an expensive habit, and I was hoping that this trip to Italy would rekindle my interest in architecture-a passion two before the plant obsession. Because Italy was so old, the gamut of architectural styles was not to be sneezed at. I knew English Architecture like the back of my hand-English, Scottish and Irish architecture was what Australia was all about, but Italian styles such as baroque, gothic and renaissance were less familiar to me, and I wanted to be informed.

So far, it had been the Gothic styled churches of the North which had piqued my interest, but I was looking forward to exploring more of the tiny hilltop churches with the Austrian-styled sloped roofs and thick wooden frames, dotted all over the countryside we would be covering in the next few days before we completed the full circle and arrived back in Milan. My guidebook had hinted at a marvellous grandiose church in Genoa, which was to be our first port of call this morning.

Genoa was literally a port of call. The most important maritime city in Italy. It was the city from which my father, and plenty of other eager Italians had sailed from on a quest for a new life in a new country thousands of miles away. Genoa had been on my list-and now we were almost there!

The old Francesca was back! It was incredible what a good night's sleep could do! Her wild red mane was flying past the seats like the trans-Siberian as she raced up and down the aisles checking we were all comfortable and ready to leave the lakes behind. Once she had reached the front of the bus, there were a few whispered words to Marcello, before she picked up her old friend, the silver-fox microphone, and began her lament.

"So, we leava the lakes eh? How many of you are sad to go, and how many of you are happy to be seeing the real gem of the trip, Cinque Terra?"

There were murmurings amongst the passengers, but no one really answered her rhetorical questions. I was sad to leave the lakes, but I knew Cinque Terra would be the highlight, and loving the sea as I did, it was probably Cinque Terra which would be claiming me. Alice was not swaying either way, so we didn't really pursue Francesca's quandary, but took up our respective occupations.

Mine involving categorising photos on my iPhone, and Alice's, naturally, her needlework. Francesca prattled on for a while, but then gave up and let us all relax or sleep. The scenery outside was stunning, even though we were viewing it from a wide concrete motorway. It was the source of the Italian Riviera, and as I had visited the French Riviera before, I could easily envisage why this stretch of coastline had been dubbed the Italian Riviera. The replicated green and yellow, pink and apricot squashed-in Lego-piled apartments in deep valleys brushing the cobalt blue sea. The same rocky outcrops and limestone cliff faces.

Glimpsing these townscapes, I was transported back twenty-five years, to when I had been holidaying in Nice. We were too far away from the towns, which were really no more than blurs from the bus windows, but I'd be willing to bet there would be clean washing to be seen flapping from lines strung across from apartment to apartment, the closer one got to the towns themselves. It was intoxicating to dream about life in these towns. We were the tourists who would descend upon them, soak in the history and architecture, and spend our hard-earned dollars on pizza and gelati, but we would never be the true partisans.

This was their 'paese' and we were the visitors. I had friends who had lived in Italy for extended periods of time, and the nearly all of them had insisted that despite becoming entrenched in the culture and daily lives, they would never be true Italians, because it was not their birth right. There was something in that notion-for sure. I was glad my father had been Italian, and that he had helped us to love all that was Italy. My father and Frank Sinatra. It was easier to love something with which one was familiar. Not so easy to love the unknown.

Francesca was announcing that we were nearing Genoa-the city between the mountains and the sea. Italy's largest seaport, and the place from which my father had set sail for Australia more than sixty-five years ago. Francesca made us laugh when she related the story of how last year this time, on the very same trip we were taking, some of her passengers had misunderstood her accent, and thought she had said "Geneva", when in fact she had said Genoa.

They believed they were in for a long day on the bus en-route to Geneve, and that the trip would involve crossing the alps a-la-Hannibal. Francesca had made sure, from that day onwards, that everyone knew exactly where they were headed every single day. There would be no confusion between place names on any trip she was guiding!

It seemed we would need to take an alternative route into the centre of the city, as there had been a recent and catastrophic bridge collapse, and many of the roads around the port were still closed. "Hava any of you heard about our bridge which collapsed?" Many of the Americans were nodding, and we had certainly watched the horror unfolding from Australia, but the Singaporeans didn't seem to know much about the catastrophe, so Francesca seized on the opportunity to enlighten them.

Looking out from my window seat I could see huge piles of rubble and tangled steel which resembled a set for a futuristic science fiction film. The last of the bridge! Then, I thought of the loss of lives in the bridge collapse and of how scary it would have been to have been sucked off the bridge through a cavernous vortex, with no warning. I decided to concentrate, for once on Francesca's instructions. She was standing in the aisle at the front of the bus, explaining the procedure for the morning in minute detail, complete with hand

and body movements. She saw me watching and with this added encouragement, her voice seemed to become higher and louder. (Francesca had told us on Day One that Italians speak in a higher voice tone than we do, but she had forgotten to include herself in the group.)

She was, therefore, high-pitched and excited, to say the least. "When the bus pulls up to the port, I don't want any of you to jump on one of the cruise ships you will see. This is not a bus tour with a cruise ship had-on. You will need to follow the new guide whoa you will soon meet, around the old part of the city, and she will show to you the real Genoa. Then, as our usual custom you will have the free time eh? Time to buy some more gifts and souvenirs that you love, and time to look at the wonderful art and music that Genoa has for you. Just remember eh. No cruising on the ships!"

We were coming to a stop in a huge, bland carpark which ran alongside of the pier and boardwalk. Lording it over the landscape, the expanse of flat concrete appeared to be a breeding ground for buses, as there were already at least ten empty buses lined up. There must have been some early-bird tourists out there, or else they had stayed in hotels in Genoa overnight. Perhaps space in which to park buses had been tight? (We had experienced the same thing in Milan.)

It was also scooter headquarters by the looks of things, and a game of Connect Four, using the scooters as giant tors would not have been too farfetched. There were hundreds of them. When I'd been planning the trip, my mother had insisted I write down the name of the street down by the port where one of my older cousins had a newspaper stand and kiosk which sold cigarettes and chocolates and the like. I'd done as she'd asked, but the piece of scrap paper on which I had scrawled down the address had gone astray, and I couldn't remember anything about it except that the stall was close to the pier. Which was where we were now parked, but I couldn't see any kiosks or newspaper stands, only stretches of iron and steel and containers which could have housed thousands of boat people trying to get into Italy.

It was desolate, and quite depressing, and I hoped we weren't in for a tour of the docks. I didn't think we would be, as there had been no mention of spending any time in such a seedy area. Cousin Gloria and his kiosk would still be there (wherever that was) when I next visited Genoa.

It took us a little while to get organised, and Francesca and Matteo did their best to help everyone off the bus, Francesca ushering us over to a sheltered side of the car park to await the arrival of our Guide for the morning. At this rapid succession of extra guides olive groves would be taking over Northern Italy. (Southern Italy being already spoken for.)

The new guide asked us to call her Lottie, and as soon as Francesca had completed the introductions, she disappeared back onto the bus. I could see her making her way up to the sanctuary of her backseat with the little fan and the pink cushions-Francesca's boudoir-through the large gleaming bus windows as she bobbed past by each one.

Lottie, dressed from head to toe in black—a mourning widow with no ring, so perhaps an elder in the ranks of the Italian Goth party? She came across as overly stern, but in the course of the hour-long tour, turned out to be quite harmless-single minded and totally focussed on steering us away from the maritime port-up hills and down dales on a quest to cover the entirety of the old town in under the allocated hour. Actually, not the whole of the old town-rather the entirety of Banks and Government Offices in the old town. The promised church never got a look-in. Lottie was fast on her feet, tall and stately.

From her first hello to her acceptance of the token olive branch from me, she remained wrapped in a grey trench coat belted at the waist, despite the warmth of the day. (Secret agent attire in my book.) Although Lottie carried the customary umbrella, not once was it thrust skywards, as we were all constantly by her side, no one daring to loiter or lag behind in the presence of this stately woman. I decided she was German, mainly because of her name, her stature and her obvious obsession with German banks.

The highlight of the tour came towards the end, when we had exhausted all the banks and bank foyers with renaissance paintings in what seemed like the whole of Genoa, and Lottie had marched her small army into a maze of quaint, ancient corridors, tight winding streets (caruggi) and alley ways lined with stone and filled with bumper-to-bumper shops selling meat, bread, fruit and vegetables, cheeses, ice creams and pastries. The smells were delectable, and the insides of the shops looked as though they had been untouched for hundreds and hundreds of years.

It was a thriving marketplace with people and shopping baskets everywhere. There was no time to buy, only to window shop, although Lottie was gracious enough to point out to us that the shops would not close until one o'clock, and that we would still have half an hour to find our way back to the caruggi to pick up any gifts we fancied. I hoped Roy and Yolanda weren't going to get any ideas about buying legs of pork or oversized tins of tomatoes, both of which were on display in the windows of quite a number of shops.

If they did, they would be on their own with the cartage, unless they could find some other gullible passengers to help them carry their loot. Alice and I would not be venturing back to the little cobblestoned streets, as we would be on a mission to find some soothing creams for Alice and some Panadol for me in a chemist. I was developing an extremely sore throat, and I wanted to nip it in the bud before I became laid up with full-blown tonsillitis.

Brielle, Natarsha and Gloria invited us to join them for lunch in one of the little restaurants which were everywhere along the streets, but we politely declined, given our medical mission. "We'll see you back at the bus." I had been insistent. The other three had looked disappointed, but I knew the meaning of self-preservation and intervention at point of need. The chemist it would be. If we managed to squeeze in some lunch along the way—all the better. After we split up from the group, with a little hand-drawn map from Lottie stating where the bus would pick us up (I had given Lottie an olive branch for her troubles), we wasted five precious minutes mesmerised by a man on a wooden crate on a street corner waving a small Italian flag and spouting *Dante's Inferno*. (I recognised parts of it from having studied the epic poem in school.)

The man was so earnest in his delivery that I could not help myself and I quickly placed an olive branch into the hat he had positioned in front of him on the concrete. Another person who would be surprised by the nature of the gift, but he did not falter from his prose.

We managed to find a little coffee bar which also did sandwiches, and the owner, a gangly Genovese native, was excited to learn that we were Australian, as his brother had just left on an Australian holiday, and he had promised to share all his Australian stories with the family when he returned to Genoa, as well as bring gifts of koalas, kangaroos and possums. (Not the real ones, he had assured us.) The choice of fillings for our sandwiches was endlessly Italian, and not knowing whether or not there would be traces of meat in the diced-up dishes, I lashed out on a limb and ordered pasta with a typically Genovese creamy pesto sauce. (Basil, pine nuts, garlic, parmesan and of course, the liquid gold—olive oil!)

The area surrounding Genoa was famous as the birthplace of pesto, and it seemed the perfect opportunity to sample the local produce. I have to say, it was the most delicious, fresh pesto sauce I have ever been forced to swallow, and of late in an effort to prepare myself for the big trip to Italy, I had partaken of more than my fair share of pesto.

Next door to the restaurant was a marvellous shop selling all manner of jumpers, jerseys, and sweaters-all in that delectable green usually reserved for English motor vehicles. I had seen a jumper in the shop-window next door as we had passed, and it was the exact coloured jumper for which I had been on the look-out. The green of the Italian flag, the green of Ireland's rolling hills, and the green of the sumptuous pesto I was devouring. Alice was still munching on her sandwich when I jumped up, telling her about the jumper in the window next door, and how ordering the pesto had convinced me to race in and buy the jumper.

"Don't be too long, Fil. We only have half an hour until the bus leaves, remember?" I did remember. I also remembered the chemist we needed to find. Still, there are some things that need to be done in life and buying a Genovese jumper the colour of the green Ligurian sea which tagged Genoa was one of them.

A I entered the shop, there was the customary tinkling of the bell above the door. Even though I knew it would happen, I was still caught off-guard. Immediately, a tall thin blonde boy appeared, meticulously dressed in a pesto green polo and tanned trousers which complimented his green and tan loafers. He was bright, bubbly and welcoming, yet not over the top, and he assured me throughout the transaction that he would be as quick as he could manage. I impressed on him that I had less than ten minutes or so to spare.

The shop was shirt-heaven, and even though it sold women's as well as men's ware, I felt as though I was in the backroom of a gentleman's club with pastel-polo shirt padding for walls. There were racks and racks of shirts, and piles of polos all neatly stacked in open wooded frames which looked like half-caskets in an undertaker's best mahogany. The counter was as wide as the bottom of a Genovese fisherman's boat, and along the counter was a thick cotton black and white tape measure which looked like it was replaced every time a new customer was measured up. (Hygiene was obviously taken very seriously in this shop) The sales assistant had his name badge in a prominent position on his polo, so it was easy to read—Ernesto.

I called him 'hey presto Ernesto', as he was so deft with the packaging of my jumper and the two pint-sized pesto-coloured t-shirts I also purchased, that I was out of the shop and back beside Alice in under eight minutes. I hadn't been measured and prodded, but I'd assured Ernest that the sweater we had chosen together would fit me perfectly, and that if it didn't, I would gift it to one of my many sisters. For good measure, I gave him an olive branch, and left him there clutching the branch as I hurriedly retreated to the café next door.

Alice had finished her meal and was practising her Italian on the proprietor. They were both gesturing madly, and although the man wanted to keep talking to Alice, I had to drag her away. She was quiet for a block two, probably cheesed off because I had dragged her out of the shop, but she soon cheered up when we passed a needlework shop with two women madly churning out embroidered garments, their heads bent in intense concentration.

"Oh Fil. Let's quickly pop into this shop. They might sell me some pink cotton. I've run out of it."

They didn't sell any pink cotton, but they did sell embroidered items of clothing, sheets, pillowcases and towels with names embroidered on them. Alice ended up with a pair of bootees for her great-niece, Anastasia, and I ended up with three blue towels for two of my godsons and an infant nephew—Beau, Callum and Johnny. The apprentice girl who was furiously making up my order asked me to write down the names of the three boys, and she was to copy the names onto the towels with her sewing machine skills.

She may have been a promising and gifted seamstress, but she couldn't spell for peanuts. All three boys ended up with one or more letters in their names incorrectly positioned so that the names were changes entirely. We didn't have time for her to rectify the damage and begin again, and as I had already paid for the towels and was unable to make her understand her errors, we cut our losses and fled the shop.

Alice had done so much walking around Genoa that she was done in. "I can't go any further, Fil. Can you find the chemist by yourself? I'll wait on these steps for you." The wide steps were those leading up to one of the grandiose banks the guide, Lottie, had shown us an hour or two before (we had come full circle) so at least we had our bearings, and Alice would be close to where the bus was expected to pull up.

I thought I'd seen a chemist near the corner where the man had been spouting *Dante's Inferno* to nobody in particular, so I left Alice on the steps and raced back to the corner. The orator had gone, but sure enough, there was a chemist shop two doors up. I had been right.

The chemist was reluctant to sell the paracetamol I needed for my sore throat and aching ears, but in the end, he agreed to the request on the condition that I would only swallow two tablets at a time. I speculated as to whether he might have had me pinned as a druggie from one of the cruise ships trying to score, but I didn't bother to stop to plead my case as I was really, really late by then, and I still had to get back with the baton to Alice. I was halfway back up the hill when I remembered the bandages I had promised to buy. Too late.

Alice would just have to make do with some towels wound around her leg Yasser Arafat style. I doubted there would be any fair-sized chemist shops open in Lucca tonight, as from what I'd heard about the town, it was fairly small and very, very old. Interestingly, we would not be all that far away from Florence—home to the oldest pharmacy in the world (founded by Dominican friars in 1221)—the city of Florence was not included in this trip, but I'd been there before, and when they said old, they meant old, where Florence was concerned.

I was approaching the steps where I had left Alice, and although the heavy stone slabs were crowded with tourists and time-on-their-hands locals, Alice was nowhere to be seen. Admittedly I was five minutes late, but Alice could have waited! There had been so many people jostling and shoving on the narrow streets that I had missed the corner to the steps where I'd left her, and five minutes had been wasted backtracking. There was nothing for it but to head for the piazza, where the bus was supposed to be waiting for us.

Thank heavens! It was still there waiting for me, and I could see Alice's head by her window, encouraging me to hurry and get onto the bus. It was a wonder she wasn't throwing a water bottle at me through the window, just to bolster me up on my last leg. The engine was already revved up, and Francesca was standing on the last step encouraging me to move faster. As I staggered down the aisle to my seat, the others (led by Brielle) started slow-clapping and wolf whistling.

I knew I was expected to give some sort of explanation for my tardiness, so I blurted out the first thing that came into my head. "Sorry everyone, I got lost, and I couldn't find a chemist, then the assistant overcharged me, and I was going to tell them, but I was out of time and I didn't know the Italian word for 'cheated'."

Everyone laughed, and Francesca picked up the microphone. "Well, my friends. Here we have Fil, who wants to make the complaints about Italy. She has perhaps not heard of the little group called the Mafia. You hear that Matteo?"

Matteo probably could hear, unless he had his earplugs in his ears, which was a definite possibility sitting as closely as he was to Francesca and her beloved microphone. Francesca was playing tit-for-tat with Matteo, ignoring him and continuing with her teasing and banter. She seemed to be enjoying herself immensely, and it was no skin off my nose to let her continue chastising. "So, Fil. Did you not remember that I specifically asked everyone to make the complaints at the beginning of the trip and not at the end? Or in the morning and not the afternoon? It is too late to fix things now. We have to go. Andiamo Matteo. Fil, sitting down please."

I should have acted there and then, and raced back down the aisle, back down the stairs and reinvented my persona with a more forceful appearance. I should have exclaimed out in a loud exasperated voice, 'I've been robbed! This is a city of squalor, thieves and plunderers! I want to make a complaint to the mayor.' But of course, I did nothing of the sort. I took my cuts like the brave woman that I was and sank dutifully and demurely back into my seat. The scathing for being late hadn't really been that bad, and as Francesca was still chuckling at her own jokes, concerning mornings, afternoons and trip beginnings, it was full steam ahead. Time for a much-anticipated nap.

We had two hours of travelling to anticipate, and when I next embraced the world it would hopefully be to the beautiful open sea of Viareggio—our home for the next two nights. Something spectacular was definitely in store for every one of us.

Chapter 27
Viareggio-On-Sea

Except that there was little peace on the bus. Francesca had realised, not long into the journey, that there were still quite a few of us who had not been provided the opportunity to formally introduce ourselves to the whole group. What she didn't know was that every single one of us had already bonded, over countless food stops, photo stops, meals and even late-night cocktails and nightcaps. Our day on the island of San Giulio had been the turning point, when ten of us had sat together in the little stone café and sipped coffees and sweet teas.

Then there had been the swimming pool incident when the fearsome four—Brielle, Natarsha, Gloria and I—had made the pilgrimage to the pool, along the wide underground tunnel, only to find that it had already closed. Friendships had been forged and sealed right under Francesca's nose, but she seemed unconvinced.

To be fair, Francesca had not been privy to any of these interactions, so it was understandable that she wanted us to introduce ourselves to the bus. I assumed this to be part and parcel of the bonding ritual, so I kept quiet and prayed that Alice and I would not be called upon to disclose any family skeletons. Thinking about family skeletons made me wonder about how many, out of the twenty of us were coveting momentous secrets.

The secrets may not even have been about themselves. There might have been a Lizzie Borden or James Mason, Jack the Ripper or even a Fred in their family, which should only ever be disclosed on a "need to know" basis. Admittedly, I myself had a handful of little secrets, none of which I would be disclosing this morning, should I be called upon to speak my mind. Alice was a notorious blabbermouth, so it would be necessary to monitor her microphone time, should our turn pop up.

"I will be making it easier for all of you with the microphone this morning. I will come to you and you can talk, or if you do not wish anyone to get to know you, just say, 'Pass'."

I was wise to Francesca. It was not that she didn't want to follow bus-etiquette and allow everyone the opportunity to speak. It was more that she had developed a special relationship with the microphone to the point that it had almost become her alter ego. How would she cope in an electrical storm with no power for the microphones? Did she have a megaphone hidden up in the back seats of the bus? It wasn't worth thinking about.

A few passengers humoured Francesca with snippets of their lives in twenty-five words or less, but, as on any trip, there were also those select few who opted to pass. I passed, but Alice joined the ranks of the chatterboxes, almost certainly exceeding twenty-five words with her first sentence. We heard all about her dual citizenship, the two dogs and the quiet court in London where she lived even before she took a breath. I'd heard it all before, so I didn't really pay much attention. Others were interested though, and Alice became an instant celebrity.

People kept stopping by on the way to the back of the bus, or to the restroom, to ask Alice about the dogs, Holly and Looby, or to get her to talk about life in London, and whether or not she spent a lot of time at Hampton Court Palace, which she'd mentioned was ten minutes from her home? If nothing else, it passed the time and Alice lapped up the attention. Halfway through the trip we had to change places, because Alice had been on the window side when she had declared herself to the world, and people who wanted to talk to her had to keep leaning over me whilst I was attempting to doze. Most irritating!

The world flew by. Distant snow-capped mountains, masses of valleys and deep ravines with masses of red roofed houses and villas, and whole country perimeters of stone walls. It was approaching four o'clock when we hit Viareggio, and the light and the whiteness of the whole sea-side town was breathtakingly bedazzling. The dips and curves of the mountain side motorway and long dark tunnels had suddenly, and unexpectedly declared latent virginity. Francesca and Matteo, having witnessed this transformation in scenery and landscape countless times before, were non-committal about the field of white and muted reds and yellows we encountered at the end of the line.

It was like an enormous, extensive, flat Swiss clinic. Even the stone walls were white or a light sandy colour, and Francesca was delighted to announce that we had "arrived to the seaside!" Although Marcello would surely have been tired from all the driving, he valiantly steered the bus past our hotel (which Francesca had triumphantly pointed out) and crawled down to the promenade, where we stopped for ten minutes or so for people to take photos of the glorious water.

There was a slight whiff of a breeze, and the sun was slowly weakening. The presence of the bustling port in Genoa had marred the beauty of the water there, but here in Viareggio it was nothing but sea, sand and white bricks. No grime, no grot no squalor and definitely not a scrap of rubbish.

With the technology of iPads and iPhones, it is hard to keep track of how many photos one takes. Historically, a roll of film should have sufficed for the entirety of a trip, but no way were people taking less than twenty-four shots of this promenade alone. I couldn't remember, but there must have been at least a thousand photographs on my iPhone, and probably a third of them were of Italy alone. Fillip was a stand-out among the seascape snappers, and he was trying to set up his tripod alongside of the bus for protection from the wind (which had picked up) when Francesca approached him and explained that there was no time for extended photo shoots, and that he could come down later in the evening and get some terrific sunset shots.

Fillip wasn't very pleased with Francesca and insisted that it would be too late by evening—he needed to take the photographs now! Lizzie intervened and tried to drag Fillip and his tripod back onto the bus, but to no avail, as Fillip had dug his heels in, and was a dog with a bone and a tripod. So, what did Francesca do? She called his bluff and pointed out the direction of the hotel (two blocks up a straight pristine pale grey road). The bus then left, with Fillip still adjusting the lenses on his camera, and stubbornly ignoring Lizzie's pleas to "stop being so stubborn and get on the bus!" That was twice we had left Fillip behind!

To diffuse Lizzie's embarrassment at her husband's antics, we all laughed about what a card Fillip was and how this was the second time in a row he had gone AWAK. Francesca made light of this potential Code-Red, tapping her microphone noisily, assuring us that Fillip would probably be back at the hotel before the bus, as we would be stopping at the other end of the pier for a gelati treat—her treat!

She made a point of reiterating that Fillip would not be included in the 'shout' as the gelati would have melted by the time we were reunited with the frustrated photographer. Had the bus been leaving for another town or even a neighbouring country, Francesca and Matteo would surely have insisted that Fillip jump back on the bus, tripod and all, but the hotel was only about two hundred straight as a die metres up the road, and Fillip was a big lad, old enough to make his own decisions.

Twenty minutes later we arrived at our hotel for the next two nights. They suited me, these back-to-back stays. It provided me the luxurious opportunity to rearrange my suitcase (yet again) and engage in some much-needed handwashing in the bathroom or in the laundries often provided by the hotels. We had landed in carpark heaven, in front of a fairly plain looking hotel compared to the opulence of the hotel in Stresa, but the whole place was so spectacular it didn't matter that the fountain and the gold edging on the revolving doors were missing.

Despite the lengthening afternoon shadows, it was about as picture perfect a town as we were going to get. It would have been useless entering Viareggio in any 'tidy town' competition, as it would have been lay down misery every single year. I couldn't believe I had never heard of the place before today. Who had never heard of Portofino or Sorrento or even Cinque Terra? Not many people on the face of the earth, I was willing to bet. But Viareggio! That was an entirely different ball game. I felt like I may have grasped whisperings of the place before, as I'd most certainly bandied around the place name, "Reggio", and the "Via" part, well, that just meant through, didn't it? But together? I just wasn't all that sure.

The reception desk was gleamingly long and wooden, and the foyer cool and welcoming. It didn't take long at all for Francesca to hand out the room keys, and for Matteo and the porters to deliver our suitcases to our rooms. Alice and I were back in our usual spots on the beds within twenty minutes of having left the bus. Francesca had given strict instructions for us to reassemble in the foyer at six pm, for our anticipated evening tour of Lucca-a small city about an hour to the east of Viareggio. Now Lucca, I had heard of! Lucca, the entirely walled city, the Renaissance architecture and the scattered towers. Lucca the aging settlement on the beautiful river, and Lucca, the epicentre of gourmet delights as ancient as the great Julius Caesar, himself.

Before I had left Australia, a teacher friend of mine had extolled the virtues of Lucca to the point that I questioned her undevoted loyalty to the town. "Oh, that's an easy one to answer. Matt (her Italian husband) is from Lucca, and the kids' Nonna still lives there." Katie, my friend, had it in one with the word 'Nonna'. Straight from the horses' mouth (Francesca) the Nonna of the household ruled the roost. Katie and her family had lived in Lucca for ten years, having only recently moved back to Australia. I wished I had paid more attention to her tales of life in the laneways of Lucca-but it had just been merely a place name to me, and of no real interest at the time. Now, having read all about the cobblestoned streets, sumptuous architecture and the beautiful river setting-I couldn't wait to explore the city.

The washing didn't take long, and in true Italian style, I hooked up a clothesline on our balcony facing fancy white villas with large backyards and joined the locals in the washing rituals. The villas reminded me of similar ones I had walked past on evening promenades, years ago-staying on the Lido as part of a European bus tour. The trip had been in the distant past, but villas of the north didn't change much over the centuries. Especially the properties of the affluent Northerners, whose homes were distinguishable by sprawling green gardens, often a bespoke mix between overgrown weeds and beautifully crafted topiary.

It was probably too late in the day to be hanging washing on the balcony ropes, but here in this pre-dusk paradise, we could leave the clothes out all night in the warm air and even into the next day whilst we were falling in love with Cinque Terra. This was the land of vague epicureanism. A place where people lived out their lives according to simple, lowly attachments with God and nature, and sometimes tiny little digressions of corruption and profiteering if it meant an easier, lay back lifestyle.

None of this was visible, but I would never underestimate the Italian psyche when it came to putting food on the table and drinking their morning coffees. I respected that lifestyle. This was their country, their seaside town, and their prerogatives to live their lives as they saw fit. We were the guests, the tourists, all twenty of us on our select bus tour. We would obey the rules, even if the Italians didn't care to.

Alice, desirous of a shower before the intended evening outing, had locked herself in the bathroom as soon as I had finished the handwashing. (To my great disappointment had been no laundry room at the hotel) Despite the neat rows of clothes I had arranged in the tiny space, I managed to find enough room for myself to squeeze into an opening by the wall, and sit there on the cool concrete in the fading afternoon light surveying the world. It was almost six o'clock and Alice still hadn't appeared from the bathroom, so the best thing I could do was sit and wait.

I was still sitting there, back to the wall, head and shoulders embroiled in the wet washing, when I heard a soft rapping on the wall next to me. Then a head appeared over the balcony. It was Brielle. I'd forgotten she'd been allocated the room right next to ours, and that we were to be neighbours for the next two nights. I wasn't sure who was on the other side of our bedroom, but it didn't matter, as the wall directly behind me was a shared balcony wall with Brielle. I could see her head, but that was about all. "Fil, are you there? I could hear you singing. I was sitting on my balcony, sipping wine and admiring the view."

I forgot to mention the view. The wonderous ocean at the end of the road, beyond the back garden of the last villa. In Australia, where most of us living near the coast and own beach houses, this would have been quite a common view, and not one to whip out the cameras and recording devises over. But here in the North of Italy, where so far, we had only seen lakes and more lakes, followed by mountains, this view of the sea was something to be savoured. We were possibly two blocks up from the water, but it felt like I could touch it if I stretched out hard and long enough.

Brielle must also have felt the call of the sea, as she asked me if I'd like to go for a wander down to the promenade when we returned from Lucca this evening. I didn't hesitate to accept. "We could see if any of the others want to join us, couldn't we?"

Yes. We could. Especially if we got back early enough, as with a few of us for protection, I might even have been tempted to indulge in a midnight swim. It had been weeks since I'd swum, and my feet were itching to dive into the Italian ocean. I wasn't sure if the water was called an ocean or just a sea. It would be a question for Francesca on the bus.

At first Francesca did not seem to quite understand my question. "What do you mean, Fil? It is the water, no? Who is caring if it is the ocean or the sea? In Australia, you go to the ocean, and in Italy we follow the English and go to the sea. What is the problem here, eh?" No problem. There was no problem. I could cope with 'sea'. When in Rome, do as the Romans do—and all that.

I was careful to ask only polite, non-specific questions of Francesca for the rest of the ride into Lucca. Alice had blamed me for asking silly questions and getting Francesca riled. I hadn't meant to. I was genuinely interested in geography, and just wanted to know where I stood (or floated) when I plunged into the water at midnight tonight.

Francesca was getting in with the anecdotes and stories surrounding the little towns we were passing before the new guide took over in Lucca. I was a fast learner and had already sussed out the pattern with these tour guides. If no new guide was expected, Francesca would let down her guard, and spend the travelling time sorting through papers, wrapping little presents for us, and paying daily homage to her mobile phone. We wouldn't see her for dust, as all this fussing, humming and action occurred at the back of the bus, which was always empty.

Only if a guide were expected, would Francesca come alive with information and stories, sometimes even jokes. This evening, though, she had warned us that a new Guide would be waiting for us by the river in Lucca, and we were advised to make certain we had some coins with which to grace her palm at the end of the city tour.

For the rest of the journey, Francesca was very quiet and subdued. She let Andrea Bocelli do all the entertaining and we were happy enough to join in the choruses we knew. Especially the duet he sang with Ed Sheeran, *Perfect*, which just about summed up the scenery outside the windows. Perfect rolling green valleys and hills, perfect towers and churches in perfect little villages. And then, 'Perfect Lucca'.

Chapter 28
Lovely Lucca

It was lovely. That was the one word I could think of to describe the little town by the river beside which we had just pulled up. it was gorgeous, but even more than that, it was clean, deep, fast-flowing and covered in greenery. The river was a focal point, and it was obvious that in years gone by, river life would have predominated. I came to the conclusion that it wouldn't really have mattered what time we arrived, as there would always be buses there before us. We had a fighting chance, having left the tour of Lucca for so late in the evening, but even with only a couple more hours of daylight, they were there. Giant colourful dominoes, all lined up in a row along the winding river-flashes of red and pink and green in the shadowing sky.

As soon as the bus had come to a halt, a young woman with a flashing smile, brown corduroy beret, a corduroy pinafore and matching knee length boots bounded up the front steps. It would not have surprised me if she'd announced that her horse was tied up along the river, having a well-earned drink. The woman announced herself as our 'Guide' for the evening and began ushering us off the bus in an orderly fashion-row by row.

When she approached our seat, I pointed to the wide blue bandage on Alice's leg, indicating that we would wait until everyone else was off the bus and then join the rest of the group. I looked around for Roy, but he must have been seated in one of the first few rows, as he was nowhere to be seen on the bus. The guide shrugged, flashed a second bedazzling smile and left us in peace. By the time Alice and I got organised, the little party of twenty or so explorers had already crossed the bus-resting bays and were grouped on the ridge beside the river.

It was drizzling slightly, and umbrellas were everywhere. The guide (whose name we still didn't know, but whom I had decided to call Calamity (after Calamity Jane), had a voice like a foghorn, and therefore had no need for a microphone. (If she did have that horse, it was fortunate that she had procured employment as a local guide, as she would never had made the cut as a horse whisperer). On the upside, it was a pleasant, lilting foghorn voice which would have been perfect in a Gilbert and Sullivan light opera. The Gondoliers perhaps?

She was busy pointing out a villa on the other side of the river to the group, explaining that the villa had been used in a film set in Florence, but had actually been filmed here in Lucca. No one was any-the-wiser, and as Florence was not that far from Lucca, nor could they really have quibbled. Near enough was good enough.

When Calamity saw Alice hobbling over to join her flock, she called out to both of us in recognition.

"Oh, here you are. The sick lady and her old nurse. Mr William Shakespeare could have used the two of you in one of his plays. Welcome." This time the smile was so wide, all that was recognisable were two identical rows of gleaming white buck teeth. If she did have a horse tethered for the next couple of hours on the riverbank, the apple hadn't fallen far from the tree. As for the sick lady and her old nurse, I wasn't sure who was supposed to be who, but the mention of age should have given me all the clues I needed.

I took an instant dislike to this toothy cowgirl. She had failed miserably, just by hinting I'd had a few too many years weighing me down. (She would do well not to start on my weight as well.) However, my aversion to Calamity didn't last all that long, in fact the ill-feeling dissipated almost instantly, once she'd opened her mouth to continue the spiel on the lovely little town of Lucca.

We'd had some promising guides but this one was superb. Worth her weight in gold. As we walked, and walked, and walked, she left no stone unturned when it came to descriptions in the finest of detail, of all that was wonderful and historical, and architecturally endearing about the walled town. I didn't think it looked big or dirty enough to be called a city, and although there were people everywhere, most of them were traipsing around in herds led by men or women on missions with umbrellas. The very same umbrellas which had been held up twenty years ago. The age-old 'guide from the group' distinguisher.

Some of our group were asking questions (not Fillip this time, the woman must not have been his type). They were calling the woman by her first name, and I had not been far off with my dubbing her Calamity. Her name was Carla, and she lived in Pisa, the land of assorted towers not far from Lucca. I had been to Pisa, but had never managed to make it to Lucca, so tonight would be an eye opener for me. Alice had been to Lucca twice before, and she was very keen to point out everything she recognised to me and the other three—Brielle, Natarsha and Gloria, with whom we'd caught up, and had, by now, reformed our tight little quintet.

It would have been nice if we'd been able to find another single traveller floating around, but the only real person of interest was Devo, the doctor son of Joe and Armenia. Devo was very quiet and very studious, his head always bent in a book. Naturally, no one really ever knew what he was behind the book-cover Devo had been displaying, as he had a seat to himself. I suspected it was notes on medical procedures such as triple bypasses and the likes, but Alice was convinced he was studying our behaviour patterns.

"I'll bet he is involved with finding out how groups of middle-aged women engage and interact with each other on trips. You wait and see. It'll be published this time next year, and we'll be the subjects. Five women from five different places in the world." Alice may have been correct, as the five of us would no doubt have made for a very interesting study—Gloria from Texas, Brielle from Martha's Vineyard and Natarsha from Seattle. Alice had lived in both England and Australia, and I had lived for long bouts in two capital cities in Australia—so we all had something to bring to the table.

I didn't believe Devo would be so devious, and looking at his proud, happy parents, it would have been even harder to assume he had ulterior motives for sometimes listening in on our conversations, and sometimes positioning himself next to one of us at the evenings out at restaurants and pubs. It would be a simple task to creep up to his seat when he was sleeping and examine the book. That was if anyone could be bothered. Now, had it been Fillip in question-then maybe? Poor Fillip was never going to live down his harmless filtration with the anorexic Kiki back at the Palace in Isola Bella yesterday.

It was becoming something of a competition between Carla and Alice as to who had the most interesting information to impart. Carla was very knowledgeable about the river in front of us, pointing out astutely that river life had been a very important part of the culture of Lucca for hundreds of years. She was quick to point out to us that the real power of the land would always be on a river. In its heyday, the river had determined what the townspeople had on their plates. Rivers had been the life blood of trade and centres for transport. She also pointed out to us as we made our way slowly towards the centre of the town, that we would be spoilt for medieval marvels-churches, abbeys and grand villas as soon as we entered the old town.

Then it was Alice's turn. Having visited Lucca twice before, for periods of two weeks and then for a month, albeit five years apart, Alice was something of an international commentator on the wonderful Lucca. While Carla was taking a break, sipping bottled water and lubricating her throat with a sweet peach she expertly peeled (so this woman was also handy with a knife,) Alice came to life. We heard of perfume, lace and silk factories as well as fresco-filled libraries and churches-all that set Lucca apart from equally stunning and profitable neighbouring towns and villages. I had to hand it to Alice. The two years she had spent studying the Italian language and culture had paid off, and many of the passengers were now wanting to gather and huddle around Alice so that they might gain a better understanding of the town.

It didn't last long though, because as soon as we marched into the town centre, with its rabbit warren of mazed streets and tiny alleys, Alice lost all confidence, and it was easy for Carla to swoop in with a suite of aces.

"So, we are now here. To the Tuscan square. The centre of the town. We hava just walked through the Santana Gate." (Not Santana the American rock group, but Saint-Anna-di Lucca. There is a slight difference.) Everyone laughed, and encouraged by our response, Carla tried her hand at a second joke.

"See the square in which we now stand? It is not a square at all, but an enormous round courtyard, built and paid for by the Emperor Napoleon for his sister Elisa, anda he could not stand the sight of her. He wanted to getta rid of her, and she wanted to live in Lucca. The fifty-three arches you can see in front of you were built for the wild animals to come through, and Napoleon had his sister down as one of them."

More laughter, and some clapping, which prompted Carla to go in for the kill with her final joke. "Which record did the tour guide lose when she took her group into the mini-Colosseum in Lucca?"

No one could think of a quick, witty response, so Carla burst forwards with the punchline. "The record of losing the most tourists to the shops on the evening tour. And they were not even open!" Alice chuckled, and the other three nodded in affirmation, but I didn't really get it. What did that mean? Would all the shops be closed tonight?

Carla was informing us that we had one hour of free time, and that we could either follow her for a guided tour of the old city or eat at one of the many restaurants to either side of us in the circular walled courtyard. "There will also be many little restaurants and cafés along the way where I will be taking you, so the choice is yours." The five of us looked at each other and burst out laughing. There was never going to be any way on earth that we would be following a zigzagging red umbrella through mazes of cobblestone streets on empty stomachs. It wouldn't be possible.

Alice could barely walk as it was, and I wasn't all that far behind her. A compromise might be a good idea if we were served quickly enough. Then we could catch up with Carla and enjoy her little quips and stories about the old town. There wouldn't be time for restaurant choosing according to appealing menus, and thankfully we were all on the same page with the idea to sit down at the first available table, and to order the first food on the menu (providing it wasn't tripe or tongue, brains or pigs trotters, which Francesca had told us were delicacies in these parts. Or pate.

No pate!

Luckily, there was a table right in front of where we were standing, so Alice did not even have to move. Gloria very kindly left the four of us to guard the table and raced over to the waiters little 'outside-booth' to ask if we might have the table straight away. She was nodding from the booth, and giving us the thumbs up, so we took our seats. The whole process was swift, and delicious. Pizza and an organic green salad for three of us, with the other two opting for the lighter choices of grilled chicken and salad. It was so light and fluffy and mouth-watering.

There was just something about the Italian food which was just so irresistible. It would be too easy to get fat in Italy. Fat and happy, and what was not to like? Brielle and I exchanged some knowing glances towards the end of the meal, tacitly and secretly sealing a pact amongst ourselves to keep that promised rendezvous in the foyer tonight at eleven, so that we could saunter down to the beach for a moonlight walk. Once again, I feared I'd have to abandon all ideas of a swim in the moonlit ocean, as once again, I had eaten so much that I felt I might sink. Thank heavens the bus was so far away from the outside restaurant. We could all use the exercise.

The waiter was so obliging, and so attentive, that I slipped him an olive branch even though we'd hardly exchanged more than a few words. He did manage to tell us he was a university student, in between balancing our wines on a very small round silver tray. I recognised that very tray from my childhood, on occasions when dad had invited Italian guests to dinner. The aperitifs had always made an appearance in tiny chalice-like glasses accompanied by gasps of delight.

Masses of them on the little silver tray, and my sister and I would watch the guests downing the shots in delicate swallowing motions from our hide-out behind the couch.

Just the fact that the boy was balancing the glasses with the same leverage and distance of arm was enough for me to want to give him that olive branch, in the hope that he would branch out (so to speak) from his lowly job as a waiter and reinvent himself as the prosperous owner of an extensive olive grove-producing the famous olive oil of the region. The world-famous Virgin oil which was in plentiful production thanks to the rich red soil so characteristic of Tuscany. I had read a lovely phrase describing this region which led all the way back to the coast as the "Olive Riviera." How marvellous!

After we'd eaten and drunk to our heart's content, there was just enough time left to wend our way back through the delightful tourist-crowded old town to the bus which was waiting in the same spot where we'd last seen it. The alleys and laneways were inspirational and very, very, old Italy. Shops which had changed names and direction over the centuries-and lived to tell the tale. My favourite had been a shop with a colourful façade, and rows and rows of tiny little cabinets selling perfumes and oils. The other had to literally drag me out. It was heaven!

Darkness was enveloping Lucca with the slow and steady familiarity of an old friend. Lights flickered on and a second crowd of tourists began arriving in buses as we pulled away from the kerb. Carla had left us in Lucca, and I had managed to hand her the little package with the olive branch just as Matteo was shutting the doors. Carla had smiled and then disappeared down towards where no doubt her lift home, across the plains, was waiting patiently, still gnawing at the stubbled grass and slurping the warm river water.

The trip back across the valleys and plains to Viareggio by the sea was much quicker than making our way there had been and given that we were all so exhausted and sleepy after the big day, the bus was very quiet and still. So still that the soft purring of the wheels on the motorway was a comforting accompaniment to the equally soft music Francesca had chosen for the trip back. (A harpist plucking out the melodies of well know Italian songs.)

We arrived back at the hotel around ten pm, and if you turned around to blink, you would have missed the lightning exit routine from the bulk of the passengers. Alice, Brielle, Natarsha and I were the last four standing in the foyer, marvelling at the emptiness around us. (Gloria had disappeared with the rest of them) Brielle had not forgotten our pact to wander down to the water's edge, and she tried her best to persuade Natarsha and Alice to join us. Natarsha begged off with a cold and I had to admit she did look dreadful. And Alice? Well, Alice did an Alice, and took herself off to bed. That left the two of us, the Yank and the Aussie, to fly the flags for our respective countries down at the seaside.

I was so glad I pushed myself to go. Tiredness, restlessness, and general lethargy had almost claimed me, and watching Alice and Natarsha disappearing towards the lifts very nearly caused me to abandon Brielle and join them in the tiny little mobile box which would carry us to our beds. But, with a supreme effort on my part, and some pushing and heaving by Brielle who had managed to secure a heavy grip on my arm, I somehow found myself outside the hotel, headed for the sea.

We had to follow the canal down to the sand, and I was relieved that there were tiny little fairy lights guiding us towards the sea, or we may have ended up in the canal ourselves. Brielle was studying the canal intently, convinced that she had seen some sort of sea creature swimming upstream from the ocean.

"Look Fil. Can't you see the movement, the ripples and the displaced water over there. Look!" She was crying out to me to look as though we were on a quest to locate the Loch Ness monster, and because she was so excited, I feigned interest. I even pretended I could see some sort of slinky creatures cruising the dark, murky waters of the canals.

In truth, I could see nothing, because I'd forgotten to wear my long-distance glasses for the walk. As I was peering and bending into the darkness, I suddenly saw some movement on the other side of the canal and a couple of what looked to be large eels or sea snakes, reared their ugly heads. Both Brielle and I screamed and started running towards the sea, which is the exact opposite of what one is told to do in the presence of snakes. (Even if they were supposed to live in the water.) Living in Australia, with the ever-present threat of snakes and poisonous spiders, we were taught to stand perfectly still and try not to breathe. (The non-breathing part being the hardest.)

Now we were running and squealing, holding hands as tightly as two runaway brides.

We only stopped running when we reached the safety of the deserted promenade, with the striped deck chairs and the closed down bars.

"I think I remember reading that the canals in the North were full of oversized rats. They must have been rats we just saw!" Brielle shuddered as she came to the realisation that in a few minutes we would have to tackle the return journey, past the canal, as neither of us had come prepared to explore an alternative route back to the hotel.

"We'll have to make a run for it back to the hotel." Brielle was laying down the law left, right and centre, and I was so rattled by the revolting rats, all I could do was nod in agreement.

"Yeah. I guess so!" My disappointment at not being able to wander into the water for a brief encounter with the sea was a very real, very deep ache, but there was also the very real fear that the rats or eels or whatever they were, would also be up for indulging in a midnight frolic, and I didn't want any part of that. We were probably standing on the very spot where the ashes of the revered English poet Shelley had been scattered.

That was the only real useful piece of information I had managed to unearth about Viareggio—the fact that many English writers and poets had lived along the coast both in this century and the last, and that many of them had spent their dying hours on the Italian coast. Shelley had met his fate in a small sailing boat off the coast of Viareggio. I had read that he had grown up as an adept sailor on the dependable rivers of England and was therefore ill-prepared for the uncertainties and treacheries of negotiations in the open sea. To look at it now, in the eerie light between day and night, it was hard to believe that the tides could ever turn hostile. Nothing in the universe, it seemed, was sacrosanct-even the mighty oceans.

Brielle was shaking me into action, so we turned and ran, but not before I had taken some shots of the beautiful beach in the moonlight.

It turned out to be a better run home than either of us had anticipated. The ravenous rats did not appear; in fact, no one appeared, and we were back in the dimly lit hotel foyer before the stroke of midnight. As we had neighbouring rooms, we rode the lift together, the indefatigable couple, bonded for life over the trauma of Italian canal rats.

Stoically, we bade each other good morning at our respective doors.

At the risk of repeating myself—What a day!

Chapter 29
Uno, Due, Tre, Quattro, 'Cinque Terra'!

When I was old enough to appreciate my Italian heritage, my father decided to do something about enculturation and took me to Italy to meet the relos. All I am able to clearly recall from those three weeks one freezing December in my youth, was calling out, 'Buon Natalie' to all in sundry, and the bizarre New Year's Eve custom of tossing out any old, or infrequently used household items only, to scavenge for other people's cast-offs in a frantic effort to replace whatever useless appliances had been hurled over balconies from great heights.

An ancient Italian custom, and one provenly responsible for more than a fair share of apartment dwellers ending up in the local hospital with concussion from flying fry-pans. That year had been a ripper of an event. My sister Mary and I had been watching all the action from our Zia's fifth floor balcony in a fair-sized city in Southern Italy. My Zia (aunt) was Rosa Cinquefiori. So, when I noticed our tour was to include a full day excursion to Cinque Terra, Zia Rosa came instantly to mind, and of how she had lived for more than fifty years with the much-maligned, yet gawkishly glamorous married name of Cinquefiori! (Meaning literally, five flowers.)

Now I was being presented with the opportunity to utter the indisputably related word, Cinque Terra, as many times as I so desired. The word had a wonderful ring to it and was possibly the main reason I had been drawn into selecting this trip. Cinque Terra. It was a place I'd heard of, but only just. Nowhere even close to the big guns of Romantic Italy—Positano, Amalfi Coast, Venice, Florence and Rome—but of late, it was edging in. My theory was that it was all in the name. The crisp vowels seemed to roll off the tongue, and I could not stop the word from tumbling from my lips over and over again.

Alice was not so smitten! "Fil, can you please stop counting to five and repeating yourself? It's very annoying!" She was under the misapprehension that I was counting and stopping at cinque—five.

"Alice, I'm not counting. I'm merely getting myself ready for our big day by repeating our destination over and over. I like the sound of the word 'Cinque Terra'. Any word with a 'Q' in it appeals to me. Quirky, quiver, quicksilver, quintessential…" I was teasing Alice by then, and she had stuck a pillow over her head in frustration and exasperation. The clear signal that it was time for me to go down to the foyer and wait for the bus, leaving Alice to half an hour of needlework peace and solace.

"OK. I'll stop. I want to see if I can take some shots of the beach this morning and I've got half an hour to spare, so I might just nip down the road."

There was something about the beautiful desolate endless stretch of beach at Viareggio which kept claiming me. I wanted to pay endless, fathomless tributes to such a soul-stirring expanse of clear greeny-blue water. The sea was one place from which I could never be too far from. It was in a class of its own, leaving stupendous lakes and rolling rivers for dead in my books. Anything that contained ninety nine percent of the earth's living-room space demanded an army of followers. I was not relishing tomorrow morning, when it would come to a choice between leaving the sea behind, or bouncing back on the bus, bound for a tour of the much-accoladed mountains. But such unavoidable wrenching was still twenty-four hours away, and I would be delighting in plenty of aqua-related pursuits before we would be leaving the sea behind and heading back up into the mountains.

Snapshots taken, I was on my merry way back to the bus when a young man with a heavy German accent stopped me, to ask directions for the nearest big shopping Centre. I had not the faintest clue, as we had arrived late yesterday, and driven straight to Lucca. It had been dusk when we'd returned to Viareggio, and now, this morning, I was down on the sandy beach taking photographs. I couldn't really imagine there being a large shopping Centre close by, but then I had a flash of the extended family of white and blue deck chairs which had been on show last night, when Brielle and I had snuck out for our midnight jaunt. The place would be crowded with families in the height of summer, and these families would need to feed and clothe children, which meant supermarkets!

The German tourist accepted my tirade of excuses as to why I wasn't the best person to be asking for help in locating the shopping centre, if it even existed. He tipped his cap to me, called out, "Aufviedersehen" and disappeared along the boardwalk, possibly looking for a reliable local who would give him the real drum. I kept my head bent all the way to the hotel, so preoccupied was I with finding a 'perfect shot' of Viareggio in this translucent yellow-grey light.

By the time I reached the hotel I had selected a possible ten photographs to present to Alice. One snap in particular, stood out for me. It was dreamy and almost celestial, with a tiny sleek yacht dotting the horizon, and to look at it was to step into a Caravaggio painting. I had to pinch myself to remember this was real life.

The hotel foyer was packed to capacity by the time I arrived back. There were possibly two further busloads of tourists crammed into the small space but I knew exactly where to go, because Francesca was calling out to those on our tour to "please make your way out to Matteo who is waiting to take us to Cinque Terra." I wasn't sure whether this meant Matteo would be driving us all the way to there, or whether a boat would be involved. I did know, from studying the map, that we would need to travel for a good hour or so if plans included cruising around the coastline further north.

From my reading, I knew we would not have sufficient time in one day to explore all of the five tiny hamlets which made up Cinque Terra. I also knew that Monterosso was the most famous of the five villages in terms of the village have the most accessible stretch of beach-front, and I therefore assumed Monterosso to be our destination.

We were back on the road within ten minutes of my having left the seashore. Having had the foresight to have left my backpack and handbag with Alice-all I was now carrying was my mobile phone, so it seemed fitting to help Roy up the steps and onto the bus where Alice was already seated. She had carried my backpack and handbag on board, and by the time I'd found our seats had managed to cram both our backpacks in the roof rack and was sitting cradling the handbags. She seemed pleased to see me, which was a nice change.

"Did you get any good photos, Fil?"

I was relieved to be able to report back that yes, I had managed to do myself proud with my photography skills this morning. "Don't be surprised if you see my photos on the front cover of next year's Italian Beaches Calendar, Alice." About twenty minutes into the trip, I decided I needed to wash my hands in the microscopic coach bathroom, which was situated down the little circular stair indentation, halfway down the bus.

Three days ago, I had been seated directly opposite the gaping cavity in the bus and passing traffic had been light. For some reason, this morning, every man and his dog needed the bathroom, and I'd had to wait until now for a lull in the slow procession. There were possibly five rows between our seat and the stairs. I crept along quietly, and almost made it to the stairs, when Matteo unexpectedly swung the bus sharply to the right to avoid a truck full of oranges (I saw what happened because I had been the only one standing.)

I struggled to maintain an upright position, but the pull of gravity was too strong and I was Neil Armstrong, slow motion floating towards the Armenian couple and landing in Mrs Armenia's plump arms. Which would have been more than a suitable place to have spent the next few minutes napping, except for the fact that Mr Armenia (Joe) was looking perplexed and quizzical. Throw suspicious of my motives into the mix, and we have a fairly accurate picture of his disposition at the exact moment of propulsion.

As far as I could tell, there was no reaction from the woman in whose arms I had landed. She was dead to the world, and I sensed snoring. I quickly struggled to my feet, apologising to the husband and turning towards the stairs. One massive leap down the stairs and I would be in the safety of the cubicle. Poised at the edge, I hesitated for a fraction of a second, and that was a fraction too long. Someone was tugging at my jumper, forcing me to turn around.

"Fil, right?" I was directly in front of the couple from the United States, with whom I'd only had the briefest of conversations so far. They lived in California. That much I knew, but beyond that piece of useless information, not much! The woman was sitting in the aisle seat, directly behind the snoring Mrs Armenia.

"You are Fil, aren't you? The girl with the good leg?" I assumed she was trying to establish if I was Fil of the good leg or Alice of the bad leg, as we had both owned up to being Australian.

"Yes, I'm Fil. I'm just on my way down there." I tilted my head towards the bowels of the bus and poised myself for my leap (which would avoid tackling the five steps) but the woman had a tight grasp of my jumper.

"Before you go dear, can you help clear up a discussion my husband and I are having? Can you tell us approximately when we will arrive at the Northern Lights, only we can't seem to find an exact day on the itinerary?"

I looked at her in alarm, my leap forgotten. "The Northern lights? Do you mean the green lights that people travel miles to see?"

"Yes. Those lights. We booked this trip especially, as soon as we saw the that we would be travelling to the Northern Lights and Cinque Terra. Will they be after Cinque Terra tonight?"

I didn't have the heart to disappoint her big time with the retort that we were nowhere near the Northern lights; possibly two thousand miles away from the green goblins of the night skies, so I stood there, mute.

"John, I'm right, aren't I?" The woman had turned to her husband for confirmation. "The trip said, 'Northern Lights and Cinque Terra', which must be our big day today."

What the trip had actually billed was 'Northern Lakes and Cinque Terra', and if you didn't know the difference, it was probably a simple mistake to make. I didn't know what to say when the two of them started arguing about being on the entirely wrong trip. Thankfully, one green light was close by—the green light shining above the entrance to the tiny bathroom, so it was safe for me to make myself scarce in there. I'd probably have to bunk down until the coast was clear, but it was still a few hundred kilometres to Cinque Terra, and I could do with the peace and quiet.

Twenty minutes later, I tentatively popped my head out of the rest-room door and scanned the section of the aisle I could make out from so far below. The customary quiet was hovering like a low, elongated cloud over the seats, and all that was really visible to me were tops of heads, like treetops on a rainforest- roughly the same sizes, and mostly dark brown or bald. Francesca was not standing up anywhere, nor was her mass of red curls visible. The only safe bets I could make on people being in their rightful positions were with Matteo, Alice and Roy. The driver and the physically impaired.

I crept up the steps one by one, such a different routing to the way I had taken that one giant leap for mankind down into the bowels of the bus twenty minutes earlier. Still all quiet on the Western front! Once I reached the even ground of the aisle, I bent down low and skulked back to my seat, questioning myself as to my guerrilla warfare behaviour. Alice was still stitching.

"Where have you been all this time, Fil? We're nearly at Cinque Terra you've been gone so long."

I didn't want to mention I'd been distancing myself in the rest-room for fear of having to talk to everyone on the way back from there, had my visit been shorter. So, I twisted the truth as best as I could without misleading her. "I was just chatting and then I had to wait for the green light for the rest-room. That's where I've been!"

"Yes. We know." That was the extent of Alice's cryptic response.

Alarm bells went off in my head, but then again, I knew Alice well enough to realise she liked to pull the other leg whenever the opportunity arose. Alice didn't answer me, just kept on stitching, as though she had been commissioned to complete a throw rug for the King of Italy to wear during the coming winter. "Alice, what do you mean by that comment?"

"What comment?" I knew when Alice was being cagey.

"The bit about how everyone knows where I've been. How could they all know? Most of them were asleep or reading when I crept down to the restroom."

Alice had conveniently slipped a stitch and was intent on picking it up, disregarding me as one would a pesky little flee on a collar.

I was about to continue badgering her, whipping her into submission, when Lizzie, who was in the seat in front of us, popped her head over the headrest and blurted out, "I could tell you, Fil, but I'm not one to gossip and you could get a little embarrassed over the whole incident."

What on earth was Lizzie on about? And why was everyone around me suddenly sniggering and laughing and supposedly pointing the finger at me?

Lizzie caved in when she saw the extent of my agitation.

"Fil. We all saw you. You must have flicked on the emergency button instead of the light when you went into the rest-room. We didn't see everything, just you smoothing down your hair and drying your hands. Matteo accidently activated the big screen and we all saw it happening. Lucky for you, Francesca was playing Andrea Bocelli again, so it looked like a video clip of the song with you washing your hands."

I was aghast. What? Why hadn't anyone come up and rapped on the door and told me to turn off the emergency camera switch? Or better still, why hadn't anyone told Matteo to turn off the television screen? I knew the answer, of course. It was because they were all too busy laughing to get up out of their seats and tell me what was happening. Francesca couldn't be blamed.

According to Lizzie, she had been lying with her eyes closed on the back seat in extended glory, counting the clouds through the gleaming skylight and savouring Andrea Bocelli. Mamma Mia! What a fiasco.

I decided to go with the glass half full notion. Instead of ranting and raving, and making everyone on the bus feel uncomfortable about not having averted their eyes when they'd had the chance to do so, I smiled at Lizzie and assured her that it would have been an entertaining few minutes, and that perhaps I could whip up another routine in the bathroom tomorrow when we were to tackle the plains of Parma?

Only tomorrow, I would choose the accompanying music. It would be Shirley Bassey belting out *Hey Big Spender*, if I had my way. Lizzie looked relieved and I could see Fillip nodding vehemently beside her. Heavens knows what he was imagining, but I left it there. I had saved face and moved on. Clearly, Alice had not been in the least perturbed. Her head was still bent into her needlework. I settled back into my seat, murmuring to Alice, "I'm having a snooze. Wake me up when we reach Cinque Terra." Then I must have fallen fast asleep.

When I opened my eyes sometime later, I had no way of knowing whether or not we had we had reached Cinque Terra. One thing was for sure, we were in some sort of tropical paradise. There were beautiful big, bushy palm trees, gleaming promenades and state-of-the-art jetties everywhere. There were boats and yachts and beautiful people. Oodles of them. The whole place looked to be the Central Station of the Italian waterways, and it was busier than the departure cove for the Sydney to Hobart yacht race.

If this was Cinque Terra, then where were the cliffs clumped with pastel-coloured shops and houses? Where were the ancient donkeys clip-clopping along with loads of polenta and corn? And where were the churches and the promised cafes serving delicious take-away coffee? This couldn't be right! Ten million tourists couldn't have gotten their descriptions wrong.

I'd just have to wait and see where Matteo had taken us. Perhaps he had turned too sharply at some stage on our journey here, and we had sped along a Suspension-bridge to one of the Italian islands off the West coast? One thing was for sure. This pristine plastic, palm-tree studded jetty was not Cinque Terra, and if it was, thousands of guidebooks would need reprinting—pronto!

The puzzle was solved soon enough. Not by Francesca, who had clammed up again and was skulking in the shadows of her alter ego somewhere up the back of the bus. (She must have known we were about to be landed with a new guide for Cinque Terra, with whom she was possibly already acquainted, because she really had made herself scarce this time.) Matteo was there though, in all his glory, his shirt still crisp and white despite the morning's hair-raising driving and embarrassment at having inadvertently pushed the button activating the big screen so that the entire bus got to witness my ablution idiosyncrasies. (It could have been worse, had it been ten minutes earlier, but that wasn't worth thinking about.)

We were all standing like stunned mullets outside the bus, clasping onto our bags, umbrellas and coats, in the coastal breeze. We had left Viareggio so early this morning that it was still only around ten o'clock, and the sun hadn't fully emerged from behind grey clouds. I was becoming more and more used to the erratic Italian weather. It could be just as punishing as it was beautiful and benevolent. I looked up into the non-descript sky, knowing it would be a warm sunny blue-skied day—soon.

Some of the passengers were discussing what would happen today, as our itinerary had been frustratingly vague and non-committal. The place name "Cinque Terra" had taken pride of place on the glossy internet page advertising the trip, but so far there had not been a shred of evidence to suggest we were even still in Italy. It looked more like Egypt or the South of France to me. (It turned out to be 'La Spezia', and we were on a gulf.)

Served me right for closing my eyes, and for not leaving a trail behind me, ensuring I'd eventually find my way back to Viareggio and our bedroom with our suitcases. Hansel and Gretel had it nailed when they left a trail of pebbles behind them leading out of the dense woods. There was a sudden flurry of movement, and I looked up to see a little spitfire of a woman propelling herself towards the twenty of us, as if she had been fired from a nearby row of round-barrelled canons I could just make out at the far end of the Lido.

A few people scattered, and Fillip let out a long wolf-whistle, which caused some laughter and chuckling. Lizzie started hitting him on his outstretched arm with her rolled up magazine, and Fillip whistled again. The woman who had caused this consternation seemed pleased with Fillip's whistling, and he in turn looked to Lizzie as if to say, 'See Lizzie. I've managed to notch up another one already.' Lizzie had to smile.

The propulsion of the woman, and the perfectly timed wolf whistle had broken the ice, and everyone seemed relieved that we were in for some direction. What we didn't know was that Francesca had not deserted us, as suspected, but that she had been busily putting in her euros worth of negotiations at the ticket booth near the row of canons, attempting to secure a group ticket for us all to board a private boat which would take us around the coast to Cinque Terra—the five coastal villages perched on the cliffs overlooking the blue Ligurian sea.

I had seen plenty of photograph of Cinque Terra in the days of postcards and long letters describing idyllic days on the Cinque Terran beaches, but its exact location remained a mystery to me. This morning finally put an end to my curiosity.

It was so exciting to be within a stone's throw of Cinque Terra. This new Guide could, at any minute, announce to us that the first fishing village of the Cinque Terra quintet was up around the corner behind the palm trees and the cannons. It would be any minute now, I could feel it in my bones. I could also feel the rain, which had decided to make a matinee appearance-just to ensure that we were all wet enough for our trek around the villages. The guide was speaking—introducing herself as Sandra, our guide for the day—and flashing around a wad of pink tickets which she began handing out to both Singaporean couples who happened to be hovering next to her.

She made a point of telling us that Francesca had been lining up at the booth for the last ten minutes to secure our boat tickets, as today was predicted to be warm and sunny and the visitors to Cinque Terra would be out in their thousands. Hence the early morning start. She then proceeded to inform us that we would be stuck with her for the day, and that if anyone needed anything, then please ask her and she'd try to oblige as best she could. I wasn't sure where Matteo and Francesca would be spending the day, but it wasn't looking like it would be with us on Cinque Terra.

With Francesca's track record, she had probably already been to all five villages scores of times. I was glad she was having a break today. Sandra looked 'interesting' and if I could become more adept at second guessing what she was trying to convey, it would be fine. One thing stood out. She had definitely slipped the word 'boat' into her spiel when she'd begun handing out the tickets. It was not my favourite word. Neither was ship, ocean-liner, canoe, barge, dinghy, vessel, raft nor punt. No mode of transport which involved crossing bodies of choppy waters.

The sign to my left had let me know that we were standing on the shores of the Gulf of Stresa—and that sign had made me nervous. The bus disappearing out of the giant carpark made me doubly nervous and looking down at the ticket clenched in my fist which read, 'All day hop-on-hop-off shuttle' caused me to almost hyperventilate. Why hadn't it sunk in before? We would be exploring Cinque Terra by boat, more than likely stopping at a base village and surveying the other four from the slippery deck of an ancient fishing vessel.

Sandra had found her feet with Francesca's microphone, and since we had, all been instructed to 'batten down the hatches' with our earpieces, she was alive and kicking in my eardrums. And loud! The loudest guide to date, as far as I could rank them at this ungodly hour of the morning. "Please everyone, follow me to the boat which will take us to the cliffs of Cinque Terra!"

My heart sank with the phrase but lifted again slightly at the size of the boat. Dinghies, yachts, rafts, canoes, paddleboats and tugboats could be ruled out of the equation, but then again so could sailing boats, ships, catamarans, hovercrafts ferries and ocean liners. That left the fair-sized, halfway decent-looking vessel in front of us, with the slippery white plank leading up then down into the cabins. It reminded me of the Manly ferry, an iconic Australian ferry in bright yellow and green which ferried half the population of Sydney around on a daily basis, connecting the heads and the quay on the outskirts of the city. Sydney Harbour Bridge took care of the cars.

We weren't the only boat bound for Cinque Terra this morning. By the looks of it, there were more than ten boats ready for take-off. A veritable armada. I wondered if there would be a starting gun fired to signal the 'Take-off' of the fleet. I wondered if there would be seatbelts, should the waters turn choppy with the movement from so many similar sized boats. And I wondered why I had not feigned illness and given up the golden, once in a lifetime opportunity, to glimpse the famed UNESCO listed villages of Cinque Terra. I was never going to be able to endure more than five minutes on this bumpy boat without feeling sick, let alone the twenty minutes Sandra had just informed us it would take to reach the main landing point—Monterosso Village.

"Hurry up, last Signora. We go onto our boat now." That had been directed at me, and as I snapped out of my forlorn and dismal daydream, I saw that I was alone with Sandra at the foot of the plank, her outstretched hand and eager smile urging me to take the plunge. I froze! My feet wouldn't work, and my throat constricted. Where was Alice and where were the others? Sandra was now coaxing me as one would a little child on their first day of school.

"We go onto the boat now. We are getting bored."

That did it. The complete incongruity of words which allowed me a slip of a smile, and for a second to forget that I was about to surrender myself to the perils of seasickness. If there was one thing we were getting-it would never be bored! Who in their right mind could ever be bored with the magnificent vistas surprising us every day? Just when you thought Italy could not get any better, along came the next breath-taking assault on the senses. Bored? Never! Aboard? Just about…now!

Sandra's ploy, her inadvertent play on words had worked, and before I knew it, I was bobbing my head and squeezing through the slippery stairwell. A strong aroma of sardines or maybe even anchovies niggled my nostrils. The boat lurched forwards-and we were off to Cinque Terra. I was so proud of myself for having conquered my seasickness fear, that I couldn't keep standing. I sunk onto the nearest bench, beside a tall, thin, German woman munching popcorn. I had never seen her before. She definitely wasn't part of our tour.

I looked around in a panic, and with sinking heart realised that none of our group were anywhere to be seen. Where was Alice? And where were Lizzie, Fillip and the Armenian family? Where were my American buddies? All I could hear was German, and all I could see were backpackers and hairy-legged hikers in shorts with Swiss army knives dangling from their belts. This was not good.

Then I saw Sandra, babbling away ten to the dozen to another German-looking woman, similarly touched with severity, who wore a name-badge and had an enormous green umbrella tucked under her arm. Another guide! The two of them were bantering off each other on German. So, Sandra was multilingual! Italian, German and English. A neat little package, if one were looking to employ the perfect tour guide.

Sandra noticed me staring towards her and beckoned in the direction of the open doors which led out to the front of the boat. Then she mouthed something indecipherable, which I decided must have meant that the others were outside. I stood up, swaying dangerously towards the German woman scoffing down the popcorn. She must have thought I was eying off her snack, but her body language informed me there would be no sharing of food any time in the near future.

Probably a throwback mannerism from the war was my first thought, as the woman clutched the bag of popcorn protectively around her chest. A little too protectively as it turned out, because with the next lurch of the boat, she lost her grip on the bag and the little yellow perils went toppling all over the wet slippery floor. Instantly soggy, and instantly my fault. I wasn't sticking around to be labelled a meal-wrecker and I shuffled as deftly as I could manage towards the doors which led out to the open deck at the bow of the boat.

It was old-home week out there. Instantly, I recognised ten of my surrogate family, including Alice. They all seemed happy to see me, and Alice moved over to her right to let me squeeze in, forcing the man on the end to stand up, as he attempted to regain his balance with all the shoving and squeezing. He was very chivalrous and tipped his hat towards me. "Allow me, madame. I am happy to oblige you, my seat."

It was a very gregarious gesture, and one which earned him smiles and accolades from the rest of the crowd out there who were also standing. Alice wanted to know where I had been and where Sandra was, as she wanted Sandra to buy her a drink from the little kiosk on the boat but didn't want to lose her prime position at the front.

"I don't think Sandra meant she would fetch and carry for us when she said she'd try and accommodate our needs, Alice. She's not a woman-servant, she's a tour guide."

The others on our bench laughed at my good-humoured dismissal of Alice, and just as we were about to settle back into a comfortable silence, gazing at the high limestone cliffs and into the azure water, Sandra herself appeared, waving her hands around excitedly and jumping from one side to the other of the narrow-necked boat. "Come quick, my group. No, this side, notta that side!" (We had all jumped up and run to the side where Sandra was leapfrogging.)

"Look, my group (all groups on the boats were looking by now, not just Sandra's group). Look, my group, we can see the 'black boys' swimming if we looka carefully."

Now that piqued my interest! Black boys swimming, their wide shoulders cutting the ocean and the raw skin glistening in the hot Italian sun which at that very minute had decided to make a grand entrance. Did anyone mention black boys?

Half of the men slumped back quickly onto their seats, disinterested, or pretending to be disinterested, in black boys. All women remained standing, and some newcomers had even raced out from the main cabin to the deck where we jostled for a better view of Italy's answer to the Chippendales—when they'd heard Sandra's booming voice alerting us to the black boys in the water.

"Look, there they are! The black boys! Many, many of them." I peered, I squinted, I wielded my long vision glasses with a small damp square of tissue, but for the life of me, I could not locate a single black boy! Our boat had picked up speed and I could see that we were about to launch out into the 'real' ocean. I doubted any black boys would be swimming this far from the shore.

Then Angelique suddenly called out, "I can see one. No, two. I can see two black boys." She did not seem to be taking Sandra seriously, and was laughing so hard she lost her balance. Don had to jump up to catch her.

Still nothing from me!

Then it was Alice's turn to start laughing. Sandra was still screeching out, 'black boys, black boys', as if she were reciting English verb conjugations.

Then I saw them! The black boys! There were no broad shoulders, no glistening, shiny skin. No men at all! The black boys were out there alright, but they were black wooden buoys, bobbing away merrily in the waves, entirely black, and entirely to guide the boats through the choppy channel and out to the open sea. We were all laughing by then, all of us except Sandra, who could not work out the source of our amusement—and the Germans, who hadn't really understood in the first place but had just gone along for the ride.

I had tears in my eyes as I sank back on the uncomfortable wooden bench. The spray hitting our faces was in full force by now and would only ever have been welcomed in the dead centre of the Australian desert at midday. At ten in the morning, despite the strengthening sun, it was beyond annoying.

"I'm going back into the cabin," I announced to Alice and a few of the others. "It's too wet and too glary out there." I followed Sandra back into the cabin, and bravely took up my former position beside the German woman who had been eating the popcorn. It wasn't as if we were ever going to become lifelong friends, and there really wasn't anywhere else to sit. The woman completely ignored me, and despite my wheezing, I relished the dryness and relative peace. Some of the hikers had taken up singing. It sounded like a German folk song, but not a very popular one, because it wasn't ringing any bells with me. It might have been the German National anthem, but I couldn't tell, as no flags were raised, and no medals forthcoming.

I lay my head back in my seat, willing the boat to stop rocking and riding the waves, praying for the sanctuary of dry land. My ears had begun ringing when the singing had become louder, and when I'd stood up to move away from the revelry, I'd felt dizzy and nauseous. This had forced me back onto the seat beside the German woman. I must have looked overly pale, because she kept staring at me, making me feel even worse. It was getting harder and harder to keep the nausea at bay. Finally, I decided I needed a precautionary sick bag, but I didn't want to disturb Sandra and her old pal the German Guide. Yet, it had to be done. Sandra would know what to do.

"Excuse me Sandra, but I feel very queasy. Would you have a paper bag, or could you please ask the captain for one for me please? A non-returnable bag?" Sandra seemed not to have had the foggiest idea what I was asking her to come up with, but the quick-witted empathetic German guide quickly threw half a bottle of water at my face and grabbed a spare plastic oversized shopping bag she had at her feet, emptying it of its few contents and shoving it under my chin.

The nausea was welling by the minute, and I sensed that I was changing colour as the seconds ticked by. Shrek would have fancied me big time at this rate!

Sandra was spinning me around to face the front of the boat, presumably with the intention of directing me back outside, to take in the air (or to lean over the side) but all that did was increase my overpowering dizziness.

After a couple of minutes of steadying myself in the far corner of the boat, I managed to slump down on the nearest seat. Other passengers had made themselves scarce when they'd seen the state of me. I probably looked like an inebriated Brit, back from Ibiza. But I didn't care what they thought or for that matter what anybody thought, as long as the boat stopped moving and I could breathe in some crisp mountain air. A few minutes later, the captain announced that we had made it to Monterosso, the first of the Cinque Terran fishing villages. I lifted my head from the bag and tossed it into the nearest bin. (The shopping bag, not my head.)

I was going to be just fine!

Chapter 30
Village Life

More than eight centuries ago, hardworking, driven farmers, labourers and townsfolk fashioned the village of Monterosso al Mare into the limestone cliffs along a stretch of rugged, unforgiving coast on the far West coast of this beautiful country. Despite hundreds and hundreds of years of weathering, the sea has remained a constant, and the glorious coastline still boasts five perfectly preserved villages which make up the collective known as Cinque Terra.

We had docked at the most Westerly hamlet-Monterosso. We could just as well have pulled up to shores of any one of the other ancient, medieval villages which spanned five miles of the rocky coastline-Riomaggiore, Manorale, Corniglia or Vernazzo, but Monterosso had won out.

My first sight of the stunning rocky hamlet, hugging the harbour and the hills in front of me, left me rooted there on the shore, gaping and gasping. Never had I seen any conglomeration of civilisation pulsing out such authenticity—so beautifully poised—from the harbour to the cliff tops. It just wasn't possible that such stark rare beauty could tangibly exist. What sheer majesty!

We could have been in the Southern Caribbean, so kaleidoscopic was the colour of the sea and the rows of tall narrow houses. I wasn't the only one gobsmacked! Every single person, standing motionless on the pebbly beach surrounding the small, snug of a fishing-harbour appeared to be overtaken with similar heady emotions. Awe. Wonder. Silent respect.

Again, I had difficulty moving. After about two minutes of my stunned staring, unaffected Alice, who had gone on ahead, called back impatiently. "Are you coming, Fil? They have a gelato shop at the top of the hill." That snapped me back to the present, and I momentarily forgot that the almost surreal village of pastel pinks and yellows, greens, oranges and purples, with the long narrow slate roofed abodes and darkened stone alleyways, would—on her next birthday—turn 'Otto-cento-uno' (eight hundred and one).

I turned to follow Alice, who was following Roy, who was following Sandra. The others were a little further up the hill, and Sandra was screeching out raucously to us to meet her outside the gelato shop, where she would deliver her introductory talk, and that we would then be free to 'take to the hills' as they say in the classics. Those of the group who wanted to tag along with Sandra for the next two hours were free to do so but should anyone decide to wander off by themselves for the next three hours or so—that option was always there.

She was quite the card, Sandra, and her little jokes and quips about the landscape and the village people kept our minds off the steep climb up the hill towards the old town, with its rabbit-warren of alleyways and rock covered tunnels. There were stairs and little tucked away shops everywhere. Pink Floyd could very well have penned their hit single *Stairway to heaven* at the opening to the old town. It was hot. It was dusty and smelly, and it was crowded with tourists, but nothing could take away the sheer pleasure of anticipation at what the day might bring in Cinque Terra. Three exhilarating hours of exploration awaited us.

"So, we have everybody here now. And who wants a gelato, or should we wait until later?" Most people were up for guzzling a creamy gelato and were happy to sacrifice a precious fifteen minutes of our time in the village cooling down and lubricating their stomachs for the second time that morning. Just to feel the cool fruity ice cream sliding down my throat was worth it. The rum and raisin and blood orange double-gelato I scoffed down was the perfect elixir to my slow-fading nausea.

Earlier on, Alice had been short with me when I'd blurted out how Sandra had taken care of me in my hour of need, and of how her friend, the German tour guide, had doused me with water to cool me down and had supplied me with her shopping bag—just in case.

"I though you said that Sandra wasn't our woman-servant? Those were your exact words if I recall, Fil. I wanted Sandra to help me, and you put her off. That wasn't fair of you."

I failed to see how seasickness and inertia could be lumped into the same category, but I forgave Alice her irritation at not having received equal treatment. Sometimes we just can't see the wood for the trees.

Alice soon forgot my wrongdoings towards her. (Although she persisted in wanting to know the difference between seasickness and boat-sickness and I didn't really have an answer for that one.)

Once Sandra had moved us all along, raving on ad-infinitum about every stone, rock, shopfront and Monterosso resident, Alice and I gradually slipped towards the end of the group and continued to follow on from metres behind. Sandra was still with us all the way, filling our heads with stories via the tiny headphones, but we didn't need to be on top of her to appreciate all that she was unravelling about the pretty little village.

After half an hour of Sandra's chatter, it was time to split up and venture out on our own. Most of the others wandered off in groups of twos and threes, and even though it would have been nice to have teamed up with the American girls for lunch, Alice and I were quite happy with each other's company. We'd see the gang at dinner tonight in the hotel, and because Alice had been slightly chuffed when I'd crept in at midnight after having been to the beach with Brielle, it was fortuitous that I was able to spend some quality time with her this morning.

We mostly shopped and then rested. Cinque Terra seemed as good a spot as any to load up with souvenirs, and there were so many pretty little figurines and plastic memorabilia-bottle openers and plates to choose from, that I ended up buying much more than I'd intended. Luckily, I had brough my expanding backpack with me, so it was easy to keep shoving in my purchases and worry about whether I had catered for everyone in the family later that evening. Tomorrow we would be caught up all day in the factories, and that only left Parma and Como as potential locations for more souvenir shops. It was best to go the full hog whilst one could.

By lunchtime, we had both had it. I was still half-alive; however, Alice looked as if she were about to shake off her mortal coil in the very near future. Food was our utmost priority. It was still only midday and we had only really been shopping for an hour or so after we had splintered from the group. Within the first ten minutes of our solo expedition, we had established a pattern. List in hand, I entered shop after shop in a quest for sought after items such as plates, bowls and condiment shakers. The trouble was, I had little idea of how to convert the wad of euros I had set aside for souvenirs into Australian currency, so I really had no true picture of how much I was spending.

More often than not, I would emerge from the shop empty-handed, and Alice's exasperation at me would increase tenfold. To make up for my indecision, I would position Alice on a seat outside the next shop along, determined to buy the first hand-painted plaques I set eyes on, and cross them off my list as plates and souvenirs cups. Who hasn't ever grabbed something for a friend or relative in haste and frustration? You knew it was never going to be the right gift for them, but you chose it anyway, because it was conveniently there.

This ingenious plan worked in the first few establishments, but I came a cropper in one particular shop which was enormously long and stuffed with every imaginable souvenir in the whole entire universe. I was spoilt for choice, but I made the mistake of asking the grumpy old Italian shopkeeper to wrap each of the twelve plates individually, as I figured it would save Alice and I one tedious job in the bedroom tonight. The proprietor had been reluctant to oblige, but then surprised me by painstakingly wrapping each individual saucer firstly in multicoloured tissue paper and then thick brown paper. As a final touch, she carefully tied a colourful raffia bow on each completed parcel.

I ended up with a dozen of them, and my shopping for the morning was done! In return for her hard labours, I presented the woman with an olive branch and she excitedly called to her husband who must have been fossicking around in the back of the shop, as there was an awful racket coming from there. I could also hear braying, which meant either a whining grandchild or a hungry donkey out the back of the shop. So they kept pets in there as well.

The husband was unresponsive, turning his back on me, the woman and the olive branch. He was probably late for a game of 'Bocce' with the other old vestiges of the village, although one over exertive throw on the part of the player, and the ball would end up in the swirling blue sea. Thanking the woman for the final time, I picked up my sagging, overstuffed backpack and left.

Alice was more put out than ever when I emerged from the shop (down at least a dozen steps) with my goods.

She greeted me with the usual, "Fil, where have you been all this time?" For once I had a fool proof excuse, and one which should have brought her great joy, as it meant we could now enjoy an early lunch, and she could take the weight off her feet. But we were talking about Alice here, and she was not one to let fellow travellers off lightly when she had been kept waiting for twenty-five minutes outside the shop which boasted the most number of souvenir in one establishment in the whole of Europe.

"Fil, since you've been gone, I've had my bottom pinched, my bag nearly stolen and then a man came up and asked me to go with him into his house for a coffee. I think he thought I was on the take, and he fancied me."

What ridiculous rubbish Alice was spouting! She was either delirious with hunger and thirst, or sunstruck from when she had been out on the bow of the boat this morning.

"Sorry Alice. I'm finished now. Let's get some lunch." The old 'answer a question without actually answering'.

That was how we ended up sitting in all our splendour in the outside trattoria in the central piazza, gobbling down pureed pesto (made from the freshly picked basil leaves from the surrounding hills), Mediterranean herbed and anchovy-soaked pizza (a specialty from the area) and guzzling fresh bloodred orange juice. Followed by a second gelati for the day. Simple, but delicious. As we lingered there, we watched the world go by. Most of the avalanche of bodies surging past the thick ropes sectioning off the outdoor restaurant were tourists like ourselves, although I didn't see a soul from our bus.

After lunch, we came up with a revised plan. Alice and I would split up and meet back at the little fishing harbour at three. She wanted to poke around in some art shops, and I wanted to savour a few more churches, and maybe a clothes stall or two. I was eager to buy a glamorous outfit from Italy to wear to the wedding I would be attending in Poland in a few weeks' time-Italy being the house of fashion and all that. We decided to walk up the rocky path together and then go our separate ways. A bit of distance between us would work wonders and afford us both the opportunity for some well warranted introspection.

About halfway up the hilly path Alice stopped and tugged my arm. "Fil look up ahead, there's a man having a massage. Maybe my legs could get massaged? I'm having such trouble climbing these hills."

She was pointing to outside a run-down shop, where a woman who looked as though she had just returned from the most burning planet in our Solar system, had set up a couple of umbrellas and a wooden bench and was energetically massaging the shoulders of a shirtless man with a mixture of very brown and very red skin. He looked as though he had been out at sea for a couple of weeks or more and had lived to tell the tale. Just. As we edged closer to the scene, Alice called out to the woman, asking the price of a massage and whether or not she did legs as well as backs.

The woman came right back at her with the cheeky, and somewhat inappropriate retort that she was up for anything, on whichever part of the body the client desired. Alice was a little taken aback, but her legs must really have been playing up, as she nodded to the woman that it would be her legs which needed massaging and that she was prepared to sit on the nearby upturned wine barrel and wait. This arrangement did not entirely suit me as there was no way of knowing how long the massaging of the man's shoulders would take, and by the looks of things, the masseur and her delighted groaner seemed to be deriving mutual pleasure from the whole thing. Too much pleasure really when I thought about it. I felt uncomfortable about leaving Alice with the couple, and I had a sneaking suspicion that a menage-a-trois was not out of the question in this isolated outcrop on the Western Italian coast.

"Alice, why don't you wait until tonight, and Natarsha and I can do a leg each? That will save money and time. What do you think?"

Alice looked doubtfully at me. She knew darn well that my version of a massage would consist of three minutes of furious rubbing, followed by a decent slapping of 'Deep Heat' and two Panadol. Done! Natarsha might have given Alice a glimmer of hope, being a doctor, but she had excused herself with a suspected cold for two nights now, so tonight was not looking good for roping in Natarsha. Maybe Gloria, who lived on a cattle ranch with her Texan husband and five thousand cattle? She may have had some experience rubbing down cattle, and realistically, how far from humans were the creatures?

I was wasting my time. No amount of pleading and justifying was going to work with Alice, so in the end I left her sitting on a dirty, dusty upturned wine barrel to the side of the sandy path in full sun, and with full knowledge that her fate lay behind the rickety wooden door to the left of the pale pink house. The masseur had whispered to us in a deep husky voice that her name was Cici, and I wasn't sure if that was her real name, or a stage name she had adopted for the punters.

Cici was clothed in skimpy, faded-blue jean-shorts which showed off her long, tanned legs. Her top was a crisp white tank top and her brown muscles rippled as she massaged. The man moaned. Alice's eyes widened, and I fled. Too bad. Alice had brought it all on herself. I couldn't hang around forever. I had people to meet and places to go.

I was on an almighty quest to find a church, a convent and a dress shop. Oh, and maybe a shoe shop if I was to struggle up the hill and disappear forever in my brand-new hiking boots. (Thongs and sandals were banned, and I could just imagine the guards sitting at intervals along the cliff top path checking tourist footwear.) If I did manage to traverse the path for an hour or two, I would need to dodge any Passport Control booths as Australian hikers did not have the best of names around these parts after three of them had been victims of a small landslide forcing the main path to close for years, and villages to be cut off from one another if one favoured the pedestrian route over boats and trains.

Given my physical condition and my tendency to become out of breath should I attempt to conquer even the slightest of inclines, it would not be likely that I would be put in a position where I needed to show my Australian passport. I would leave all that to Brielle and the other American girls. Australians had done their dash around these parts. They would not be needing me to reinstate them today.

Two hours later I was back at the meeting spot on the warm sandy shore where the boat had dropped us. Surprise, surprise! No Alice. The rest of the group was there, sitting under trees and on stone walls along the shore, eating, drinking and talking away in true holiday spirit. I spotted Brielle and the Singaporeans (both couples) and I made a beeline for them. These were the people who had scored prime seats outside on the bow of the boat on the way here this morning.

If I was to have a fighting chance of not having water thrown over my flushed face for a second time, I would need to secure a prime position out in the fresh air on the boat for our return journey. If I played my cards right, it would be right alongside the Singaporeans who must have been used to a healthy lifestyle back home. Despite the age differences, the four of them always looked so young, fresh and energetic. I would do well to take a leaf out of their books.

It was a bit of a worry that Alice had not yet turned up, but we still had ten minutes until Sandra. I gave Alice the benefit of the doubt, and wandered over to the little group on the stone wall, telling them I was still waiting for Alice and asking them all to keep an eye out for her, as she might have gotten lost by herself and may have been waiting at another sheltered harbour. She may even have been in one of the other four villages if her legs had been miraculously cured and she'd felt like a sprint over the alto Way, past 'Lovers Lane' (Via dell' Amore) and onto the next village.

I knew the rough, narrow path above the village was colloquially referred to as 'Lovers Lane' because I had read about it, and also because I had run up the hill and back down again in record time just so that I could tell them I'd traversed the Blue path. Truth be told I didn't see any markers for either the Blue path or Lovers Lane, and I was quite possibly on the wrong path altogether. My hike had been short. Definitely no Camino Way. More likely the 'Wrong Way', but at least I'd had a go.

Despite an intensive search, I had not managed to find a suitable wedding outfit; my hopes would now need to be pinned on Como. Surely, I would find something suitable in the posh shops of Como? Money would not be an issue, as I'd held onto my little booty for so long it should more than suffice. It would be more a matter of finding an outfit which suited me, and more importantly one which fitted me. I'd been at far too many weddings in Australia not being able to breathe in a too-small dress, nor able to walk in 'too tight' shoes. No one would be that fussy in Poland, I was sure of that.

The other thing I had wanted to do in Cinque Terra had been to find a convent and to have left an olive branch for the silent nuns. I had been unsuccessful in my search, and no one I'd asked had seemed interested in helping me locate a convent. I would leave it till next time, when I'd had time to research the locations of convents in the five Cinque Terra towns.

While we were waiting for Sandra to show up, our little group exchanged stories of what we had seen, what we'd missed due to time restrictions, and what we had liked best about Cinque Terra. Overwhelmingly, people favoured the pastel-coloured houses, the castle and the narrow little alleys and shops of the old town. Second came the churches (they definitely got my vote, especially the black and white stripped liquorice church I had stumbled upon at the very end of my exploring) and a steady third position was taken up by the interesting, quaint and bespoke shops which were so prolific in the town that they almost outnumbered the houses.

We were interrupted in our conversations by Sandra, flying along the promenade, gathering up the group and ushering us towards a long pedestrian tunnel, which she informed us led to the train station. At that very same minute as Sandra was shepherding us towards the station, who should appear around the corner, looking like a million bucks and positively running, but Alice. We all stopped chatting and stared at her. When had this transformation occurred? Was there a Lourdes-like shrine at the of the hill, where ailing tourists could be revived and even cured of their ailments for good?

I couldn't believe it was Alice, but it was, and she wasn't saying much! Simply parading around everyone like a prized tiger. I kept quiet about the massage, not having been with Alice for most of the afternoon. It was easier just to ignore her mysterious metamorphosis and concentrate on the words Sandra had just uttered. "Hurry, my group. You are all so slow that if you take two steps by yourselves you will end up lost. Stay close with me and we will find the station."

What had she meant about a station? Were boat ramps and jetties referred to as water-stations in Italy? I remembered back to the vaporetti of Venice and had a distant recollection of the piers on the Lido being referred to as stations. That must be it. The boats would be all lined up on the little pebbly beach beyond the wide tunnel. My fate was sealed.

But no! There was no water beyond the pedestrian tunnel, and there really was a dinky-di station. Lots of wrought iron, hanging baskets filled with Spring flowers and polished wooden pews to sit down upon and await the train. A station from which George Bradshaw would have been proud to have boarded a train. I couldn't help but notice similarities with Malpensa Airport Railway station we had stumbled upon when we had first flown into Milan. Whereas Malpensa Station had been inside the airport itself, this picturesque train-stop was outside, in the beautiful lemon fragrant air. (One of the Singaporeans had visited the famous monastery above the station where the monks made limoncello.) The smell was wafting down through the iron grates, and it was heavenly.

I was in double heaven. Heaven that there would be no more water-travel today, and in heaven with the intoxicating smell of citrus. This was truly the Italian Riviera, and we were the luckiest tour group of them all! Sandra was again practising her handing out tickets skill, but this time the tickets were for the approaching train which would take us to another station where Matteo would be waiting with the bus. I liked their style, these tour guides. Pushing us to the limit with hundreds of stairs to climb, only to find a couple of hundred more at the next hill, and then pushing us some more with tunnels to traverse and trains to catch. The plush comfy seats of the bus would be worth it though, and for me, it was the best outcome ever. No boat meant no seasickness and a clear head for the rest of the day. It was a win, win!

The train was on time and quite spacious inside. Everyone managed to secure a seat, and we were all so exhausted that there wasn't much movement at all in the carriage. Sandra kept talking and talking, but it was easy to tune out and stare at the lush passing countryside. After two picture-perfect stations, Sandra informed us that Matteo and Francesca would be waiting at the next station, and that we should begin collecting our possessions and be ready to jump off the train as the station was small and the stop would be short and sweet.

I raced up to Sandra and thrust an olive branch and ten euro at her. "Thank you for a wonderful tour of Cinque Terra, Sandra. It's been spectacular, and you are a very funny guide. You made us all laugh so much. Don't forget to plant the olive branch, will you?"

Sandra was still smiling and waving as we all tumbled off the train. I looked over towards where our bus was parked, and when I looked up again to wave goodbye to Sandra, the train had disappeared. And that, as they say in the classics…was the last we saw of Sandra.

Matteo and Francesco were very pleased to see us all returned safe and sound. Matteo didn't talk, but Francesca made up for him, bubbling over-enthusiastically all the way back to the hotel, quizzing us on our fav parts of the trip, and promising to give us the opportunity to dissect the day over dinner tonight which we would be sitting down to partake of, in the hotel restaurant. Wine would be included with the three-course meal, and it was to be an early sitting, as many people had expressed a desire for an early night. "We will begin now with the practise! No music. No talking. No breathing. Just rest until we arrive back into Viareggio."

Despite our vows of silence, it still took a long time to get home. There had been no noise, no music and no sharing of stories. Everyone was subdued and wanting to get back home as soon as possible. The hotel was a welcome relief by the time we dragged our weary bodies up the stairs to our bedroom on the first floor. Francesca had insisted we all be down in the foyer by six pm, so that we might have the opportunity to eat drink and be merry at a respectably early hour.

Which we were. The meal was again magnificent. I couldn't say I'd had one forkful of any product on the Italian gastronomic landscape which was not top notch. Whether it was in the picking, the mixing or the cooking-the food was superb.

After the meal it should have been bedtime, but a few of us weren't quite ready to hit the hay It was still early, and Brielle suggested we hit the bar in the hotel instead. It wasn't the worst idea anyone had ever put forward.

We didn't have to walk very far.

The bar was behind a partition in the dining room, and no sooner had we settled ourselves on the white, comfy chrome and leather couches, than a waiter appeared to take our order. He was the same young strapping lad who had served us the three-courses and the vino-rosso in the room next door, along with three young waitresses who had been so young and so sweet, that most of us had left all three of them a healthy tip. Seated at the table next to us were two English looking women, and from the sounds of their accents they were from the north of England.

Apart from those two women, the bar was deserted. The German tour group who had shared the dining room with us were still finishing off the last of their dessert, and from where we were sitting the raucous rendition of the German National anthem filled both rooms. If we encountered the German group in Parma, and then again in Como, we should just about know all the words to the anthem by the end of the trip.

Brielle had invited the two English women to join us at our table, and then there were seven! Brielle, Alice, Natarsha, Gloria, myself and the two English ring-ins. The waiter took our orders, carefully scribing our preferences and then bustling off to the bar as if he had been commissioned to prepare drinks at the Last Supper. It was nice to see him taking his job so seriously. Five minutes into our chatting away with the English ladies—Betty and Rona—we had visitors. The older Singaporean couple, Kate and Hoc, had seen us slipping into the bar and had decided to join us. "Sorry we are a little late," Kate explained. "I was cold, so we went to fetch my shawl from the room."

"No worries. I'll get the drinks for you. The waiter's already back at the bar. What'll you have? Name your poison." Kate looked panic-stricken at my mentioning of the word 'poison'.

It was insensitive of me to have thrown in the phrase, as I was well aware that idioms and colloquialisms do not always translate, and that to Kate, poison would literally have meant poison. Her husband, Hoc, an international banker was not as easily fooled, and he was quick to assure her (in Chinese or a related language) that I was offering to buy them a drink of their choice, and not to poison them on the spot and steal their credit cards.

To placate Kate, Hoc ended up accompanying me to the bar. Alice, who had been intensely studying the cocktail menu whist the other ladies had been chatting and I had been plotting the Fall of Singapore, decided to put in a second order. "Seeing as you are going up to the bar, Fil, can you please get me a banana daiquiri? I've always wanted to try one, and where better than in romantic Italy?" (I knew she was hoping Matteo would saunter into the bar for an orange juice nightcap any second now; I could read Alice like a book.)

"OK. Anyone else want anything else?"

Betty and Rona looked up at me expectantly. "We would like a banana-split if others are having one, wouldn't we, Betty? We'll pay for our own, of course!" Rona handed me a twenty euro note and nodded her head in gratitude. "A banana split! I haven't thought about one of them in a long, long time. Probably not since the last war."

With the exception of Hoc (who had already disappeared off towards the bar) and Kate (who was still trying to work out what the word poison might mean in English) and Betty (who must have been hard of hearing as she was busily adjusting the tiny earpiece I glimpsed protruding from the corner of her right ear), the rest of us dissolved into fits of laughter.

We had also all grown up with hearing about banana splits as a dessert. The dish had been a favourite of my Irish grandmother, back in the day.

I had to put Rona straight in-between gulps and clutching my aching side. This was the best laugh of the day. Better than the Black Boys and the little quip Sandra had slipped in when she'd insinuated, we would all get lost after three steps, or that we wouldn't be seen for 'a very long time' if we had ventured up the one hundred and twenty-eight steps to the Dominican church at the top of the village this morning. This innocent phrase, "I'll have a banana split" when all desserts had been digested hours ago, and we were now onto banana daiquiris, had to take the cake.

It would not do though, to continue embarrassing Rona, Betty and Kate. I explained to them, as gently as I could manage, that a banana daiquiri was a potent alcoholic drink, and that it had nothing to do with a banana split, which, to my knowledge was a retro dessert, composed of fresh bananas, sugar, ice-cream and a sprinkling of crushed nuts, served in a long thick glass boat-like bowl.

"That's alright, dear," Rona piped up with the 'not-to-be-sneezed-at' news. "We're both normally tea-tottlers, but we'll be adventurous and have daiquiris like everyone else at the table. We've got a big day of hiking up into the alps tomorrow, haven't we, Betty?"

This time Betty must have had her earphones turned up, because she was nodding and clapping her chubby little hands together in glee. "I'd love a Banana-Zachery, I've never tried one of those."

It was daiquiris all around after that. By the time we called it a night, Betty and Rona had to be escorted up to their bedroom by Hoc and Kate, and the rest of us had waited a bit and then staggered towards the tiny lift, and up to our own bedrooms, which were all on the same floor.

It had been a 'pearler' of a day. So much had happened that it would have taken the next hour for me to have recapped all the events of the thus far biggest day of the trip—the day we'd visited Cinque Terra. The next few days would be slower and less action-packed. I wouldn't be saying no to that after the colossal day we'd had. I'm sure Alice would have agreed with me, had she been awake, but she was dead to the world even before I'd finished cleaning my teeth.

Chapter 31
Nothing Compares to Prosciutto

If, for whatever reason, you happen to find yourself sauntering along a deserted stretch of seashore at six am, and you gaze back at your footprints in the sand, try not to be too alarmed at your heightened reaction to the sheer, raw, impact of those endless stark indentations in the sheet of whiteness. The enormity of realisation at the minuscule place one occupies, on this planet obsessed with virtual footprints. Carbon footprints, eco footprints, environmental footprints-it had become too easy to jump on the political bandwagon. Entire governments have been built on 'footprint policy' guised as Brexit or World Aid, but in reality, no more than a particular party's commitment to a vision of footprint.

The footprints I had just created existed-sinking indentations on a blanket of sand-seemingly far more tangible than political banter, and only ever mine! More often than not, survival is no more than 'chance' for footprints such as these, with tidal waves and tsunamis forever in the wings. One swift dosing and the footprint ceases to be.

And, was it ever really a wave responsible for snuffing out the indentation? Or just some nark on the tube who spitefully stood on your toes, or that self-centred interviewer who was never in a million years going to give you that job? We live in a world full of wipe-out waves, most of which engulf individuals and worst scenario-even entire countries, when you least expect.

This morning, on the beautiful, warm Viareggio beach, I was up for making a life-changing decision. From this moment on, my life would change, and I knew how to make that happen. I would walk a little further up on the sand, away from the breaking waves, where my footprints would still indent, but the waves would be unable to reach me. I would seize this opportunity to leave my footprints rest for a while longer in this slice of morning heaven which was Viareggio.

I knew of multiple ways to reduce my footprint on the world. I was already a vegetarian, grower of organic vegetables and nurturer of organic compost with added valerian for a suitable gestation time, not to mention an avid plastic avoider-but this morning I wanted to preserve my footprints for a while longer. So that by lunchtime, when our tour bus was high up in the craggy mountains, little children might wander down to play on the sandy shoreline with their buckets and their families, and marvel at a long line of footprint snaking along the sand and U-turning up to the embankment.

They would probably laugh at the size of the imprint, or maybe even try to fit their own tiny feet into the blueprint, even count the number of wet indentations, but they would notice them and I would have left a little bit of me behind on the North-Western coast of Italy. They would not have had the slightest clue as to the owner of the footprints, but dried out on the warm white sand, I could be assured they would look pristine and spectacular.

It suddenly hit me why certain 'overly-egotistical' celebrities so eagerly accepted pseudo-immortality in a paltry 'terrazzo and brass' star set in concrete on an ordinary Boulevard in Santa Monica California. It was a way of ensuring they would not be forgotten to the world. Well, judging by the time (already seven thirty) and the threatened disappearance of my footprints in the wink of an eye (I had not checked the tides before setting out for my walk, so the children might be missing out if they didn't appear soon), there would be no second chance for me this morning to witness the beguiling beauty of my bare feet in the sand.

Or anytime soon in Italy, as in twenty minutes, we were scheduled to leave this magnificent coastline behind and head up into the beckoning mountains. Had I really wanted to leave my footprints in Italia, I could always have found a farmer, or labourer on his or her way to work in one of those tiny tut-tut trucks and a concrete mixer hooked up behind. I'd grown up with concrete, spades, trowels and cement mixers as my father had been a master concreter from birth. His greatest desire had been for all of his eight daughters and one son to follow in his footsteps. He'd ended up with plenty of teachers, public servants and counsellors, but no offspring had come even close to getting their hands (or feet) dirty with concrete or sand.

With time being of the essence, I flew back to the bus without any real sense of direction. No need for a compass. It was a fool-proof two straight blocks back to the hotel. Past the silent, sleeping green and yellow striped deck chairs, past the closed bamboo gelato-hut, past the murky, smelly channel where Brielle and I had come face to face with the rats swimming the night before, and straight onto the bus, where the gang were all belted up ready to go.

"Fil. Buongiorno. So nice of you to remember us, your friends who want to take this journey with you up into the mountains of Italy." I couldn't tell if Francesca was serious or not, but Matteo was smiling, and a teeny little smirk was forming in the corner of Francesca's mouth. Yes. She was humouring me.

I sighed with relief, mumbled out a feeble apology to everyone and no one for having kept the bus waiting and sidled over to my seat. What with the daily seat-rotations, Alice and I were now only one seat back from the front row, which meant tomorrow would be our day for identity disclosure. I could see the sense in this practice on the first few days of a tour, when everything and everyone was new, but after a few days of being together almost 24/7, we really should have dug out all there was to know about our fellow passengers through natural attrition.

Not that I would be telling the bus my life history. It would be enough for them to know that I was Australian, a fun-loving person with no apparent dark side (I had no cookies left since the little Italian girl on the train into Milan had scuttled off with them) and that I loved beach combing and gardening. Surely that would suffice.

Alice was talking excitedly to me about the trip today, and of how we would be touring a prosciutto (ham) factory this morning. Prosciutto-di-Parma was world renowned, and peculiar to the mountainous terrain into which we were about to drive. I remembered two things about the prosciutto which Francesca had been keen to impress upon us yesterday—that the pigs were specially bred in the mountainous area, and that sea salt was an important ingredient in the curing process. Possibly Viareggio sea salt?

"How are you going to cope, Fil? You know the sight of raw meat sets you off. What will you do?"

The way Alice was speaking made it sound like I was the world leader of the vegetarian movement, shunning meat as one would certain lifestyles choices. My problem was not looking at rows of carcasses as Alice had intimated, but the fact that I was eating animal flesh. No matter how well cured or how thinly sliced, it would forever remain ham to me; in fact, the thinner the slices, the more unsavoury the product became to my mind. Irrational, I know! I was perfectly respectful of those who regularly indulged, and fully aware that meat was a plentiful source of iron, but it just wasn't for me. I accepted the fact that today we would be presented with the opportunity to visit a factory where a thousand-year-old (pre-Roman) process was surviving and thriving on a daily basis.

If I were to make a bucket-list of factories I wanted to visit, a prosciutto factory would possibly be number five thousand, meaning it would never happen in this lifetime for me. Today, I would gratefully remain resting on the bus but, ever open to new experiences, I was willing to give it a go.

There was some good news in store for me. It wouldn't only be a prosciutto factory we would be visiting. A tour of a cheese farm/factory was item number two on today's riveting itinerary, and cheese, I could do! I was aware that some cheeses contained rennet, an animal by-product, but I wasn't a purist and happy to overlook it. They also made glue out of horses' hoofs, but that had never kept me from my scrapbook before the days of social media.

I also knew that the pigs responsible for the prosciutto we would be encouraged to taste today were fed on a strict diet which include whey from the cheese produced in the Reggio-Emilio district. (This detailed information had also been courtesy of Francesca, but my guidebook on the gastronomy of Italy and this area in particular had confirmed this fact.)

Apart from the back-to-back factory visits, we would be having a 'lazy day', the afternoon looking to be relatively free at this stage. Francesca had suggested we take advantage of the opportunity to sit in front of the mirrors in our bedrooms and glam up for this evening's extravaganza—a night on the town! (Not really, it was a dinner in a former monastery on an isolated farm turned five-star restaurant, with music and entertainment provided.) Francesca had been plugging this evening since Day One of our trip, so it must have been something to write home about.

I had been daydreaming for so long, mulling over the plans for the day, that we had pulled up at our first photo stop, and people were piling out of the bus, eager to snap the glorious poppy infested fields with the snow-capped mountains in the background.

Alice wanted to stay and admire the view from the bus. "I'm saving my legs for the dancing tonight, Fil," had been her excuse. I could have written an entire book with Alice's excuses for not overtaxing her legs. But that would have been cruel, and not my style. Alice was in pain; I could tell by the pained look on her face.

"I'll get some perfect pics, Alice, and send them to you."

Alice looked a little happier. There was also a smothering of something else on her face. Satisfaction that yet again she had me fooled? I think not, Alice! Undeterred by my scowl, Alice was pushing on from the victory seat. "Thanks. I think the flowers look beautiful against the blue sky. Can you try and get most of the poppies in the shot? I might do a stitching of them next."

Poppies?

Alice was entirely correct. The field massed with rich red the poppies and a single solitary grey-stoned castle in the background was superb. I kept snapping away from all angles, bending over and even crouching down on my knees to capture the moment, especially when the wind whipped up and the poppies began to dance. Alice had been uncannily close to the mark with her excuse that she was saving her legs in anticipation of tonight's dancing. If she couldn't manage to hit the dance floor, gazing at the picture of the sunlit-kissed poppies, trumpeting their heads in regal glory, from the sanctity of the long wavy green grass, announcing the imposing castle on the hill would make a good second-best option.

I overdid it with the fitness routine in the field. The next thing I knew I was flat on my face and up to my shoulders in wet grass and crushed poppies. Getting up was no mean feat, but Brielle and Natarsha came to my rescue, and we all laughed at my unfitness. I was well aware I didn't match the Australian profile of a 'tanned and fit traveller' but I was one mean photographer, and Alice would be pleased. After about five minutes Francesca started up with her clapping and stomping routine, calling out "Fa presto" which by now was a familiar catch cry for our group. Time to move on.

Once resettled on the bus, Francesca got it into her head that it was time for some music, and we travelled the next twenty or so miles as Andrea Bocelli and Pavarotti groupies, as the two native sons belted out plaintive Italian love songs. I felt very happy listening to two of my favourite performers, and I had a good feeling about facing my fears at the prosciutto factory, our next step. Twenty minutes later, we were there. As had been the case with the castle at our last stop, the factory was perched at the top of a hill, yet the scenes were in complete contrast to each other. The castle had looked to be a stately affair, from where I had lain in the wet grass with my iPhone.

The low flat building in front of us could have been modelled on a Russian prison camp. A duller, more mundane-looking building, one would be hard pressed to find in the entirety of Italy. Things could only have been progressively worse inside, as there were no windows to speak of, and not an ancient stone wall, marbled sculpture, fresco or gold edged plaque within a stone's throw. All was dull. All was monotonously flat. It was depressing, with that 'after the war' feeling in the air. We had pulled up in one of the largest carparks I had encountered so far on our tour. (Double the size of the one in Genoa.) The carpark could easily have accommodated twenty tour buses, at least fifty cars and numerous motor scooters. At this early hour, it was semi-deserted, with only a few cars, a battered green truck and one solitary scooter. (They probably belonged to the farmworkers.)

No people. No dogs. No cats. No horses. Not even a pig or two. And no other buses! Francesca was pleased to see we had the place to ourselves. "It is funny, eh? We arrive and everyone has disappeared. Where are the Germans and the French? Still sleeping in their rooms, or stuck in the Brenner Pass?" She was making little sense to Alice and me with her mumblings about the French and German tourists, but Francesca had visited the factory before, and maybe those particular nationality groups had given her some grief? It didn't matter. They hadn't yet arrived, and by the time they did, with a bit of luck, we'd have already left for the cheese factory.

I couldn't really imagine how the prosciutto farmers were going to keep us all entertained for the next couple of hours, but it must have been a regular haunt for the tour buses. If I had been asked to choose a factory to visit in these parts, it would only ever have been the Barilla Pasta factory on the outskirts of Parma- the city we would be visiting tomorrow morning. The Barilla Pasta factory was world famous, and one thing was for sure—there would be no associative smells.

I'd watched a television documentary on the making of the pasta in that very factory, not long before this trip, and although the cameras hadn't panned to the outside of the building, it had been clean and easy on the eye on the outside. Francesca could have been planning a surprise visit to the factory tomorrow morning. The itinerary had hinted at a surprise somewhere along the way. We'd just have to wait and see.

"Watch your step as you jump off the bus. It is very muddy. You know how they say about the pig in mud, yes? If you do not watch your step, you will end up as the pigs who fly, eh?" A few people laughed, but most of us were just trying really hard to keep a straight face over the incongruity of an excursion to a pig farm, when we'd had our hopes built up over the last few days with high culture, spectacular architecture and gastronomic delights. This was certainly a bit more down to earth, and quite obviously not to everyone's taste.

Francesca soldiered on. "I knowa that some of you would rather stay on the bus and look at the photos when we return, but this is Italy, and we have the high range of the activities. One day the opera and the next day the 'Three Littla pigs'." Again, a polite murmuring of laughter, and in that instance of hesitation and distraction, Francesca casually leant on the enormous button behind her, closing the big front doors of the bus with a satisfied smirk.

I couldn't help thinking that action had not been without precedent. How many tourist-passengers had given the prosciutto factory a zero rating on their evaluation sheet at the end of the trip when ten meant high satisfaction and zero meant they would never again be visiting a pig farm in this lifetime?

Francesca had us exactly where she wanted us. Poised outside the piggery, like rats in a trap.

Before I had time to topple down the grassy slope a-la Maria in the *Sound of Music* opening scene, Francesca had dumped two gigantic blue and red striped bags down directly at my feet, and was encouraging the group to make their way over to where I stood so that they might delve into the bag and reach for a paper lab-jacket and a hairnet with which to cover their bodies and hair. (Or their hairy bodies?)

"Even if you are the bald gentleman, you must follow the regulations of the hairnet. For you, it should be called the 'bald eagle net', but we are working on that." Not a soul was chuckling this time, and I was really getting worried that I'd pass out in the factory and miss out on the cheese tasting, something I was really looking forward to.

There was nothing for it but to dress up in the doctor's and nurse's uniforms. It felt quite familiar to me, as I had done nursing for a year in my early twenties, before my career was cut short by an overexaggerated misunderstanding between myself, the matron and an injured patient. The best part of the job had been eating 'patient food' in the linen presses and dressing up in the comforting blue uniform. Id loved the feel of the giant fob watch ticking against my chest, and the fact that I'd had to spend a fair whack of my pay each week on bobby-pins to keep my hair from running amuck.

Alice was having a little more difficulty getting the uniform over her head. "Fil. Can you help me, I appear to be stuck." She was stuck, and it took a supreme effort on the parts of the 'three little maids from school'—Brielle, Gloria and

Natarsha to disentangled her completely. Francesca came to the rescue with a wider outfit so that Alice could manoeuvre her legs more easily. Roy was privy to the same treatment.

After ten minutes, we were all suited up and ready to cross the threshold into the factory. Francesca had also donned the protective wear, but Matteo was lying low somewhere and no one was asking about him. I could see Alice looking towards the bus, probably wondering where Matteo was hiding out, but she didn't say anything either. Alice was smart enough to keep her trap shut in public when it came to Matteo.

Francesca insisted we have a group photo, stressing that in years to come, when we'd forgotten all about the trip, dressing up in the blue protective wear would stick in our minds. "You will get the laugh which is the last one!"

Francesca had such a way with words.

I hadn't really paid much attention to the man who'd taken our photo, but now Francesca was introducing him as Carlo, our host for the morning. We were to address him as Signor Carlo, and he would love for us to be thinking about questions to ask of him, once we had completed the tour of the factory. I had my question ready even before I'd darkened his doorstep. "Do we have to stay in the factory even if we find the smell of the pigs offensive?"

I would try to hold off with negative questioning for as long as I could manage, but my track record in olfactory-challenging factories was not one to write home about.

By now we had moved as a mass of blue nylon towards the huge, iron factory door, and although he was not charging admission as such, Signor Carlo was counting us off as we stepped inside. I tried to trick him by teasingly placing my foot half inside and half outside of the building, but he was not smiling—just looking contemptuously at me. Francesca came up from behind and gave me a hefty no-nonsense shove, and that fixed that. I was in. We were all in.

Strangely, there was no smell of farms or pigs, slops or even fertiliser. The whole area was clean and appeared to have been freshly scrubbed down. The predominant smell was a strong antiseptic. Alice had done her usual pushing of her way to the front, but it was proving difficult as the obstacles were everywhere. The first room we had stepped into was adorned with hanging ham carcases. They weren't actually pigs hanging there in hundreds of neat rows, but they must have been pigs at some time in the process.

I took a deep breath and moved on towards Alice. Brielle was also taking some deep breaths of her own. She looked very pale and was nodding her head furiously as if in the throws of a panic attack. I forgot all about Alice and sidled over to my walking pal as unobtrusively as I could.

"Brielle, Brielle, are you OK? What's wrong?" She could not answer, just kept shaking her head and when I tentatively touched her arm it was burning hot.

"I can't be in here, Fil, I just can't."

"Can't what?"

Had Signor Carlo asked for a volunteer to slash the side of one of the hanging hams whilst I'd been fishing around in my pocket for a tissue? Had Brielle suffered a bad childhood experience with pigs, which had all come flooding back to her at this very moment, or had she treasured Charlotte's Web as her favourite bedtime story, and couldn't bear thinking one of the hanging hams as one of Wilbur's relatives? (Every child growing up in America would have read the classic story of the doomed pig!) Since Brielle wasn't talking, only hyperventilating, the source of her discomfort was not so much issue as was her inability to breathe.

"My ventilator. T…top pocket," she managed to squeeze out in between loud wheezes. Mr. Carlo was speaking so loudly and with such rapid animation, relating the curing process of the 'magnificent hams' that no one else was noticing either of us. We were standing near the exit door, through which Brielle wanted badly to escape. The trouble was Signor Carlo had finished his address in record time and was now calling for volunteers to ask questions of the process of turning the fat happy pigs of his farm into prosciutto.

Fillip was obliging. The question was long-winded, and seemed to have many sub-questions, but that was good, because it gave Brielle the opportunity to falter out through the exit, past the buses and into the fields beyond. The door remained ajar for a few seconds, and I watched her fleeing down the hill. (Probably from the fat to the frying pan, as I could also see the bent heads of slurping pigs and collections of primitive iron troughs scattered throughout the fields.) These were premium free-range pigs, feasting on premium leftovers and copious amounts of fresh mountain air, and Brielle was in for a shock if she had ideas of flopping to the ground like an 'angel in the field'.

As the door shut on Brielle, I realised I had glimpsed a row of gleaming buses lined up next to ours. The buses hadn't been there ten minutes ago. There hadn't been any tourists about, so the passengers must have been waiting on their buses for their factory tours. It would be interesting to see if the next group would be required to reuse the protective clothing we had been forced to wear, or whether it was just the first group of the day who needed to subject themselves to this tedious embarrassment. Brielle must have looked a right sight to those passengers who'd been peering out their windows admiring the pigs as she rushed past them and down the hill towards the waiting pigs. Talk about living out your fears.

Had I been sitting propped up on one of those buses, and I'd witnessed Brielle streaking past in her head-to-toe protective gear, I would most definitely not have budged from my spot when the Tour guide had called for everyone to assemble outside.

Our group had moved on from where Brielle and I had left them, and were now weaving in a long, snake like line in between rows and rows of thick triangular ham legs. There were so many of them, that all I could see were the legs of our group, and sometimes it wasn't easy to tell the difference between the hams and the humans, especially some of the women of our group.)

I decided the 'ham hunt' wasn't for me, and stayed put, leaning against the door, waiting for Signor Carlo to conclude tour.

As I was standing there, half-listening to his monologue, leaning against the thick metal door, it suddenly swung open, and a woman with a black umbrella a dead-ringer for the wicked witch of the West), tried her best to hold the door open with her umbrella, and once she had pried an opening large enough for a small person to slip through, began ushering her group inside. By the looks of things, some of the heavier Germans in her group were in for a challenging squeeze.

I knew it wasn't raining outside and that her umbrella was for leading her group around the factory floor. The woman looked at me as if I were a bouncer at the entrance to a precious museum, which in a way, the factory was. Prosciutto ham was famous all over the world, and many a time my father had forced us to go to school with precious prosciutto sandwiches. (Even though I'd pleaded with him for stras, corned beef or lamb with pickles—something more Australian.)

Signor Carlo saved the day by coming over to me, and the woman guiding the next group booked on today's busy schedule seized the opportunity and opened the door wide enough for her group to enter. I looked around for my own people, but they seemed to have disappeared through a back exit. If I didn't hurry up, I'd end up part of the tour with the incoming group, and probably never see Alice and the rest of my new-found friends again.

I raced towards the back of the factory from where the last person (Hoc) was disappearing. I just made it. Two minutes later, and the doors would have been locked. It was beyond me—all this heightened security. The factory was at the top of a hill, miles from anywhere and the only people who had arrived so far this morning had done so on buses. How likely would it be that any one of us would be strong, shifty or bothered enough to steal a ham and lug it to the bus? And then what? We still had three more days of togetherness, and someone would have to notice something, sometime!

By the time I caught up with everyone, they had disrobed and were busy tossing their paper suits and jackets into a large green bag. There was a separate container for the hair nets.

Brielle was with Gloria and Natarsha, so she must have made it up the hill, past the staring passengers on the other buses and then spotted her friends getting changed. She explained to all five of us over brunch that she had felt very queasy and had thought she would faint, therefore she'd had to leave. I vouched for her disturbed state.

It took ages for everyone to get ready for the next exciting episode which Francesca assured us would be, "Something so wonderful you will all squeal like pigs."

The wonderful surprise was food. Glorious food, and almost 'hot sausage and custard' the two longed-for forbidden delicacies in *Oliver*. I felt as if I was ticking off all the musicals which had meant something to me in my childhood, up here on the hilltop. First, *Sound of Music*, now *Oliver*. What was next, *Kinky boots*?

I'm certain Signor Carlo would have obliged, had a pair of long pink boots be called for. He'd been quite the entertainer throughout the Factory tour. His serious face, and earnest description of the plight of the pigs and the top-notch products we were sifting our way through, was laced with more than a thread of humour. His voice was so deadpan commanding, it was almost comical, and the expressions on his face when he described his beloved pigs being churned out as prosciutto were equally slapstick. Signor Carlo the card! I had wanted to slip him an olive branch there and then, but he must have disappeared when he'd shown the people up the front the back exit, because I didn't see him again once I'd reached the little outside courtyard.

At least I didn't think I would see him again!

The back exit had led to a little vine covered alcove with pots of geraniums and earthen tumblers with wild poppies. In comparison to the sterility and punctuated pinkness of the factory, it was heaven out there.

We had the place to ourselves.

One group were in the factory, the others were waiting their staggered turn on the buses in the roomy carpark, and there were possibly ten more buses on their way from Genoa or even as far north as Switzerland at that very minute. Francesca had told us the factory welcomed at least twenty bus loads per day- and that would have meant more than five hundred daily visitors-if you counted the smattering of interested locals and tourists in cars. (I didn't suppose there would be many of them, since no one was forcing them to look at caucuses.)

Once we were all fresh in our 'travelling clothes' as Maria Von Trapp had informed the commanding German Officer when the family were preparing a getaway over the alps into Switzerland.

"These aren't travelling clothes Herr. These are our costumes for tonight."

Julie Andrews, accomplishes actress that she was, had convinced the German Captain that the clothes they were wearing were costumes, whereas in fact, they were genuine travelling clothes-almost identical to the clothes most of us were now wearing.

Francesca was leading us up a flight of narrow stone stairs, reminding me of the steps up to the blue path yesterday. At the top of the stairs there was another enormous foyer, again, beautifully and tastefully furnished, and set off with jars of poppies which had been placed at intervals on white lace runners. It was the scene a French impressionist painter would have gone mad for!

Standing at the entrance to what looked to be a grand eating room with two of the longest, narrowest tables I'd seen since the Borromean palace-was a man, dressed impressively in a black suit, complete with a poppy-red bow tie and a shiny red belt. (They knew how to milk the aesthetics of nature up here in the hills)

I squinted as I stared at him, trying to make out where I'd seen him before. Turning to Alice, who was again rearranging the bandage on her leg, I whispered, "Alice, have you seen that man before? He looks very familiar."

Nobody looked familiar to Alice because she rarely bothered with scrutiny in the first place. Alice was one of those people who has a lot to say about what everyone should be doing, without ever really making eye contact. She was skilled and extremely proficient and would have been very useful in a war. No eye contact with anyone was her motto. Kept one out of trouble.

I wasn't going to stop whispering though, until she looked up to study the gentleman. We were in Italy and would never again grace this hilltop factory, so it would be no skin off her nose to steal a glance. "Alice, just have a quick look at him. Pretend he's Matteo." That got her moving! It was a wonder she wasn't fishing around in her bag for her mini-binoculars or, better still, a wide lensed telescope.

After a long, studied look at the man, who was busy ushering Roy and Yolanda and the two Singaporean couples into the bosom of his restaurant, Alice turned back to me with a disappointed expression. (Perhaps she had thought the man might be Matteo dressed up for the occasion and working as an usher in the piggery restaurant).

"I've never seen him before, Fil. Now hurry up. The line is moving quickly and I'm starving."

Except that she had seen him before. Also suited up, but the last time Alice had seen the man, he had been wearing a white suit that had covered him from head and to toes and a hair net. And gloves. The man was Signor Carlo of the factory floor. He hadn't appeared in pink boots, but he had managed to do a two-minute costume-change and was now transformed.

We had reached the front of the queue into the restaurant. Alice smiled at the man and started limping towards the long table closest to the entrance, which still had seats left at the end. She called back to me, "I'll save you a seat, Fil." She must have thought I would do my usual thing of talking to doormen, because she didn't even glance back at me as she made her awkward way over to the table.

There was no one else behind me and I should have moved, but I was too preoccupied with staring at the man. Was it really the loud, matter-of-fact man from the floor below us who was now standing before me with a huge smile on his face and an incessant wink?

"Are you the man from downstairs?" He pretended not to understand me, but I was one step ahead of him, even without the aid of babble.

"Sei l'uomo dal piano di sotto?" Still he didn't respond. Just kept smiling. I thought I may have mixed up my nouns, and that he may have thought I was asking him whether or not he played the piano softly. That's what the words sounded like to me.

Then he spoke, in perfect English. "No Signora. That was my brother, Cervo." Then he burst into peals of laughter and immediately confessed that yes, it had been him all along. He added that he was so used to bluffing people with his routine, he had managed to dwindle the costume change down to three minutes. With a little help from his daughter, Serena, he added.

I was more than impressed with his feats.

A theatre veteran myself, I would have experienced enormous difficulty peeling off the layers in such record time. Given his age and heavy schedule, Signor Carlo was a real trouper. He may have already been wearing the shirt and pants under his protective garb, but it was nevertheless impressive to have raced up all thirty stone steps and still appear composed and welcoming.

Signor Carlo was still chuckling to himself that he had snagged yet another gullible tourist. He probably had a list pinned up in a prominent position the bar where he ticked off the records for the day. If there were still ten tours to go, today might turn out to be something of a record.

Chapter 32
Nothing Compares to Parmesan Either!

We were having a ten-minute breather in the bus. Matteo had driven like a Formula One entrant and managed to ferry us to the next offering on our itinerary—a delightfully provincial cheese factory, which would been the worthy recipient of the prize for the smallest of its kind in Italy. At first, we had thought Matteo had taken a wrong turn and had pulled up in a farmyard to ask directions to the real factory. The yard was a neat and compact package with chickens and ducks running freely around the perimeters. (They must have been wise to the traffic.)

It was the size of a suburban block, and Matteo had excelled himself manoeuvring the giant tyres across the iron grids along the makeshift road which led to the farm. As soon we had come to a bumpy stop, Matteo and Francesca had both jumped ship. Francesca was normally very fussy about explaining the rules of any place we were about to visit, and since she had bounded away without a word, I could only assume she was following Matteo into the farmhouse to ask for directions to the real wonder of the north-the Italian cheese factory.

But, as it turned out, we were all wrong. When Francesca and Matteo had returned to the bus, there had been an entourage in tow. A tall gangly elevation of a man, followed at a distance by a dressing-gowned ancient Italian Nonna (as short as the man was tall) who by the looks of things, had been enjoying a lie-in before our bus arrived. The four of them looked up at the twenty of us on the bus, waved (well, three of them waved, not Nonna, who was shaking her fists) and disappeared back into the farmhouse which was attached to a tall silo-like building I had failed to notice when we'd pulled up in the yard. Not a word was spoken, and left with no direction, and the opportunity for another snooze, the bus fell into a silent reverie.

Unquestionably, there were still a few inebriated souls taking up more than their fair share of the seats, as they lolled about in semi-dipsomaniacal states. Fillip most definitely fell into that category. He and Lizzie were seated directly opposite, at arm's length to us, and if Fillip turned over one centimetre more, he would be in Lizzie's arms. (With my luck I would be next, as I had the aisle seat.)

Under normal circumstances, falling into Lizzie's arms would have been acceptable, as they were, after all, husband and wife, but the look on Lizzie's face would have informed even a perfect stranger that she was not amused by her husband's behaviour.

It hadn't entirely been Fillip's fault he had ended up in such a state in such a picture-perfect farmyard. To wind the clock back an hour or two, after Signor Carlo had ushered our group into the eating area, he had quickly detoured to the bar where he'd picked up as many decanters of vino Rosso and vino Bianco as he could juggle without losing his balance. Before too long, it was a case of 'in vino veritas' for many of the group. It had been a very pleasant surprise to have been offered such copious amounts of wine at such an early hour, and although there were plates piled high with delicious looking prosciutto, wedges of cheese and little crusts of bread for dipping into the highest quality virgin olive oil and Modena vinegar, the strong fruity, fast working wine put everything else in the shade.

Not all of us drank though, and I noticed Matteo and Francesca at a little table by themselves which had been positioned surreptitiously by a pretty waitress with a blonde ponytail at the end of one of the long tables. The waitress must have had a strong grip to have carried the table by herself. When she approached our end of the table to fill the wine glasses, I asked her (in haltering Italian) if she was part of the family and whether or not she enjoyed working in the family business.

I also asked her if she attended one of the nearby universities. I didn't think it would be a young person's cup of tea—stuck out on a hill in the middle of nowhere with hundreds of loud tourists to contend with on a daily basis. The girl was young, pretty and hardworking. She told me her name was Serena, that she was studying agriculture at one of the universities in Parma and that she intended to take over the farm one day. It was an ambitious vision for one so young, but she might have had extended family to help her along. Not knowing how much longer we would be staying in the restaurant, I handed her an olive branch and an additional one for her father.

"Try to plant these, and they will be here for your grandchildren to see in twenty years' time." I had observed children playing in front yards studded with olive trees as we'd passed through one of the little towns this morning on our way from Viareggio to this Prosciutto factory. There had even been a swing attached to one of the olive trees in a front garden of one town which had the longest red traffic light in existence. I'd seen the rope with a makeshift seat tied to the olive tree when Matteo had been idling the bus.

Serena had looked tickled pink with the gift and had promised to plant an olive grove when she took over the farm. "I'm not sure thisa branch will helpa, but it has given to me the idea." By the way she had moved the heavy iron table into position for Francesca and Matteo, I didn't doubt for one minute that in a decade or two, Serena would have established an olive kingdom to rival the prosciutto sales. I'd read an article in the Milan newspaper of how Italian school children were being steered away from sugar and encouraged to enjoy snacks of olive oil dipped in thick crusts of bread which was being provided freely in many Italian schools. The hearty, nutritious olive was making a comeback not to be sneezed at.

Half an hour later we had been herded back onto the bus by Francesca, and I noticed she was carrying a moleskin pouch of water (at least she told us it was water) from which she was taking swigs as she led the way down the stairs. Had we encountered breathalysers set up in a nearby field, Francesca may have been in strife, but then so would many of the passengers. Fillip had been one of the suspect contenders, and now he was championing the way of the inebriated in the bus. Two others had preceded him.

First Roy, and then Macey had tripped on the stone stairs. We'd all rushed over to help them struggle back to their feet, even Signor Carlo, who had come running down the stairs from the eating area with all the commotion. Francesca was trying to break up the party, alarmed that we might be taking too long, and Matteo might be forced to move the bus out of the carpark to make space for new arrivals at the factory. (Very tight windows.)

All that had happened almost two hours ago, and in the meantime, most of the group had enjoyed a little snooze, allowing them to sober up in readiness for the cheese factory. But, as on any bus trip, there would always be that select few who stood out from the crowd, and Fillip, who couldn't win a trick with Lizzie- was one such contender.

"We have sorted it out. Finally."

Francesca was standing at the front of the bus, clutching the microphone, and behind towered the tall Italian. Behind him stood the old nonna, but all that we could make out of her was her head. She looked dazed, but happy to have been invited onto the bus as part of the welcoming team. It turned out that we had been at the cheese factory all along. It wasn't a factory at all, but a tiny, artisan cheese farm which was big on production, but less fussed with the grandeur of enormous flat factories and, hopefully, tourists.

The whole setup looked like a film set for 'Escape to the Continent-Italian countryside'. It was with much anticipation that we traipsed off the bus for the third time this morning. Francesca was not handing out any blue paper space suits, which was a promising start, and the tall guide (who turned out to be the proprietor living on the farm with his family and old mother) was chatting to the senior Singaporeans as if they were long lost relatives.

Matteo, still sexy, immaculate (no wonder Alice had persisted with the crush), was standing to attention close to his beloved bus, probably glad of the opportunity to stretch his legs. The rest of us were just hanging around waiting for whatever was going to happen. Finally, the farmer stopped talking to Hoc and Kate, and turned around to face the rest of his audience for the afternoon with the measured professionalism of a well-versed, performer in an open-air madrigal. His voice was a high-pitched birdsong, matching his long lanky body perfectly.

If he intended to hold court with each of us, or with couples, we would be there well into the afternoon, and the likelihood of our beauty treatments for tonight's expected singing, eating and dancing extravaganza would be severely jeopardised. Thankfully, no one else took his fancy. Could the reason have been that the bulk of us were not so noticeably from another country as were the Singaporeans? (Kate told me later that the proprietor and Hoc had been talking high finances when she had slipped into the conversation that Hoc was a merchant banker in Singapore.)

The birdman was introducing himself with a touch of the "Friends, Romans, countrymen, lend me your ears" tone.

"Gooda afternoona to usa all. My name is Benito, and this is mya farm. I will be your ost for the next owa, and together we will see the floors where the cheeses lay sleeping." From where I was standing, it sounded like Benito had said, "where Jesus lay sleeping", and looking around the farmyard, I could well imagine an outdoor nativity scene unfolding around Christmas time, with a chubby Italian infant (baby Jesus) sleeping in a makeshift manger set up underneath the eaves.

I whispered to Alice that I thought I'd heard Benito saying, "Where Jesus lay sleeping." She smothered a giggle and passed the joke on, like Chinese whispers, to Brielle who was standing beside her. Brielle then passed the joke on to Gloria, who passed it on to the next person, without really looking up to see who was standing to their left.

Had Gloria been more observant, she might have realised it was Francesca, as that mass of red curls was a dead give-away every time, but Gloria must have been mid-sentence before the realisation struck home. Francesca suddenly began laughing, so raucously that Benito was forced to abandon his history lesson and look quizzically at her.

"You have something to share with us all, dear Francesca?" He spoke to her with a decent lather of familiarity and affection and we could tell he was humouring her—old friend that she was. This visit to the cheese factory turned out to be Francesca's twentieth, and over the years she and Benito had become old friends. She had watched his children grow up, and Benito had even visited her in Venice, where she lived with her family.

"No, Benito." The monosyllable was all Francesca could manage to blurt out, and Benito was left wondering what had caused the outburst from his amiga. He moved on quickly, determined to make historians and agriculturists of us all before the day was done.

It was his fierce-looking little mother who put a stop to his ramblings, by calling out sharply to him in Italian, "Fai presto Benito. Vogloi fare un bagno." It was the firecracker to his posterior that Benito had been itching for. They made me laugh, these male proprietors turned guides. First Signor Carlo with his deadpan expressions and phone-booth costume changes, and now Benito with his total disregard for time and the fact that we were on a tight schedule with more places to see and savour before the stars made an appearance in the pitch-black Tuscan sky.

The reason the tour had started late was because Benito had been out chasing one of his errant cows out of a herd of five hundred. There would be no way Benito could cope with more than three groups per day, and even then, it would be a tight squeeze if every preamble took as long as this one had.

With no-nonsense-Nonna leading the way, and Alice and Roy the limping bridesmaids, the twenty-two of us squeezed though the miniscule red door leading into a barn which housed the cheeses. Inside, it was 'Prosciuttoville' revisited, only someone had switched the hams for big yellow wheels of cheese. In place of the chlorine smell, which had been a rude assault to our nostrils in the prosciutto factory and had more than likely been the sole cause of Brielle having to flee down the hillside, we were met with a wave of maturing cheese odour. I didn't know which was worse, but at least Brielle looked a little happier.

Although there had been no insistence from Benito to suit up, Francesca was assisting him, roaming the floor and handing out thin paper gloves, more hairnets and matching white gowns to anyone whose intention it was to handle the cheeses. I obliged her by taking the bundle of stiff whiteness and struggling into costume, but I wasn't fussed with the whole stroking ritual.

Benito was demonstrating the manufacturing process with little diagrams and models. The cheeses were piled up sixteen rounds high, and unlike the hams, were stacked on metal shelves about thirty centimetres apart from each other. What I couldn't get over was the sameness about them. The wheels were all the same size (a given because of the moulds) but to be exactly the same colour and seemingly the same texture—that was remarkable! I wanted to ask Benito to explain how long the cheeses were expected to sit still in the vertical pews of eerie, bizarre silence, but he had moved on. From my position in the back stalls, it was difficult to see all the stroking of the cheeses that was presumably going on, and in the end, I gave up and just listened.

After ten or so minutes of my being in the complete dark about what we were doing there staring at resting rounds of cheese the size of six footballs, Benito beckoned everyone towards a steep, sandstone staircase and offered us the choice of following him up to where life began for the huge cheeses—where, in a neophyte form (milk), they were stirred to perfect consistency—or waiting bus-side until he returned with those who had been brave enough to battle the steep steps.

Alice was at the exit door before you could say 'Jack Robinson'. Roy, Yolanda and Gloria quickly followed suit. The remaining nineteen of us, including Francesca and good old 'skulking-in-the-shadows Nonna', braved it behind Benito and took to the steps.

That trip to Italy when I'd been thirteen, and my sister Mary eleven, and we'd met our grandfather for the first time, kept coming back to me in this cheese factory. As mentioned earlier, Nonno lived in a sparsely populated little village not far from the port of Brindisi in the South, and the dusty dirt roads into his little walled town had been lined with olive groves. My recollection of the olive grove was still clear to this day. Scruffy, mangled, withered olive trees would have been our best description, but we had been impressed, the landscape being so different to Australia.

The second thing I remember about the town was the number of narrow steps up to the tiny stone villa. Twenty stone steps up to the wooden front door, and twenty-three more in the three storeys of the house. Nonno had lived there-across the street from the town square for sixty years, with his second wife and her unmarried sister, Zia Rosina. My great aunt had been confined to a wheelchair her whole life, so she never really left the house. These steps in front of me reminded me vividly of the steps to Nonno's house. Nothing like a bit of nostalgic déjà vu to put you in the mood for a wine and cheese tasting.

The sole worker on the upper floor of the cheese factory was a small, hunched over man who looked as if he hadn't slept for the last three days. He did not speak. Benito spoke for him as we approached every new intersection, describing the stirring, heating, and thickening processes to perfection. When Benito spoke, it was with a velvety voice choked with love and admiration. His life was obviously devoted to cheese, and woe betide anyone who was lactose or cheese intolerant. The worker was stirring one enormous vat after the other, so vigorously he looked as if he might end up airborne with the force of his gyrations. Benito could not resist throwing in one of his little jokes.

"Seea that stick Giuseppe is stirring with? That belongs to my mother over there! (The old school Nonna, Benito's mother, had been with us all the way.) When she was hangry she would beat us with the stick, but nowa I have tricked her. We keep the stick up here to stir the cheeses."

At the mention of her name, Nonna took a giant step forwards and began a mock handshaking towards her son. She was good at it, and I guessed the joke was part of the daily routine for the tourists. Giuseppe must have heard it all before and did not flinch from his single-minded stirring. His motions reminded me of stirring the warm Valerian-infused water for the compost heaps I was forever making back home, so that my organic vegetables would taste better. That was bad enough, but I wouldn't want to be doing it for a living as was the case with the unfortunate milk stirrer.

We had been touring the upper floor for possibly ten minutes. The layout was not unlike the floor of a big Department store, with little sections everywhere. Once you'd witnessed the stirring, and the rows and rows of cheeses, there was little else to savour. Nonna was the first to slip away, and the rest of us weren't far behind her. I felt a little sorry for the solo worker, stirring day in day out, but he seemed happy enough with his lot in life.

I lagged a little behind the rest of the group and handed him an olive branch. He didn't register at first that I was leaving it for him, and he might have preferred a 'Get out of the cheese factory free' card, but he was gracious in his silence. I hurried to catch up with the group who had disappeared into a large lift. A man in our group I hadn't yet had much interaction with—Stevie—quickly wedged his foot between the factory floor and the lift, and it stayed open for me. I squeezed in, and the lift moved slowly back down to the ground floor where we had started off the tour.

I'd half expected a new tour group to have taken up our former positions on the floor, delighting in the large round lumps of Parmesan cheese, and relishing the distinctly Italian aroma, but the ground floor was deserted. Benito was a man on a mission once he'd led us out into the bright sunshine. I could see Alice and Roy sitting companionly on a seat behind the bus, a shade umbrella protecting them from the heat and adding a hint of respectability to their closeness. It was very warm in the full sun, and no sooner had the group assembled there, than Benito raced off towards a barn opposite the main building which must have housed spare umbrellas, as he emerges with one in each hand. The two he had retrieved were almost identical to those Brielle and I had rushed past on the Viareggio beach a few nights ago. The deckchairs must have been regional favourites.

The reason we were all congregating in the Italian sun was because Benito had promised us a cheese-tasting picnic, complete with a glass of cold Prosecco. He was flat-out hacking into the large wedge of cheese his mother had laid out on the little card table. Placed beside the table were two upturned chairs, one of which held a large decanter of red wine and the other a tray with a mass of tiny crystal glasses. That was it. A traditional Italian wine and cheese tasting affair, standing up in the full midday sun.

Old customs aside, the interlude was authentically provincial. A bunch of Tarantella folk dancers appearing whilst we watched Benito painstakingly pile up the cheese wedges onto an enormous wooden breadboard would have added to the charm of it all, but we were suitably entertained with the antics of the farmyard chickens, ducks and geese. What with the farm animals and the wind and Benito's rendition of *Oh Sola Mia*. (Three times in between racing back to retrieve more provisions.)

The entertainment was better than an afternoon 'Opera on the Farm'. I decided singing was the life blood of Italians. It kept them living to a ripe old age. Singing and virgin olive oil! Unselfishly, they had shared their talents out with other countries so that the voices of Italy, and Italy's sons and daughters and even grandchildren had resounded throughout the world—whatever the epoch. From as far back as the forties, it had been the velvety voices of Frank Sinatra, Tony Bennet and Dean Martin. The Holy Trinity of American-Italians had been followed by the likes of Zucchero, Andrea Bocelli, Madonna and Lady Gaga. In which area of the Arts had Italy failed to excel?

Alice had shuffled back to the tandem seat she had been sharing with Roy whilst the rest of us had been preoccupied on the first floor with Benito. She had buddied up with a fat stray ginger cat which she was stroking. Action destined to go on for hours!

The creamy, chewy cheese was delicious, and there was plenty of it-enough to go around for the next twenty minutes. Not many of us touched the wine and observing this abstinence, Benito raced off and reappeared with two large decanters of water. He must have considered our group a cheap shout or perhaps a convention of Catholics who had given up alcohol for Lent and just hadn't gotten around to taking up drinking again. (No one was mentioning the restaurant at the prosciutto factory.)

I was becoming accustomed to having my life timetabled into one or two-hour blocks and then moving onto the next slot. During the course of the picnic, Francesca announced that the family had set up a little take-away cheese shop inside their home-on the ground floor. Collecting Alice (who insisted on handing me the cat to carry over with us), we wandered over to the little makeshift shop on a quest for tea-towels with cheeses motifs or prints. I had bought a dozen or so tea-towels in Monterosso with lemon prints, and it would have been nice to have had some more.

Alice had discovered that tea-towels were the ideal gift, and something for which everyone had a daily use. Nonna was there again, this time behind the counter, keeping an eagle eye on anyone who might have been considering lifting anything from the shop. I attempted to strike up a conversation with her in Italian, but she was non-communicative. She did, however, grudgingly cut a mean slice of cheese (the tasting had continued in the shop). The younger Singaporean couple were purchasing slabs of cheese to take back to Singapore with them. We didn't bother; I'd had enough of Customs on the trip over without inciting riot by importing cheese back into Australia via England.

All too soon, our time at the country cheese factory was up, and through the open shop windows we could hear Francesca rounding up the troops and shouting out farewells to Benito and his youngest daughter who had appeared to help pour the Prosecco. I pressed two olive branches into Nonna's wrinkled, gnarly hand, asked her to pass one branch on to her son. She looked at me with not the faintest clue in the world as to what I was giving her, but I figured her granddaughter would be learning English at school and would have been able to read the instructions on the bag.

After much waving and honking (Matteo's horn and the geese), we left the little farm and factory behind and began the last leg of our journey on our circuitous route back to Milan. We were headed for Parma, and tonight would be a night to remember. If only I could remember where Francesca had said the momentous evening was to be held.

It would have to be a surprise!

Chapter 33
Glamming It Up in the Bedrooms

Our penultimate hotel looked to be a let down from the front, as we pulled up in the big carpark resembling the parking bays for Tour-buses at Stonehenge in England, or Graceland in Memphis Tennessee. At both sites, the buses had needed to park hundreds of metres from the attraction, and in the case of Graceland, a shuttle bus was used to shuttle passengers to the venue. Matteo hadn't needed to employ such drastic measures this afternoon, possibly because we were early, and most of the Tour-buses were still out on the roads or stuck on narrow mountain-passes up in the Alps.

Once the nondescript, 'verging on home-brand hotel' was in sight, Francesca jumped back on the microphone. "And a nowa, ladies and gentlemen, we will come to the last hotel you will have in the countryside of beautiful Italy. Tomorrow it will be in Milan that you will sleep, and after that. Poof! Off you all go. Back to your own countries to spread the news about how wonderful is Italy."

It was no secret to any of us that this trip—out of all twenty-five trips of Italy offered by the Tour Company—was Francesca's favourite. It had to be. Each place we visited caused her to break out in a visibly pleasurable sweat, and she couldn't wait to infuse us into her enthusiasm. I had to admit, Italy had been pretty damn good, but then so had many other places I'd visited. It was probably about patriotism, and love for one's own land which spurred Francesca on to the heights of wonder and praise for Italy.

I took another long, hard look at the three-storey, flat-roofed hotel in front of us and tried to be inspired, but it just wasn't happening. Where were the fountains in the driveway, the stone walls, the frescos and the portico? The wrought iron, the crumbling red tiles and the pastel coloured, vine-clad walls? Where were the olive groves? It looked like Signor Carlo's prosciutto factory of this morning, minus the add-ons of the green hills and mountain streams. It looked like the ends of the earth.

I wasn't the only one disappointed. Fillip was voicing our collective reservations. "What's this all about, Francesca, do we stay here tonight, or is this another factory?"

Francesca was a little taken aback at the indignation in his voice, but she was quick with her retort. "No Fillip, it is not another factory, unless you want to join the staff in the kitchen and prepare the evening meal for the guests on the other buses who will be arriving soon, and yes…not joining us at the surprise extravaganza dinner tonight."

"Them there's fighting words," I whispered to Alice.

It was Fillip's turn to be taken aback.

"I was only saying…" His voice petered out as Lizzie yanked him back into his seat. She then stood up to address the whole group.

"My apologies for Fillip, Francesca. He tends to get a little carried away. Don't you, Fillip?"

There was no answer from the floor where the unfortunate Fillip had ended up. He must have realised he'd put his foot in it again.

From our position opposite Fillip and Lizzie, Alice and I had scored front row seats to the standoff, and it was hilarious. Neither Fillip nor Francesca was one to give up without a fight, but Francesca, in particular, stood her ground. No one else dared to voice any dissatisfaction with the accommodation for tonight. Francesca had one last shot at silencing the lot of us. "Anybody else have something to share with us about the hotel? Anyone?"

Not a soul stirred in their seats. Most of us were too tired to put in a complaint and, as Francesca had reiterated on the first day of the trip way back in Milan, "any complaints, see me before midday. I only take complaints in the mornings."

Fillip, the sacrificial lamb, had been offered to the Gods for nothing. For nothing at all! Never judge a book by its cover, and never judge a hotel by the size of its carpark and the blandness of its exterior.

Inside, it was a whole different ball game. The foyer was vast, the wooden floors gleaming, the flowers perfect, and the staff, all ten of them standing straight-backed behind the long front desk, were attentive to our every need. Keys were distributed with efficiency and a smile, and our suitcases were outside our rooms even before we had a chance to reach them ourselves.

The hotel was enormous. A sprawling expanse of concrete and red bricks. I would hazard a guess at there having been more than three-hundred rooms. The main reason being that we had not pulled up in front of any ordinary hotel. This was a Convention centre, with all the perks of a big showy establishment, too far out of the city of Parma for nipping out for milk and the paper, but self-sufficient enough not to warrant leaving the premises. Had we wanted to, we could have stayed put until the next morning when Matteo would be driving us into Parma and then on to Lake Como.

The room we scored was very big, very airy and furnished in sparse but chic Italian fashion. There were twin double beds, a snazzy bathroom and a fabulous balcony overlooking the green courtyard. I was becoming quite partial to the balconies of Italy. No wonder the Pope spent so much time on his, it was the place to see and be seen.

All the rooms were clustered in an L shape around the courtyard which housed an enormous swimming pool covered with a huge green tarpaulin. I did not need to consult the room-guide to ascertain that the pool was closed. At this rate, my swimsuit would remain dry for the duration of the trip. I had been looking forward to taking a dip this afternoon, before showering and dressing up for the evening-but that would not be happening! We had two and a half hours until the bus departed for the converted monastery in the nearby countryside where the evening's twilight festivities were to take place.

I had two options. Either to walk in the fields beyond the hotel, or to take a long nap. I decided on a walk, even though we'd already endured a deluge of exercise today at both the prosciutto and cheese factories. But the field had looked so green and inviting from the back window of our second-floor bedroom, and I didn't want to attend the wedding in Poland fat and lethargic.

Alice had decided not to join me. Not that I blamed her. It had been a long day and it was still only four pm. We had two hours to ready ourselves for the evening and Alice wanted to be fresh. I toyed with the idea of knocking on Brielle's door to see if she wanted to join me in my frolic in the fields, but I then remembered that Brielle had used her time wisely in Cinque Terra when she'd hiked into the next village and back, in the time the rest of us had trudged around the covered stone alleys, buying souvenirs and gorging ourselves in outdoor restaurants. It probably wouldn't have been the best decision to sprint with Brielle when such a big night had been planned for us. My walk would be leisurely, and I'd be doing it alone.

I wasn't gone for that long. Probably only twenty minutes. The field had been muddy, and my shoes were in no way suitable. Should there be another opportunity to walk tomorrow, I would do things a little differently. For starters, I would wear suitable clothing and footwear. The one good thing about my meander was that it had allowed me some time for self-reflection and a mental check of all the good things that had happened in Italy so far. I didn't get past day One when we'd lost our suitcases and had been forced to hide-out inside the hotel because we were so tired from the flight and the endless hours of waiting at Lost Property at the airport. By the time I had churned over the goings-on in Italy on day one for Alice and myself, it was time to return to the hotel.

A shower was a priority, and I also wanted to wash my hair with the miniature shampoo bottles I had seen lined up like soldiers in the beautiful roomy bathroom. (I hoped Alice hadn't beaten me to it and used up all the shampoo, body wash and conditioner.) When I poked my head into the bedroom half an hour after I'd set off for my walk, the room was in semi-darkness.

Alice must have pulled the curtains and blinds down as far and as tightly as possible, and the room was very quiet. I wasn't sure whether flicking the light on would wake up Alice, or even if she was asleep in the bed near the window— the one she had claimed for herself as soon as we'd entered the room. It was either fish around in my backpack (which I'd taken with me for the walk) or fumble around for the light switch and explode the room with light.

I went with the second option, hedging my bets that if Alice were asleep, she'd need to wake up pronto, and if she were not in the room, it wouldn't matter.

"Fil. What are you doing?"

She was in the room!

"Why are you making us get up so early in the morning?"

I breathed a sigh of relief. Alice wasn't mad with me for having turned on the light and woken her; she was just confused about the time of day, and probably even what day it was. "It's okay, Alice. I've just gotten back from my walk. You'd better get up. We've both got to have showers before tonight, and I was going to ask you to French-plait my hair."

Ah, the powers and intricacies of the French plait. Had I asked Alice to polish my shoes for tonight, or to have ironed my bolero top taking care to smooth down the collar, she would have flatly refused and been in a bad mood for the rest of the evening because I had disturbed her sleep. But ask her to French-plait my hair? I couldn't have come up with a more suitable request had I shouted out "Rumpelstiltskin!"

Chapter 34
Off to the Land of Monasteries Under the Stars

The bus was hurtling along the dirt road with an imposter pretending to be Matteo at the helm. The driver couldn't possibly have been 'Our Matteo' or he would have realised we were travelling at a speed grossly excessive for the bumpy, dirt road beneath us, and that he would be causing much angst amongst his passengers. Fillip would start complaining, and the 'real' Matteo would by now have been compromised by Francesca, who was desperately trying to keep her feet steady in the aisle, gripping the microphone as if her life depended on it.

It turned out to be Matteo alright, as no sooner had people begun to scream, than he immediately checked himself. We slowed down to an acceptable crawl. The only explanation I could come up with was that the affable, obliging Matteo we had come to know and love over the past week, must have an episode of imagining himself alone on a grand-prix circuit driving the bus.

"Matteo. Enough with the boy's games. We are hungry and we want to arrive aliva. We hava seen enough dead animals already today." Brielle let out a little shriek from her seat across the aisle from us. She still hadn't gotten the sight of the hanging hams out of her system. Whenever I thought back to the hams, images of Judas hanging from a cypress tree in the Garden of Gethsemane overtook me, and it wasn't a pleasant image to be harbouring before an anticipated feast.

The bus was slowing down to pass through a farm gate, and it appeared Matteo had again achieved a lunar landing in the middle of nowhere. What a shame Alice and I had made such a concerted effort to dress up in our finery. (The last of the clean outfits we had saved for this special occasion tonight.) My hair had been French plaited to within an inch of its life (so tight was the braiding) and then sprayed with enough VO5 hairspray to have extinguished the Great Fire of London.

After Alice had finished spraying and slicking down my hair, it had been difficult to negotiate our way around the bedroom, even with the main downlights and both bedside lamps ablaze, so thick was the fog of hairspray. Anyone passing by our bedroom would have ended up in a heap outside the door, having collapsed with a VO5 overdose. Alice had explained her gay abandon with the tins of hairspray as being for the good of the community—in that when perfect strangers came to her aid with her suitcase at the airport in two mornings' time, they would not be in fear of slipping a disc with the weight of her luggage.

"They weigh a tonne these cans of air, you know, Fil, and without them and the bottles of water in our cases, they will be so much lighter." I believed her, although thousands wouldn't, and urged her to take the giant rollers out of her own hair, or we would end up walking to the dinner tonight, we'd be so late for the bus.

"Fil. Chill. It's all good." I could tell Alice's "I'm on the home stretch now" voice.

She had suffered a great deal with her legs and knees in the course of the last week and was probably ready for home. I, on the other hand, was just revving up. As a rule, it took me a week to shake off jet lag, and this time it was taking two. I was at my premium when a trip lasted a month, and my favourite escorted Bus Tour to date, was our American trip which had lasted for sixty days, taking in half of the United States and parts of Canada and Mexico. Heaven to a travelaholic like me!

Thinking of the American trip reminded me of the character who had led our tour into Mexico-City on a day trip. In some ways, he could easily have been a male Francesca, but in other ways he couldn't have been more of a contrast. Sammy—the American guide—had been overly tall, overly flamboyant and overly dark-skinned. Francesca was of average height, decidedly not gay, judging by the way she interacted with Matteo and the young Singaporean hunk, Jimmy, and her skin was as white as snow. Had she been entered into the annual 'Rose of Tralee' pageant in Ireland, she would have won outright on the whiteness of her skin alone. I was glad I had suddenly remembered Sammy. The brotherhood of the tour leaders was a strong bond no matter where in the world one was based.

Francesca had us all lined up in order of height, outside the bus. She then divided us into two rows—a row of gentlemen and the other of ladies. She let it slip to Lizzie (who had informed everybody who'd been awake on the bus at the time) that one of her better party tricks on evenings such as these was to organise her groups into couples. In our case this evening, it was so that we might parade into the massive courtyard of the converted monastery, our venue for the evening.

The instructions were clear. We were to link arms, straighten our backs and hold our heads up high. I prayed there would not be a need to balance a book on our heads, as that was me gone straight away. My tiresome middle-ear affliction caused me to be off balance for most of the time, and balancing books was out of the question. Earlier on in the afternoon, before my muddy walk, Francesca had urged us to dress up for the evening in our finest clothes.

"Ladies, I will expect earrings, bracelets, necklaces and even tiaras if you happen to have one stashed at the back of your suitcase. No mantillas please! We are not the travelling Italian choir come to entertain guests who will arrive later this evening for their weddings and parties."

So, it would not only be our busload dining in the barn tonight! I didn't mind that we would have company, and given the early start we were having, our evening could more than likely be done and dusted before the natives even lifted the farm gate at the end of the field. (At least that was how I had imagined the monks had kept themselves cloistered.)

We were ready to be presented to the empty courtyard. Matteo was the only audience to the procession, and to make himself comfortable, had dragged a white plastic chair from inside the venue which had been draped in white silk and tied with a matching white chiffon bow, from the outskirts of the enclosure. He had then sat smugly in the centre of the courtyard, mock-clapping and whistling as we paraded past him. From the corner of my eye, I could see a huddle of apron-clad young men and women, stifling giggles and pointing towards us. Let the games begin!

Francesca led her troops with a slender golden umbrella which had not yet seen the light of day on our trip. (Saved for this very occasion?) Directly behind Francesca were the Singaporean couples, only the wives had been reversed, and Hoc and Kate kept turning around looking at each other in confusion at the wife-swap. "Eyes to the front, troops! No unnecessary turning. Backs straight and eyes on the prize."

Francesca must have had eyes in the back of her head to have known that there were people turning around in confusion. The 'prize' was a cluster of small tables and stone benches to the side of where Matteo sat calling out, "Bellissima and bravo, brava!"

The prized tables had been puffed and prettied up with vases of fresh field-flowers in purples, yellows and reds. There were giant white umbrellas to the side of them, which must have been reserved for lunchtime festivities. A tall, bushy cypress hedge skirted the perimeter of the courtyard. All we needed were the horses and we could have been in the mounting yard at Buckingham palace with the Queen's Garden within marching distance.

The procession leaders had already reached the tables and stone benches, and Francesca had wordlessly motioned for them to stop and wait, whilst she tended to the couples at the rear, whom she began fussing over like a lady-in-waiting at a same-sex wedding. Brielle and Gloria been one of the last couples, and Gloria's ranch-style hat had been whisked off her head when an unexpected gust of wind had blown up. (No wigs went flying past me in the squall, so everyone must have sported their own head of hair.)

One thing was as sure as the sun coming out each day, my hair was going nowhere! Alice had plastered it down so firmly and held it in place with almost two containers of hairspray, so I could be assured of an impeccable hairstyle for many decades to come. Hankering to look me up some time? Take a squiz in the Guinness Book of Records. You'll no doubt find me there, alongside of Bob Marley and his dreadlocks and the Corleone clan with their horses' heads. Varied hairstyles can cause such a stir!

As soon as Francesca had reinstated Gloria and Brielle to coupledom, she raced up to the front of the line and began to indicate to the first three couples that they should sit at the first outdoor table. "Please, Hoc, Kate, Jimmy, Yvonne, Lizzie and Angelique. Sit down here and the waiters will pour you a glass of Spumante. You too, Lizzie and Fillip." The next three couples, Natarsha and Devo, Armenia and Joe (whom Francesca had allowed to walk in together as tomorrow was to be their thirtieth wedding anniversary) and Marsha and Stevie were shown their digs for the next half an hour. That left the remaining couples, including Alice and myself, to take up our positions at the big round table directly behind where Matteo had sat cheering and clapping when we had processed into the courtyard.

I wasn't sure where Matteo had scuttled off to, but I had an idea what he'd look like when he reappeared. If the whole entire history of Italian men out for an evening stroll was anything to go by, Matteo would reappear from Francesca's boudoir at the back of the bus dressed to kill. (I forgot to mention that Francesca had been conducting her affairs in her Sunday best for the last hour, having already been suitably attired when we'd left the hotel.)

The hors-d'oeuvres of olives, pickled vegetables, little risotto balls, tiny, crunchy asparagus rolls, slithers of prosciutto (which I passed on) and local cheeses were mouth-watering. I kept stuffing olives into my mouth (bocca della lupa) and trying to be as unobtrusive as possible with the pips, but it was difficult. At one stage, I had five of the gnarly little blighters in my mouth at once.

Gloria was asking me to help her fasten a pin to her hat to keep it from flying off again. It was very warm and very still in the courtyard, and I was positive there would not be the likelihood of an Edinburgh wind whipping up in the next twenty minutes, I obediently obliged her whim. I had made up my mind on day one to keep sweet with Gloria.

If she were to be believed, she had fallen on her feet when she'd arrived penniless as a dressmaker from the Philippines in Texas twenty-five years ago, and had snared a millionaire widower with five children and a ranch the size of Hawaii. I quite fancied another trip to America, and I'd never been to Texas, just to the surrounding state of Louisiana and the Gulf of Mexico where I'd swum in the tepid green waters. I had no reason to doubt Gloria; it was just that she never mentioned her husband or her children and grandchildren unless prodded to do so, and when I'd been shopping with her that one time on the island of St Jules, she had only bought presents for herself—nothing for the husband or the grandchildren.

There had been children's toys galore in the little shops on the island, from tiny wooden Pinocchio toys with extra-long red noses to jigsaw puzzles of the Colosseum and even Paw Patrol t-shirts. (I'd bought a few of the tee-shirts in various sizes.)

She was an enigma was our Gloria. I couldn't help thinking she had a bit of Jason Bourne about her. Brielle and Natarsha had confessed their lives away to us, but Gloria? There was a real Cinderella story lurking beyond the flying hat.

Time was up! Francesca had reappeared with a firm grasp of Matteo, and she was ushering us excitedly towards the barn which had been converted to a huge, twinkling restaurant. From the outside it looked as though it could accommodate several hundred people, but as I wasn't sure about the size of the dancefloor, I compromised with a conservative estimate of a hundred and fifty. There were only twenty-four of us, so that meant either five more busloads of tourists were expected, or we had hit the jackpot and scored the whole place to ourselves until the storm of the locals scheduled for after nine pm. (The waiting staff had supplied me with that morsel of information.)

I had my answer with Francesca's next breath.

"Don't look too worried that we are the only people in the barn tonight. It is much better and much more intimate. Who knows what kind of romances will come your way? Single ladies only, of course!"

Lizzie was walking in with Alice and I when Francesca had been talking, and was quick with the retort, "Move over single ladies, I'm in!"

The three of us linked arms and crossed the threshold to the barn raucously belting out Beyoncé's *I'm a single lady* as we entered the room. Matteo and Francesca were highly amused, and encouraged by their appreciation, Brielle, Natarsha and Devo joined in with the chorus, making us six abreast, and a chorus line. (Devo was singing, *I'm not a single lady* and for that his parents, Armenia and Joe, were grateful.)

It was the prosciutto factory restaurant all over again only this time someone had replaced the brown paper cloths with stiff white starched clothes, had added candles and bottles of red and white wine, flowers, and little welcome gifts of bonbonniere-Italian pink, blue or white almond sweets packaged in tiny fishnet bags. Another flashback to my childhood. I had literally not given those sweets the time of day for over fifty years, and now, here they were, making a memory-stirring comeback in a monastery-barn in Northern Italy.

I almost cried when I picked up the bag which had been placed alongside the real cloth serviettes, gold tinted crockery and matching cutlery denoting my place at the table. I had to tell someone what these little net bags meant to me, but no one seemed particularly interested. Francesca had been correct when she had pinpointed this trip as the best in the whole of Italy.

There were two long tables, exactly as had been the case this morning at Signor Carlo's place, but instead of just Signor Carlo and his daughter waiting tables, it was silver service with one waiter or waitress per couple. I leaned back on my chair which had been covered with a white satin cover to rival a royal wedding party and looked up to the skylights in the gabled barn roof. I was trying to pick out a star on which to make a wish in the fast-fading light. None out yet, but give it an hour or two, and I'd be singing that Disney song to death.

Alice's dreams were also coming true. Matteo was sitting directly opposite, at a little round affair for two, which had been placed about ten metres away from our long table. (There were plenty of other long tables just as exquisitely set in other parts of the room.) Alice's hopes were irreversibly dashed as she watched Francesca making her way over to the little round table and clinking glasses with Matteo.

"They're probably arranging a rendezvous for later tonight when we're all asleep." Alice was a misery guts for the next ten minutes, sulking over her missed opportunity with Matteo and stealing glances over towards the little rotund island in the midst of a sea of white reflected from the other long tables and chairs whenever she dared, or whenever Francesca let out an extra loud cackle.

"It's just not fair, Fil," Alice complained to me. "That should be me over there with Matteo. He could help me walk up to the buffet and he might even have had a slow dance with me as I can't move my legs all that well after all the walking today."

Brielle and Gloria had been listening in, and Brielle burst out laughing at the notion of Alice and Matteo slow dancing.

"I don't get why you'd want to, Alice." Brielle had tried her best to buffer Alice's disappointment. "They are probably going to discuss how many more miles we need to do tomorrow, what time we should leave Parma and then what time we should leave Como—all the boring stuff. We don't want to listen to all that. We want to sing and dance and have fun. And drink. Lots of drinking!"

Brielle had a point with the drinking. The great thing about having a bus to drive you home on a pitch-black star-studded night in Northern Italy is that you can drink as much as you like without having to drive. With that cheery point in mind, I joined Brielle, Gloria, Lizzie Angelique and Natarsha in a 'chin-chin' which was a toast in Italian and not a group chin-scratching session.

After the first course (Prima-piatti), Francesca called everyone over towards the kitchen where another long table had been set up with a portable stove, a large frying pan, some pots and a couple of saucepans, some flour and a punnet of ripe red tomatoes. It looked like a set for a cooking demonstration and guess what? It was a set for a cooking demonstration. Only it wasn't Jamie Oliver, Hugh from River Cottage or Mary Berry who emerged from behind the white chiffon curtain, bur a pretty 'thirties something' woman, completely kitted out in chef's garb, including a chef's hat and apron.

The woman was coveting a large shiny steel knife. No wonder there had been no chickens or ducks or geese running around the monastery courtyard. They probably had the chop earlier this afternoon. It was a Saturday night, and the owners would have been anticipating big crowds.

The woman was a genius with the pots, pans and produce. Within the course of twenty minutes she had produced a large bowl of pasta she made from scratch right before our very eyes, and a creamy tomato sauce she also made from scratch. The pasta was delicious, and I made sure I took lots of shots depicting the process as it was an easy dish, and one I felt sure I would be able to replicate at home, as long as I could source the particular flour. In my suburb back home, we had quite a few Italian shops, and many Italian restaurants, so it shouldn't be too difficult a quest.

We all clapped wildly when the woman, Mara, had finished her demonstration, and of course, we couldn't leave the table without slipping her a small token of appreciation of her culinary skills. I also managed to also slip her an olive branch complete with the planting instructions, and with her affinity with food I did not doubt that that there would be an olive grove leading down to the monk's vegetable garden when next we visited the monastery.

Next came the main course, which was help yourself from the buffet table. There were hot meats, grilled and battered fish, oysters, lobster and squid, hot vegetables, salads, more pasta, lasagne and more pasta, polenta, risotto and pizzas. Lots of pizzas with various toppings. It was the most extensive range of food we had seen on the trip so far, and it was all laid out solely for our group as we were still the only tourists in the restaurant.

While we were eating, a young girl in a glittering black cocktail dress and shoes so high they looked like stilts, had busily set up a microphone and a karaoke machine and had begun singing. Everything from Italian folk songs to Abba and Madonna. She was very engaging, very good and not too loud, so we were able to still talk. The singing was followed by dancing, and because I adore dancing and there was an empty dancefloor, I couldn't resist rushing over to Matteo and dragging him to his feet for a dance. It was harmless fun, and I did it for Alice as I knew she would never be able to dance, but that she'd love looking at Matteo while he was preoccupied with which foot to put forward in the waltz.

Matteo must have been tired from all the driving, because he began to waver after our second dance, and I let him off the hook by beckoning Devo to join me on the dance floor. We danced and I sang to *Mamma mia*, and the audience (our group and the watching staff) seemed to enjoy the performance. (While I'd been singing with the girl, and we'd had our backs to each other for the dramatic chorus of *Mamma Mia, here I go again, my, my how can I resist you?* I had slipped the girl an olive branch I had brought with me onto the dance floor. She looked Italian. I just hoped she was).

Fillip had even called out, 'encore' but I thought that was taking it a bit too far. The dancing was followed by dessert and coffee or tea. Throughout the evening, the wine had flowed freely, and more than a few of us overindulged. Neither Alice nor I though. Alice didn't drink, and I had exercised all the drink away with my dance floor antics. Water was all I desired.

It was the best time I'd had in a long while. It felt good to be letting my hair down, even though that was wishful thinking on my part, as the French plait would not budge when I tried to shake my hair free, but it was wrapped as tightly as an Egyptian mummy, and I would most likely be sporting the fashionable French look for a few weeks to come. As we were gathering our things to leave, Francesca asked Don to make a presentation to the Maître-D of the venue on behalf of our group. She had collected ten euro from each of us, and Don happily handed the proprietor the handsome donation.

The man was very humble in his acceptance of the gift and pledged to donate the money to sick children in the region who could not afford medical treatment. It felt good to have given, and not to have frittered the ten euro away on water bottles and crisps. The monastery food had been delicious to the point of every mouthful tasting better than the one before. No one at our end of the table had room for dessert, but Hoc and Kate at the other end were up at the buffet perusing the layout.

I made a mental note to ask them about the quality of their choice tomorrow. This converted monastery certainly was a place to be remembered. Just as we were stumbling out, the floodgates opened to the locals and visitors who had driven their own cars to the farm. One family who passed us at the door had two old Nonnas in tow, and one of them reminded me of Benito's mother. I would possibly never see either of them again, but if I did, I would say to Benito, "Well done on a lovely family and for taking such good care of your mother."

It was a wonderful thing, the Italian family, and many other countries would do well to take a leaf out of Italy's book when it came to protection and provision for older family members.

Another group was hot on the heels of the extended family. This time it was a posse of young men, about ten of them, all buttoned and suited up, reeking of aftershave, and ready for an evening of song and dance. They were not aware of their magnetism as a group or the effect they were having on the women in our group. Reactions varied from coy smiles (Lizzie and Angelique) to full blown, "Come and get me tiger" (from Brielle and Natarsha).

I was so tired from all the singing and dancing it was all I could do to smile at them as the team passed us by and drag Brielle back to the rest of our group. She had taken a fancy to a small wiry lad in a black leather jacket who was hanging around holding the white curtain back so that his mates could pass under. The boy was extremely good-looking—that I had to admit—but he far too small to be useful to any of us, except perhaps as a drinking partner. He had a cheeky grin and called out to us that his name was Dominic, and that he was here with his soccer mates for a good time. He certainly knew how to call a spade a spade.

"You girls wanna join us?" Dominic spoke very slow, but also very clear English, and Brielle was looking longingly at him. Perhaps she had noticed that the collective age of the team would not even come close to a quarter of our collective ages.

Francesca came to the rescue yet again. "Hurry ladies, Matteo is afraid of the dark and we do not want to be attacked by wolves on our way back to the hotel." She then looked directly at Brielle. "You want to stay, eh? You want to drink and dance and maybe even fall in love with the beautiful Italian boys?"

Brielle started laughing and joined Francesca in the banter. "Yes. I would like to stay with the boys, Francesca. But I want to sleep more. If I stay here and drink and dance the night away, I'll be fit for nothing tomorrow, and nothing, nothing is going to stand between me and Lake Como. These past few days have been wonderful, but Lake Como is the sole reason I'm here. Let's go home. I need my beauty sleep."

"Brava Brielle! A wise decision. Andiamo to the bus. Fa presto!"

That was how we came to leave the lads in the doorway to the restaurant. They were going in, and we were going out. Spontaneously, I handed Dominic a keepsake. I was down to my last few olive branches, but his team would have to practise somewhere, and maybe he was a bit of a gardener?

We flew home in record time. Matteo saw to that! Neither was there any music talking or interruptions from Francesca. The only time she spoke into her beloved microphone was when we arrived at the hotel, and that was to remind us to place our suitcases outside the bedroom doors by seven, and to be at breakfast by seven-fifteen. The bus was scheduled to leave at eight-thirty sharp. We were in for a big day-our last in the countryside. First up would be Parma, followed by Lake Como (had anyone heard of it?) and then, finally back to Milan, late tomorrow evening. Our last meal together would not commence until eight pm, and then we would be back at the Milan hotel tomorrow night by ten thirty at the latest, as some passengers (including Alice and myself) had early morning flights to catch.

People had listened in silence to the final instructions from Francesca. It was sinking in with all of us that in less than twenty-four hours, we would be saying our last goodbyes. Alice was right. We'd do well to get a good night's sleep.

Chapter 35
Early Morning in Parma

The early morning light dipping across the fields where I had walked yesterday afternoon was like a swift passage of athletes in an Olympics' Opening ceremony. A fester of coloured silk approaching the winning post-a giant kaleidoscopes of speckled rainbow morsels, being scattered across a misty terrain. I had to shake myself to make sure I wasn't hallucinating. All the dancing and drinking last night may have disturbed something in my brain, causing me to see this ethereal display of morning colour every time I squinted up.

I was lying flat out in the field behind the hotel. Any community-minded hotel-patron with a pair of binoculars and a half decent imagination would have alerted the authorities by now, and the police would be on their way. Inspector Montalbano, that's whom I wanted. I would not be moving an inch until he was summoned. (I seemed to recall the Inspector operated out of Sicily-nowhere near Northern Italy, but I could wait.)

If Matteo was not turning out to be an option for Alice, and Brielle, with all her blonde charm and full suite of American coquettish moves hadn't managed to snare Dominic, then the least I could boast would be a visit from Inspector Montalbano of the Italian Carabinieri. I would take great pleasure pointing his smouldering good looks out to my friends and family next time the reminder for my upcoming slide night popped up on my google calendar alert. Slide night! I hadn't thought about slide nights for years.

At a pinch, the last time was probably when I'd had moved houses ten years ago, and the filmy white-edged slides had come tumbling out of their neat little rectangular yellow-edged boxes and ended up in one higgledy-piggledy heap on the floor of my loungeroom. I'd had the brilliant notion to hold an impromptu house-leaving party that very night, with a party-game I would entitle, 'Pick a slide-any slide'. My guests would be encouraged to allow themselves a blindfold (usually a cast-off from a long-haul flight) and sink to the faded carpeted floor-selecting three slides at random.

Nowadays, it would be eco-friendly carpet designed to leave no footprints (carbon or real) nor any indentations. These slides would be slotted into the projector, and the guest would need to come up with a plausible story using the locations of the slides in under a minute. The most entertaining story would win the grand prize of, wait for it, 'a bottle of Leibfrouwine'. There would also be a consolation prize (a half-bottle of Leibfrouwine) for the most boring story, because that was the other thing on the topic of Slide nights that remained firmly cemented in my mind. Boredom to the point of death. A slow. Suffering, interminable, sleep-deprived death.

Needless to say, my inspired idea for a board game featuring thousands of slides never paid off. Somebody beat me to it with Trivial Pursuit, and we all ended up pushing little dull-coloured wedges around a board in the wee hours of a Sunday morning, claiming to know what colour the hankie was in Napoleon's pocket when he coughed at the Battle of Waterloo. Or something like that. If anything was missing from post travel nowadays, it was 'Slide night'.

Thinking about Olympic ceremonies and jockeys flying past, kaleidoscopes and Leibfrouwine kept me occupied for five minutes at least, but after that, I was just plain cold, wet and uncomfortable-flat on my back in the sodden field. Were we too far North for this to have been a paddy field? I couldn't be sure, but I thought I'd better move quickly in case an angry Italian Signora McGregor came chasing after me with a pitchfork or a giant rice cooker.

It was fully light by the time I reached our bedroom. Six thirty and full-blown sunshine. Alice was in the shower when I'd crept back into the room, and I noticed she had laid her clothes for the day ahead carefully out on her bed, and had also managed to drag her suitcase across the room so that it was behind the door-ready for the trip back to Milan. I was nowhere near as advanced as Alice with the preparation of my own suitcase, but who would know if I just picked up all my clothes and threw them into the case? I would only need clothes for today and tonight, and I would be wearing my tracksuit on the plane back to England-as was my pattern.

It would be strange not to be heading back to Rome and then straight back to Australia from the airport tomorrow morning, but I still had six weeks of travelling around Europe before I would see my friends and family again. One plan had been for me to remain on the Continent and fly straight to Poland to enjoy the sights and sounds of Warsaw for a month before the rest of the party arrived for the wedding, but I couldn't see myself sitting still in one place for so long, unless I enrolled in a short course at the University and spent my nights hauled up in a hotel room studying and writing. I had been yearning to write for some years now, and so many writing courses had paraded their way before me, coaxing me to jump on board, but so far, I had procrastinated, assuring myself that I would settle down and write when I'd retired from the important work which was keeping me from realising my dreams. Teaching took its toll, but I loved it. The only real disadvantage of teaching was that it got in the way of my travelling, but to be fair, teachers probably had double the holidays of Public Servants.

Consequently, I would not be travelling to Rome, or Warsaw or anywhere else other than London Heathrow, where I would assume my duties as 'lady in waiting' to Alice who was struggling through these last few days with her knee and legs. A true humanitarian, putting the wants and needs of others before me. That was the me I wanted to present to the world. I had one more full day to prove myself with my fellow passengers, and an extra day with Alice when we'd be airborne on our way back to Heathrow. After Monday-I would be on my own in London. My accommodation was booked for a week in central London, and I had made my plans to visit a different English town every day, using my First-class British Rail Pass which extended out from Victoria station in all directions for a radius of one hundred kilometres. That would be something of an experience, especially as I would be on my own.

By the time I had finished squashing my crumpled clothes into my suitcase, remembering to leave enough out for tonight's farewell dinner and tomorrow's travel day, I dragged both cases out to the corridor for the last time. Tomorrow, there would be no Matteo. We would need to call on the bellboy for assistance as we would be leaving Milan at five in the morning in order to catch our eight o'clock flight. Alice must have heard me struggling with the cases, as though the open bedroom door, I could see that she had appeared at the bathroom door, clad in the hotel terry towelling robe, her head bandaged in a matching turban. She looked a sight for sore eyes with her face streaked in white face cream. As usual, she was in no hurry to get moving and was on for a chat, leaning against the bathroom door, watching me readjust the cases.

"Fil, I was looking everywhere for you. I even used the binoculars from the back window, but I couldn't see you anywhere. There was someone working in the field behind the hotel, but apart from that man, there was no one else. Did you go back to the field for your walk, or a different way?"

It was safer to tell the truth, so I answered truthfully that I had been in the field this morning, but that I hadn't seen anyone picking produce. Alice hadn't yet finished. "But Fil, the strange thing about the worker was that he suddenly disappeared. One minute he was bending over, and the next, I couldn't focus on him. Do you think he was OK?"

In my head I was answering her, "Yes Alice, I'm okay. It was me. I was laying in the grass going over our trip and thinking about this being our last day with the group." But aloud, I was saying, "No idea, Alice, now we had better get a wriggle on or all the eggs will have disappeared."

Alice moved like a rocket at the mention of breakfast, and in ten minutes we were ready to go downstairs. Because the hotel was a convention centre, and there were probably three or more conventions happening today, the breakfast room was chock-a-block full. Fortunately, Francesca had booked a section of the room for our group and although Alice and I had to sit at different tables because we had arrived so late, we still managed to fill ourselves up with the delicious breakfast. I was getting mad with myself for harping on and on about the quality of the food in Italy, but I couldn't stop singing the praises of the chefs in every place we visited.

I had taken my father too much for granted when I'd sat down every evening with my sisters and brother to the delectable Italian meals he'd prepared. Mum was also a good cook, but she really was at a disadvantage when it came to a choice of vegetables and meats. Coming from Irish stock, she was proficient at concocting stews, lamb chops with veg, and on Fridays tinned salmon with mashed potato and white sauce. That was the extent of mum's repertoire. But dad? He could cook like a king. All vegetables were fresh from Uncle Frank's market garden and everything dripping in olive oil. That was the real secret to Italian cooking. Lashings and lashings of olive oil. My heart went out to all those unfortunate souls who had never experienced the joys of Italian cooking. It was something everyone should experience, and something purely enticing.

After breakfast we had precisely fifteen minutes to race back up to the bedroom to collect our smaller bags, clean our teeth and be back on the bus ready to leave at the promised hour. It wasn't far to the centre of the town where we were scheduled to meet our last guide for the tour in the town square at nine am sharp. Francesca had dressed flamboyantly for our last morning on the bus.

She greeted us at the steps in long flowing gypsy skirt and a billowing blouse. She had tied her hair back with a colourful scarf and had looped large silver earrings through her ears. Even though she had made a noticeable effort to dress in costume for the mountains, I wasn't sure whether this was the last outfit in her suitcase, so I refrained from commenting on her appearance.

Alice, on the other hand, made up for my nonverbal reserve. "You look pretty, Francesca. Are you going to demonstrate the Tarantella for us this morning?"

Francesca looked at Alice in deadpan surprise. "No Alice. I thought you and Roy might like to do the honours and give us a demonstration in the main square in Parma. It'll be good exercise for the two of you. I'll call out the steps." She winked at me as she spoke, and I winked back. Both of us knew she had Alice bluffed, and that there would be no dancing in the town square this morning. A hanging perhaps, but no dancing.

Before we'd even had time to recline in our seats and listen to Francesca for the umpteenth time, we had arrived in the centre of the town. It was very quiet, almost deserted save for a few hurrying students late for Saturday university classes, a couple of old Nonnas on ancient bicycles complete with wicker baskets brimming with bread sticks, pedalling furiously through the stone streets and alleyways. Parma reminded me immediately of Lucca. Sister towns, possibly twins? There was a river, there were churches and masses of shops and row after row of tall narrow buildings which stretched up to the brilliant blue sky. It was beautiful. Early morning, crisp air, beautiful surrounds-just as it had been out in the field three hours before. Everyone was happy. Parma was making us happy with its simplicity of surrounds, and hint of a fascinating, extravagant history. Hard to explain, but definitely a special place.

We didn't have to wait long for the local guide to appear. She must have been chatting in the patisserie behind where Matteo dropped us off, because she materialised from the shop as soon as the bus moved off.

Francesca was hugging her and shaking her hands vehemently as if she were a long-lost relative who had not been sighted in years. I was smiling to myself, thinking that Francesca was like a sailor with a girl in every port, the way she was with the guides. She had done the Tour Company proud with her relentless dedication to catering to our every whim and fancy. It took a bit to impress me when it came to tour guides, but Francesca was one out of the box. We would all miss her terribly for the first few days after the trip.

I knew that was on the cards. Just like the inevitable jetlag. Matteo would also be missed, but he'd been a quieter presence than the extraverted Francesca and hadn't been with us 24/7 since the beginning of the trip as had Francesca. It was part of life—moving on. I knew that. It was just sad that things had to change.

Our last local guide turned out to be a formidable force. She was immaculate and meticulously dressed in flowing robes and scarves. She reminded me very much of an English Dame, and I wouldn't have been at all surprised to have learnt she had a hyphenated surname. Not a hair on her head was out of place. Her fascinating monologue was delivered in the record time of forty- seven minutes, and not one of those minutes left a single stone unturned as to the extreme significance of a place like Parma, a name I had only ever associated with specials in Australian pubs –'Parma and chips'.

The real Parma shared nothing with often cheap, slapped together meals in Australian bars. The real Parma was pure class, and the woman skilling us up about the place was a perfect match. Actually, she was informing rather than telling, and effusing rather than bubbling over with enthusiasm. Everything about the woman delivering the history of Parma was pure class. She was, of course, English, but her Italian was perfecto, and she had lived in Parma as a University lecturer for almost half of her life.

She was a true Parmense, and fiercely proud of her heritage. She had married an Italian Art Historian and their children and grandchildren were categorically Italian. There was no getting past the fact that this woman was in a gold-carriage of her own. I was glad Francesca had stuck around, as that showed there were no hard feelings when it came to who made the better guide. Penelope may have had Parma, but Francesca, like Puccini, had Italia!

Penelope began by setting the scene and letting us know where we really were. This morning it had been enough for me to know that I was in a field bordering a hotel on the outskirts of Parma, Northern Italy. This morning, according to Penelope we all needed to be much better informed about our exact location. Knowing that we were in Italy was one thing, but being able to report back to family and friends that we had spent our last full morning together as a group in the province of Emilia-Romanga-home to roughly four-point-three million people, and bordering the world-famous Tuscany-now that would have been something to have written home about!

Once she had begun speaking, there was no stopping Penelope. She knew her stuff and was determined to educate the twenty-two of us to the point that if we had to remember anything at all about Italy, it would not be the cliffs of Cinque-Terra nor the alpine peaks of the little village of Santa-Marie high up in the foothills of the alps. It would not be the beautiful beaches of Viareggio nor the gulf of Poets where writers and Poets from all corners of the earth had, for centuries, lived out their dreams. It would not even be the exquisite walled city of Lucca, nor the heaven felt gardens of Taranto. It would be Parma!

Architecturally outstanding, historically unrequited, and aesthetically so pleasing to the eye that it was difficult to know in which direction to turn. The quality of life in Parma was second to none. Children played in their gardens and academics rode their bicycles to work. Crime was down, if even existent, and morale was high. Food was plentiful, places of worship in abundance, and the beautiful river provided a place to relax and enjoy all the sumptuous life Parma had to bring.

Those words were all from Penelope. Normally, I was one step ahead of the local guides. I was proud of the fact that I had done my homework the night before we were due to visit a new place, and I would have been able to step in as a substitute guide had the real guide fallen ill and no replacement had appeared. I was well versed with the duties of an understudy, having understudied to many a protagonist of musical theatre in my younger days. I just never really got that big break.

No one was ever ill, and even if they were suffering from laryngitis, most of them wouldn't have given up their lead role for quids. In a way I was relieved to have spent my theatre days in the chorus line. It was a place where I could be part of the action yet slink away into the background like a greasy oil slick whenever I so chose. I could kick my legs high and exert all my energy, or alternatively slack off and let the person in the line next to me do all the work. No one was going to notice! No one ever did. That rubbish about stars being discovered in the chorus line, belting their hearts out or busking to a crowd of three on a street corner in Dublin? Poppycock!

Back to Penelope of Parma. The reason I was not prepared for the commentary, and therefore not in a position to question Penelope's authority or legitimacy of opinion or fact, was because I had been so tired last night after the monastery extravaganza that I had gone straight to sleep without having even turned on the bedside reading lamp.

I think I got as far as the title, 'Parma' in my guidebook by the light of my phone and had then promptly fallen asleep. Then, this morning I'd had the field debacle and…well, you know the rest.

Penelope had moved us on from the streets with the early-morning shoppers to an enormous bare, stone-square with an enormous stone church propped up in the right-hand corner. She was in raptures over the church. I could see Francesca on her phone some way from our group, back hunched, and engrossed in intense conversation with someone.

For Alice's sake, I hoped it was her husband and not Matteo, but we would never know as she was too far away from us. I realised I was daydreaming and not concentrating on Penelope's dissertation. I tried to brighten up and join in the questions. Fillip was in fine form. He was in his element when it came to churches and public sculptures, and although he'd left his run a little late on the itinerary, Fillip was doing his best to help us all understand the intricacies of the architecture with his questions.

Finally, Penelope stopped for a breather, hoisted her umbrella, and ordered us to follow her towards the grand array of steps leading into the colossal Cathedral. The action was redundant, as there was nobody else in the square, but it was something she did-like the mason handshake, and if nothing else, it alerted Francesca to the fact that we were moving, and she'd be wise to curtail her call and follow us in. With twenty-four hours to go, she wouldn't want anything happening to any of us and end up with a lawsuit on her hands.

If anyone were to file a complaint against Francesca, or even against one of the local guides we'd had the pleasure of meeting on the trip, the complaint most definitely would not have been from an Australian traveller. It wasn't something we did. It would have been un-Australian. But Americans and lawsuits? Well, that was a whole different scenario.

Twenty years ago, on my 'Grand Europe' trip which lasted for forty-nine glorious days, my friend Maryanne and I had teamed up with a rich American woman, an English woman and a New Zealander. The New Zealand woman had been the thirty-year-long pen-pal of the English woman. There was an incident on the trip which resulted in a lawsuit being filed; my point being that it was the American woman who had successfully sued the Tour Company.

Her complaint had been that she'd paid for a double room yet had been allocated a tiny single room for three days in Lucerne, Switzerland. Adele had been ropable, and every morning when we met up with her, it was to the same catch-cry, "I'm going to get my lawyers onto this. This Tour Company is going to wish they'd never started up. I'm suing them for all they've got!"

I hadn't been very happy it had rained for the whole three days we were in Lucerne and the Tour Company had promised us all a wonderful time in the sun, but I wasn't suing anyone, was I? That was it; the different responses to expectations. We Aussies gave them no grief, and despite the lawsuit, the company lived to tell the tale and go on to become one of the most well-known travel providers in the world today.

Chapter 36
Exploring Parma

The steps leading up to the magnificent cathedral which, stood slightly to the right, yet still managed to dominate the pristine Square, were as steep as they were wide. Most of us were climbing three or four abreast with Penelope at the helm and Francesca to the rear, struggling to keep up, and clutching on to her mobile for dear life. It struck me that we all had lives to live beyond this cathedral, the Bishops' Palace and the expansion of sandstone slab in this deserted quadrangle.

Also bearing consideration were the lives of the many famous townsfolk who would have walked the square over the centuries. Back in front of the Patisserie, when Penelope had outlined proposed sight-seeing for the next three quarters of an hour, she had proudly announced that Giuseppe Verdie-Parma's very own son, had bought his ham from the 'Ham-curers' on the street where we were standing, and that the ham with which he left the shop was always wrapped in pig skin. Verdi liked it that way.

Penelope then gave us a little Verdi quip which I quickly noted in my moleskin notebook. (Maybe I could get myself a pig-skin notebook in Parma if they stocked such items.) Verdi's quote was worth noting down: "Let me look intelligent and you can look like peasants." I admired the frankness and audacity of the man. Verdi would have been quite the character to have met on the street.

Like Francesca today, Giuseppe had his life to live, and he had lived it out well, bringing joy for centuries to come to thousands of music and Opera lovers. Similarly, with Penelope. Her story, had time permitted her the opportunity to unravel the last sixty years, would have been equally meritorious. Not one of us in the group would have been without something interesting to say about our own lives, or those of our children, parents or grandparents. It was no wonder 'Ancestry.Com' was such a billionaire business.

So simple a notion, yet so worthwhile a cause. To give families a sense of where they came from, and of who bore responsibility for the lives they were living today! It was hard to pinpoint which century was more wonderful an epoch in which to be alive. Fate had brought us together for the seven days but once midnight struck-it would be the turn of a new group of excited travellers-eager to further their understanding and appreciation of this ever-changing landscape.

Francesca was probably missing her family. It wouldn't be the easiest of jobs-being so far away from loved ones, and she had mentioned her family, especially her mother-in-law quite a few times during the trip. I remembered Francesca's first mention of the woman. "My mother-in-law. Now there is a force, huh? She lives on her little farm quite close to us, all by herself, and she picks the tomatoes also alone. In the spring she fishes for frog's legs in the stream behind her house, and she eats these for tea to keep her string and healthy. In winter she chops the wood fora the fire and in summer she sweeps the house ever day to make the cool air. She is in a charge of us all and next week it is her birthday!"

Well, that might have gone some way towards explaining Francesca's current agitation. Besides Easter and Christmas, a mother-in-law's birthday would have to have been one of the most important events on the Italian calendar. Easter had gone, Christmas was still to come—that only left her mother-in-law's birthday which was probably around about today.

No one else was bothering about Francesca not keeping up with the group. I just wanted her to get through the last couple of days without a hitch. So far, we had been the perfect tour group. No bus romances, no brawls in hotels, and nobody had been arrested for wearing the wrong footwear in Cinque Terra nor wearing too skimpy an outfit in famous churches. No one had endured an altercation with the police, and no one had contracted food poisoning. Oh, and not even Fillip had spoked out of turn, or shown rudeness towards the local guides.

We were squeaky clean, and now, in these last hours, it was up to a Francesca and a Matteo to follow our lead. Of course, Francesca knew all that. She was probably just suffering from a little cabin fever and needed a break. We had already notched up hundreds of miles, and there would be another hundred to go before we had completed the full circle and ended up back in Milan. I would put Francesca out of my mind. She was a big girl who would survive perfectly well without me as a minder.

Penelope was already inside the building and the rest of us were still shuffling along as if en-route to a religious escape room. No choice to relax on the bus had been offered to us this morning. We were in for one final dousing in the Baptismal font whether we liked it or not. I was easy either way. The church looked and sounded interesting and it would fit nicely into my new Pinterest folder 'European Churches' if I could manage to get a clear enough shot, but after seeing more churches than gelato shops, I was pretty much past it today. If I couldn't get a good enough photo, I'd buy a postcard. Or two! An easier and more reliable a solution.

We finally caught up with our Parma-obsessed local guide. Penelope had ground to a halt inside the foyer and in an exaggerated 'cloak and dagger voice' made us all swear to secrecy before leading us in her click-click-clickety red high heels across a wide-open space, past rows of pews and frescos. I was becoming a little blasé about the whole 'marvellous insides of a church thing' and having not a clue in the world what we would be searching for did nothing to improve my deflating mood.

Penelope, on the other hand, knew exactly what she sought, and with a personality such as Penelope leading you, it was best to offer no resistance and follow blindly. We were literally following blindly it was so dark and high ceilinged in the echoing spot where our illustrious Guide had come to an abrupt halt. She had extended her neck as far as it could go and was pointing out "The Assumption of the Virgin Mary" which she enthusiastically reported had been painted in the sixteenth Century by the famous Italian artist Antonio Correggio.

I'd had no idea there would be Correggio to savour and was slightly disbelieving that it had been played down so much. (Served me right for forfeiting my homework last night, and for being such a sceptic about the Cathedral.)

Where were the crowds one had to fight at the Louvre, Uffizi and Vatican?

Where were the signs and the barricades, witches' hats and the security staff?

And where were the lights?

It was so dark it was impossible to make out anything. Penelope was wielding one of those thin blue halogen torches I'd seen astronomers lovingly directing towards the roofs in Planetariums. She was busy crisscrossing the ceiling and walls of the smaller chapel we had entered. The torch became a frenzied blue firefly and it was moving so fast I started to feel dizzy trying to keep up with it.

I tried to see where Alice had disappeared to, but it was too dark. The feeling of vertigo continued, and I must have faltered where I'd been standing, because the next thing I knew, it was the 'water over my face of the boat trip' revisited, and I was being led back outside into the open air. Dripping wet, I was propped up against the sandstone wall of the cathedral, on the top step—adjacent to the heavy wooden double doors.

Brielle was sitting cross-legged, yogi-style by my side.

"Well, Fil, that was a good party trick."

I tried to protest that it hadn't been a trick at all and that I had been very interested in all that Penelope had to say but that I had been overcome by the fumes. It was coming back to me slowly. The darkened interior, the buzzing blue light, Penelope's voice rising to countless crescendos in her excitement of revelation, and the pungent smell of incense wafting from a small room to the side of the arches. (Perhaps the incense barrels had needed changing and they'd left it until a Saturday to do so.) I began to feel better within minutes and strong enough to stand up and re-enter the ring, but just as Brielle and I reached the doors, they were opened from the inside by Penelope. The tour was over.

I don't think Penelope realised Brielle and I were part of her tour, as she marched down the stairs on a mission, without giving us a second glance. She made have assumed us to have been a couple of church beggars and had not wanted to draw attention to the fact that every city had its fair share of the downcast, even a prize-winning city such as Parma. But, regardless of her excuse, we were passed by. Once the others saw us slumped against the wall, most of them stayed to help us up, and in Fillip's case, to find out what had happened.

Penelope and Francesca and a few of the others had already reached the piazza and were looking up to us and waving. There was no time to humour Fillip with a blow-by-blow account of my misfortunes in the House of God. "I'll tell you all later. It was no big deal. I just felt slightly dizzy and Brielle helped me out into the fresh air. I should feel better now."

I did feel better with fresh air. I decided incense did not agree with me and that the next time I sniffed the strong smell, or when a priest tried to wave the little gold lantern with the sickly smelling ashes in my face at a Benediction, I would whip out my face mask and scare him off. (Not with a horror mask but a little white face mask similar to the ones worn when trying to escape paint fumes.)

The whole ten of us who'd been loitering at the top of the stairs copped it on the chin when Penelope lost some of her composure and threatened not to persist with the tour if so many of us could not muster up a little more interest. No one dared speak up and let her know what had happened, and after one final contemptuous, sweeping dismissal of all ten of us, she turned on her heels, and with her head held high marched off into the distance.

This time we all quickly followed. There were still ten minutes of life with Penelope, so it was best behaviour all round. Even Alice and Roy managed to keep up with the group as we whirl winded past fashionable glass panelled shops and restaurant after restaurant which had still to open its doors. The streets were still deserted, and the outdoor chairs and tables which would transform the pavements and kerbsides by lunchtime and well into the evening, still had yet to see the light of day. I picked up my phone to check the time and was surprised to see that it still wasn't even ten o'clock. Penelope had informed us that Saturday and Sunday mornings were late opening mornings for the conventional shops, as they would be staying open later in the evenings on the weekends.

We window-shopped for a while as we sauntered back to where we'd met Penelope, almost an hour before. Our illustrious guide had shaken off her irritation at the slight hiccup I had unwittingly caused at the cathedral, when people had denied her by not demonstrating their full attention, and in the end, we left as friends.

Penelope had been a fitting climax to the local Guides, and if I were forced to choose between which of the Guides had been the most informative-Penelope would have found herself in my last three. We were handing her the coins and notes of appreciation for her informative and eye-opening talk, and I slipped her an olive branch.

She was delighted, and like many guides before her, promised to plant the cutting at her earliest convenience.

"I have a marvellous cottage garden with lemon trees and a cypress hedge right down the driveway. I've always dreamed of an olive grove at the bottom of the garden. Thank you so very, very much." I was aware of my policy of non-Italians not qualifying, but Penelope was more an Italian than many a person I had met on the trip, and I was glad she'd been so delighted with the gift.

We still had an hour before Matteo would whisk us off to Como. Brielle was so excited that she decided to skip the markets (which were around the corner and due to open at ten) and walk back straight back to where the bus was to pick us up. "I don't want to miss out on Lake Como. If I come to the markets with all of you, then we might get carried away buying treasures, and miss the bus. Francesca was very insistent that the bus will wait for no one."

I tried to reason with Brielle that we had at least an hour, time enough for a drink, ablutions and perhaps a quick browse around the open-air Saturday morning market for which Parma was famous. "Matteo won't leave without five of us, Brielle. It wouldn't look good on either his or Francesca's resumes, if they wanted to change jobs."

But Brielle would not be convinced, and once we reached the first corner after farewelling Penelope, she bounded off in the opposite direction. I wasn't sure that was the right direction to have taken, but Brielle had a map, and seasoned walker that she was-a shortcut or two up and down hills would be on the cards. She'd insisted she'd remembered just where along the river Matteo was waiting with the bus, no doubt double-parked and reading an Italian newspaper.

Thinking about Matteo by the lapping river in his old black deckchair and his torn straw hat reading the Italian paper, made me think of my own father and his determined reading of the 'Canberra Times' every single day from cover to cover. There hadn't been one scrap of information that had been relayed in the paper which had escaped dad's eagle eyes. Every Saturday he would drive to the Italian shop in a neighbouring suburb and pick up the Italian paper the Italian shop-owner had put away for him under the counter.

The paper—Il Globo—contained all things Italian. That was how my sister and I came to be something of authorities on Italy when we took up Italian in secondary school. Dad would fill us in with all the details of life in Italy, and we would relay this information to our teachers. It kept everyone happy, and we always passed Italian with flying colours.

Right in front of us was the bustling market, in complete contrast to the Cathedral precinct which had been dead, and the classy shop district which had been closed. I'd been disappointed that our timeframe did not allow for any serious shopping in the little Parma boutiques, but there was still Como, and maybe even Milan if we got back early enough this afternoon and the evening meal was pushed back a little. Ideally, I would have hung around the shop where I had seen a great-looking jumpsuit in summery colours which I'd rather fancied as my wedding outfit.

The mannequin in the window looked to be about my size, and I would have purchased it regardless of the fit. Having seven sisters came in handy for some things. There would always be an ugly stepsister or two willing to squeeze into a too-small outfit if it meant scoring a fashion garment from Italy. But it would have been too risky to have waited until the shop opened, tried on the jumpsuit and then raced back to the bus all within an hour.

Alice had offered to wait with me when she'd seen how much I'd had my heart set on wearing the outfit to the Polish wedding, but she was realistic enough to point out that there was no way she would be able to race back to the bus in time. "I just couldn't manage it, Fil, then Matteo would be mad at me for holding us all up. He'd probably have to bring the bus back here to pick me up, and there'd be nowhere to park."

Alice was becoming quite stressed with the notion that Matteo might go off her; I had given in and accompanied the other four to the bustling open-air market.

Now we were seated close to the front window, of a small family-friendly restaurant which sold coffees, soft drinks and toasted sandwiches. None of us were hungry, but we were all thirsty, and all in need of the bathroom. After ordering our drinks, we took it in turns to visit the bathroom. It was cool in the shop, and I was tempted to stay sitting there with another lemonade and ice, whilst the other three browsed the market. We had thirty-five minutes. Twenty-five, if you counted the ten ministers it would take to find the river and the bus.

When the other three stood up to go, I remained seated. Alice was surprised. It was usually she who was going nowhere. "What are you doing, Fil? We only have a short window of opportunity to buy things, you know." Alice lived for markets. Markets and fetes and bazars. Every year she took charge of a stall with her friend Robyn at Hampton Court Palace. The proceeds of the stall were gratefully accepted by the Needlework Association of Hampton Court Palace.

Alice had completed a two-year needlework course at the Palace and had made many friends there. Then there was the annual school fete which caused her no end of excitement and anticipation in the preceding weeks. Alice was always commander in charge of the bookstall, and for more years than I care to remember, I had sent pre-loved cookbooks and novels over to England (at great expense) so that they might be sold at the fair for five pence. I couldn't see how this morning would be any different as far as markets were concerned. Alice would be as excited to mingle in the market as she had been at the castle in Milan to have mingled amongst the dogs.

"I'm just going to sit here and wait, Alice. I can see everything that's going on."

The little trattoria we had stopped at was in the thick of things. If I stepped out of the front door, I would be up to my knees in shoes, or, were I to move a little further up the hill, it would be pots, pans and brooms. Next to the metal and steel appliances stall there were piles and piles of women's clothing, heaped on the racks, with no particular distinguishing layout. I was about to sink back into my comfortable retro armchair and order myself a café late, when an item of clothing on one of the hangers displayed in the women's clothing stall (above the haphazard heaps) caught my eye. It was hard to make out, and it could have been a dressing-gown, because there were a few of them flung about in the breeze which had picked up, but it wasn't a dressing-gown, or even a kimono. It was a jumpsuit. A beautiful jumpsuit in greens and reds and golds and navy.

I could see when I wanted to without my glasses.

I'm not much of a television or movie buff. I prefer to read or write in the evenings, but one television programme I would not miss every weekday evening was *EastEnders*. I loved the characters and the East London setting. I loved the Queen Vic pub and Albert Square. Most of all, I loved the buzzing little market where clothing was cheap and fruit and veg fresh. The jumpsuit I was staring at was jumping about in the breeze, begging me to venture over for a closer look.

An Italian family who were ambling past the stall were almost hidden in the flapping material—all six of them! This alarmed me to the point of action. Gloria and Natarsha had left the café ten minutes ago, and Alice was about to leave me here if I wasn't going to join her. That much was clear. "Hold on, Alice. I'll come. I've just seen my outfit for the wedding."

Alice looked delighted that I would be joining her on the short bargain hunt, but she didn't know I had little intention of sticking with her. I would be spending the next twenty minutes modelling the jumpsuit for anyone who cared to take a break in shopping and bartering, and from their reactions decide if the garment was the right choice. I wanted to be irresistible at the wedding next month and maybe even score me a Polish fella. I had always been partial to the Poles with their round faces and 'ski' tacked onto the end of every surname.

That jumpsuit had my name all over it!

Chapter 37
Second Last Outing

We were on our last leg of the journey. Most people had reverted to a semi catatonic state, slumped in their seats or looking at maps and reading. Every morning of the trip, Francesca had briefed us on the day ahead, and many of the group had taken to highlighting yesterday's path with different coloured highlighters, zigzagging across the top of Northern Italy-following the bus route. It didn't look all that far on paper, but I knew the fatigue was setting in for Matteo, and that was understandable, because apart from that one day when…had taken over and Matteo had enjoyed a morning sleep in, he had been on board pretty much every day. So had Francesca, but she had the local guides to bat off, so it had been a little easier on her. Francesca even had time to buy some souvenirs for her grandchildren, whose pictures she had shown me, last night at the monastery barn restaurant.

Francesca did her best to get us talking, but everyone was well and truly spent, and we still had romantic Lake Como and tonight's farewell dinner to live through. I lay back in my seat and thought about the last hour I'd spent in Parma: working backwards from when I had been sitting sipping lemonade in the café, to when I'd raced back to the bus waiting by the river—face flushed with first love and the realisation that I had at last secured an outfit for the Polish wedding, and of all places to have realised my dream—in the Parma outside market. The stalls and the big tall African vendor had come good. (I also bought some cheap thick socks for walking in the hills and a couple of t-shirts.)

How cheap had it all been? How perfect was the cotton, and how long were the legs? There had been only one slight hitch to the transaction. The biggest benefit of all was that the jumpsuit had cost only one fifth of the price that had been attached in large print to the one I had fancied in the shop window. I wasn't sure what material the expensive designer labelled item had been, but it didn't matter to me in the slightest. I had the jumpsuit I wanted.

It had fit like a glove when I'd slipped it over my head behind the makeshift curtained area in the middle of the square, and I now had a great weight lifted from my shoulders for the month to come. I'd still need shoes and perhaps a shawl, but Kmart or Penny's would suffice. The slight hitch was the length of the trouser legs. Each leg was at least fifteen centimetres too long and would require curtailing. Alice was good with a needle and thread, and even handier with a pair of scissors, so I didn't fuss too much when the legs of the jumpsuit caused me to trip and topple over, and of course—because it was me—for the makeshift curtain to follow suit.

I ended up on the ground, entangled in the curtain, thankfully fully clothed in the jumpsuit. The African man and his assistant came running over to see if I was alright, which I was, and they both helped me struggle to my feet. The younger man then began reassembling the pop-up dressing room. He was taking ages, because the curtain pole kept falling over and without the older man to give him a hand, it was just not working. The older man had disappeared towards the front of the shop, and because his merchandise was so cheap, a long line of shoppers had formed.

There was no way the young boy would be able to reassemble the dressing room in time for me to change back into my travelling clothes. "Don't worry about it. I'll just pull my travelling clothes on over the jumpsuit. That'll work until I get back to the bus. We have a bathroom onboard, and I can get changed in there."

Even as I spoke, I could hear Lizzie's curt, cutting words to me, "We could all see you, Fil."

No, that would not do. I couldn't take the chance on not inadvertently activating the emergency button for a second time. People would think I was a flasher or someone, and that I needed my daily fix.

I tried to help the young boy with his struggles, but I was making it worse. We were becoming more entangled in the curtain. Finally, after ten wasted minutes, we gave up.

"I have to go now. I'm late for my bus." The boy shrugged and held out his hand for the payment. I handed him a fifty euro note and told him to keep the change. They were the right words, and he ran towards the end of the shop shouting, "Papa, papa!"

At least the tip would be staying in the family.

And now, half an hour later, I was reclining back in my seat, Lake Como bound, without a worry in the world to drag me down, when we arrived in the town. Francesca had spelt it all out for us. Arrive. Eat. Boat-ride. Sight-see. Depart. Three hours tops. Brielle had been disappointed to hear that we would only be spending three hours exploring Como, but it couldn't be helped. Had the Tour D'italia bike tour not been happening in May, our route would have been reversed and Lake Como would have featured earlier in the itinerary.

The opportunity would have been there to have spent an entire day in the beautiful surrounds, and it would have been marvellous. Would have beens! Could have beens! The world was full of them. It hadn't happened, and because of that we had managed to enjoy more places we would have, had a whole day been devoted to Lake Como.

I must have dozed off, because when I glanced at my phone it was already one thirty. My stomach was rumbling and my neck was stiff from having been in a compromising position for so long. Alice was still asleep. I was glad she was resting, because it meant I wouldn't need to face the barrage of questions inevitably headed my way when Alice discovered I was wearing a jumpsuit from an Italian outdoor market underneath my travelling clothes. She hadn't seemed to have noticed I'd inexplicably gained weight in the course of an hour, when I'd rushed up from the river-path, late as usual, and ready to have the tomatoes thrown at me.

But no red-splattered stoning had been forthcoming, and I'd managed to get away with it. The tardiness, the extra baggage and the non-apologies for having kept everyone waiting. Matteo's only desire had been to have put his foot down and navigate his way along the river towards the motorway, and everyone else was just so used to me being late, that nobody had batted an eyelid.

There was a sudden tapping on the microphone and Francesca's loud, clear voice was urging the bus to awaken and for everyone to prepare for arrival. The tour guides and the flight attendants must surely have worked closely together on training days, as the wording was near perfect. "Ladies and gentlemen. We will shortly be arriving to Como, the beautiful lakeside town. Please ensure you are sitting uptight in your seats and your seatbelts are fastened."

Alice had the giggles. "Fil, did you hear what Francesca just said? She asked us to make sure our seatbelts were fastened and then she said we should be sitting uptight in our seats. That's funny, isn't it?"

It was funny, but I didn't want to join Alice in her giggling, as I was sitting in the aisle seat, three back from where Francesca was standing, and she may have seen me and realised her mistake. She was probably right with her Freudian slip, as many of the passengers were looking a little uptight.

Most of them were tired, as was I, but a few of them were disappointed that they would not have as long as they'd hoped for in Como. By the law of averages, people start getting unsettled after a week or so of being out of their normal routine, and a smattering of our group sitting uptight in their seats as we cruised into Como was not such a bad thing. A boat-ride out in the fresh lake air would do wonders, and they would return revived for the last twenty-four hours we would be spending together. I say 'they' would look revived, because I had no intention of sitting on a boat for an hour circumnavigating Lake Como, even if I would be missing the opportunity to glimpse George Clooney, his villa and his family.

I planned to inform Francesca that I wouldn't be joining the boat trip due to my sea sickness and that I would be perfectly happy dipping my feet into the lapping waters of Lake Como, slurping on a gelati and people-watching. The reason I hadn't already told Francesca of my plan to boycott the boat was because I hadn't been able to scrape up the courage to tell Alice and the other three—Brielle, Gloria and Natarsha—that I was chickening out.

Alice still had no idea I'd spent the last hour sweltering in double layers, and if my luck was in, I would be taking my secret to the grave. Just to be on the safe side though, I would be sticking to Francesca's mantra of 'arrive, eat, sightsee, boat ride and depart', which meant that I wouldn't have to break the bad news to anyone until after we had eaten and had an opportunity for a little sightseeing.

We arrived ten minutes after Francesca's bungled announcement, and all uptightness was forgotten, as each one of us stepped down from the bus and exclaimed aloud at the sheer, sheer beauty of our surrounds.

Words could not describe the light, the lake, the air…the list would extend any potential superlatives to infinity. Even if every single one of us had offered a word to the Gods as we'd stepped off the bus-they would have been a drop in the ocean. The real descriptions were untenable. This was a place beyond description. There were simply no words to describe Lake Como. And this was coming from someone who had been blown away by so much on the trip already.

So much lush rich vegetation, so many delights of nature, so much good food and so many happy, happy Italians. The opportunity for description was there, but most of us couldn't utter a word. We were speechless. What we really needed to happen was for Francesca to line us all up, single file this time, and for her to slap the first person in the line hard on the cheek, and in so doing snap them out of the collective stupor which had overcome us. The slapping would have had a domino effect down the line, so that by the time the slapping reached the last person, we would all have felt the sting of the slap and have come to our senses.

That did not happen, of course, so it was with a sense of incredulity that Alice, myself and the other three staggered towards the nearest restaurant and claimed the last table in the outside section with the view of the spectacular Lake with mountains in the background. Although I had not had time to brush up on Parma, Como had been the one place about which I had excelled myself, having taken copious notes on the rich lakeside history and prolific architectural gems. I was able to tell the others that the mountains behind the lake were the Grigna mountains, famed for darkening the waters of Lake Como in certain spots and at certain times of the day, and that we were on the South west shore of the lake which was shaped like a 'Y'.

Alice was impressed with my knowledge of the area. "Fil, you should go and walk around with Francesca. She'd love to have you as a sidekick. We can save you some pizza."

Alice just didn't get it that I wanted to sit in an outdoor café with unobstructed views of the shimmering blue lake. That there was no way I would be shadowing Francesca and some of the others who had decided to skip lunch and gone off sightseeing. I could feel my face reddening. I hadn't wanted to show off in front of the Americans, but I had wanted to impress them with my information. If Alice had found it presumptuous of me, Natarsha who fancied herself as a bit of an historian, seemed delighted, and gently coaxed me to continue. "Please Fil, it's interesting, and it saves us reading the guidebooks."

So, while Alice and the other two waited for their pizzas to be served, and Gloria waited for her fish of the day with lobster on the side (that she could still afford lobster at the end of the trip spoke a thousand words), I entertained the table with little anecdotes about Lake Como I had committed to memory. I was able to tell them that the lake enjoyed pleasant thermal winds, and that on a beautiful day like today, it would soon be packed with afternoon windsurfers and sailboats.

I told them about how the lake was surrounded by beautiful Italian villas and of how it was perfectly positioned between Milan and Switzerland. I told them there were hundreds of fascinating small villages around Lake Como, and that it would take months to do justice to the history and architecture of the area. Lastly, I told them a story I had read which told of a villa on the shores of Lake Como which was never occupied, and nobody, to this day, knows who built it, who owns it or why it has been unoccupied for hundreds of years. "They call it the ghost villa. Maybe we'll find a souvenir tea towel with a picture of the villa. But we probably won't be able to see it because it will be invisible."

Everyone laughed at my little joke, and we raised our glasses in a 'chin Grinna' to more happy trips together. I didn't think that would be very likely, as we all lived so far away from each other, but maybe fate would throw us together for a reunion trip.

The pizzas were delectable. Authentically Italian and dripping with olive oil and over-ripe tomatoes. The best so far, and a real credit to Como, given that it was normally an accolade reserved for Rome. Gloria shred her lobster and fish with the rest of us, and I could taste the morning freshness in the fish. Our waiter was gregarious and happy, and as well as a tip, he received an olive branch, which he was happy to immediately slip into his pocket.

"Grazie signora. We have three olive trees in pots in the tiny back garden here. When I planta thissa, we will have four. Grazie tante!"

Francesca had left explicit instructions for those of us who had needed to eat, to meet her at the boat-ramp directly opposite the main piazza at three o'clock sharp, as our private charter was booked from three-fifteen until four. After that we would be in a hurry to leave Lake Como, as we needed to be on the road back to Milan before the traffic built up too much.

"Our hotel in Milan is on this side of the city, so we will save half an hour. It will give you all more time to make yourselves beautiful, and for those of you who didn't manage it last night…wella, you will have the second chance." I assumed Francesca to have had Brielle at the forefront of her mind when she had been prattling on about having a second chance.

Brielle would have not only a second, but also a third and a fourth chance at a romantic interlude, as she was the only one of us who would be staying on in Milan when the tour ended. She had told me on the night of our beach escapade that she was going to stay for a couple more nights on Milan, and then take the train up into Switzerland, where she intended to do some hiking. So, at least one of us would not be giving up on romance after tonight.

It was already a quarter to three, and we hadn't yet done our sightseeing. After the main meal, and before the coffee and mouth-watering lemon crème Brule, I had excused myself and raced off in search of the bathrooms. A waiter leaning against a stone wall puffing on a cigarette as if it were his last before the announcement of a breakout of a World War pointed me in the right direction, and I was thankful when I saw there were two cubicles. I'd brought my backpack with me to the bathroom, even though Alice had wanted to know why it had been necessary to have taken it with me, when they were all at the table and could have minded it. "I might need something from it, Alice. Or, there might be an earthquake or a flood, and I'd need my passport. Those natural disasters are always in the cards in Italy."

As I'd retreated, I overheard Alice whispering to Natarsha (who was next to her), "I never know whether to believe Fil or not. She tends to overexaggerate. Do you think there'll be a flood, Natarsha?"

I was really going to miss Alice when I was on the trains next week.

Once I'd locked myself into the cubicle, I started to peel off the layers. Sweat poured off me, as it had really been quite hot in the open-air restaurant. Normally, the giant umbrellas would have shielded patrons from the glare, but over the last few days, it had been raining on and off, so the waiters probably hadn't yet gotten around to erecting them. Today was the first of June. Halfway through the year already. Time was flying by. They had better get their skates on.

It took me a while, but I finally managed to wriggle out of the precious jumpsuit and stash it in my backpack. It would be crumpled, creased and crushed when I pulled it out tonight, but at least Alice hadn't found out. She would have gone on and on and on like a veritable fishwife about the market incident. By the time I'd arrived back at the table, everyone was already halfway through their dessert, so I slipped into my seat and began slurping the lemon Brule.

Nobody noticed I had lost weight!

Chapter 38
More of Como

We cut it fine, but the boat was still moored when we arrived at the designated dock. It had been directly across the road from the restaurant, but we had all been too focussed on the beauty of the lake to have noticed the mooring docks, and we'd had to ask quite a few tourists from other buses if they knew of the dock. None of them did, but then, none of them spoke English either, so it was a little problematic. I did my Marcel Marceau impressions, but they fell on deaf ears.

Alice even had a go at sign language, but even she failed miserably. People were just not interested in our plight. Luckily, the last couple we accosted were Dutch, and Gloria spoke a little Dutch, and was able to semi-communicate with them. They also knew where the boat we were looking for was docked, as they had been out on that very boat themselves this morning.

Natarsha the doctor was pragmatic about the whole incident. "See, you just need to find the people who look like they will know the answers to all your questions. Eventually, you will meet that person."

I had to disagree.

"True, Natarsha, but you could take a lifetime to find a person who would give you the exact answer you were looking for. And it would depend on the type of questions you asked, and whether or not there even was an answer."

Natarsha was looking at me as if to tell me that I would never make a doctor if I went around spouting philosophies to all and sundry, but it was water off a duck's back to me because I would have made a rotten nurse all those years ago. Nothing in the medical field for me. Far too analytical and regimented. I would stick to watching reruns of *MASH* and new episodes of *Casualty*.

Natarsha looked a bit put-out, and I immediately regretted having made the smart comment. I would have done better to have just agreed with her and kept my mouth shut. When would I ever learn the power of silence?

We were about ten metres away from the boat, and I still hadn't opened my mouth about my fear of seasickness, and the fact that nothing short of an underwater volcano exploding would convince me it was a sightseeing tour.

Five metres.

One metre.

At the one-metre mark, Francesca stepped forward and began hurrying us onto the boat. The Captain was a big smiling sailor who looked as though he ate wild boars for breakfast and then again for tea. If my fear had been a fear of the boats themselves, I probably would have given it a go this afternoon, but it wasn't the boat I was afraid of—it was what the boat might do to me. A bit like not being afraid of snakes but being very afraid of what it felt like to be poisoned and laid up in intensive care.

Half a metre.

In Francesca's arms.

"Fil, I'm happy to see you too, and I like very much the warm hug you are giving me, but we are late and everyone is already on the boat. See. Look up there!" I looked up onto the upper deck, and there they all were. Every single one of them including Alice. (I had no idea how Alice had managed to climb to such great heights in such a short time.)

It was now or never!

"Francesca, I can't do it. I can't come on the boat-cruise. I can't see George Clooney's villa and I can't look for dolphins. I just can't! I get terribly boat-sick and after Cinque Terra, I swore to myself I was never getting on another boat, ever again."

I had expected a severe reprimand for having left it till the last minute to tell her I wasn't going, and I didn't even know if it was against the rules to leave a passenger behind and sail off into the distance with the rest of the group, but I was not budging from the shore. They would have to carry me on, and although the Captain looked as if he could pick me up with his row of broken teeth and still have a firm grasp of me, he didn't look as if he cared whether I was coming or not.

"We go now, Signora." He was speaking to Francesca in the voice of a notorious gangster-of-the waters, but Francesca simply ignored him, smiling at me and reassuring me in her gentlest voice that it was my choice to stay, and that if I sat under that tree over there and waited, then she would come and get me in an hour.

"Then we will take you to Milan where you can rest. We need you to come to the farewell dinner full of the beans."

I laughed and with a huge sigh of relief, turned back towards the little park directly across the road from the jetty.

Only when I had collapsed onto the park bench beside a couple who were not coming up for air any time soon, did I look back to the boat and wave to Alice and the others. I'd hoped Francesca would have gone straight up to the upper deck and told everyone that I was giving the boat trip a miss, but I couldn't see her mass of red curls, no matter how hard I squinted.

The boat was pulling away from the shore, so I waved and shouted to them, but there was a road in between the park and the departing boat, and there was quite a bit of traffic about, so they must not have heard me. Neither was anyone waving, so they must not yet have known I wasn't on the boat. Time would tell!

At first, I'd thought all the noise was coming from the busy road that lapped the lake, but there was also a commotion coming from over my right shoulder, beyond the park. I got a shock when I turned to see what was happening. There were vintage cars everywhere, lots of tooting and calling out on a loudspeaker in Italian, and families everywhere waving little Italian flags and jumping up and down excitedly. There was a huge banner, but I couldn't read it from where I was sitting. I was too far away.

Apart from the kissing cousins to the left of me, there weren't many other people about in the park. I now knew why. They were either out on the lake having their senses topped up, were sauntering alongside the lake with not a care in the world except that they had made it to Lake Como or were watching the car-show. Not one of those three options appealed to me, so I decided to wander up to an extravagant-looking hotel with lake frontage I could just make out on the corner, and settle in the outside courtyard with a nice cold glass of crisp white wine. That would be the kind of Como heaven I needed.

Not being out on a pleasure cruise boat with my stomach churning. Not jumping up and down in delight as the Ferraris, Maseratis and Lamborghinis paraded by, and not even strolling along the lake, keeping a lookout for my friends to return. None of those options appealed to me. It was hot, and I wanted to rest. Some anti-social, introspective drinking in an olive-potted courtyard was presenting as a very viable option.

The bar was dark and cool, and the sole bartender was engrossed in mixing, dicing and flipping lemons onto an enormous platter, stirring drinks and placing olives delicately on the rims of the glasses. I was leaning nonchalantly on the bar watching him, and he appeared to be in no hurry to serve me. It was not arrogance on his part, nor even the slightest slither of contempt for single women in his bar-rather, it was a sense of proprietary. I was standing on his turf, and he would be making the rules. I would be served-certainly, but all in good time-his time!

Ten minutes later I was still standing there waiting. The bartender had disappeared out the back and had not returned. For the first five minutes of his absence I had kept myself occupied-looking at the photos on the wall above the bar and trying to make out the seasons in which they had been taken. The photographs had been framed in gold edged aluminium, and the brilliant blue matting set the lake off beautifully. There were at least ten photographs, which would more than likely have been taken from a boat, as the townships and little villages were always in the background. Some of the photos were taken at sunrise, and others at sunset. The shadows on the lake were an easy clue to the time. The photographers must really have known their craft, as they were sensational. It was like being alone in Tate London. All that was missing was my glass of bubbly. Which was not forthcoming. No bartender appeared, no waiter followed with the drinks tray, no police on the lookout for pickpockets and no vagrants loitering around the nooks and crannies of the best hotel on the foreshore. It was close to the lake alright. On a quiet midweek morning it might have been possible to hear the water lapping-or at least to hear the boats out there honking at each other to free up the waterway, but it was Sunday afternoon and the families were all out in their hundreds for their weekly 'passigiata' along the streets and promenades, or watching the expensive cars strut their stuff.

The last five minutes of the bartender's absence were excruciatingly and interminably long. There was a rectangular steel clock with strokes in place of the numbers ticking above the sleek green tiled bar which I was tempted to throttle into silence. I had no reason to feel out of place in the bar, but I just couldn't help it. Everything around me was so opulent, so shiny, and so deserted.

I could wait no longer! The boy was never returning-was possibly in Switzerland tobogganing with his university chums by now, and a bar like this would never have a machine for self-serve 'all you can drink' Lemon Lime and bitters, no matter how hard I longed for one to materialise. It was possibly my thirst which was driving me to such an insanely agitated state. We were in Italy, and everything and everyone was operating on Italian time. Had I booked into the hotel for week, and was wanting drinks on my terrace, time would not have been an issue, but I was in no position to be aimlessly drifting through this hotel in search of the bartender. It was action stations for me!

With half an hour until the meet-up with Francesca, I worked it out I had five minutes to locate a bathroom and fifteen to find a shop. (I had just remembered my promise to bring my favourite nephew Paddy back a polo shirt from Lake Como. Up until this very minute, it had completely slipped my mind.)

Surely one of the closed doors must be a bathroom? I tried three rooms, all of which led to identical little snugs with potted palms and ashtrays on stands, art deco lampshades and little round, silver drinks trays. Clearly not what I was after at this hour of the afternoon.

I struck gold behind the fourth door. There were three toilets with icons of women and little vases of white roses everywhere. It was simple, sumptuous and completely understated. I was not sure whether I was expected to be leaving a ten euro note for the privilege of being there.

I left a fiver, which was my last note. I still had a few emergency coins in my backpack, but I was saving them for the last batch of beggars I expected to encounter on the streets of Milan later tonight. Francesca had impressed on us to save energy for the walk to the restaurant, as had been the case on our first evening in Milan, it would be difficult for Matteo to get close enough to the trattoria where we were expected. Knowing Alice, she would already have hurled the last of her coins into the last fountain we had admired in the driveway of the petrol stop Matteo had taken between Parma and Como. It had only been a small, inconsequential fountain, not a patch on the real McCoy in Rome, but I'd noticed Alice loitering near it when I had emerged, refreshed, but still struggling with the jumpsuit under my clothes, from the road-stop bathrooms.

The great benefit of the bathroom was the little fire escape door at the back, which led to and outside courtyard, which led out into the back alley. Which, in turn, led me straight to the shop selling Polos. I hadn't really wanted to march into the first shirt shop I found, and pull a polo off the shelf, but I was getting really nervous by now that Francesca's and my paths would never cross again if my time ran out before I had time to run back to the lake.

Working in my favour was the fact that the shop, like the bar next door, was empty. Where were all these trusting proprietors and bartenders? The only thing I could think of was that they must all have been opposite in the park watching the car display and dreaming of taking to the hairpin bends of the Italian Riviera in one of them. I was making a lot of assumptions. One, that it would be a man who owned the shop in which I was pacing up and down impatiently, and two, that it wasn't Siesta time. Because if it was, the proprietor may have inadvertently left the shop door open and was at this very moment snoozing in the couch upstairs.

"Yessa, Signora. Can I elp youa?"

My fairy godmother was alive and well and living in Como, Italy. She was about to grant me my last wish of the trip which was to find a Polo shirt for Paddy with a tag that proved it had been bought at Lake Como. My instructions had been that if I were, for some reason unable to fulfil my promise, then I would be the best aunt on the planet if I managed to source a polo from his beloved Liverpool Football team, should I happen to add a trip to Liverpool to my jam-packed itinerary for touring England before the Polish wedding. A lot was at stake in this shop, and although I was at eye-level with a stack of polo shirts in every colour of the rainbow, something was not quite right.

Actually, two things were bothering me.

The first one being that it baffled me just how these Italian knew we Australians weren't Italian. I had not opened my mouth, and yet she had gone straight for the jugular. She might well have been asking me if that was all I wanted to purchase today, because I was obviously in the shop as a rich tourist, wanting to buy a shirt or two or three as gifts for someone dear to my heart.

"You want to get the special present so that you will get the special present too?"

That was the second thing about the Italians. That raunchy undercurrent—always there. That confronting, dangling tease, hugely inappropriate. The woman was looking at me, goading a response. All I was thinking was how presumptuous of her it was to assume that I was interested in buying a polo shirt for anyone other than myself or my one brother, and of how wrong I'd been with my assumption that the proprietor of a Men's shirt shop would need to be a man, and that if he wasn't there, he would be either watching the car race or sleeping upstairs.

I should have known it could never have been man when the door was left open. Never in a million years would a woman such as the gung-ho little tank of a Signora in front of me, dripping in jewels and sweat ever leave the door open by mistake, or step outside for a breather or cigarette. Speaking of which, I could smell smoke! The strong smell of tobacco in the shop was indication enough for me that Italy had not yet caught up with the rest of the world when it came to indoor smoking laws, or, in the case of the woman glaring at me, the fact that the customer is always right-no matter what.

I was the customer here, and demanding of fast efficient service, not condescension at the fact that I was a woman in strictly male territory. The woman selling the shirts must have realised I was not one to be fobbed off or sent scuttling out of the shop because I had not reacted to her abrasive manner.

I hardly recognised my own demeanour. My voice was low and authoritative.

"I am looking for a Polo shirt, possibly Lacrosse brand, and in a size medium. White please."

It had been the correct thing to have said. Some might call it the coward's way, because I wasn't giving her any information to go by. I was pretty sure she thought the polo was for me, and that I was a world circuit tennis player, spending my day off soaking it up in Como. I didn't really care. My mission was to source a medium, white, polo shirt in…five minutes.

The woman had found one, selecting it with clear disdain from the neatly stacked wooden shelves (the same setup as I'd encountered in Genoa with the green pesto shirts). She was wrapping the parcel as swiftly as her tough little fingers could fold and knot. I handed her fifty euro, even though the price tag had red 'forty-seven euro' and fled. No olive branch for her until she learnt some manners!

Past the hotel, past the flag-wavers and back onto the park bench. The lovers had been replaced by an old man who had set up his microphone and was crooning out *Oh Solo Mia* to an audience of one.

Me!

Francesca turned up two minutes later, and without a word, grabbed my arm and started hurrying me towards the waiting bus. All the window-side people, including Alice and Gloria, were waving at me, cheering me on to the bus and up to my seat as if I had been missing for two decades and not only two hours. Even Matteo had smiled at me from his sunken driver's seat as I'd been dragged along past him by Francesca.

It felt good to be wanted, and back within the bosom of my family. Matteo started up the engine and we were off.

Off to Milan for the very last time!

Chapter 39
Farewell to Arms and Legs, Bodies and Heads!

I couldn't speak for the others, but with Alice, the welcome I'd received when Francesca had thrown me to the crowd on the bus was definitely a throwing to the wolves.

Alice was cold and upset with me. "Where were you, Fil? We were all worried. Someone said you had run off with one of the Lamborghini drivers, because you'd mentioned that you wanted to feel the wind in your hair on the way to Monaco in a soft top sports car. Did you go for a ride with anyone, Fil?" Alice looked so innocent when she asked such ludicrous questions.

I knew we had at least an hour of travelling to go before we'd be back in Milan, and I just could not resist one final opportunity to hold court on the bus. I would speak to Alice, but in a loud, exaggerated voice. I could tell everyone around me had their ears pricked up, ready to hear about the gorgeous, young sweaty Formula One driver who had stopped for me to cross the road, and in so doing had offered to take me for a spin around the Lake in his brand spanking new Maserati worth at least one hundred thousand pounds.

"It was just after you all left that he stopped. He was supposed to be in the parade, but for some reason, he was on the road, and he stopped to let me cross over. As I walked past, he couldn't resist asking me if I wanted to go for a ride in his car. Actually, his very words were, 'You beautiful seniorittass, where are you off to all by yourselfa? Hop in and I will take you for the ride of your life'."

I stopped to take a swig from my water bottle, and I noticed that quite a few of the others had congregated in the aisle beside my seat. They could not all have been on their way to the bathrooms. Inspired, I continued my story, taking care to lower and raise my voice where appropriate.

"Then the man did a U-turn and headed for the mountains. The Gringas, remember I told you about them before, Alice."

"Oh yes!" the response had come from five voices, not just Alice's. One of them had been Fillip who had not even been part of our table at lunchtime. Good old Fillip. He would be another person for me to miss.

Alice was really hooked by now. "What did you do when you got to the mountain roads, Fil? Weren't you scared he would kidnap you and steal your money?"

I looked around at the expectant audience and wondered how I could manage to bring this baby in without disappointing anyone, and then just sleep for the next half an hour. I'd had my appreciation and self-stroking with the (hard to be believed) opening line from the fictitious driver, "You beautiful Seniorita". I would be pushing my luck to try and convince my entourage that the driver had promised to drive into Milan tonight and meet me for a nightcap around eleven. Looking at Brielle's expectant face, I really, really wanted to continue on with the charade, but enough was enough. I'd had my fun.

Better still, I had diverted the conversation from why I'd been nowhere to be found on the boat to, "what had happened in my hour with mysterious driver." Mission accomplished. They would never know the real truth. Once Alice saw the white Polo, she would certainly be asking me where it had materialised from. As we'd run out of time for sightseeing after the pizzas and lobster, Alice would know I must have bought the polo in Como whilst they had been on the boat.

I was dying to know all the details of the boat ride, and whether or not they had seen anyone famous hanging out private washing near their private jetties. Or tending to their tomato patches or lemon and olive groves by the foreshore. However, sleep was more important, and we only had half an hour to go. I'd hear all about it tonight; that was a given where Fillip was around.

The bus came to a sudden stop, and I realised we had arrived at our hotel. Our last hotel, and although not on the same grandiose scale as this afternoon's hotel of the missing bartender, it looked perfectly acceptable, and a welcoming place in which to lay our heads. In Alice and my case, we would have less than twelve hours in the hotel-four of which would be spent at the restaurant tonight. Consequently, there would be no searching for swimming pools, no walks in the park, and no Room-service of drinks and nibbles before we left for the trattoria around six.

Time was of the essence again. It seemed to have been a day of rushing, and it probably wouldn't stop now until we were on the plane tomorrow morning. Francesca had delivered her last set of instructions to everyone, and although her voice was tinged with sadness at the fact that our time together was nearly over, she wasn't letting go that easily, and in the last five minutes of the bus trip, she had wandered up the aisle with her little wicker basket, delivering gifts. There were two different types—Cinque Terra coffee cups and Lake Como fridge magnets. There were also coloured Italian lollies wrapped in a little lace doily (bonbonniere) and a tiny Italian flag-just like the ones the car enthusiasts had been waving this morning. It was lovely of Francesca to have gone to so much trouble for us. Lizzie thanked her on behalf of everyone, and Fillip had given her a big hug on behalf of everyone (but mostly from himself.) We were almost done!

Getting ourselves dolled up for the farewell dinner had some of the shine taken off it by the fact that we were in a hurry and wouldn't have time for long steamy showers. Alice had insisted she'd need the longest shower, her reasoning being she had been on the boat all afternoon, and the wind had blown her hair in all directions. Her hair needed emergency washing and curling if she were to be presented to the world this evening.

I could have pointed out that I too had commitments this evening, but since it wasn't true, I wasn't really fussed if Alice hogged the shower. I ended up having a quick shower and then repacking my case whilst Alice lathered her body and hair with hotel toiletries. (We'd run out of our own supply even though Alice had bought such a big bottle at the hairdressers only last week.) I hid my new jumpsuit underneath the new socks. That way, Alice would not find out until after we arrived back in England.

By the time Alice reappeared, I was all packed and ready to go. I could have hopped straight into the taxi and been early for tomorrow's flight, but we still had an evening meal to savour, good company and lots of goodbyes to get through.

"Ready, Alice?" For once we were early, and when we arrived in the foyer, there were only a few people already there. The Singaporeans and the Armenian family were sitting in the armchairs waiting patiently to be told that the bus doors were open.

As soon as Devo saw Alice, he jumped up from his seat and offered it to her, but she politely refused, as at that same moment Francesca had appeared from outside to announce that the bus was ready to take us to our final outing of the trip. The Farewell dinner in a little trattoria near the canals. A trendy part of the city, and somewhere very fitting for a valedictory celebration.

Chapter 40
Valedictions and Arrivederci

The private room which had been allocated to our group was a tinier, cosier version of where we had enjoyed the three-course meal, singing and dancing the evening before. Possibly one tenth of the size, and there was no dance floor, but it was intimate and perfect. Tiny fairy light had been massed across the ceiling, and two long tables had been perfectly draped with crisp white tablecloths. There were candles and vases with sprigs of lavender. It was the heart of simplicity and starkly welcoming.

Getting to the room had involved the same rabbit-warren zig-zagging we had succumbed to on the night of our Welcome dinner across the city from where we sat tonight. Matteo had done his best to deposit us as close as he could manage to the trattoria, but in a city as large as Milan, it had been no mean feat. Ron and Alice had been forewarned by both Francesca and Matteo that walking would be involved, and that if they so desired, a taxi could be arranged to ferry them to and from the restaurant from the hotel.

Naturally, their faithful companions would be included in the taxi ride-which would be offered courtesy of the tour company. Both Roy and Alice had insisted that they would be able to manage the three blocks to the restaurant from where Matteo intended to stop the bus, and that they'd reassess how they felt about struggling back to the bus once the evening had wound up.

Yolanda and I were both plugging for travelling to the restaurant on the bus with the rest of the group, but we'd made a pact that we wouldn't be deserting either Roy nor Alice, should they choose to take up the offer of the taxi. Francesca had also come up with a second solution and that was to park the bus near a bicycle hire depot, and for the whole group to support Roy and Alice by riding up to the restaurant and leaving the bikes parked outside.

I could think of three flaws to that plan right away, the first being that no one had any idea of who could ride a bike and who was still on training-wheels, and the next two being the difficulty of finding a bicycle holding station (even though the city was overflowing with them) able to offer more than twenty-two bikes ripe for the picking. And the third? Well, that would depend on Matteo.

How would he feel not being able to deliver and return us safely from our very last congregation as a group? Would his days and days of driving, the hundreds and hundreds of kilometres he had notched up in a superlative effort to present Italy at its finest-all have been in vein, when he found himself unable to deliver at the last post? Of all three reasons I was putting forward, the last seemed the most convincing case for the affirmative. The affirmative being to walk the five or so blocks to the restaurant after Matteo found a suitable parking spot. It was the decent thing to do and arriving on bicycles may have worked in eighteenth-century Milan, but tonight, in our finery and high heels, it would be an impractical backward step.

I need not have agonised over the bicycle debate (which had been knocked on the head by quite a few of the non-bicycle riders amongst the group even before Francesca had finished her sentence) because it ended up being Roy and Alice putting their heads together and deciding to go for broke—and walk. Francesca had insisted we weren't in a hurry, as the entire room had been reserved for our group, and even if we ended up eating at midnight it would be a good night. "Good food, good company and a good outlook on life, whata more is there here in Milan?"

Francesca had not mentioned Milan once since we had left the city a week ago, but she was making up for it this evening as we crawled up and down the streets in the gleaming, coloured bus-restaurant bound. Every corner we rounded was described, every park we passed was praised for its greenery and architectural layout, and every block of apartments we stopped at to admire had been designed by the best architects in the world, and the most eco-friendly of landscape artists.

It was all true—Milan was a wonderful metropolis, but I had preferred the exquisite paradise of the lakes, and the majesty of the mountains to the grid-flat blocks and blocks of shops and buildings with trees scattered here and there which had stretched out before us to the horizon.

No one had any idea where we would end up, so when Francesca came to an abrupt halt in front of an insignificant doorway flanked with identical chestnut trees on either side of the architraves, we all thought it would be to ask for directions. That she must have taken a wrong turn, and that we were all lost. But it had been a purposeful faltering as no sooner had we all caught up than the door was opened from the inside, and we were greeted by the maître-D, decked out in white, and flashing his equally white teeth towards the group.

"Welcome to the best restaurant in Milan. We have been expecting you all day-every day in fact, since you have made the booking! And now the time has finally arrived, scusi, the tour has finally arrived."

The man was outrageously handsome, and Brielle, who had been walking by my side for most of the way since we'd left the bus, was panting out to me, "Isn't he gorgeous Fil? What a hunk!" I prayed the man was hard of hearing, or that he had no clue of the meaning of the word 'hunk'.

Francesca, who held an unblemished record for never missing a trick, noted Brielle's comment and she looked at her approvingly. "Yes Brielle. He is truly a chunker!"

I giggled, and we moved past the 'chunker' and into the body of the restaurant. A grungy young waitress had appeared, complete with short cropped purple hair, tiny black-studded bangles up her left arm and a crisp white short-sleeved shirt over tight black pants. She was missing an earring, as one of her ears sprouted a large hooped earring, and the other was noticeably bare. I didn't make any comment because it would have been rude to alert her to the fact that she'd lost an earring, and there was always the possibility that wearing one earring had been a deliberate fashion statement on her part. She was a sweet, mousey little thing, and we all followed her into a room studded with the fairy lights, and sat down pretty much according to how we had walked in.

During the course of the evening's conversation, Alice had the opportunity to retell the story of how she had not known whether I had been dead or alive for most of the boat ride, and it was only when Francesca had come up to the top deck to see how everyone was going that she thought to ask her of my whereabouts. "But Alice, why did you take so long to ask her? Couldn't you have gone to find her, or sent Brielle if the stairs were too much for you?"

Angelique really wanted to know.

That stumped Alice, and the rest of the story fell flat.

Gloria came to the rescue with a long-winded story of life on the Texan cattle station, and Fillip and Lizzie filled in the gaps with tales of their own particular corner of the United States. I sat listening to them, trying to get my head around how they lived in a country with more than two hundred million people. Compared to Australia, it was inconceivable.

We had the best night. Not because anyone was over-exuberant or bursting with energy and wanting to dance on the tables. Quite the opposite really. We were all tired and ready for bed, but being together for the last time, easy in each other's company, and perfectly bonded made for an evening to remember. We laughed, took photos and exchanged emails and mobile phone numbers. We ate together, drank together, and took more photos. Slide nights may have died a natural death, but WhatsApp, Twitter and Facebook were in for a thrashing when we all returned to our homelands.

Inevitably, it was time to leave. A time of great sadness yet tinged with appreciation and gratitude that we had been privileged and honoured in Italy, a land where everything was so completely different to anywhere anyone has ever been before or was yet to visit.

Alice and Roy were able to walk back to the bus. We all were. It was a quiet progression.

No one felt much like talking, and even Francesca was taking a backseat. When we reached the bus, Matteo was there in all his glory ready and waiting to help us on. "Women and children, first," Francesca had called out jokingly, and that broke up the cloud of gloom which had settled on many of us towards the end of the night, when it had begun to sink in that the party was over. We joked that Francesca had meant for Armenia and Devo to be first on the bus, as they were the only two truly fitting her instruction.

"Come on everyone, we will sing the one last song together, and then we will all run away to our bedrooms." Francesca slipped a disc into the player, and Frank Sinatra's smooth, perfectly pitched voice took over the bus. Frankie was right.

The end was near!

Chapter 41
Homeward Bound

It was still pitch dark in the bedroom when the alarm did its thing. When I say 'alarm', that's exactly what I mean. No soothing meditative music, or gurgling rivers and streams coaxing me into opening one eye.

Even better!

A loud tingly alarm-sound, emanating from my iPhone, but wholly identifiable as the unmistakeable sound of an alarm clock in frenzied flight. The slim rectangular phone from which the incessant burring and clanging was deliriously resonating may have looked like butter wouldn't melt in its mouth, but rest assured it could be relied upon in all conditions known to the history of civilisation to spitefully churn out the loudest din in the universe if it meant doing its job of awakening hapless sleepers.

Disoriented, I turned over sharply and promptly fell out of bed. The polished wooden floor was cold and hard, and I bumped my head, but that was a small price to pay for having my memory reinstated. Plans for the day loomed up in front of me like a huge hot air balloon. It was the morning of our departure from Italy.

The morning of extraction, the morning of separation from everyone and everything I had come to know and love in the past ten days. The morning of mourning. It would also be the morning when Francesca and Matteo found themselves burdened with Alice and myself for the next week on the next tour—with a new group of strangers if I didn't stop dwelling on the inevitable and hurry up. That couldn't happen. We'd said our goodbyes, and the trip was done.

It was coming back to me now—fast and furious.

Last night's farewells had been difficult, and leaving Brielle, Natarsha and Gloria probably the most difficult and wrenching of all. All three of them had displayed a different reaction to our parting. Brielle was super airy and fluffy, caught up in the fact that she was yodelling off to Switzerland by train, and that she would "Catch up with us again soon!" We were to pop over to the East coast of the US and visit her. That was a given. I tried to encourage her to come to Australia, insisting it to be the most beautiful place in the world in which to travel (outside of Italy, of course) but she was insistent that any reunion needed to be at her home, on her turf, by the ocean.

"You'll appreciate how I can't be away from the sea for too long, won't you, Fil?" I could, and did, appreciate the pull of the water. I'd been hooked on the ocean for most of my life, but Martha's Vineyard, or wherever it was that Brielle called home, seemed a long way from Australia.

Moving onto Natarsha; she had hugged us both, despite her raging cold, and had then run for the lift, calling back that she would never forget us and the wonderful time we'd all had together on the trip. Alice tried to call out to her to take our addresses which she had written down on little cards to hand out to our new friends, but Natarsha had already dissolved into a fit of tears, and Alice didn't want to embarrass her any further. (There had been a group email list sent around the bus by Francesca, so we already had Natarsha's address and email.)

That had left Gloria, whom we never really got to farewell, as no sooner had everyone began the hugging and kissing ritual, customary at the end of a tour or a wedding reception when the bride and groom are farewelled, Gloria had disappeared into thin air. Several of us waited around for twenty minutes or so to no avail. She was a no-show, and we were upset that we hadn't managed to say goodbye to her.

Ever hopeful Alice was still pinning her hopes on the fact that Gloria might invite us to fly over to Texas and stay with her on the ranch, but I told her not to hold her breath. Gloria had been a great chum for the last week, and was very quirky in her habits, especially with her tendency to wear wide-brimmed Texan hats every day, but once we'd all separated, I felt fairly sure that would be it, and people would get on with their lives. If our paths crossed again, we would be very happy to see her.

The others from the group had disappeared from the foyer in dribs and drabs, and soon there was only Alice, Francesca and I left at the entrance to the lifts. Francesca was very happy with her olive branch and the generous tip Alice and I had slipped into her palm. We had also handed her a sealed envelope and an olive branch with Matteo's name printed on both the envelope and the little plastic package, in Alice's best calligraphy style. Francesca had promised to deliver the envelope and the olive branch to him in the morning, when they would both be departing form Milan, and making their separate ways to their home-towns. Alice had said not a word about Matteo having disappeared, but I could tell she was greatly disappointed.

The lift had arrived, and we had stepped inside without taking much notice of a man already occupying half the space in the squashy receptacle, as he'd been facing the wall, fiddling around with the floor buttons. He spun around to ask us (in Italian) which floor we required, and neither Alice nor I could find a voice with which to respond. Speak of the devil. The Italian stallion himself—Matteo.

I finally found my voice. "Second floor, thanks Matteo." He smiled and looked at me coyly. Was it only last night that he had clasped me in his arms as we'd whirled and twirled around the dancefloor to the applause of the entire room?

The sooner we got out of the lift, the better.

Alice and I fumbled our way out on the second floor, thanking Matteo again for all the driving and the wonderful company. At least I did. Alice still hadn't spoken. The handsome contribution to Matteo's wallet and the olive branch—both of which were still with Francesca downstairs—were not mentioned. Not in his presence in the tiny lift that is, but once the lift door had closed on that finely chiselled, almost Romanesque face we were never to see again, Alice suddenly found her voice, and it wasn't soft.

"Oh, Fil! We missed our chance of hugging Matteo and letting him know how good he's been to us. I just couldn't talk. I was so stupid! Fancy acting like silly schoolgirls the last chance we had. We were probably the only two lucky enough to have seen him for the last time, and that was only by chance. What idiots we are!"

"Now hang on, Alice. Fair crack of the whip. We weren't both Carmelite nuns in the lift. I spoke for the whole team. For you, Roy, Yolanda, the Singaporeans, the Armenian family, Brielle and the others—actually, for everyone. I told Matteo he had been wonderful, remember?"

Alice couldn't remember anything. The evening had been ruined for her. Without a satisfactory signing off with everyone in the group, Alice felt cheated. She told me, from her position on the floor near the lift, that she just couldn't sleep, knowing that Matteo had thought she'd ignored him in the lift. I tried to rationalise with her. Tried to tell her that the mere mortal of a man had been driving tour buses for twenty-five years, and with an average of one trip per month, would have driven over five hundred people every year, which meant well over two thousand people over twenty years.

We were insignificant if we stopped to think about it. If anything, Matteo would remember Alice because of the number of times he'd needed to help her off the bus. Up steps, down steps, into lifts and into chairs. (I'd seen him pulling out seats for Alice in many of the restaurants and breakfast rooms of the hotels in which we'd stayed.) He was extremely polite, thoughtful and courteous. And good-looking.

If Alice could just remove smouldering sex-appeal from the equation, then all would be well, and Matteo, reduced back to the status of efficient, caring bus driver. But in Alice's mind, things had gone just that little bit too far, and there was no possibility of reversal. The only thing we could hope for, if Alice was ever to get over this holiday romance (most of which was in her head), was for Matteo to reappear, and for Alice to have one last chance to say goodbye.

"Come on, Alice, get up. I don't know why you're slumped up against the potted palm anyway. You're crushing the leaves. Let's just get to our bedroom and have a last limoncello. A final toast to Italy!"

That got her moving! It also started her laughing. "Fil, it's funny really, isn't it? You and me in the lift with Matteo on the last night of the trip. What were the chances?"

We'd reached our room, which was only two doors down from the lift, and could have been reached by crawling, had Alice not wanted to get up from the floor. I nailed it in two strides. That part was easy. The hard part was fitting the key in the lock. Nothing was working. I jiggled, pushed and banged on the wood to the side of the keyhole in case the door had moved slightly with the heat or the cold, but to no avail.

Then Alice had a go, but still no success.

"We'll have to go downstairs and ask for another key. Unless we ring them and see if they could bring one up. It's quite late and the reception desk is probably already closed." I had hoped Alice would come good and fish out her phone and do the talking, but she had begun laughing again, and would have been in no fit state to explain to the person on the front desk why we required a replacement key. Besides which, I couldn't remember the word for key. (Had I ever heard it?)

I had one last go at forcing the key into the lock, resolved to making a trip back downstairs, but it would not turn in the barrel. Totally exasperated, we turned to go, and had both only taken a couple of steps forward when the door was flung open. A tall man in a navy woollen dressing-gown towered there, clasping an umbrella. His face was thunderous, and I realised at once that we had been trying to open somebody else's door. Somebody who had probably been asleep, and somebody who was holding an umbrella in the exact same pose as Francesca had adopted every day of our tour this last week. Only this time the umbrella had not been hoisted in peace.

It really wasn't worth trying to explain that we were not burglars dressed in our finest clothes, high heels and jewellery out on a joyride, but that we were simply misguided and totally confused about our room. Perhaps we wouldn't be having that limoncello nightcap after all. The corridor was beginning to blur and I suddenly lost all sense of direction. Where was the lift? The irate gentleman who'd thought his room was about to be ransacked had taken a menacing step forwards and the scene was rapidly turning ugly.

Then, the most unlikely thing happened. Alice took control! She yelled an apology at the gentleman and dragged me forwards. I didn't look back to see if he was still standing at the door, but there was no noise of slamming, and no heavy breathing down our necks, so he must have been startled into inertia. We were back in front of the lift, and I instantly regained my bearings.

Alice was looking at the key. "It definitely says 'Room 3'. Do you think they gave us the wrong key, Fil?" I thought back to when we'd come out of the room this afternoon, and of how all the rooms in our corridor had been left open for us. Then I remembered that the whole floor had been devoted to our tour group, and that Angelique and Don had been allocated the room to our left, and Lizzie and Fillip were to our right. We had been talking in the corridor and had then taken to our rooms to taint ourselves up for the Farewell dinner.

"Hang on a minute, Alice. Something's not quite right here." My dalliance with dizziness had disappeared and left me with a crystal-clear head for some late-night detective work. I had not watched countless episodes of Midsomer Murders, Miss Marple, Inspector Jack Frost, Endeavour, Morse or Colombo (to name a few) for nothing. If Matteo had driven thousands of people all over Europe, then it would be no exaggeration for me to assert that I had watched many more than a thousand murder mystery episodes on television, not to mention the countless number of crime books I'd read since my teens. The clues were in my hand with the keys.

Think!

Suddenly it came it me. Of course! The key was never going to fit in the lock, even though it was labelled 'Room 3'.

We were on the wrong floor!

We should have been on the third floor, and I had told Matteo we'd wanted the second floor! Eureka!

"Alice, Alice, I know what's happened! We're on the wrong floor. This must be the second floor and our room must be on the third floor. The man with the umbrella was probably asleep and he thought his room was being burgled. It's too late to tell him we know what happened, and he probably went straight back to sleep. We don't look like burglars, do we?"

The real Alice had been returned to her body, and the proactive Alice had dematerialised—possibly for good. She was almost asleep by now and didn't seem in the least interested in my Eureka moment and deft solving of the "Mystery of the unobliging key".

"Just hurry up and get the lift to come, Fil. I'm so tired now." I pushed the button and glanced at my phone. It was just after midnight. We would only be getting five hours sleep at this rate, but we could sleep on the plane, and England wasn't that far away from Italy. As long as we could find our room, everything would be good. We'd sleep and awaken refreshed and ready for the flight.

We did find the room and we did sleep. No limoncello nightcaps, no last-minute packing, no showers to wash off the grime and sweatiness of the evening, picked up when we'd walked block after block back to the bus. Just straight to bed. Then nothing.

Then, the wretched alarm!

Chapter 42
Happy Endings

It was curtains for that condemned ringtone on my phone. Even though it was only four thirty am, and even though I hadn't yet doused my face with hot steaming water in the luxurious shower, I still found the time and energy to delete the hugely annoying application and revert to something far more sedate. It took me a precious five minutes (I couldn't decide between Ed Sheeran or Nina Simone) but I was not going to rest until the potential disturbance to tomorrow morning was totally eradicated. Silenced for the term of its natural life.

After the act, I went into "Do not disturb" mode. Neither Alice nor I spoke for the next twenty-five minutes. We were on a mission, and someone out there had set the time bomb to explode in thirty minutes. If we weren't downstairs, collecting the breakfast we had pre-ordered last night and waiting for the chauffeured car (also pre-ordered) to arrive, then it would be the end for us making the plane. But that wouldn't happen.

Nothing was going to stand in our way. Nothing and no one.

Not even Matteo, if Alice happened to glimpse him biding his time with a newspaper and a torch in the dark shadows behind the bus (which had been parked at the front of the hotel for safe keeping until this morning when Matteo would drive it singlehandedly, and carrying no passengers back to the head depot on Rome.) Francesca was training it back to Venice where she lived, but she had assured the group she would be hanging around until after lunch to ensure everyone got off to the airports on time. There were two airports servicing Milan, and about half the group were flying out of Malpensa and the other half out of Linate.

Except Brielle, who was staying on in Milan for a couple of days and, like Francesca, training it. Only Brielle would be on a different train, bound for Switzerland.

Alice and I would be the first to depart Milan just as we had been the first to arrive. The reason being that originally, we were not booked on the nine-day trip of Northern Italy, but the five-day trip, which had fit in nicely with Alice and her holidays. But there had been a mix-up, and the Tour Company had offered to accommodate us on the next trip, which would best fit in with our inflexible airline itinerary. (It was late spring and most flights to Milan were fully booked.) It had worked out well for us, allowing Alice and I extra time in Italy, but it had meant leaving early on the last day. Today.

By five am we were downstairs, showered, dressed and ready for departure. Alice had phoned the bell boy whilst I'd dragged the cases to the door. The front door concierge had told the front desk boy, who'd told the Bell-boy to tell us to leave the suitcases by the door and to head downstairs, as the chauffeur had already arrived, and was on the lookout for us. I got the giggles with the Little Red Hen story. Delirious at this early hour.

"Do you think he will walk around the foyer with one of those little signs that have customers' names printed on them, looking for us, Alice?"

Alice didn't answer but did manage a weak smile. I told myself she would be better company after she'd eaten. Already, I was missing Francesca. She would have laughed at my joke. I could just hear her now, "Fil, why do you make the fun about your driver. Don't you know you should make the joke after you arrive safely to the airport, and not before. You learn slowly, Fil." Then I would have laughed at her retort, and we would have been tit-for-tat.

No sooner had we stepped out of the lift (overloaded with countless small bags, coats and jumpers even though we had left the two bulging suitcases upstairs for the porter to bring down) than the chauffeur appeared. He was dressed impeccably, from his cap down to his boots. I could tell he took his job very seriously, even though my eyes were not really adjusting all that well to the dark.

"You are the two laddies who have ordered the car to take you to the airport, or would it be that lady over there and just one of you?" He pointed over to a dark corner of the lobby where Alice and I could just make out a small figure, covered in a thick coat, huddled in a corner, presumably sleeping. It was the wide-brimmed Texan hat which instantly gave her away.

"Gloria!" Alice and I chorused aloud in unison.

"And praise the Lord, the Jesus Christ!" (That came from the driver.)

We both looked at the him in surprise. He must have thought this was a common morning greeting in our countries—steeped in Irish Catholicism and all that.

I tried to explain that we were calling out to our friend, Gloria, the woman in the corner.

"But yes, more to the point, we are the ladies who booked the car. Would you please take this hand luggage to the car whilst we say goodbye to our friend and collect our breakfast?" The man was happy to oblige. Unlike the two of us, he did not look as though he had just tumbled out of bed. Maybe he had been on a nightshift, and this was his last pick up and not his first for the day. Or maybe he was just one of those people who never looked any different at any time of the day.

The driver swiftly picked up our luggage and disappeared through the revolving doors. Time to bring down the curtain.

In a commanding voice, I ordered Alice to shuffle over to Gloria and tell her that we were in a hurry and that I said goodbye. Once Alice had moved off, I ran up to the desk and tried to make the non-English-speaking boy behind the desk understand that we needed to pick up our breakfast right away, as the chauffeur was ready to leave.

The boy was doing his best to understand me, and kept picking up items on the desk, looking at me and nodding.

No, I did not want a stapler. No. I had no use for the fax machine (he hadn't picked up the machine, just pointed to it). No, we were not after a vase of flowers, although he was getting warm. (If you counted flowers as food, and I knew they did that sometimes here in Northern Italy—the headquarters of the Slow Food Movement.)

Just as I was about to give up, the bellboy appeared by my side with our suitcases, the sole occupants of his huge steel bird cage on wheels.

"La Signore vuole la sua colazione."

"Ah, si, si!" The boy was off in a flash and returned with two enormous, pristine brown paper bags, handing them to me with so much pride that I wondered if he was personally responsible for the cold contents. (Sadly no bacon and egg rolls, unless they were the stone-cold version.)

In the next three minutes, three things happened. Number one, Alice and I met at the doors and I handed her one of the breakfast bags. Number two, the bellboy met the chauffeur at the revolving doors and helped him load the suitcases into the car; and Number three, Gloria's waving hand was the last we saw of the hotel or indeed any of our tour group. It was far too early, and far too dark.

Once we had settled into the backseat of the sleek, silver Mercedes and we'd made sure the driver knew which of the two airports we were headed for, we could relax back in our seats. The driver introduced himself as Peppino and asked us if there was anything he could do to make us more comfortable. Short of his waving a magic wand so that we might reclaim another three hours sleep, there was nothing he could really do.

We were extremely comfortable, had exquisitely embroidered lace-pillows for the backs of our necks and all the food and drink our hearts desired in the enormous paper bags we were both nursing. Peppino chatted on amicably, describing Milan and pointing out statues, churches and fresco-painted walls whenever we came to a standstill. Everybody was still sleeping, but I knew from last week that in under two hours, the roads would be clogged with cars, trucks, buses bicycles and scooters—people on their way to work at the beginning of another busy working week.

I also knew it was June second, Italy's National day, so maybe many of them would be having a holiday? Whatever the reason, the roads were deserted. It was so early that we were the only car on the northbound road out of Milan. Peppino let us know we had about an hour or so to go as soon as we left the city behind.

The countryside was beautiful in the half light. The city had been lit up, but the countryside was still bathed in early morning fog-a thick swirling coating the colour of fairy floss, which looked as though it could be swallowed up by hungry dinosaurs roaming the hills.

After about ten minutes or so of undulating topography, Peppino offered us each a bottle of water, and took a long swig from his own bottle. He was still chatting. Prattling on about everything, possibly trying to keep our minds off the fact that this would be the last we'd be seeing of the Italian countryside. I knew what he was up to and I thanked him for it in my heart. It was fitting that the last person we had contact with in the countryside around Milan was a decent bloke, doing his job in the best way he knew how and trying to do his best for his family and his beloved country. Italia!

Just as we were pulling up into the main thoroughfare of the airport, I tapped him on the shoulder and handed him an olive branch. He accepted graciously, not even bothering to ask me what it was for, or why I would be handing him such an unusual gift.

I hopped out of the car and ran around to the other side to help Alice. Then, I turned a full 360 degrees and, borrowing four succinct heartfelt words from Francesca's heartthrob, the silky-smooth heart-whisperer we had relished every single day of the tour, belted out to anyone who cared to listen:

"Time to…say goodbye!"